New Explorations

Critical Notes

ON PRESCRIBED POETRY FOR THE 2007 EXAMINATION
(HIGHER AND ORDINARY LEVEL)

EDITED BY
John G. Fahy

CONTRIBUTORS
Carole Scully
Bernard Connolly
Marie Dunne
John G. Fahy
Ann Hyland
Seán Scully
John McCarthy
David Keogh

GILL & MACMILLAN

Gill & Macmillan Ltd
Hume Avenue
Park West
Dublin 12
with associated companies throughout the world
www.gillmacmillan.ie

© Carole Scully, Bernard Connolly, Marie Dunne, John G. Fahy, Ann Hyland, Seán Scully, John McCarthy, David Keogh 2005
0 7171 3830 5

Design and print origination in Ireland by O'K Graphic Design, Dublin

The paper used in this book is made from the wood pulp of managed forests. For every tree felled, at least one tree is planted, thereby renewing natural resources.

All rights reserved.
No part of this publication may be copied, reproduced or transmitted in any form or by any means without written permission of the publishers or else under the terms of any licence permitting limited copying issued by the Irish Copyright Licensing Agency, Irish Writers' Centre, Parnell Square, Dublin 1.

Acknowledgments

Harcourt Publishers for 'The Figure a Poem Makes' by Robert Frost which was published as an introduction for *The Collected Poems of Robert Frost*.

CONTENTS

1. JOHN DONNE (1576–1631)
   The quest for certainty 1
   P The Flea 11
   P Song: Go, and catch a falling star 14
      The Sun Rising 16
      The Anniversarie 18
      Sweetest love, I do not go 21
      A Valediction: Forbidding Mourning 23
      The Dreame 25
      Batter my heart 27
      At the round earth's imagined corners 29
      Thou hast made me 31

      Developing a personal reaction to John Donne 33
      Questions 34
      Bibliography 35

2. WILLIAM BUTLER YEATS (1865–1939)
   A literary life 37
   P The Lake Isle of Innisfree 43
      September 1913 45
   P The Wild Swans at Coole 48
   P An Irish Airman Foresees his Death 51
      Easter 1916 53
      The Second Coming 58
      Sailing to Byzantium 62
      The Stare's Nest By My Window 65
      In Memory of Eva Gore-Booth and Con Markiewicz 68
      Swift's Epitaph 71
      An Acre of Grass 72
      Politics 74
      From 'Under Ben Bulben' 75

      Developing a personal understanding 77
      Overview of a selection of themes and issues 77
      General questions 78
      Bibliography 79

P = POEM ALSO PRESCRIBED FOR ORDINARY LEVEL 2007 EXAM

3. Robert Frost (1874–1963)

	A literary life	80
	The Tuft of Flowers	84
	Mending Wall	86
	After Apple-Picking	88
	Birches	91
P	'Out, Out –'	92
P	The Road Not Taken	95
	Spring Pools	97
P	Acquainted With the Night	99
	Design	100
	Provide, Provide	101
	An overview of Robert Frost	103
	'The figure a poem makes'	108
	Questions	111
	Bibliography	111

4. T. S. Eliot (1888–1965)

	Timeline	113
	The Love Song of J. Alfred Prufrock	114
P	Preludes	124
P	Aunt Helen	130
	A Game of Chess (extract from *The Waste Land II*)	132
	Journey of the Magi	138
	Usk (extract from *Landscapes III*)	143
	Rannoch, by Glencoe (extract from *Landscapes IV*)	145
	East Coker IV (extract from *The Four Quartets*)	148
	T. S. Eliot – An overview	151
	Eliot – a dramatic poet	158
	Questions	158
	Bibliography	159

5. Patrick Kavanagh (1904–1967)

	Kavanagh overview	160
	Inniskeen Road: July Evening	164
	Epic	167
P	Shancoduff	169
	The Great Hunger	170
P	A Christmas Childhood	174

P = POEM ALSO PRESCRIBED FOR ORDINARY LEVEL 2007 EXAM

	Advent	176
P	On Raglan Road	178
	The Hospital	181
	Canal Bank Walk	182
	Lines Written on a Seat on the Grand Canal, Dublin	183

6. Elizabeth Bishop (1911–1979)

	A literary life	186
P	The Fish	188
	The Bight	191
	At the Fishhouses	193
	The Prodigal	196
	Questions of Travel	197
	The Armadillo	200
	Sestina	203
	First Death in Nova Scotia	204
P	Filling Station	206
	In the Waiting Room	207
	An overview of Elizabeth Bishop	211
	Forging a personal understanding of Bishop's poetry	217
	Questions	218
	Bishop's writings	219
	Bibliography	219

7. John Montague (1929–)

	Praising the burden	220
	Killing the Pig	229
	The Trout	232
P	The Locket	235
P	The Cage	241
	Windharp	244
	All Legendary Obstacles	247
	The Same Gesture	251
P	Like dolmens round my childhood . . .	254
	The Wild Dog Rose	257
	A Welcoming Party	259
	Developing a personal reaction to John Montague	262
	Questions	262
	Bibliography	264

P = poem also prescribed for Ordinary Level 2007 Exam

8. SYLVIA PLATH (1932–1963)
	Introduction	266
	Black Rook in Rainy Weather	270
	The Times Are Tidy	273
	Morning Song	275
	Finisterre	277
	Mirror	280
	Pheasant	283
	Elm	286
	Poppies in July	290
P	The Arrival of the Bee Box	292
P	Child	295
	Overview of the poems	297
	Forming a personal view or response	303
	Questions	303

ORDINARY LEVEL, 2007 EXAM
EXPLANATORY NOTE	305

Alternative Poems (Ordinary Level, 2007 exam)
Henry Vaughan	306
Peace	
Christina Rossetti	307
Remember	
Edward Thomas	308
Adlestrop	
W.H. Auden	309
Funeral Blues	
Edwin Morgan	311
Strawberries	
Howard Nemerov	313
Wolves in the Zoo	
Denise Levertov	314
What Were They Like?	
Patricia Beer	315
The Voice	
Richard Murphy	316
The Reading Lesson	
Fleur Adcock	317
For Heidi with Blue Hair	
Sharon Olds	319
The Present Moment	

P = POEM ALSO PRESCRIBED FOR ORDINARY LEVEL 2007 EXAM

Paul Durcan	320
Going Home to Mayo, Winter, 1949	
Paddy Bushe	322
Jasmine	
Paul Muldoon	323
Anseo	
Carol Ann Duffy	324
Valentine	
Simon Armitage	325
It Ain't What You Do, It's What It Does To You	

1 John DONNE

Carole Scully

The quest for certainty

John Donne was born in 1572 in Bread Street, London, into a family that was prosperous, educated and, as Catholics, part of an unpopular religious minority. He was the third of six children. His father, also called John, was a successful merchant and a prominent member of the Company of Ironmongers. His mother, Elizabeth, a devout Catholic, was the daughter of John Heywood and the granddaughter of John Rastell, both popular writers in their time; even more significantly, she was the grandniece of Sir Thomas More, who had been beheaded by King Henry VIII in 1535 because he would not swear the oath accepting Henry as supreme head of the church. More had famously declared on the scaffold: 'I die the King's good servant, but God's servant first.'

This staunch religious devotion in the face of oppression was very much in evidence in Elizabeth's family. Two of her brothers, Donne's uncles, became members of the Jesuit order – an extremely dangerous choice of career, as Jesuits were considered, with some justification, to be the main leaders of the Catholic revolt against English Protestantism. It was treason, punishable by horrific forms of death, to be a Catholic priest, or even to help a Catholic priest. One of Donne's uncles, Jasper, led a secret Jesuit mission to England between 1581 and 1583; he was caught and sentenced to death, but this sentence was reduced to imprisonment and exile. There have been suggestions that the young Donne accompanied his mother to visit Jasper in the Tower of London, but there is no proof of this. In all likelihood, Donne was fully aware of his uncle's situation, as he was about eleven years old at the time and still living at home with his mother and stepfather.

Donne's father had died when Donne was four years old, leaving about £3,500 to his wife and six children – a large fortune at the time. About six months later Donne's mother, still only in her thirties, had married Dr John Syminges, a wealthy widower with three children. At one time Syminges had been president of the Royal College of Physicians; more significantly, he was a Catholic. Donne continued to live, therefore, in a family where education was valued, affordable, and Catholic.

EDUCATION

Donne was educated at home with his brother Henry for the early years of his life. There are strong indications that the boys' teachers were Jesuits. In later years Donne wrote of these men: 'I had my first breeding and conversation with men of suppressed and afflicted religion, accustomed to the despite of death and hungry of an imagined martyrdom.' This early exposure to religious intensity had a profound effect on Donne and may partly explain his constant intellectual struggle to find some evidence of certainty in existence. Izaak Walton, Donne's first biographer, relates how Donne, at the age of twelve, entered the University of Oxford with his younger brother, Henry. By starting university at a slightly younger age, Catholic boys could finish early; in this way they left before taking a degree, as that involved swearing the Oath of Supremacy, which declared the English monarch, and not the Pope, to be head of the church. The boys attended Hart Hall, a college with Catholic sympathies, for three years. There are suggestions that they then transferred to the other great university town of Cambridge. Even though he was still unable to take a degree, Donne benefited from this time spent in studies and in mixing with the intellectual group that lived around the colleges.

THE WORLD'S PLEASURES

At some time in his youth, most probably between 1589 and 1591, Donne appears to have travelled on the Continent. Travel was very much a part of a young gentleman's education at this time. He seems to have been fluent in Italian and Spanish, and in later years he kept a great many Spanish books in his library; indeed at about this time he chose a Spanish motto for himself, *Antes muerto que mudado* (Sooner dead than changed). The dramatic nature of this motto expresses the type of young man Donne was, or at least wished to be. An early portrait shows him beautifully dressed, with long, dark, curly hair, his intelligent, educated gaze looking into the future while his hand grasps a sword. He is the epitome of the Elizabethan gentleman. Perhaps Donne had discovered, as so many of us do, that there is a comforting certainty in belonging to a recognisable group.

In 1592 Donne was admitted to study law at Lincoln's Inn, London. In this he was following the strong family tradition on his mother's side. However, as the student lawyers were from wealthy families, they spent more of their time pursuing the pleasures of London life than in studying law. A friend of Donne's from this time, Sir Richard Baker, described him as 'not dissolute but very neat: a great visitor of ladies, a great frequenter of plays, a great writer of conceited verses'.

At this point in his life the twenty-year-old Donne was living a life that was radically different from the one he had learnt from his Jesuit teachers and his family. He was Master of the Revels (the title explains his role) for the Christmas celebrations at Lincoln's Inn. His poetry was circulated, with much praise, among the learned of London. He went to the theatre and socialised with fashionable women; he was on the way to becoming a popular celebrity. This may simply have been the natural rebellion of a young man against the beliefs of the older generation, or it may have been a reaction to seeing his younger brother, Henry, die from the plague while imprisoned in Newgate prison for helping a Catholic priest. It could have been another attempt to find the elusive certainty in life. Whatever the reason, Donne gave himself up to living the life of a gentleman about town and expressing his view of the world in bright, clever, sensual poetry:

> Put forth, put forth that warm balm-breathing thigh,
> Which when next time you in these sheets will smother
> There it must meet another.

Gradually, he drifted away from the law. In 1596 he joined a band of volunteers, under the leadership of Robert Devereux, Earl of Essex, and Sir Walter Raleigh and sailed to Cádiz. He experienced a violent sea battle and wrote with grim honesty of the terrible scenes he witnessed: 'They in the sea being burnt, they in the burnt ship drowned.' He returned to England briefly, but in 1597 he joined another expedition under the command of the Earl of Essex, sailing to the Azores with the aim of capturing the Spanish treasure fleet.

It was socially acceptable for young men from the upper classes to take part in these expeditions. At the time relations between England and Spain were uneasy. As recently as 1588 English forces had narrowly defeated the Spanish Armada, more by luck than by design. Queen Elizabeth, though officially disapproving of her subjects' attacks on Spanish vessels and territories, was perfectly happy to receive a share of the booty. Certainly the sense of drama and adventure seems to have appealed to Donne, as can be seen in his poetry:

> Here take my picture, though I bid farewell;
> Thine, in my heart, where my soul dwells, shall dwell.

The trip to the Azores was not a success, with violent storms battering the ships. Donne described the damage vividly:

> And from our tattered sails, rags drop down so,
> As from one hanged in chains, a year ago.

There is a feeling that Donne may have gone on these voyages hoping to find that elusive certainty he craved, but came home with the realisation that it was not to be found in the role of adventurer.

THE WORLD OF POLITICS

On his return to England, Donne, who by now had largely exhausted his finances, became a rather lowly member of Queen Elizabeth's court. He was twenty-five years old, charmingly ambitious, entertainingly educated, and had proved his valour on military expeditions. Not surprisingly, his fortunes soon improved. In 1598 he was offered a post by the father of one of his fellow-volunteers to Cádiz, and he became private secretary to Sir Thomas Egerton, Lord Keeper of the Great Seal. This was a great opportunity for Donne, as he now had steady employment and a clear connection with an important member of the court. The Lord Keeper presided over the House of Lords and the Court of the Star Chamber, where religious trials were conducted, and he organised the Court of Chancery. As was customary, the Lord Keeper lived at York House; so Donne came to live in a large palace with beautiful gardens that swept down to the Thames. He became part of Egerton's extended family group, which included his fourteen-year-old niece Ann More.

There is no doubt that Egerton was very fond of Donne. When his son died of his wounds in Dublin Castle while serving with Essex in Ireland, Egerton asked Donne to carry his son's sword in the funeral procession at Chester Cathedral. In 1601 he made Donne member of Parliament for one of the boroughs that he controlled. It seemed as if John Donne was destined to play an important role in the world of Elizabethan politics. Perhaps he had found his certainty at last.

THE RELIGIOUS DIFFICULTY

In all likelihood it was about this time that Donne began to move towards the Church of England. He had already considerably loosened his connections with the Catholic Church. In his pursuit of certainty he had been drawn to study the religious controversies that abounded at the time, and he seems to have developed the view that the different religions were simply different representations of the one truth:

> As women do in divers countries go
> In divers habits, yet are still one kind,
> So doth, so is religion.

By taking up the post with Sir Thomas Egerton, Donne in effect committed himself to practising the religion of the court: it would have been impossible for a Catholic to act as a private secretary to one of Queen Elizabeth's more senior courtiers. There is no doubt that Donne was fully aware of the opportunity he now had. A man could advance himself at court if he came to the attention of those in power. Donne carried out his duties diligently and enthusiastically.

Marriage and its consequences

In December 1601, in what could be seen as a foolish and impulsive action or as yet another attempt to find certainty, Donne, now twenty-nine years old, eloped with Ann More, who was seventeen. Ann's father, Sir George More, was a man known for his violent temper. When the couple finally confessed the marriage to him he was furious that his daughter had tied herself to a penniless private secretary. Donne was instantly dismissed from his post by Egerton, Ann's uncle, and was for a time imprisoned. Sir George More used his influence to ensure that Donne was unable to find employment to support his new wife. Donne, with his customary honesty, summed up his situation in six words: 'John Donne, Ann Donne, Un-done.'

Luckily, Ann's cousin, Sir Francis Wolley, offered the couple shelter in his home in Surrey. For the next few years Donne struggled to provide for his growing family. By 1608 Ann had given birth to five children. He spent some time assisting Thomas Morton, a chaplain, who was fiercely anti-Catholic. Indeed there are some indications that Donne may have collaborated with Morton on a number of writings against the Catholic Church, though his name does not appear on any of them.

When Morton was made Dean of Gloucester in 1607, he tried to persuade Donne to take holy orders in the Church of England. Donne's letter of refusal expresses a change in his approach to life. He appears to be ashamed of the heady days of his youth:

> . . . Some irregularities of my life have been visible to some men, and though I have, I thank God, made my peace with Him . . . yet this, which God knows to be so, is not so visible to man, as to free me from their censures and it may be that sacred calling from a dishonour.

Donne may have been using his past life as an excuse to avoid taking holy orders, because he was not yet fully convinced of the religious doctrines of the Church of England. Perhaps he still harboured the desire to succeed in Elizabethan politics. Or it could simply have been that Donne was not sure whether he could make an adequate living in the religious world to support his ever-increasing family. Nevertheless, whatever their motive, these are the words of a man who has sought certainty but has yet to find it.

Happily, in 1608 relations between Donne and his father-in-law improved, and Ann finally received her dowry. They were able to move to a small house in

Mitcham that was, to Donne's delight, convenient to London and his old friends.

There has been a great deal of debate about the nature of Donne's relationship with his wife. On the one hand, he seems to have felt extremely guilty about the way in which their marriage changed her life. He wrote to a friend, describing himself sitting

> in the noise of three gamesome children, and by the side of her whom I transplanted into a wretched fortune, I must labour to disguise that from her by all such honest devices, as giving her my company and discourse.

On the other hand, he wanted to escape from the house at Mitcham, calling it a 'prison' and a 'dungeon'.

Donne travelled extensively on the Continent with Sir Robert Drury and his family between 1611 and 1612. Ann remained in England with their seven children. Finally, in 1615, as a result of continual urging from King James I, Donne broke from the Catholic Church when he was ordained deacon and priest at St Paul's Cathedral, London, and became a royal chaplain. He quickly became known for his brilliant and moving sermons.

THE DEATH OF HIS WIFE

In 1617 Ann died, a few days after giving birth to a stillborn child. She had borne twelve children in fifteen years, seven of whom lived; the eldest was fourteen, the youngest only twelve months. Donne was devastated. Walton describes how he 'became crucified to the world ... a commensurable grief took as full possession of him as joy had done ....' When he wrote a sonnet in her memory Donne clearly stated that he intended to channel all his passion into his life as a cleric and his new religion:

> Since she whom I loved hath paid her last debt
> To nature, and to hers, and my good is dead,
> And her soul early into heaven ravished,
> Wholly in heavenly things my mind is set.

He did indeed become extremely successful in his new religion. In 1625 he preached a sermon at the lying in state of King James I, and then another for the new king, Charles I. His sermons were noted for their use of striking metaphors. In the 'Sermon of Valediction' he challenged his parishioners to consider their relationship with God in the following terms:

> No man would present a lame horse, a disordered clock, a torn book to a king.... Thy body is thy beast; and wilt thou present that to God, when it is lam'd and tir'd with excess of wantonness? When thy clock ... is disordered with passions ... when thy book ... is torn ... wilt thou then present thy self thus defac'd and mangled to almighty God?

Donne was by this time deeply ashamed of his youthful adventures, and he adjusted his life story so that the biography written by his contemporary, Izaak Walton, largely omits his early years. Nevertheless he was sympathetic towards the extremes of youth:

> An old man wonders then how an arrow from an eye could wound him when he was young, and how love could make him do those things which he did then.

He came to believe that his difficulties in supporting his family were part of God's plan for him:

> ... And looking back on my past life, I now plainly see it was his hand that prevented me from all temporal employment; and that it was his will I should never settle nor thrive till I entered into the ministry.

His sermons were popular because they were filled with a sense of the common humanity of mankind:

> No man is an island, entire of itself; every man is a piece of the continent, a part of the main.... Any man's death diminishes me, because I am involved in mankind. And therefore never send to know for whom the bell tolls. It tolls for thee.

THE FINAL QUEST

In 1631, having got out of his sick-bed, Donne delivered his last sermon, entitled 'Death's Duell'. He spoke of the interconnection of life and death, once again using vivid images to convey his message:

> Wee have a winding sheet in our Mother's womb, which grows with us from our conception, and wee come into the world, bound up in that winding sheet, for wee come to seek a grave.

In a gesture that recalls his youthful fondness for the dramatic, Donne ordered a large carved wooden urn to be brought to his room. He stood on it wrapped in his own shroud while an artist made the life-size sketch that was later used for a stone figure.

It is generally agreed that had Donne not died when he did, on 31 March 1631, he would have become a bishop. He was buried in St Paul's Cathedral.

Donne's apostasy

There has been much debate about Donne's apostasy (giving up his religion) and the sincerity of his conversion to the Church of England. Perhaps he was motivated by the desire to succeed in a world where Catholics were definitely second-class citizens. There is no doubt that King James greatly influenced his decision to be ordained by refusing to grant him a secular appointment. Or it may have been that his early experiences led him to rebel against the religion that had caused so much distress in his family. Interestingly, his mother, who was always a staunch Catholic, came to live with Donne and his family in the Deanery at St Paul's. Was his change of religion simply another attempt to find that emotional and intellectual certainty he so badly craved?

Whatever his motivation, Donne's conversion did not end his quest for certainty. His sermons may have expressed an unwavering faith in God, but his poetry still trembled with uncertainty. In his final poem, 'A Hymn to God the Father', Donne begs God for mercy. There is a poignancy in the uncertainty that still haunts his very being after all his years of searching. Yet behind the overwhelming need and the religious language there is still the glimmer of the man who, in spite of the terrible uncertainty he could see, lived life with a passion, the man who was made Master of the Revels, sailed the seas, married impulsively and preached inspiringly, the man who even at the last could not resist punning on his own name:

> But swear by thy self, that at my death thy son
> Shall shine as he shines now, and heretofore;
> And, having done that, thou hast done,
> I fear no more.

Perhaps he did find his certainty after all.

John Donne and metaphysical poetry

John Donne wrote poetry throughout his life. Whether he was on land, at sea, at court, in prison, Catholic or Protestant, single or married, Donne wrote poetry. But, surprising as it may seem, he did not write for publication. For Donne lived at a time when the writing of poetry was considered to be the accomplishment of a true gentleman. Rather like mastering fencing, it was a skill that defined a man's social status. A gentleman wrote to amuse, to impress and even to seduce, but he never wrote to publish. Donne circulated his poetry among a select group of friends and patrons. His point of exhibition and distribution was generally the Mitre, an inn frequented by intellectual gentlemen. He rarely dated his work and all too often did not keep copies of the poems he had written. But although Donne followed the customs of the day in the way he viewed his poetry, he was rigorously individual in the way he wrote.

It is ironic that the term 'metaphysical', applied so often to Donne's style of writing, was first thrown at him as a term of critical abuse. In 1693, some sixty years after Donne's death, John Dryden wrote that he

> affects the metaphysics, not only in his satires, where nature only should reign, but perplexes the minds of the fair sex with nice speculations of philosophy, when he should engage their hearts, and entertain them with the softnesses of love.

In truth, this passage says more about Dryden's expectations of poetry than it does about metaphysical poetry; but his use of the word 'metaphysics' is important, because it captures in one word an essential aspect of Donne's poetry: his desire to go beyond the physical confines of existence. When Donne wrote about love he did not list his beloved's physical qualities, as was customary with traditional poets: instead he ignored these 'softnesses of love' and told her of the ways in which she filled his emotions, his mind and his every waking moment. Donne united the intellect and the emotions in a way that had never been done before. As T. S. Eliot put it, 'a thought to Donne was an experience; it modified his sensibility.'

In an effort to communicate this unified experience of thought and emotion, Donne made use of the *conceit*. Conceits, in the form of far-fetched comparisons, had long been used in traditional love poetry as a device for emphasising the beauty of the poet's beloved. But Donne discarded the traditional in favour of his own unique approach. Once again it is a negative interpretation by a critic that provides the key to what Donne was attempting to do. Samuel Johnson famously commented that in metaphysical poetry 'The most heterogeneous ideas are yoked together by violence; nature and art are ransacked for illustrations, comparisons and illusions . . . .' His use of the words 'violence' and 'ransacked', though intended to be a reproach, suggest the uncompromising way in which Donne combined ideas in his poetry. He disregarded convention, both in thought and taste. He can use the image of a flea in a love poem and urge God to ravish him in a religious one.

Because he was trying to communicate an incredibly complex experience, Donne used the conceit as a device whereby he could connect apparently unconnected images in such a way that the gradual uncovering of a connectedness between them conveys both an intellectual and an emotional message. T. S. Eliot called it a 'telescoping of images and multiplied associations . . .' It is a way of dramatically and rapidly communicating complexity of both feeling and thinking. So Donne could summarise the essence of Elizabeth Drury's being in three words: 'Her body thought.' As readers we can react to this statement on an instinctive level. By combining two images that are accepted as relating to two distinctly different aspects of human existence, Donne succeeds in communicating a unity of message. The three words, and the mental images they carry, amalgamate into a new and complex concept that simultaneously appeals to the intellect, the emotions and the spirit. There is an instinctive quality to our reaction to Donne's conceits that arises out of this challenging combination, a quality all too often lacking in more logical and expected comparisons. In his writing Donne released himself from the accepted norms of appropriateness; in our reading of his work we should endeavour to do the same.

To be able to make these connections, the metaphysical poet had to be finely tuned in every fibre of his being. Here again, those who were suspicious of metaphysical poetry regarded this as a weakness. Johnson rather huffily pronounced that 'The metaphysical poets were men of learning, and to show their learning was their whole endeavour . . . .' In a way, Johnson both hit and missed the point with this statement. The metaphysical poets, and Donne in particular, were indeed men who had benefited from the privilege of education; but instead of simply exhibiting their education by reproducing skilful copies of what they had previously studied, they confronted the very foundations of that education: they questioned the logic they had been taught and tested the substance of the rhetoric they had practised. In this way Donne takes the framework of the traditional Petrarchan sonnet and subjects it to the stresses of unexpected conceits; he fills the dramatic opening, so long the poet's comfortable starting point, with a tension of contradiction, and rejects the conventionally artificial language and rhythm of poetry for the words of everyday speech and the rhythm that comes from the sense of these words.

To be able to do all this, he had to have 'wit' – not in the simplistic sense in which we use that word today but, in the words of the critic Josef Lederer, as 'a brilliant result of long study, a quintessence of deep learning'. Samuel Taylor Coleridge expresses his view in more detail:

> Wonder-exciting vigour, intenseness and peculiarity of thought, using at will the most boundless stores of a capacious memory, and exercised on subjects where we have no right to expect it – this is the wit of Donne!

Of course the fundamental question with Donne is whether his poetry grew out of some inner, inescapable urge that demanded expression or was the calculated posturing of a man who was ambitious for fame and fortune. Did Donne possess a mind that was, in T. S. Eliot's words, 'perfectly equipped for its work' of 'constantly amalgamating disparate experience'? Was this mind tormented by the vision of the uncertainty of existence and forever searching for some evidence of certainty? Do his unconventional conceits and 'wit' simply represent the spiritual, intellectual and emotional insecurity that Donne felt throughout his life? Or was his poetry merely a brilliant exercise in self-advertisement, a cynical publicity stunt to attract the applause and admiration of his peers?

The Flea

Text of poem: New Explorations Anthology page 2
[*Note: This poem is also prescribed for Ordinary Level 2007 exam*]

One of the difficulties with Donne's poetry is that he never made any attempt to keep his poems together, or to organise them in chronological order. Izaak Walton deeply regretted this attitude, commenting that Donne's pieces 'were loosely, God knows too loosely scattered in his youth'. Publication did not appeal to Donne, and on the rare occasion when he allowed the 'Anniversaries' to be printed he wrote to a friend: 'The fault that I acknowledge in myself is to have descended to print anything in verse.' It was not until 1633, two years after his death, that the first collected edition of Donne's verse appeared. The order and grouping of the poems was largely a matter of guesswork on the part of his friends.

It has been said that 'The Flea' was one of Donne's most celebrated and most widely known poems while he was alive. Though there is no definite evidence to support this, there are indications that it was translated into Dutch.

A READING OF THE POEM

Donne opens the poem in a dramatic fashion. He is talking to his lover, but it is definitely a one-sided conversation. It is almost as if he is lecturing her. His use of the image of the flea, though a common poetic device in the seventeenth century, adds to the drama and the tension. There is a feeling that Donne has already tried a number of arguments and has been rejected. Perhaps somewhat at a loss in the face of constant refusal, his eyes wander around the room and suddenly light upon the flea, and inspiration strikes.

The first line appears to be a casual comment on the appearance of a flea. We can imagine how it would catch his lover's attention, how she would probably feel rather puzzled at this sudden change of topic. But the second line quickly undercuts this apparent simplicity. Donne uses the flea to make a very important point to his lover. She is denying him something he wants, but so far he does not specify what it is.

In the next two lines he returns to his comments on the flea. He describes how the flea has bitten both himself and his lover, and their blood is now mixed together in the flea. A basic physicality is suggested in his use of the blood image, which prepares us for the sixth line. Donne's use of the word 'maidenhead', along with 'sin' and 'shame', leaves little doubt about what it is his lover is denying him.

Donne reinforces the connection between himself and the flea in the final three lines of the first stanza. Unlike Donne himself, the flea is able to enjoy an intimate relationship with this woman, even though it has not gone through the rituals of courtship. The use of the word 'pampered' implies a feeling of contentment and satisfaction – two states that Donne most certainly does not feel. The suggestion is that he has played the wooing game according to the rules, and he feels that, in all fairness, his lover should play her part in the game.

It is evident from reading this first stanza that how this poem is interpreted, and what reaction we experience to it, depend on how we view the tone of the piece. Donne would probably have read this poem aloud to a small group and in this way could have coloured the tone. But our interpretation has to develop as a result of careful reading and rereading. If we consider Donne to be approaching his lover in a mock-dramatic or charmingly pathetic manner, we can react with amusement; we can join in the joke that is trembling between Donne and his lady. But if we think he is behaving in a thoroughly unpleasant fashion, exerting considerable emotional blackmail on his lover with his selfish, adolescent whingeing, we are bound to feel anger and annoyance.

Finally, it may be that Donne deliberately wove this ambiguity into the poem as a way of adding a sense of danger. He knows he is skating on thin ice, and so do we. In this way he deliberately moves away from the safety of creating straightforward amusement and into the perils of humour that challenges our preconceptions.

Donne ended the first stanza on an extremely dramatic note, lamenting in mock-heroic terms – evident in the use of the word 'alas' – the fact that he and his lover have not experienced physical intimacy. He continues this approach in the second stanza. His dramatic plea, 'Oh stay,' asking her to not to squash the flea, carries with it a wealth of understated comedy. In an age when fleas and their destruction were commonplace, the drama Donne attaches to this incident can only be interpreted as humorous. He asks that the flea's life be spared, because in killing it his lover will destroy the flea's life and, because it contains their blood, her life and Donne's. He urges her to remember that the mingling of their blood is intimate and special: it is like their 'marriage bed' and their 'marriage temple'. Here again Donne overstates the situation in a humorous way: linking the image of a temple with a flea is patently ridiculous. Donne races on, carried forward by his own eloquence and perhaps by his lover's lack of response despite his best efforts. Nevertheless, in the midst of all these theatricals he produces a stunningly vivid image of their blood within the flea, 'cloistered in these living walls of jet.' Barely pausing for breath, he launches another argument at his lover. If she is unmoved by his death and that of the flea, then she must be concerned about causing her own suicide and thereby committing a sin to add to that of two murders.

Donne uses religious language in this stanza to provide a framework for his argument. His implication is that he regards physical intimacy with his lover as something sacred and special; but there is an undercutting awareness of the humorous incompatibility that lies in linking a flea sucking blood with religion.

Though Donne's lover never speaks, we can clearly visualise her reaction to his arguments in the way that she behaves. She may be verbally inactive but she is far from being passive. The third stanza opens with the death of the flea. Donne is horrified by her action. It is 'cruel and sudden,' perhaps as cruel and sudden as her rejection of his advances. She has spilled the 'blood of innocence'. The clear suggestion is that the woman is callous and cruel in her behaviour towards the innocent flea, just as she is with the innocent Donne. This, of course, is obviously ridiculous. Donne is far from innocent in his desires. He continues this line of thought, stating that she triumphs in the flea's death because she has proved the arguments that Donne put forward in the second stanza to be wrong.

At this point it appears that Donne is completely beaten. He gives the impression that his lover has outwitted him. But he is simply lulling her into a false sense of security. The last three lines of the poem are produced with a magician's flourish. Donne concedes that the woman is absolutely right: she has lost nothing with the death of the flea. But, in a breathtaking reversal of the balance of power, he tells her that, in exactly the same way, her yielding to his advances will not cause her to lose her honour. He is, in effect, using the well-worn argument that he will respect her in the morning!

STYLE

Donne uses a popular device from sixteenth-century love poetry as the framework on which to hang his poem. The linking of a male lover with a flea had been used in Greek, Latin, French, Spanish and Italian poetry. The image was usually developed along very bawdy lines, with the flea wandering over the woman's body; the death of the flea at the hands of the woman was regarded as ultimately blissful.

This poem could be viewed as Donne testing the limitations of the device not simply to achieve a humorous effect, but to challenge the conventionality that the device represented.

Alternatively
Samuel Johnson wrote of the metaphysicals: 'Whatever is improper or vicious is produced from nature in pursuit of something new and strange; the writers fail to give delight by their desire to excite admiration.'

This piece may be nothing more than the poetic equivalent of a dirty joke. It causes a reaction simply because it uses rude images. Donne takes an 'improper' idea in the belief that he will be able to give it a new slant, purely in an attempt to impress his friends at the Mitre. It is neither 'new' nor 'strange', nor does it 'excite admiration' or 'delight'. In short, it is the perfect piece to be read in a dimly lit room filled with immature men.

Song: Go, and catch a falling star
Text of poem: New Explorations Anthology page 4
[Note: This poem is also prescribed for Ordinary Level 2007 exam]

This poem appears to have been written during the time Donne spent at Lincoln's Inn, when he was beginning to make a name for himself as a poet. Poetry at this time was one way in which an educated young man on the fringes of the court could bring himself to the attention of those in power.

STYLE

The listing of impossible tasks was popular in Petrarchan poetry. This use of *hyperbole* (an exaggerated statement not meant to be taken literally) was a device to emphasise the poet's devotion to his beloved.

There is a strong element of *satire* in this poem. Broadly speaking, satire is used to expose and ridicule folly and shallowness. It is frequently driven by anger, but it is more refined and sophisticated than an angry outburst. The writer generally expresses a one-sided view of his subject, in order to ensure that the satire works. The use of satire suggests that the writer feels superior to those he is satirising, that he can see the folly while others are unaware of it.

A READING OF THE POEM

The first line of this poem has a magical, fairy-tale quality about it. The catching of a 'falling star' belongs to the romantic world of handsome princes and beautiful princesses. Donne deliberately creates specific expectations in the reader by using this as his opening line. However, the second line introduces a sense of unease, as it is a much darker image. The phrase 'get with child' is brutally unromantic. The mandrake is a plant that people at the time believed had human qualities, such as screaming when it was uprooted. Though this image, like that of catching a falling star, is meant to represent an impossible task, it is very much the stuff of nightmares.

The tone changes again with Donne's rather conventional question about the passing of time. But we return to a darker world of images with the question about 'the Devil's foot'. The 'mermaids singing' could belong to the world of falling stars and passing time; however, Donne appears to be deliberately exploiting the ambiguity that existed around the image of the mermaid at this time: while it could refer to a beautiful half-woman, half-fish creature, it could also be used to denote a prostitute. The final image of 'envy's stinging' has a deeply personal feeling about it.

Donne is deliberately playing with his reader's perception of the nature of this poem. He alternates between images usually connected with the Petrarchan view of love and images that are radically and disturbingly opposed to it. He is consciously confusing his reader in order to create tension. All this tension culminates in the final three lines of the stanza, where Donne uses both the sense of his words and their rhythm in a most unsettling way. There is real vehemence in his statement about the lack of success for the 'honest mind'. Does it reflect the frustrations of an ambitious young man not yet able to break into the powerful world of the court? By interrupting the rhythm of the stanza with two lines of only two words, Donne skilfully emphasises this final image.

The second stanza continues this tension but in a slightly different way. Rather than alternate between pleasant traditional images and more unpleasant unconventional ones, Donne remains in the world of the unpleasant. A series of disquieting images is hurled at the reader: being 'born to strange sights,' able to see 'things invisible', riding 'ten thousand days and nights,' hair turning 'snow white' and returning with stories of 'strange wonders'. It is not accidental that Donne repeats the word 'strange' in this stanza, for it is unsettlingly strange.

In a final flourish Donne ends the stanza on the strangest concept of all: the fact that it is impossible to find 'a woman true and fair.' He has propelled us along a roller-coaster ride of emotions, and we are left gasping at the end of this outburst. Are we speechless from shock at the strength of emotion underlying his opinion of women? Or has the tension that fills every word in the poem become unbearable?

The tone of the final stanza is more controlled; it is as if Donne has been emotionally drained by the first two stanzas. There is a sad vulnerability and longing in the line 'If thou find'st one, let me know,' for, despite his best efforts, Donne still yearns for the 'woman true and fair.' Quickly he changes his mind, asking not to be told of such a woman, not even if she were living next door to him. Once again Donne's bitterness returns, perhaps even more effective now that it is more understated in its expression.

In the last five lines of the poem Donne summarises his attitude to women. He no longer rants and raves: he simply states the fact that even if a 'true' woman were to be found she would inevitably turn 'false' in the length of time it would take for a letter to be sent to him while travelling to meet her. It is a shocking ending to the poem; or is it?

As with 'The Flea', this poem is a mass of unresolved ambiguities. Is Donne being serious or not? Is he expressing his real views, his longing for certainty, or is he simply acting out an attitude? Is the 'me' in the poem Donne, or a persona he has taken on? Did he write this poem as a satire? If he intended it to be a satire, what was he satirising? Was he satirising women, perhaps as a result of something he experienced? Or was he drawing attention to the stupidity of the conventional Petrarchan love poem? Was Donne fighting for women to be treated by men as real human beings? It is up to you to decide.

Alternatively
William Hazlitt commented on the metaphysical poets: 'Their chief aim was to make you wonder at the writer, not interest you in the subject . . . .' This poem could be seen as the work of a self-absorbed man. Donne was determined to gain notoriety by being outrageous and controversial. Though this poem may have been written as the words to a song, it is not pleasantly amusing. His images are deliberately disturbing, his views on women are offensive and his tone is nastily pompous. He may pride himself on having an 'honest mind', but on the evidence of this poem it is little wonder that he was unable 'to advance'.

The Sun Rising

Text of poem: New Explorations Anthology page 6

Donne made no attempt during his lifetime to date the majority of his poems, nor to keep them in any kind of order. As very little of his work was published and the poems were simply distributed in manuscript form, we have few indications of when most of the poems were written. In the first printed edition of his poetry, in 1633, the love poems are scattered through the book. However, in 1635, four years after his death, an edition of Donne's poetry grouped all his love poems together under the title 'Songs and Sonnets'. Generally, later editions have stuck to this arrangement, because not enough definite information is available to organise them in any other way.

STYLE

Donne frequently places himself in a dramatic setting in his love poems. Whether he is attempting to seduce his lover, to remain with her or to leave her behind, the reader is brought into the scene at a very important moment. In this poem Donne uses this drama to give new life and energy to the traditional love-poetry images of royalty and the sun.

A READING OF THE POEM

The opening three lines of this poem are wonderfully dramatic. Donne balances straightforward language and natural speech rhythms to vividly create a sense of immediacy. It is as if we are there with him as he vents his annoyance on the sun. The beams of sun shine in through 'windows' and 'curtains', disturbing Donne and his lover. It is an intrusion into their close intimacy, an unwanted reminder that they will not always be able to exist in this tranquil and contented state. The sun is a reminder to the two lovers of the world outside. Their quietness is emphasised by the frenzied activities, clearly suggested by the rhythm of these lines, of the early morning. In four lines, we see 'late schoolboys' and 'sour prentices' reluctantly going on their way, while courtiers scurry around after the king and farm workers, 'country ants', set about the harvesting. All these people are governed by something outside themselves: the schoolboys by the school day, the apprentices by their work, the courtiers by the whims of the king, and the farm workers by the seasons. However, Donne and his lover are freed from such controls by their love. They have transcended time itself.

The second stanza continues this theme of love triumphant. Donne challenges the power of the sun with his beams 'so reverend and strong'. He states that he could easily blot out these beams by simply shutting his eyes. But he will not do this, because he does not want to miss seeing his beloved for one instant. Therefore, for him his lover is stronger than the sun. This links into the following image, where Donne speaks of her eyes being bright enough to blind the sun. This is a traditional image in love poetry, but Donne places it in a context where the comparison seems to occur naturally and spontaneously. As in the first stanza, he sweeps from the close intimacy of the room to the outside world by his use of vivid images. He challenges the sun further by stating that it may spend the day moving across the world, over the evocative 'Indias of spice and mine' or shining on kings, but the real, true world will be in this room with the two lovers. In this way, love transcends the confines of space.

In the third stanza Donne draws together this central theme of love triumphant. His lover is 'all states' and he is 'all princes'. There is an irresistible quality about Donne's enthusiasm, whatever his motivation. Even if he was only driven by the desire to seduce, it is hard not to be swept along with him. He is emphatic in his belief that the two lovers have everything that matters with them in the room: 'Nothing else is.' The trappings of worldly success, considered so important in the external world, are irrelevant in the world of love. The unlimited power wielded by sixteenth-century royalty is but an imitation of the lovers' power; the rewards of 'honour' are simply amusing imitations, and wealth is useless. The sun, which so rudely wakened them, is pitied by Donne, because its movement is across this external world on its own, whereas Donne and his beloved are two people united in a limitless world of love. Momentarily, he has found some certainty.

In the final four lines of the poem Donne slows the rhythm of his words to underpin the alteration in his emotions. His excited and challenging confidence changes to sympathetic concern for the sun. The sun is old and deserves some respect, particularly from two who have such power. Donne comforts the sun by allowing it to enter into their world, so that in shining on them it will be shining on the true world. Is there a touch of humour in these lines? Could Donne be, once again, practising the art of humorous seduction?

Alternatively
The critic John Carey considers the 'vaunting language' used by Donne in this poem to be a clear indication that he did not feel as confident and contented as he said he did. Rather than feeling better than those involved in the court, or richer than those who had wealth, Carey feels that Donne, who had financial difficulties, was deeply envious of the world of the rich and powerful. He was desperately ambitious to make his mark on the world. Carey's view is that Donne regards the 'private world' he inhabits with his beloved as being only an imitation of the 'public' world he so longs to join. No matter how hard he tries to concentrate on the superiority of love, he is 'irascibly conscious of the rest of the world's activities'.

The Anniversarie
Text of poem: New Explorations Anthology page 8

BACKGROUND

See the background notes for 'The Sun Rising', pages 16–18.

STYLE

Donne's poems on love are usually classified as *lyrics*. Though the term 'lyric' is a rather general one, there are certain characteristics that tend to be obvious in a lyrical poem. The nineteenth-century writer John Ruskin defined the lyric as 'the expression by the poet of his own feelings'. There is an undeniable personal quality about the lyric, in that the words are spoken by one person from a personal viewpoint. However, a problem arises regarding exactly who the 'I' of lyrical poetry is. The 'I' could be the poet himself, or it could simply represent a character the poet has created, a persona, to act as a mouthpiece for what he wants to express. Therefore, it is not always clear just how personal 'lyric' poems are.

There has been a great deal of discussion about the reality of the love experiences Donne describes in his love poetry. Some have felt that the 'I' in these poems is not Donne and that the feelings expressed are no more than the wishful thoughts of a frustrated young man. Others believe that Donne based his poems on actual experiences in his life and that the 'I' is very definitely Donne himself. What is undeniable is the fact that when Donne turned to religion he became deeply embarrassed by these poems from his youth.

A READING OF THE POEM

This poem opens on familiar territory, both for the modern reader of Donne and for those few of his contemporaries who were privileged to read his work in manuscript form. The images of the court and the sun were part of the traditional formula of Petrarchan love poetry, which was so popular in Donne's time. For modern readers who have read some of Donne's works these images are familiar because he uses them frequently in his writing. Yet, even though these two groups of readers are separated by more than four hundred years, a common sense of expectancy is stimulated by this opening. Just as Donne's friends might have glanced at each other in anticipation of how Donne was going to follow this beginning, so we are also aware that something will happen in the course of this poem that will not be totally expected.

However, the first stanza continues in a reasonably conservative way. Donne, having noted that everything from the 'kings' to the 'sun' has aged by a year since the lovers first met, states clearly that it is only their shared love that is untouched by time. In the face of 'destruction' and 'decay' their love 'keeps his first, last, everlasting day.'

In the first stanza the concept of time passing is conveyed by fairly unthreatening images. The idea of 'kings', 'beauties', 'wits' and the 'sun itself' ageing by a year is not really disturbing: Donne is simply reproducing the usual formula to suggest the passing of time. Similarly, the line 'Only our love hath no decay' is a common sentiment expressed in love poetry. Love has 'no tomorrow', nor has it a 'yesterday'. This is all fairly unremarkable. But then we meet the line 'Running it never runs from us away,' and the formulaic safety of the opening eight lines begins to tremble slightly. What does Donne mean by this line? He must have felt it was of reasonable importance to use it to interrupt the traditional approach he had followed so far. There is a kind of premeditated intellectualisation in this paradox, a conscious self-awareness that is not present in the previous lines. The verb 'running' is not one that immediately springs to mind in connection with a love affair, yet Donne obviously chose it carefully. Was it simply so that he could construct this clever little paradox to amuse both himself and his friends? Or did he deliberately use 'run' because it was definitely *not* part of the vocabulary of the Petrarchan love poem?

Donne ends this stanza with a line that is beautifully balanced, both in its meaning and its rhythm: 'But truly keeps his first, last, everlasting day.' Love remains untouched by the 'destruction' and 'decay' that haunts everything else.

The second stanza begins with a graphic image of two bodies in separate graves. The threat of death was very real to the Elizabethans, and this would have been a disturbing image, one far removed from the niceties of Petrarchan love poetry. The description of the two lovers lying in the one grave is not totally comforting. Donne continues the royalty image of the first stanza with his comparison between the two lovers and 'princes'. This is an idea that we have met previously with Donne: that mutual love makes two people special, powerful, and set apart – rather like royalty but even better. However, despite their uniqueness the two lovers, along with 'other princes', must inevitably surrender their physical bodies.

It is interesting that there is generally a marked lack of physical details in Donne's poetry: we rarely learn anything about what his lovers look like, even though his love poetry is filled with a sensuous pleasure. Yet here he deliberately writes of the 'eyes' with their 'sweet salt tears' and the 'ears' that were 'oft fed with true oaths'. The first six lines of the second stanza vividly describe the physicality of death, because Donne wants us to feel the overwhelming nature of death, so that love's ability to triumph over it will appear all the more wonderful. For love does triumph. Donne declares that their love has transcended the limitations of mere physical love: it has become a part of their very souls. This spiritual love is able to cheat death: the bodies of the lovers may go 'to their graves,' but the souls will escape to 'there above'. This was provocative stuff in an age when access to Heaven was being fought over by the Catholic and Protestant churches. Both promised eternal life to their followers and damnation to those who rejected them. Yet here is Donne, filled with certainty, saying that love shared between a man and a woman is the way to gain entry into Heaven.

The final stanza opens where the second stanza ends. When the souls of the lovers go up to Heaven they will be 'thoroughly blessed', because their love will be increased by heavenly love. There they will join all the other lovers who have also attained spiritual love, and in this way they will no longer be unique in the way that they are on Earth. However, for the moment they are still here on Earth; they are still 'kings', because their love is true, but they need not fear death. The lovers are safe, because they can be damaged in only one way: by each other. Their love ensures that they are immune to the passing of time and the horrors of death but, ironically, it also makes them profoundly vulnerable to each other. Happily, Donne is so confident in the certainty of their love that he quickly dismisses this possibility. They must simply avoid worrying about 'true and false fears' and live a long life together, secure in the protection of their shared love.

This poem ends in a way that is far removed from the Petrarchan conventions that filled the first stanza. It has travelled from the world of the court to the sun blazing in space, from the darkness of the grave to the light of Heaven. But above all it has declared the power and the certainty of the love that Donne shares with his beloved.

Alternatively
Samuel Taylor Coleridge commented on the metaphysical poets that they 'sacrificed the heart to the head'. Is this poem a sincere expression of Donne's belief in the certainty of his love, or is it simply an intellectual exercise designed to show just how stale and old-fashioned traditional Petrarchan love poetry had become? Did he write from the heart, or did his head make it look as if he was writing from the heart?

Sweetest love, I do not go
Text of poem: New Explorations Anthology page 10

It has been suggested – particularly by Donne's first biographer, Izaak Walton – that Donne wrote this poem, together with 'A Valediction: Forbidding Mourning', to his wife before he left to travel on the Continent in 1611. However, as Donne rarely dated any of his poetry, there is no proof to support this view.

In some manuscripts this poem is in a group entitled 'Songs which were made to certain airs which were made before'. Several seventeenth-century manuscripts contain music for this poem, but again there is no proof that Donne ever intended this poem to be sung.

A READING OF THE POEM
The poem opens in typical Donne style. It is a moment of drama, and we have stumbled upon two people immersed in an intense conversation. But the drama in this poem is far more understated than in much of Donne's other love poetry. There is a sense of true intimacy about the language he uses to express his feelings. He speaks simply and with apparent sincerity. There is little evidence of his sparkling wit and tongue-in-cheek humour; he is simply trying to reassure his beloved. In the very first lines of the poem he emphasises to her that he is not going 'for weariness' of her, nor because he is looking for 'a fitter love'. He then uses gentle humour to try to lighten the moment. After all, he says, he will have to die sometime, and he would rather enjoy life than spend it imagining all the dreadful deaths that might happen to him. We can almost see Donne widening his eyes and giving an appealing smile to emphasise this little joke.

In an effort to carry this lighter tone into the second stanza, Donne then compares himself to the sun. The sun, he tells his beloved, set yesterday but was still able to return. So, he must go away, but he will be back. In a simple little hyperbole he tells her that he will be back more speedily than the sun, because he has the motivation to return to her.

The third stanza approaches the main theme of the poem from a slightly different angle. Donne reflects on the ways humankind deals with life experiences. He comments that we tend to accept the good times for what they are, but when it comes to the bad times we tend to exaggerate how bad they are. He is trying to minimise the 'bad chance' of their parting in an effort to comfort and reassure his beloved.

However, in the fourth stanza he returns to the intensely personal tone of the opening stanza. In a series of beautifully constructed images and rhythms he describes just how deeply connected the two lovers are. Her sadness is so real to him that it actually erodes his life force. Her sighs diminish the strength of his soul; her tears are like a loss of blood to him. Her grief is killing him, and he urges her to remember this, to realise that she is 'the best of me'. This stanza vibrates with a level of sincerity and an emotional openness that are in marked contrast to some of Donne's earlier love poetry. There is no sense that Donne is performing or taking up a position in an effort to impress or amuse. For once, it seems that we are seeing John Donne the man as he really is, filled with the certainty that their love is true.

This emotional intensity sweeps into the final stanza. Donne begs his lover not to imagine all the terrible things that could happen to him when they are parted. He admits the possibility of something dreadful occurring, but he reminds her that they really have no control over destiny. Once again he uses a wonderfully evocative image to convey the depth of his feelings. For lovers such as they, the ultimate terror of death is simply a turning 'aside to sleep'. Their true and certain love enables them to triumph over time and space, and even death itself.

STYLE

The structure of this poem is deceptively simple. The very appearance of the printed lines on the page implies that this is a poem that should be easily understood, and in many ways it is. Donne uses the simple language of everyday conversation. There are no dramatic exclamations, no witty constructions: just the desire to express sincerity. His occasional movements away from the deeply personal tone (in the second and third stanzas) are not for the purpose of displaying his intellect, but rather are further attempts to relieve the dreadful emotional turmoil the two lovers are experiencing. His use of a light rhythm and a strong rhyme seems to be a deliberate attempt to lighten the intensity of the situation. Similarly, the five eight-line stanzas impose a definite structure on the scene, a structure that is clearly lacking in the reality of the lovers' imminent separation. However, in spite of his best efforts, Donne cannot control the emotional impact of this moment. His true feelings break through rhyme and rhythm. He cannot hide his own vulnerability. The death that he is suffering in this poem is more real and painful than the one he described in 'The Flea', because love is no longer a game.

Alternatively
'In his poems there is often a perfect equilibrium between their exact truth to mood and feeling and their acute awareness of an audience' (Barbara Everett). Is this poem simply another example of Donne using love as a vehicle for his desire to impress his little group of fans? Is he exploiting his lover, once again using their apparent emotional connection as an opportunity to display his 'wit'?

A Valediction: Forbidding Mourning

Text of poem: New Explorations Anthology page 12

As we have seen, Izaak Walton links this poem with 'Sweetest Love, I Do Not Go', suggesting that they were written just before a trip to the Continent in 1611. He comments: 'I beg leave to tell you, that I have heard some critics ... say, that none of the Greek or Latin poets did equal them.' However, attractive though it may be to connect them to Donne's life, it should be noted that parting or absence from a loved one were traditional themes in love poetry.

A READING OF THE POEM

Donne opens this poem with a vivid image of a death-bed scene. This, coupled with the title – 'A Valediction: Forbidding Mourning' – creates the expectation that this poem will be about the death of someone. It is certainly not an unpleasant death, as the 'virtuous men' are confident of a life after death in Heaven. The atmosphere is one of dignity and composure, with a group of friends present at the gentle passing.

The second stanza links into this idea of a quiet withdrawal. Donne advises his beloved that they should 'melt, and make no noise'. At this point Donne still seems to be dealing with death in its physical sense. But the following three lines have something odd about them. Donne seems to be suggesting that the two lovers should die peacefully. He emphasises the depth and uniqueness of their love by using such religious phrases as 'profanation of our joys' and 'to tell the laity'. Theirs is a love that is wonderfully special and should not involve others. In the light of this intensity it seems odd that he should be advising her to meet their death with 'no tear-floods, nor sigh-tempests'.

The third stanza makes no attempt to resolve this difficulty. Donne seems to deliberately leave the personal and move to the impersonal. He comments on the custom, popular since classical times, of viewing natural occurrences, such as earthquakes, as signs or portents. He sweeps the focus of the poem up into the skies to see the 'trepidation of the spheres', the very planets moving. Gradually this image connects with those in the opening two stanzas: the death of 'virtuous men', Donne's desire for the two lovers to 'melt', and now the 'trepidation of the spheres'. Each of these images is centred on the idea of movement, movement that is profoundly important but is nevertheless a gentle, quiet and 'innocent' movement.

Donne continues his astronomical imagery in the fourth stanza with his reference to 'sublunary lover's love'. This is the type of love that 'the laity' experience. It is a narrow, earthbound type of love that is dependent on physical presence, a love that cannot endure 'absence'. At this point we begin to realise that Donne is not concerned with death in a physical sense but in an emotional sense.

From the fifth stanza on, Donne slowly reveals the reason for his 'valediction'. He expands on the love he shares with his beloved. It is quite unlike that of the 'sublunary lovers'. It has been 'refined', purified, so that all impurities have been removed. Their love is not confined by physical nearness, the presence of 'eyes, lips, and hands': they have achieved an 'inter-assured' love that is founded on connection of the mind rather than of the body. They are able to be careless of the physical presence of each other because they are so confident in each other.

The sixth stanza reaffirms the special quality of their love. Donne has described it as something close to a religious experience, a moving of planets, a shared emotion without imperfections. Now he draws all these images together to represent theirs as a relationship of 'two souls', where a parting, reluctant though it is, is nothing more than 'an expansion'. The central theme of the poem is revealed. Donne and his beloved must face a separation. He is trying to comfort her, to stop her mourning as if it were a death. For, he tells her, physical separation takes their 'refined' love and refines it still further, so that they achieve a connection of exquisite pureness, 'like gold to aery thinness beat.'

These interwoven images of a perfect love are breathtaking; and yet they are not enough for Donne. He has to go beyond the poetically expected, to explore a dimension of imagery that is neither expected nor accepted. He takes the concept of 'connection' and searches for a way to express it further. In the final three stanzas of the poem he rejects the traditional, the quickly recognised, the easily understood, and finds the world of science. For him, the essence of their relationship is captured by the 'twin compasses'. Just as this instrument of measurement is made up of two metal legs joined at a point, so Donne and his beloved are connected in separation. In Donne's case he is the 'foot' that 'far doth roam,' while his beloved is the 'fixed foot' that 'leans, and hearkens after it'. They are mutually dependent, while being independent. So, Donne can declare that she is the certainty in his life; her 'firmness' ensures that his direction is true, and it is she to whom he will return, just as the compasses must inevitably meet together, 'and makes me end, where I begun'. He reassures his beloved that there is no need for her to mourn this separation, because for them it is no separation at all.

Alternatively
In 1837 Henry Hallam wrote of Donne's poetry: 'Few are good for much; the conceits have not even the merit of being intelligible . . . .' This poem is not only confused, it is also confusing. Donne wanders around the early part of the piece in a kind of intellectual haze. Then, in the later part, he pulls out the conceit of the pair of compasses, rather as a bad magician pulls out a bunch of flowers from a pot. There is no real sense to the trick, but it might just impress the audience!

The Dreame
Text of poem: New Explorations Anthology page 14

The idea of the poet's beloved appearing to him while he is dreaming or daydreaming originated in Classical poetry. It was taken up by Renaissance poets and became a very popular topic. Donald Guss holds the view that Donne was in a direct line of influence from the Renaissance: 'Donne sometimes expresses dramatic emotions through the gallant conceits of the Petrarchans.'

METRE
Donne's approach to metre has been the subject of much debate. Though he frequently employed *iambic pentameter* (each line having five stressed and five unstressed syllables), it is generally agreed that the reading of his poetry is controlled more by the sense of the words than by their metre. Coleridge commented on the poetry of Donne that 'In poems where the writer thinks, and expects the reader to do so, the sense must be understood to ascertain the metre.' This view was echoed by Joan Bennett when she wrote: 'Often the rhythm is as intricate as the thought and only reveals itself when the emphasis has been carefully distributed according to the sense.' Any personalised consideration of 'The Dreame' should include an analysis of the way in which Donne links sense and metre to achieve a deceptively natural rhythm.

A READING OF THE POEM
As we have seen, Donne's poetry frequently begins with a moment of drama, where the reader is swept into the piece by a dramatic statement. So, in 'The Flea' we read:

> Mark but this flea, and mark in this,
> How little that which thou deny'st me is . . .

Similarly, with 'Sweetest Love, I Do Not Go':

> Sweetest love, I do not go,
> For weariness of thee . . .

And, perhaps the most dramatic of all openings, that of 'The Sun Rising':

> Busy old fool, unruly sun . . .

However, with 'The Dreame' we encounter a slightly different opening technique. The theatrical statement gives way to a remark that is immediately and intensely intimate and, in many ways, even more dramatic. It is as if we have chanced upon Donne at his most open, caught him in those unguarded seconds between sleep and wakefulness. The very rhythm and sounds of the words in the first two lines of the poem are filled with an unexpected gentleness and emotional vulnerability. Donne tells his beloved that she acted 'wisely' in waking him. His lack of irritation at being disturbed is in marked contrast to the last time we saw Donne being awakened, in 'The Sun Rising'. He speaks to his 'dear love' in a quiet and familiar way, welcoming her arrival. His comment that she 'brok'st not' his dream, but rather continued it, is touching in its sincerity. This Donne is certainly not playing at the game of love. He tells her that she is 'so true' that she makes 'dreams truths, and fables histories'; she embodies the idealised perfection of the worlds of dreams and fairy stories. His invitation to her to 'enter these arms' is a million miles away from his attempt in 'The Flea' to entice his lover to yield to him. A desire to possess and dominate has given way to a longing for mutual submission, for them to finish his dream, to 'act the rest.'

This intense intimacy continues in the second stanza. He tells her that she did not wake him by the noise of her movement, but by the light of her eyes. Here Donne expresses a common feeling among lovers, where a meeting of eyes can have the power to set hearts fluttering and pulses racing. He is so aware of her that her very presence is enough to wake him. The level of their closeness becomes even more apparent as the poem continues. Donne tells her that he thought she was 'an angel', adding with a moving vulnerability that he is telling the truth because she 'lov'st truth'. This is not the Donne who used amusing flattery as an aid to seduction. This relationship is much too serious for anything but the truth; it is based on the certainty of mutual understanding, emotional empathy and a sharing of thoughts. It is no wonder that Donne uses the religious words 'angel' and 'profane' in an effort to convey just how special it is.

In the final stanza Donne gradually becomes more wakeful. He now begins to 'doubt'. On one level, this doubting is simply a question whether his beloved is actually there or not. However, on a deeper level it is indicative of the terrible inner doubt that Donne experienced in all aspects of his life, but particularly when it came to love. Previously, when he did not truly love he had been able to hide this doubt beneath sparklingly witty comments. Now that he does love he must lay his soul bare. He is embarrassed by his own insecurity, admitting that the strength of his love is equalled by the strength of his fear. He speaks for all lovers who know the wonder of truly loving and the terror that it will all suddenly disappear. His beloved is as a light in the overwhelming darkness, with her 'lightning' eyes and her ability to know his heart and his thoughts. She comes into his dream 'to kindle,' to set him on fire with her presence. But even more than that, there is a sense that Donne felt she had come to kindle his very life, to light up the gnawing darkness in his soul that craved some certainty.

The poem closes with an expression of the complexity of Donne's emotions. He longs to return to 'dream that hope again' with such intensity that if he cannot do so he will die. This is more than poetic over-dramatisation, or the role of the charmingly pathetic lover. Instead it is an admission of dependence: he needs to experience true love again, he needs to be close to his beloved, he needs to feel that certainty.

Alternatively
Mario Praz felt that Donne's 'sole preoccupation is with the whole effect'. In this poem Donne simply reproduces a popular poetic device so that he can, once again, display himself. For him, the 'whole effect' of this piece rests on his willingness to be the centre of attention, to describe and analyse his emotional viewpoint. To this end he sacrifices coherent structure, disciplined metre and intellectual resolution. It is undeniable that the 'whole effect' of this piece is impressive, but it is equally undeniable that it is based on a structure of shifting sands.

Batter my heart
Text of poem: New Explorations Anthology page 16

As always with Donne, the dating of this poem is the subject of much debate. Some critics like to view Donne's poetic output as occurring in two phases, which represent two distinct parts of his life. The first phase is that of his youth and marriage and traces his growth from a young man desiring adventure and romantic conquests to a mature man, who shares a deep love with his wife but is profoundly frustrated with his position in life. The second phase is seen as occurring in his later life, after his ordination and his wife's death, when Donne gave himself up to his new religion but was still tormented by doubt.

In this scheme the three sonnets 'Batter My Heart', 'At the Round Earth's Imagined Corners' and 'Thou Hast Made Me' would be seen as belonging to the second phase, while the other seven poems under consideration would belong to the first phase.

However, this is a rather simplistic view of both Donne's life and his poetry. Life is not lived in distinct phases, and poetry is more than just a rhyming diary of day-to-day events. Donne was a highly intelligent and complex man, who was fully aware of the limitations of the human condition and the profound uncertainty of existence. His life was spent in a continuous search for some evidence of certainty in the many aspects of his experience. The world of love and the world of religion were always present in the world of John Donne, as was the world of poetry. His poetry was not written for financial gain, since it was rarely published, nor was it stimulated solely by the desire for notoriety, since Donne frequently expressed embarrassment about his writing. Rather, he wrote poetry because he had no choice but to write poetry. It was his way of confronting the worlds that he inhabited. Poetry enabled him to express the very turmoil and desires of his soul, and the soul does not exist in phases.

A READING OF THE POEM

This sonnet in many ways condenses a number of the aspects of Donne's earlier poetry into a tight, fourteen-line structure and a rigorous rhyming scheme of *abba, abba, cdcdee*. It begins with the usual dramatic opening – indeed it is an opening that is spectacularly dramatic. The implied paradox of the 'three-personed God', the representation of the spiritual, being called upon to physically 'batter' Donne's heart, is both stunning and shocking. Before we can recover from it Donne launches us into a list of breathtaking verbs: 'knock, breathe, shine . . . rise, and stand, o'erthrow me . . . bend . . . break, blow, burn . . .' We are left gasping by this combination of action images, the conflict suggested in the paradox 'that I may rise, and stand, o'erthrow me,' and his clever use of the alliterative '*b*'. The first quatrain of this sonnet is a challenge not only to God but also to us, the readers.

In the second quatrain, Donne sustains this drama and intensity. He sweeps us into a wonderful conceit, comparing himself to a 'usurped town'. This combination of images to suggest Donne's dilemma enables us to understand intellectually and to empathise emotionally. It is the metaphysical conceit at its very best. Donne is betrayed by reason, God's 'viceroy', and without this support he is unable to surrender himself totally to God. He longs for God, the source of certainty, to dominate him, rather in the way that he hoped his lover might desire his domination in 'The Flea'.

The final six lines of the sonnet, the *sestet,* begin with a change in tone, though the content links to the previous quatrain. The city under siege was a common image in courtly love poetry for the woman who was reluctant to yield to her lover's advances. Violence and frenzied activity give way to courtly phrasing and language. Donne declares his intentions to God: 'Yet dearly I love you, and would be loved fain.' His confession that he is 'betrothed' to God's enemy is filled with the submissiveness and reluctance of the courtly lady; it is as if Donne has changed not only his religion but also his sex. He is trying to communicate his human vulnerability in the face of God's overwhelming power by drawing on the image of the female figure being overwhelmed by her lover's passion. It is a subtle and complex combination of images and ideas, a conceit that is both vivid and unsettling.

Donne develops the image in the following line, where he asks God to free him: 'Divorce me, untie, or break that knot again.' As his sense of fear and panic increases, so his imagery begins to intensify. He begs God to 'Take me to you, imprison me.' He concentrates all his desperation into the paradox: '. . . for I | Except you enthral me, never shall be free.'

Finally, driven to the very edge of his emotions, he grasps at a paradox that is profoundly shocking and deeply disturbing: 'Nor ever chaste, except you ravish me.' We are left reeling from this image and his total disregard for the conventional 'niceties' of expression. Does it represent Donne at his very best, or at his very worst? Only you can decide.

Alternatively
A. J. Smith commented on Donne's poetry: 'There is a calculated offence to decorum in the interests of truth.' Is this true for 'Batter My Heart'? Does Donne shock us in order to make us think? Or is it simply that his search for new and exciting combinations of ideas sometimes led him into lapses of good taste? Is there a place for decorum and good taste in the world of poetry? Or are they only restrictions imposed by those who are afraid to think?

At the round earth's imagined corners
Text of poem: New Explorations Anthology page 18

BACKGROUND
See the notes on 'Batter my heart', pages 27–29.

STYLE
Donne's decision to write some of his poetry in *sonnet* form placed a number of restrictions on his writing. His poem had to consist of fourteen lines, as that is the required length of a sonnet. In addition, the Petrarchan form of the sonnet

involved the creation of two parts to the poem, the *octet* and the *sestet*. The octet, which comes first, consists of eight lines, the sestet of six lines. A strict rhyming scheme is used to mark the two parts: for the octet *abba, abba,* for the sestet *cdcdee*. It is obvious that this rhyming scheme is quite complicated, and it requires a lot of effort to ensure that the sense and mood of the sonnet fit into the rhyming scheme successfully.

Generally, the octet describes a situation, while the sestet presents a meditation on or a reaction to the octet. The change in rhyme between the octet and the sestet is often mirrored by a similar change in the mood and tone of the poem. The final rhyming couplet, which forms part of the sestet, usually expresses the main theme of the sonnet.

A READING OF THE POEM

Donne daringly uses a paradox to open this sonnet. His image of the 'round earth's imagined corners' is at once completely illogical, since something round has no corners, and wonderfully descriptive, in that it conveys a sense of boundless expanse. Indeed the quatrain creates a scene that is the poetic equivalent of 'Cinemascope'. Rather like the legendary director Cecil B. de Mille, Donne uses a cast of thousands to populate his magnificent backdrop. Angels fill the heavens, and 'numberless infinities' of souls go in search of their 'scattered bodies'. Behind all this activity, heavenly 'trumpets' ring out a clarion call of triumph. For this is a description of triumph: it represents the triumph over death of those saved by God. On the promised Day of Judgment, the souls who have inhabited Heaven may return to their bodies to embark on a life that will stretch to eternity.

The second quatrain expands this concept. Donne uses the device of the 'list' to communicate a feeling of multitudes and to emphasise just how total this triumph over death is. No matter what the cause of death is, whether 'flood', 'fire', 'war, dearth, age, agues, tyrannies,' or 'Despair, law, chance,' those who believe in God are guaranteed eternal life, while those who are alive on the Day of Judgment, provided they believe, can join in this transition to eternal existence 'and never taste death's woe.' This promise of eternal life was a powerful one in an age when death was a real presence in everyday life; but to attain it there had to be a complete act of faith, and it is this that Donne finds difficult.

In one sweeping movement, Donne shifts the focus of his sonnet away from the swarming Earth and the crowded heavens to himself. His concern for the dead – 'But let them sleep, Lord' – may sound compassionate, but it is founded on purely selfish reasons. Donne asks God to put off the Day of Judgment, quite simply because he is afraid. He is afraid that he has so many sins that he has not yet truly repented for them all. He is afraid that he is spiritually unprepared to face the Day of Judgment. Since he understands that ''tis late to ask abundance of thy grace' when he is facing God, he begs God to show him how to repent 'here on this lowly ground'.

Donne knows that the key to his salvation is repentance, and being Donne, he is equally aware of the fact that he is finding it difficult to repent sincerely, because he still doubts the certainty of God. He outlines his predicament with an unswerving honesty to God. If God can help him, Donne knows that he will be saved, just as surely as a condemned man will escape execution by the monarch placing his seal upon a document of pardon. But in Donne's case the seal is absolute, because it will be made not of wax but of blood, the blood of God. Perhaps at last Donne is beginning to grasp the ultimate certainty, or perhaps he is once again simply trying to persuade himself that there is a certainty.

Alternatively
'Donne elaborates and decorates at the expense of theme, sometimes so far that he displaces it altogether' (Michael Schmidt). Is this sonnet an uneasy combination of vivid description and confused intellectualisation? Does Donne become carried away by his own creativity to such an extent that he loses his theme completely? Is Donne claiming to be concerned with repentance and spiritual salvation when all the time he is really interested only in his own descriptive powers?

Thou hast made me
Text of poem: New Explorations Anthology page 20

Religious exploration seems to have played a continuing role in Donne's life. Long before his decision to change his religion he was concerned with forging a personal and independent religious philosophy. This was, perhaps, just another aspect of his quest for certainty that arose from his uncompromising intellectualisation of the experience of human existence. Izaak Walton, probably influenced by Donne himself, characterises Donne's religious struggle as the central force in his life. But this is really only a reflection of Donne's own desire to minimise the importance of his earlier, less religious work.

Whatever their motivation, Donne's religious poems convey the intense religious debate that raged not just within his mind, but also within his very soul. Some critics have suggested that Donne's approach to this debate was influenced by the spiritual exercises of Ignatius Loyola, the founder of the Jesuit order. Given Donne's early education and his family connections with the Jesuits, it is likely that he was familiar with Loyola's work. These exercises encouraged the individual to develop an intensely personal and emotional relationship with God through 'conversations' that were founded on inner debate and private reflection.

STYLE

Coleridge wrote of Donne's poetry: 'We find the most fantastic out-of-the-way thoughts, but in the most pure and genuine mother English . . . .' This sonnet is a wonderful illustration of this comment. Within the strict structural confines of the Petrarchan sonnet (fourteen lines, rhyming scheme, octet and sestet) Donne presents his complex spiritual struggle in a language that is both natural and simple. He is able to communicate the agonising dilemma he faces and the real terror in his soul in such a profound way that it comes as something of a shock to realise that he has written only fourteen lines.

A READING OF THE POEM

The dramatic opening that Donne has used so successfully in all his poetry, both secular and religious, becomes in this sonnet an expression of the essence of his emotional and spiritual turmoil. In one line he captures all the anguished questioning that haunts his soul: 'Thou hast made me, and shall thy work decay?' His lifelong quest for certainty is distilled into this one devastatingly simple question to God. He has left behind the intellectual gymnastics that occupied him in his youth. For Donne those bright, brittle days are past. Now his poetry has a personal intensity that is uncompromising and unaffected.

His description of the state of his life is stunning: 'mine end doth haste'. In an image that is both vivid and disturbing he conveys just what this 'haste' is like: 'I run to death, and death meets me as fast.' There is an inescapable inevitability about this line and a suggestion of a strange intimacy. Rather like two lovers irresistibly drawn together, Donne and Death move towards each other. Donne is completely focused on this inescapable meeting. All his previous life fades away in the face of this ultimate moment: 'all my pleasures are like yesterday'. It is no wonder that Donne's request to God, 'Repair me now,' vibrates with urgency. The time for clever intellectual tricks is over.

The second quatrain maintains this intensity. We see Donne poised, frozen with terror, between despair and death. The inner vision of his soul becomes, for him, a frail rope to cling to in his desperation: 'I dare not move my dim eyes any way.' But his horror increases as he realises that his 'feeble flesh doth waste', that the very hands that grasp this rope, the very eyes that focus on the safe horizon, are rotting away. His physical self, that body that in his youth had seemed to hold the certainty he craved, is now a dead weight, putrefying with sin, which drags him down 'towards hell'.

There is only one means of escape for Donne: his total faith in God. It is a terrible irony that the man who spent his life searching for certainty in the world outside himself should come to understand that the ultimate certainty could only be found within his own soul. The pure existence of God is not the answer; it is Donne's ability to believe in that pure existence that is the final solution. If he is empowered by God, given the strength to focus his 'dim eyes' so that he 'can look,' his state instantly alters. The dead weight melts away and he begins to 'rise again'. But he has to have the faith that God will empower him. Donne sways on the brink of this 'leap of faith'. Doubt, the weapon of their 'old subtle foe', the Devil, constantly tempts him. Doubt has for him such a terrible attraction that he cannot hold himself focused for even 'one hour'. In desperation, he pleads with God to help him escape. God's grace will release him from this terrible struggle, the weight dragging him down will fall away, and like a bird he will fly from the clutches of the Devil's art. God's grace will draw him onwards and upwards as smoothly and as irresistibly as a magnet attracts iron. It is an image of wonderful ease and beautiful certainty. Sadly for Donne, who had lived his life driven by the urge to intellectualise and rationalise, the action of a magnet can be scientifically proved, while the redeeming grace of God depends solely on an unscientific and profoundly irrational act of faith.

Alternatively
William Hazlitt commented on the metaphysical poets: 'The complaint so often made, and here repeated, is not of the want of power in these men, but of the waste of it; not of the absence of genius, but the abuse of it.' Is this the truth that lay behind John Donne? He frittered away his incisive intellect on glittering verses to entertain the crowd; he used his literary skills in a calculated attempt to grasp the trappings of wealth and power. For him, poetic genius was no more than a convenient tool of manipulation. It was a way to make life easier. He used his poetry for seduction, he used his poetry for self-glorification, and finally he used his poetry as a short cut to salvation.

Developing a personal reaction to John Donne

1. Why do you think John Donne wrote poetry?
2. Was his poetry based on the intellect, or on the emotions, or on a combination of the two?
3. What does the term 'metaphysical' stand for? Can John Donne be classed as a metaphysical poet?
4. What is a conceit? How is it used in Donne's poetry? Do you feel that the conceit is a successful poetic device?
5. What themes recur in Donne's poetry? What do they tell you about John Donne himself? Do you think he was a likeable man?
6. How did Donne use traditional poetic devices and structures in his work?
7. What is your reaction to the type of language and rhythms found in

Donne's poetry? Are they appealing to a modern reader?

8. Consider what aspects of Donne's poetry appeal to you and what aspects you find unappealing.

9. Has the work of John Donne anything to say to a twenty-first-century reader?

10. Do you think you will ever return to Donne's poetry, or will you be glad to leave it all behind?

Questions

1. Read 'The Flea', then answer the following questions.

    (a) (i) What impression of Donne's attitude to love emerges for you from your reading of this poem?

    (ii) Choose *two* phrases from the poem that especially convey that impression, and comment on your choices.

    (b) (i) Why does Donne introduce the flea into his poem?

    (ii) How does Donne's lover react to what he says? Support your answer by reference to the words of the poem.

    (c) Answer *one* of the following questions:

    (i) How would you describe Donne's tone in this poem? What words or phrases in the poem convey this tone?

    (ii) Would you write such a poem to a person you loved? Explain your view by reference to the words of the poem.

    (iii) Donne seems to have read a great many of his poems aloud to a small group. Choose *two lines or phrases* from this poem that you feel would have caused a reaction among the group, and explain what that reaction might have been in each case.

2. Read 'Song: Go Catch a Falling Star', then answer the following questions.

    (a) (i) What do you think is the point of this poem? (ii) Choose *two phrases* from the poem that especially convey this point to you, and comment on your choices.

    (b) What have all the strange tasks got to do with the theme of the poem? Illustrate your view by close reference to the text.

    (c) Answer *one* of the following questions:

    (i) How does the pattern of the lines in this poem emphasise what

Donne is saying? Support your view by referring to the words of the poem.

(ii) What is the mood of this poem? Refer closely to the text.

(iii) What part does rhyme play in this poem? Explain your answer by reference to the poem.

3. 'Donne's poetry represents an attempt to connect emotions with mental concepts.' Discuss this view, supporting your answer by quotation from or reference to the poems you have studied.

4. 'Donne's deliberate avoidance of poetic language gives his poetry a sense of realism.' In your reading of Donne's poetry, did you find this to be true? Support your answer by reference to or quotation from the poems on your course.

5. 'John Donne: A Personal Response.' Using this title, write an essay on the poetry of Donne, supporting your points by quotation from or reference to the poems on your course.

6. 'Underlying Donne's poetry is a unity of experience that is not immediately apparent.' Discuss this view, supporting your answer by quotation from or reference to the poems you have studied.

7. 'Donne's poetry is generally unpleasant and occasionally disgusting.' Give your response to this point of view, with supporting quotation from or reference to the poems on your course.

8. 'The poetry of Donne is a continuous commentary on the world and on himself.' In your reading of Donne's poetry, did you find this to be true? Support your answer by reference to or quotation from the poems you have studied.

9. 'Though Donne rejected the traditional poetry of his time, he was still greatly influenced by it.' Discuss this view, supporting your answer by quotation from or reference to the poetry on your course.

10. 'The tone of Donne's poetry is often unclear, and as a result the reactions it provokes can be confused.' Give your response to this point of view, with supporting quotation from or reference to the poems on your course.

Bibliography

Bennett, Joan, *Four Metaphysical Poets: Donne, Herbert, Vaughan, Crashaw* (second edition), Cambridge: Cambridge University Press 1953.

Carey, John, *John Donne: Life, Mind and Art,* London: Faber and Faber 1983.

Carey, John (editor), *John Donne: Selected Poetry,* Oxford: Oxford University Press 1998.
Everett, Barbara, *Donne: A London Poet,* London: Oxford University Press 1972.
Gardner, Helen (editor), *John Donne: A Collection of Critical Essays,* Englewood Cliffs (NJ): Prentice-Hall 1962.
Garrod, Heathcote William, *Poetry and Prose of John Donne,* London: Oxford University Press 1972.
Hamilton, Ian, *Keepers of the Flame,* London: Pimlico 1993.
Nutt, Joe, *John Donne: The Poems,* London: Macmillan 1999.
Schmidt, Michael, *Lives of the Poets,* London: Phoenix 1999.
Tamblin, Ronald, *A Preface to T. S. Eliot,* Harlow (Middx): Pearson Education 1988.
Walton, Izaak, *Walton's Lives,* London: Methuen 1895.
Wedgwood, C., *Seventeenth-Century English Literature* (second edition), London: Oxford University Press 1970.

2 *William Butler* YEATS

John G. Fahy

A *literary life*

William Butler Yeats was born on 13 June 1865 at number 1 Sandymount Avenue, Dublin, a son of John Butler Yeats and Susan Pollexfen. John Butler Yeats originated from Co. Down, where his father was Church of Ireland rector and whose father before him had been rector at Drumcliff, Co. Sligo. The Butler part of the family name came from an eighteenth-century marriage to a relative of the Butlers of Ormonde, one of the oldest Anglo-Irish families. That marriage brought with it the more tangible asset of a few hundred acres of land in Co. Kildare, the rents from which continued to provide a measure of financial support for the family until the land had to be sold in 1886.

John Butler Yeats had trained as a barrister before his marriage but decided to become an artist instead, and in 1867 the family moved to London so that he could study painting. This was the first move of a peripatetic childhood and youth for the young William, as the family moved from one house to another in London or between London and Dublin in pursuit of the father's artistic career, which never really became financially viable.

William was the eldest surviving child, followed by Susan Mary (called Lily), Elizabeth Corbet (called Lollie), and John Butler (Jack) – all born within six years of each other. Their mother, Susan Pollexfen, was the daughter of a wealthy merchant and shipping family from Co. Sligo; and when John Butler Yeats got into financial difficulties the family spent a good deal of time there, which the poet remembered with great affection. So a good deal of Yeats's childhood and youth was spent in an atmosphere of genteel poverty, supported by better-off relatives.

He was educated at the Godolphin School, London, 1875–80; the High School, Dublin, 1880–83; and the Metropolitan School of Art, Dublin, 1884–86. At first the young Yeats found it difficult to learn to read, and when by the age of seven or eight he still could not distinguish all the letters of the alphabet, his father is reputed to have thrown the reading book at him in a rage. In later life Yeats's spelling continued to be idiosyncratic, supporting the later conclusion that he suffered from dyslexia. As it was unlikely that he would pass the entrance examination for Trinity College, his father's old university, he was tutored to some extent by his father, who regarded himself as the young man's chief mentor, and was therefore largely self-educated. Consequently his acquaintances and readings assumed a very significant role in his development.

Among the people introduced to him by his father was the old Fenian John O'Leary, and this sparked off an interest in nationalism, particularly as a subject for poetry. He was influenced also by the writings of Douglas Hyde, Katherine Tynan and Samuel Ferguson, as well as James Clarence Mangan's versions of Irish poems. But it was probably the histories and the fiction of Standish O'Grady that most impelled Yeats to investigate Irish mythology. At this time he was fascinated by the folk tales, fairy tales and supernatural beliefs found in Co. Sligo and Co. Galway, which resulted in the collection *Fairy and Folk Tales of the Irish Peasantry* (1888). He also wanted to reformulate in English the old Irish legends and so re-create Ireland's lost intellectual and cultural heritage. This found expression in his collection of poetry *The Wanderings of Oisín* (1889).

At this time also Yeats began to search for alternative philosophies to Christianity, such as Buddhism, magic, spiritualism and astrology. Influenced to some degree no doubt by his discussions with his friend George Russell, the poet, he began to explore mysticism and the occult, often through the practices of esoteric groups and cults. Among these were the theosophists (through whom he encountered the notorious Elena Blavatsky), who believed that knowledge of God could be achieved through spiritual ecstasy and direct intuition. He became involved also with the 'Hermetic Order of the Golden Dawn', a Rosicrucian order that practised ritual demonstrations of psychic power, which he joined in 1890. The Golden Dawn was based on the desire for alchemical change – the transformation of people into gods, the possibility of transforming the world. Yeats became quite dedicated to the practice of magic, believed in the evocation of spirits, and indeed was convinced that he himself was a magician.

Among the principal beliefs that he subscribed to were:
- that the borders of our minds are ever shifting and that minds can melt and flow into each other, creating a single entity or 'Great Mind';
- that there is a 'World Soul' or shared memory in nature;
- that the Great Mind can be evoked by symbols, which Yeats introduced into poetry in order to access truths.

He learnt a great deal about symbolism from Shelley and Blake. Symbols reveal themselves in a state of trance. He felt that the purpose of rhythm in poetry is to create meditative rhythms in which the mind is lulled into a state of trance. So, when poetry is working well it operates like a mantra or chant, helping us to see past the ordinary. Yeats believed that 'simple' people (those who were considered fools), ascetics and women can see beyond modern culture into the world of magical truths.

Yeats also believed that Celticism was the remnant of a former world religion, that the occult is really the remnant of this old religion or magic, and that Ireland is the place where it can best be contacted. So Celticism and the occult are important and connected twin pillars of his poetic philosophy.

During the 1890s Yeats's poetry developed from simple pastoral poetry and verses about fairy tales to the use of cycles of mythology of Ulster and the Fianna. He introduced heroes from these tales into his poetry: Cú Chulainn, Méabh, Deirdre and others. He began to use the Celtic material in a visionary way to create mystical poetry, which culminated in the volume *The Wind Among the Reeds* (1899).

Women were important in Yeats's life, and he had a number of troublesome and tempestuous love affairs. Of all the women he encountered two were to be most influential: Maud Gonne and Lady Augusta Gregory. The former, whom he met in the late 1880s, was the source of passionate romantic involvement and disappointment for him over the succeeding three decades; but she was also the inspiration for some of his work, such as the play *The Countess Kathleen,* was a frequent reference point in his poetry, and was the focus for some of his ideas on nationalism, women in politics, the aesthetic, ageing and others.

He first met Lady Gregory in 1894, and from 1897 onwards her home, Coole Park, near Gort, Co. Galway, was a summer refuge from his somewhat nomadic life. As well as helping him collect folk tales she provided both psychological and financial support and the opportunity to meet other writers, such as George Russell, George Bernard Shaw, George Moore and Edward Martyn.

Lady Gregory, Yeats and Martyn were the principal co-founders of the Irish Literary Theatre. Their manifesto clearly outlines the driving philosophy and ambition of the movement.

> We propose to have performed in Dublin in the spring of every year certain Celtic and Irish plays, which whatever be their degree of excellence will be written with a high ambition, and so to build up a Celtic and Irish school of dramatic literature. We hope to find in Ireland an uncorrupted and imaginative audience trained to listen by its passion for oratory, and believe that our desire to bring upon the stage the deeper thoughts and emotions of Ireland will ensure for us a tolerant welcome, and that freedom to experiment which is not found in the theatres of England, and without which no new movement in art or literature can succeed. We will show that Ireland is not the home of buffoonery and of easy sentiment, as it has been represented, but the home of an ancient idealism. We are confident of the support of all Irish people, who are weary of misrepresentation, in carrying out a work that is outside all the political questions that divide us.

Eventually this movement led to the founding of the Abbey Theatre, Dublin, in 1904, where Yeats was manager from 1904 to 1910. But the public did not always appreciate the movement's artistic vision. There was adverse reaction to Yeats's play *The Countess Kathleen*; and in 1907 John Millington Synge's play *The Playboy of the Western World* sparked off riots in the theatre. Yeats was deeply disillusioned by this lack of understanding and aesthetic appreciation, a feeling that was deepened by the controversy over the Hugh Lane proposal. This disillusionment is reflected in his poetry *The Green Helmet* (1910), *Responsibilities* (1914) and *The Wild Swans at Coole* (1917). In contrast, his visit to Italy in 1907 with Lady Gregory and her son, Robert, pointed up the difference between the mob in Ireland and what it had been possible to create through aristocratic patronage in Florence and Ravenna.

The Easter Rising of 1916 forced Yeats to rethink his view of Irish society, as we see in the poem 'Easter 1916'. These years ushered in other decisive changes for Yeats. After a final round of marriage proposals to Maud Gonne and then to her adopted daughter, Iseult, he settled into marriage with Georgina Hyde-Lees on 20 October 1917. The marriage produced two children and much-needed domestic stability for Yeats. And, whether by chance or design, it also produced the 'automatic writing' created by his wife, who, while in a sort of trance, transcribed the words of certain spirit guides or instructors. This seemed to offer a new system of thought to Yeats, incorporating themes of change within a new view of history, which he developed in his book *A Vision* (1925).

The central idea of his philosophy was that civilisation was about to reverse itself and a new era of anti-civilisation was about to be ushered in. The signs of this were everywhere: in mass movements in Europe, in the rise of communism, fascism, etc. Yeats examined change against the backdrop of world history. In his review of history he noticed that certain eras favoured the development of human excellence in art and learning and also produced social harmony: Athens of the fifth century BC, Byzantium, the Italian Renaissance – all of which developed political culture and artistic culture and in general fostered human achievement, creating what Yeats termed 'unity of being'. These eras were separated by a thousand years, each reaching its peak about five hundred years after it replaced the previous 'millennium'. There were two main forces at work: what Yeats called 'anti-thetical' energies, which created this unity of being, and the opposite force, which he termed 'primary' energy. These two energies grew or waned in their turn over the course of each millennium.

Yeats represented this theory of change by the symbolism of the 'gyres', two interpenetrating cones (see page 58), one primary and the other anti-thetical, each growing or decreasing in strength as the centuries pass. He felt that his own time was now reaching the end of the primary gyre and that the growing violence on the Continent and in Ireland was an indicator of its imminent collapse, to be replaced by a new anti-thetical gyre. This is the philosophical background to the bleak view he took of the current fractious age in the volumes *Michael Robartes and the Dancer* (1921) and, in particular, *The Tower* (1928). See in particular his poems 'The Second Coming', 'Sailing to Byzantium' and 'Meditations in Time of Civil War'.

This philosophy, which had as its central belief the notion that the times were out of joint and that cataclysmic changes were about to happen, may help to explain Yeats's flirtation with extreme political philosophies and movements: for example, his consideration of fascism, his exploration of the place of violence in politics, his scepticism about democracy and his preference for the political model of Renaissance prince–ruler (a model that cast the Anglo-Irish gentry in a similar role), and his engagement with theories of eugenics.

This search for solutions, for paradigms of thought and models for living, continued into the poet's old age, but it took more conventional forms in his volume *The Winding Stair and Other Poems* (1933). Here we find many elegies – to dead friends, to past times and to other more unified eras, such as the eighteenth century, from which Yeats took his chief model, Jonathan Swift, whom he wished to emulate as poet–statesman.

Indeed, he was pursuing that ideal in his role as a senator in the new Irish Free State. He devoted much energy to his work in the new senate, which first sat on 11 December 1922 and of which he was a member until 1928. During 1923, for instance, he spoke nineteen times on such subjects as law enforcement, manuscripts, the Lane pictures, film censorship and Irish, and he continued over the years to contribute on issues such as partition, divorce and the new coinage. In 1922 the University of Dublin conferred an honorary doctorate on him, and he was similarly honoured by the Universities of Oxford and Cambridge in 1931 and 1933, respectively. But the crowning international recognition was the award of the Nobel Prize for Literature in 1923.

In the late 1920s and early 1930s Yeats experienced a number of health problems, and the family began to spend more time in the sunnier regions of southern Europe. The house at 82 Merrion Square, Dublin, was sold and exchanged for a flat in Fitzwilliam Square. In 1933 Yeats took himself out of the city altogether when the family took a long lease on a house, 'Riversdale', in Rathfarnham, 'just too far from Dublin to go there without good reason and too far, I hope, for most interviewers and the less determined travelling bores'. (See 'An Acre of Grass'.) But he continued to write, indeed with renewed vigour, and *New Poems* was published in 1938. His last public appearance was at the Abbey Theatre in August 1938. He died on 28 January 1939 at Roquebrune in the south of France; in 1948 his body was re-interred, as he had wished, in Drumcliff churchyard.

Principal volumes of poetry	Poems in this selection
The Wanderings of Oisín (1889)	
Crossways (1889)	
The Rose (1893)	– 'The Lake Isle of Innisfree'
The Wind Among the Reeds (1899)	
The Green Helmet and Other Poems (1910)	
Responsibilities (1914)	– 'September 1913'
The Wild Swans at Coole (1917; second edition 1919)	– 'The Wild Swans at Coole' – 'An Irish Airman Foresees His Death'
Michael Robartes and the Dancer (1921)	– 'Easter 1916' – 'The Second Coming'
The Tower (1928)	– 'Sailing to Byzantium' – 'Meditations in Time of Civil War'
The Winding Stair and Other Poems (1933)	– 'In Memory of Eva Gore-Booth and Con Markiewicz' – 'Swift's Epitaph'
A Full Moon in March (1935)	
New Poems (1938)	– 'An Acre of Grass'
Last Poems (1939)	– 'Under Ben Bulben' – 'Politics'

The Lake Isle of Innisfree

Text of poem: New Explorations Anthology page 49

[Note: This poem is also prescribed for Ordinary Level 2007 exam]

This poem was written in 1888, when Yeats was living in London, where he was unhappy and homesick for Ireland. A somewhat altered version was first published in the *National Observer* in December 1890, to much acclaim; this really was the poem that first made Yeats's name. It is included in the collection *The Rose* (1893).

Yeats had been greatly influenced by the vision of self-sufficiency in nature found in Henry David Thoreau's book *Walden* (1854), which his father had read to him. And he too dreamed of living alone in nature in a quest for wisdom. This was a theme he explored not just in verse but in his prose writings also, an indication of the pervasive autobiographical nature of the quest. For instance, there are close similarities between this poem and the scenario in *John Sherman*, a novel Yeats had written in 1887–88, in which a young Sligo man who had left home in search of a fortune and was now homesick in London recalls an island on a lake where he used to pick blackberries. He dreams of returning there, building a wooden hut, and listening to the ripple of the water.

YEATS'S VISION AND QUEST

The vision of self-sufficiency in nature obviously pervades this whole poem. However unlikely a scene, it shows the poet as rustic woodsman and gardener, writing in the first person, actually planning to build a simple, crude dwelling and attempting agricultural self-sufficiency. 'Clay and wattles' were the traditional rural building materials for centuries past. The hive and the bees suggest the simple sweetness and richness of life, as well as providing a natural musical ambience. Altogether the vision is one of idyllic rural primitiveness, with a hint of the hermit's ascetic: a life 'alone in the bee-loud glade'.

This is a romantic view of the human being in perfect harmony with nature, at one with its sights and sounds. It is an alluring picture, sensual even, where the feminised morning is draped in veils. But there is also a strange, slightly unreal quality about it. The light is different: noon is a 'purple glow'. The archaic language in the expression of 'midnight's all a glimmer' reinforces the strange, even magical nature of the atmosphere. For representative sounds Yeats chooses the simple, rhythmic, calming sound of lake water lapping and also the repetitive rustic sounds of the cricket on the hearth, a common feature of rural stories and tales. Co. Sligo is one of the few places in the country that provides an all-year-round habitat for the linnet, a small unspectacular bird that likes rough hillsides and uncultivated lands near the sea. With accurate recall, Yeats is celebrating the indigenous wildlife of the area. His vision of happiness is a romantic one – a simple, unsophisticated lifestyle in an unspoilt habitat, surrounded by the sights and music of nature. It is a picture full of the rich textures of colour, sound and movement, in total contrast to his present environment, that of the cold, colourless and lifeless 'pavements grey'. So in one sense the poem can be read as an expression of Yeats's romanticised and nostalgic yearning for his native countryside.

But it is also more than this. For it is no frivolous weekend in the woods that he is planning: it is rather a quest for wisdom, for deep, eternal truths – an attempt to see into the heart of things. This is the sentiment that comes across in the first line. The sound of water, one of the essential elements and a life force, haunts him and seems to suggest that only in nature will he find the truths of the heart. The ambiguity about whose heart is in question here further strengthens the connection between the poet's heart and the heart of the earth. This is a move he feels compelled to make, a compulsion. We can sense the strength of his resolve in the verbs 'I will arise' and 'I shall have'. But the biblical allusions underlying this expose even more complex layers of compulsion. The repeated 'I will arise' echoes the words of the Prodigal Son, who has wasted his inheritance, led a profligate few years in exile, and finally resolves to go home: 'I will arise and go to my father.' So the words of the poem carry great unhappiness, a sense of failure and loss, the loneliness of exile and separation and perhaps even a feeling of guilt or remorse. The phrase 'always night and day' could also be a Biblical allusion. St Mark's gospel (5:5) refers to a man possessed by an evil spirit who was freed from his torment by Christ: 'Night and day among the tombs and on the mountains he was always crying out and bruising himself with stones.' This allusion, if intended, hints at a somewhat manic compulsion and mental and spiritual turmoil, or at the very least a great discontent.

THE MUSIC OF THE VERSE

The poet's feelings of unease and discontent and of being driven to take this course of action are hidden by the musical quality of the verse. Apart from the obvious repetitions of the end rhymes in alternate lines, there are subtle musical vowel repetitions throughout the poem. For example, there is a profusion of long 'i' sounds in the first stanza ('I', 'arise', 'Nine', 'I', 'hive') and a repetition of long 'o' and 'a' sounds in the final stanza ('go', 'low', 'shore', 'roadway', 'core' and 'day', 'lake', 'pavements', 'grey'). The repetition, particularly of long broad vowels, gives this a languidness and soporific calmness that belies the tension at the heart of it.

ISSUES

Among the issues that preoccupy the poet here we might emphasise:

- the yearning for self-sufficiency in natural surroundings
- the search for truth, wisdom and peace
- the poet's discontent, which impels him on this quest.

September 1913
Text of poem: New Explorations Anthology page 51

This poem was written in September 1913 and was first published on 8 September in the *Irish Times,* where it was entitled 'Romance in Ireland (on reading much of the correspondence against the Art Gallery)'. It was included in the volume *Responsibilities* (1914) under its present title.

YEATS AND POLITICS: SOME OF HIS VIEWS ON SOCIETY

At one level of reading this is just a political poem – an angry poetical response to a particular event in which Yeats was passionately involved. Sir Hugh Lane, a wealthy art collector (and Lady Gregory's nephew), had presented to the city of Dublin a unique collection of modern paintings, with the proviso that the city build a suitable gallery to house them. There were various suggestions for building a gallery, such as one on a bridge over the River Liffey; but the entire project became entangled in increasingly bitter public disputes about the location, the architecture, and particularly the cost. Yeats was furious about what seemed a mean-spirited, penny-pinching and anti-cultural response to Lane's generous offer. The opponents of the project drew attention to the poverty and slum living conditions that many Dubliners endured at the time and accused the proponents of the gallery of putting art before bread and also of an elitist arrogance typical of the Ascendancy class. The controversy developed strong overtones of class conflict and set Yeats thinking about the recent changes in Irish society.

The make-up of society, the need for particular kinds of people in a cultured society, and the responsibilities of particular classes – these were issues that had long preoccupied Yeats. In 1907, on the death of the old Fenian John O'Leary, Yeats wrote an essay entitled 'Poetry and tradition', in which he talks about the ideals that he and O'Leary had discussed and shared. Though the primary emphasis in the essay is on poetry and culture, the views reflect Yeats's notions of the ideal society.

> Three types of men have made all beautiful things. Aristocracies have made beautiful manners, because their place in the world puts them above the fear of life, and the countrymen have made beautiful stories and beliefs, because they have nothing to lose and so do not fear, and

the artists have made all the rest, because Providence has filled them with recklessness. All these look backward to a long tradition, for, being without fear, they have held to whatever pleases them.

So for Yeats, the really important constituents of society were the aristocracy, country people and artists. It should not surprise us that Yeats was bitterly disillusioned with the changes in society that were proceeding apace from the end of the nineteenth century and into the twentieth: changes in land ownership hastened the demise of the aristocracy; a new upper and lower middle class emerged. Yeats saw only a new Ireland of small shopkeepers, clerks and traders; and it is at this section of the new society that he directs his wrath in the poem.

In the main he makes two accusations. Firstly, their only preoccupations are making money and practising religion, as he ironically says:

> For men were born to pray and save.

They are a money-grubbing and fearful people, tyrannised by their religion. And Yeats is revolted by this combination of materialism and religious serfdom; it is the antithesis of his Renaissance model of a cultured society, where art and literature are valued. Secondly, these small-minded, self-regarding, blinkered people are incapable of understanding the generosity of spirit and the self-sacrifice that motivated the patriots of old. Lines 25–30 can be read in this way. The selfless patriotism of the heroes of past time would now be misinterpreted by this unenlightened generation as love-crazed emotion merely to impress a woman.

> You'd cry, 'Some woman's yellow hair
> Has maddened every mother's son'

So the present generation and society are contrasted, most unfavourably, with previous generations.

It is worth exploring Yeats's notion of the heroic past and his view of the influential figures of romantic Ireland. They all were political rebels, risk takers who tried and failed gloriously to free Ireland. They all were men of action, soldiers who willingly gave liberty or life for the cause: 'They weighed so lightly what they gave.' They were hugely energetic, forceful characters:

> They have gone about the world like wind,
> But little time had they to pray.

In particular, Yeats seems to admire their extraordinary selflessness and courage, their almost manic bravery: 'All that delirium of the brave'.

Yeats's thinking accommodated two sometimes conflicting notions of the heroic: the hero as representative leader of a people, and the hero as a solitary figure, often even in opposition to the people. There are elements of both notions here. There are some hints of their popular influence ('the names that stilled your childish play') and perhaps also in their willing sacrifice ('all that blood was shed'). But the overwhelming impression is that of the solitary figure, apart, different: 'they were of a different kind'; 'the wild geese spread | The grey wing upon every tide'; 'those exiles as they were | In all their loneliness and pain.' And it is this difference that gives them status in the poem. And, by implication, the present generation lack their qualities of nobility, courage, selflessness, and self-sacrifice for an ideal.

Tone

This poem is built on contrast – an extreme, somewhat simplistic contrast between a present and a past generation, or what Yeats sees as representative figures from these generations. The heroic past he idolises in tones of reverence and awe. There is a suggestion of their strange power in 'the names that stilled your childish play' and in the reference to their going 'about the world like wind'. He empathises with their loneliness and pain and inevitable fate:

> But little time had they to pray
> For whom the hangman's rope was spun,
> And what, God help us, could they save?

His undoubted admiration for their selfless courage is carried in 'They weighed so lightly what they gave' and in that 'delirium of the brave'.

In contrast, the new middle class is lampooned in the caricature of the shopkeeper as a kind of sub-human creature, fumbling, shivering, and certainly not capable of understanding more noble motives. The tone of savage mockery is often achieved by the use of irony – for example the perverse irony of 'What need you, being come to sense' – or the ironic statement of philosophy, 'For men were born to pray and save.' The bitter contempt is hammered home through the repetition of 'For this . . . for this . . . for this.' The sneer of disdain rings through these lines.

Altogether this is a poem exhibiting passionate but contrasting emotions.

Some themes and issues

- Bitter disillusion with recent social changes
- Contempt for the perceived materialism and religious serfdom of the new middle class of business people

- Concerns for the well-being of a cultured society; concern for its lack of altruistic principles and generosity of spirit
- A particular view of Irish history as a history of courageous failure in the struggle for independence
- A nostalgic, romanticised view of Irish history
- Thoughts on patriotism and the notion of the heroic.

The Wild Swans at Coole
Text of poem: New Explorations Anthology page 54
[*Note: This poem is also prescribed for Ordinary Level 2007 exam*]

The poem was written in 1916 and first published in the *Little Review* in 1917, and it is the title poem of the volume *The Wild Swans at Coole* (1917).

This poem is structured as a retrospection by Yeats as he records how his life has changed since he first stayed at Coole Park during the summer and autumn of 1897 ('the nineteenth autumn'). It is important to be aware that this is an artistic construction, because in reality his state of mind had changed very little. Though he chooses to say that he was more carefree ('trod with a lighter tread') at that earlier period, probably for aesthetic purposes and to set up a contrast, in fact he had been in a state of mental and nervous exhaustion during that visit in 1897. His love affair with Diana Vernon had just ended. He was 'tortured with sexual desire and disappointed love', and, as his diaries reveal, 'It would have been a relief to have screamed aloud.'

In the summer of 1916, the year the poem was written, Yeats went to France to Maud Gonne, the great, omnipresent, passionate love of his life for the previous quarter of a century. Her husband, Major John MacBride, had been shot for his part in the Easter Rising. She was working as a volunteer nurse with the war wounded, and Yeats once again proposed marriage to her. On her refusing for the last time he contemplated the possibility of marriage with her adopted daughter, Iseult. Possibly it was this turmoil and the disparity in their ages that set him thinking of time, age and immortality, the death of love or the possibility of its being eternal. But this is one instance where a biographical approach does not help very much, as the poet orders and alters events and ideals to suit an artistic construction rather than any actual reality.

When Iseult finally refused him in 1917 he married Georgina Hyde-Lees and bought a tower-house, Thoor Ballylee, not far from Coole in Co. Galway.

THEMES AND ISSUES

This poem, as Yeats's literary biographer Terence Brown says, 'sets a mood of autumnal introspection'. In a certain sense it is quite a personal poem, in which Yeats, at fifty-one, unmarried and alone despite many passionate love affairs, takes stock of his emotional situation. Primarily he laments the loss of youth, passion and love. He regrets the loss of his carefree youth, 'trod with a lighter tread', however inaccurate this nostalgia is. Now his 'heart is sore'; he is a man broken-hearted, discontented, emotionally unsatisfied. He no longer has what the swans appear to have – youthful passion.

> Unwearied still, lover by lover . . .
> Passion or conquest . . .
> Attend upon them still.

And he has not got unchanging or constant love, while 'their hearts have not grown old'. Above all else, the poet seems to resent the loss of passionate love in his life; we cannot mistake this yearning in the many references to hearts, lovers, passion and conquests.

The loss of love is just one aspect of Yeats's general sense of regret here, which concerns ageing and the passage of time. Indeed he seems to have been ambushed by time – the nineteenth autumn 'has come upon me' – and is forced to accept that 'all's changed'. His awareness of this and his resentment are accentuated by the seeming immortality of the swans: 'Their hearts have not grown old'. By implication we sense the poet's yearning for changelessness, for immortality.

Yet another kind of loss is hinted at here: the possible loss or diminution of the poetic gift, insight or vision. Perhaps that is what he fears at the end of the poem, in that final plaintive image: that the poetic sight or vision will have deserted him and passed to others. For him, the swans are in some way a manifestation of his poetic vision. So we can see that he explores

- the personal loss of youth, passion, and love
- the consequences of ageing
- the passage of time and the yearning for changelessness and immortality
- the loss of poetic power and vision – the sense of failure.

Imagery and symbolism

The entire poem is structured around the swans, real and symbolic, which have particular significance because they appear to have defied time for the past nineteen years. They give the illusion of immortality: 'Unwearied still . . . Passion or conquest . . . attend upon them still.' Our rational mind tells us that of course they may not be exactly the same swans; but the poet glosses over and even builds further on this poetic illusion. He concentrates our attention on the patterns they establish, patterns that will survive even though they may die. These 'great broken rings', the spiral imagery they create, are similar to the 'gyres' or cones of time (see pages 40–41) that Yeats saw as the cyclical pattern behind all things, time and eternity. So there is a hint of the eternal about the spiral imagery the swans establish. Also, they link the water to the sky, link earth and heaven; and so in a way they are both mortal and immortal. The swans provide an exciting, vibrant, multi-layered symbolism, but they are also hauntingly and accurately described as real creatures. The real power and energy of the movement is evoked by the breathless enjambment of the lines and by the use of sinuous and muscular verbs and adverbs:

> All suddenly mount
> And scatter wheeling in great broken rings
> Upon their clamorous wings.

The swan imagery carries great resonances and symbolic value in the poem; but there are other images also that add to the richness of texture. The 'woodland paths' can be either the straight paths of the intellect or the winding paths of intuition. Whatever symbolic weight they carry they are dry here, in keeping with the themes – lack of passion and creativity. The trees, a great symbol of permanence for Yeats, are in the ageing cycle of their lives, as is the poet.

Three of the four symbolic elements are used in the poem: earth, air and water. Only fire is not used, indeed is conspicuously absent. The suggestion is that this is more than just a poem, that it carries elements of magical divination. Even the musical image 'The bell-beat of their wings above my head' reinforces this sense of the magical. And of course Yeats believed in and practised magic. Our sense of this is strengthened further by an exploration of the degree of patterning in the poem. Notice how the swans on the lake take to the air and finish by drifting on the still water again – creating a perfect round or circular pattern. Consider the pattern of antitheses in the poem – between the swans and the speaker and between the poet now and the poet nineteen years ago. And, as the critic Donald Stauffer points out, the essential pattern is a contrast of moods, something experienced only by humans. The essential contrast in the poem is that between transient humanity and eternity.

All in all, there is a richness of imagery and symbolism here that can be enjoyed and appreciated at many levels.

STRUCTURE

There is a gradual opening out of both the voice and the vista as this poem progresses. Stanza 1 just paints the picture, unemotionally and accurately, as any ornithologist or naturalist might do. From this very anchored and particular opening we go to the poet's personal reminiscences in the second and third stanzas, before moving on to more generalised speculative philosophising in the fourth stanza. The final stanza opens up unanswerable questions, speculating on the future, leaving us with the possibility of a completely empty final scene, a blank canvas. The future is as unclear and ungraspable as that final question – incidentally the only question in the poem.

The poem goes from the particular to the general and then to the entirely speculative. Beneath the tranquillity of the imagery, the languidness of language and the sounds of the words, the ideas of the poem are tightly linked and structured. Notice how images or ideas are picked up from one stanza to the next, and so the stanzas are chain-linked.

The first stanza ends with the enumeration of 'nine-and-fifty swans', and the second stanza takes up the count.

> The nineteenth autumn has come upon me
> Since I first made my count;

Stanzas 2 and 3 are linked by the poet's looking: 'I saw . . . I have looked'. At the end of stanza 3 he remembers or fancies his carefree 'lighter treat' of nineteen years earlier. Stanza 4 opens with the still 'unwearied' creatures.

The fifth stanza picks up phonetically on the word 'still', and, though semantically different, it provides a phonic linkage. There is of course the imagery link also, where swans 'paddling in the cold | Companionable streams' of the fourth stanza are picked up in the fifth stanza as they 'drift on the still water'.

An Irish Airman Foresees his Death

Text of poem: New Explorations Anthology page 57

[Note: This poem is also prescribed for Ordinary Level 2007 exam]

This poem was one of a number written by the poet for Robert Gregory, Lady Gregory's son, including 'Shepherd and Goatherd' and 'In Memory of Major Robert Gregory'. Yeats saw Gregory as an educated aristocrat and all-round Renaissance man ('Soldier, scholar, horseman, he'). He was also an energetic boxer and hunter and a painter who designed sets for Yeats's own plays. The poem was written in 1918 and first published in the second edition of *The Wild Swans at Coole* (1919).

CRITICAL COMMENTARY

At one obvious level of reading, this is a type of elegy in memory of the dead man. But it is a variation on the form, in that it is structured as a monologue by the dead man rather than the more usual direct lament by a poet, praising the person's good qualities and showing how he is much missed, and so on.

It makes an interesting contribution to war poetry in its attempt to chart the motivation and psychological state of the volunteer. What strikes one immediately is not just the fatalism – he knows his death is imminent – but the bleakness of his outlook on life, his disenchantment with living, despite his privileged background.

> The years to come seemed waste of breath,
> A waste of breath the years behind . . .

In contrast, the war seemed an adventure, an 'impulse of delight', a 'tumult in the clouds'. The poem captures well the excitement and exhilaration felt by many a volunteer. As Ulick O'Connor put it (in *The Yeats Companion*, 1990), 'There can seldom have been a better summing up of the sense of elation which the freedom to roam the uncharted skies brought to the young men of Gregory's pre-1914 generation.'

Yet the decision to volunteer was not a heady, emotional one. The poem stresses the thought and calculation brought to the decision. The concept of balance is repeatedly stressed:

> I balanced all, brought all to mind . . .
> In balance with this life, this death.

He was not carried away by the emotion of enlistment meetings ('Nor public men, nor cheering crowds'). He was not moved by any sense of 'duty' or 'patriotism'; neither was there conscription in Ireland ('Nor law, nor duty bade me fight'). These 'nor – nor' negatives of the rejected motives are balanced against the excitement of action. The general picture is of a young man who has chosen, after careful consideration, this path of action, almost indeed chosen his death.

This heavy sense of fatalism is most obvious in the opening lines. But there is never a sense in which this fatalism is merely weak surrender or opting out. He accepts his fate, he goes consenting to his death, but more like one of Homer's heroes. Yeats gives Gregory Homeric stature by allowing him to choose a heroic death; and this gives meaning to an otherwise meaningless conflict. The airman feels none of the great passions of war, neither patriotic love nor hatred of the foe:

> Those that I fight I do not hate,
> Those that I guard I do not love;

Further, he does not think the war will make a whit of difference to his own countrymen:

> No likely end could bring them loss
> Or leave them happier than before.

But it is the self-sacrificing death, 'this death' freely chosen, that raises the young man above the events of his time and confers particular significance on him. The awareness of impending death also brings this moment of insight, this clearness of vision that allowed him to evaluate his past life and contemplate a possible future as a country landowner – all of which he rejects for the 'tumult' of action.

So, as a war poem, this is an interesting, personal, even intimate approach, charting the thoughts and motivation of this young man. But it has a more general aspect also. Gregory may be seen as representative of all those young men of talent who were cheated of their promise by the slaughter of the First World War.

We have already mentioned that Yeats saw Gregory as the all-round Renaissance man – in other words, an educated man and person of culture as well as a man of action. Yeats had felt that the 'lonely impulse of delight' was what differentiated the artist from others, that the artistic impulse was essentially lonely and solitary. Here we see this artistic impulse motivating a man of action, who is essentially instinctive rather than intellectual. Yeats felt that the impulse was sometimes hampered in the artist, who often thought too much. So the later Yeats began to champion the non-intellectual hero and the instinctive man; the sportsman and the adventurer are given the status of mythic figures. The airman Gregory is essentially a solitary figure, like other mythic figures created by Yeats, such as the 'Fisherman'.

Some critics read this poem as a classic statement of Anglo-Irishness as Yeats saw it. In later life Yeats used to talk about the 'Anglo-Irish solitude'. Is there a sense here of not quite fully belonging to either side, of being neither fully committed English nor unreservedly Irish? There is certainly a sense of emotional distance on the part of the subject, both from those he guards and those he fights. Though he has an affinity with Kiltartan's poor ('my countrymen'), he is aware that the war and his involvement in it will have no impact on their lives. In general, the feeling one gets is of some detachment from the events in which he participates, and this could be read as a metaphor for 'Anglo-Irish solitude'.

Easter 1916

Text of poem: New Explorations Anthology page 60

On Monday 24 April 1916 a force of about seven hundred members of the Irish Volunteers and the Irish Citizen Army took over the centre of Dublin in a military revolution and held out for six days against the British army.

At first the rising did not receive widespread support; but the British military authorities regarded it as high treason in time of war, and the subsequent systematic executions of fifteen of the leaders between 3 and 12 May brought a wave of public sympathy and created heroes and martyrs for the republican cause.

Though Yeats's poem was finished by September 1916 and a number of copies had been printed privately, it was not published until October 1920, when it appeared in the *New Statesman*. It is included in the volume *Michael Robartes and the Dancer* (1921).

THE NATIONAL QUESTION: YEATS'S POLITICAL VIEWS

Yeats spent a good deal of his time in England during his early life, but he felt that the English understanding of the Irish was stereotypical and condescending. One of his main ambitions was to help change Ireland's view of itself through a revival of its unique cultural identity. He had denounced the English government of Ireland, and his refusal of a knighthood in 1915 is a statement of his political stance. Yet his view did not prevent him living there, and indeed he was in England when the Easter Rising took place.

This ambiguity was further complicated by Yeats's arrogant and scathing dismissal of the current generation of Irish people as ignoble, self-focused, materialistic and priest-controlled, who were totally incapable of the idealism or courage necessary for heroic leadership and personal sacrifice. These views he had expressed very trenchantly in 'September 1913'.

The Rising took Yeats by surprise and blew some serious holes in his thinking. Firstly, he now had to rethink his public stance and views on the new Irish middle class. These people had been prepared to give their lives for an ideal. Yeats had been quite wrong. Secondly, though he was disgusted, like most people, at the savagery of the executions, he began to realise that the establishment's brutality had created martyrs, had transformed ordinary men into patriots with a strange new unchallengeable power. Perhaps Pearse's idea of a blood sacrifice was correct. Yeats had to rethink the place and value of revolutionary determination. So Yeats had to work out how this cataclysmic change had occurred in Irish society – 'all changed, changed utterly'.

A READING OF THE POEM

Though it may not appear on the surface to be a questioning poem, this work is really an attempt to answer or clarify a great number of questions that the 1916 Rising stirred up in Yeats's mind, an attempt to come to terms with:
- how everything had changed
- how wrong he had been
- how ordinary people had been changed into heroes
- the deep structure of change in society, the mysterious process, a kind of fate that directed and powered change (Terence Brown puts it eloquently: 'It seeks to penetrate beneath the appearance of history to comprehend the

mysteries of destiny.')
- the place and functioning of revolutionary violence in the process
- the change in his own position: how to resolve his own complex and contradictory feelings towards this violent process.

The diplomatic difficulty of having to recant his views on Irish society Yeats faced honestly and generously in the first section of this poem. Technically he achieved this by structuring the poem as a *palinode* or recantation of his opinions in the earlier 'September 1913'. Re-creating the drab, unexciting milieu of pre-revolution evenings, the poet acknowledges his own blindness and failure to engage with these people in any depth:

> I have passed with a nod of the head
> Or polite meaningless words,
> Or have lingered a while and said
> Polite meaningless words,

He confesses to his own unpleasant, condescending mockery ('a mocking tale or a gibe . . .') and his belief that all the pre-1916 organising was mere comical posturing:

> Being certain that they and I
> But lived where motley is worn . . .

He includes himself ('they and I') in this attempt at identification.

He spends the second section looking again at these people that he knew, as he needs to understand how they have changed. They are still the flawed characters he remembers: Constance Markievicz wasted her time in misplaced volunteer work ('ignorant good-will') and became a shrill fanatic ('nights in argument . . . voice grew shrill'); MacBride he thought 'a drunken vainglorious lout' who 'had done most bitter wrong' to Maud Gonne and Iseult. These are very ordinary, fallible, flawed and unlikely heroes.

Furthermore, the impression Yeats perceives is not one of energetically active heroes, but rather the passive recipients of this mysterious change. MacDonagh 'might have won fame in the end'. MacBride 'has resigned his part I In the casual comedy'. This smacks of an unknown actor giving up his part in an inconsequential work. The impression given is of relatively insignificant lives, out of which MacBride 'has been changed in his turn'. Note the passive voice: the change was effected on him, rather than by something he did, and it happened 'in his turn'. He waited his turn – perhaps a reference to the executions. Is Yeats saying that it was the executions that effected this change, transformed everyone utterly, and gave birth to this terrible beauty? That it was not due to the nature or any action of heroes?

Another aspect of these patriots that Yeats refers to is their feminine qualities. 'What voice more sweet' than Constance Gore-Booth's (in younger days)? MacDonagh's thought is 'daring and sweet'. Even MacBride has his passive side. So there is a sensitivity about these people that balances their more aggressive and masculine qualities, also referred to.

It is this softer, feminine quality in man and woman that is destroyed by fanaticism, something Yeats explores in the third and fourth sections. But first it is worth noticing the feminine aspect of the new order. This utter transformation of the social and historical reality is imagined as a new birth; but Yeats is so disturbed and confused by it that he can only describe it in paradoxical terms as a 'terrible beauty' – something that is partly feminine, aesthetically pleasing, sexually alluring even, but also carries suggestions of terror and of destructive power. This magnificent image carries all Yeats's confusions and contradictory feelings about the dramatic change.

In the third section he explores how change is effected. Only a stone, usually taken as a metaphor for the fanatical heart, can change or trouble the course of a stream, and it can achieve this only at a price. The heart will lose its humanness:

> Too long a sacrifice
> Can make a stone of the heart.

In the 1909 *Journals* Yeats had already written about the effects of political fanaticism on Maud Gonne, in metaphors akin to those used here:

> Women, because the main event of their lives has been a giving of themselves, give themselves to an opinion as if it were some terrible stone doll . . . They grow cruel, as if in defence of lover or child and all this is done for something other than human life. At last the opinion becomes so much a part of them that it is as though a part of their flesh becomes, as it were, stone, and much of their being passes out of life.

In this third section Yeats is exploring the dangers of fanatical devotion to a cause or ideal, and he represents this metaphorically as the conflicting forces between a stone and a stream.

The living stream is marvellously evoked. It is a picture of constant change, the flux of natural life and bursting with energy. The seasons are changing 'through summer and winter'; the skies change 'from cloud to tumbling cloud'; all is life and regeneration, as 'hens to moor-cocks call'. It is full of transient animal and human appearances, as they slide or plash or dive. And all this activity happens 'minute by minute'. Against this stream of ever-changing energy and life is set the unmoving stone, the fanatical heart. It is not difficult to conclude that the weight of the poet's sentiment is with the living stream rather than the unmoving stone. And yet out of this confrontation is born the 'terrible beauty'.

There is no easy answer to the conflicts posed by the poet. And indeed he seems to weary of the dialogue and of this dialectic in the fourth section. Having concluded that prolonged devotion to an ideal is dehumanising –

> Too long a sacrifice
> Can make a stone of the heart.

– he seems to accept the necessity of it and at the same time wishes for an end, in that sighing plea: 'O when may it suffice?'

The first seventeen lines of this fourth section are structured in questions – rhetorical questions, or questions that cannot be answered – thereby revealing the poet's uncertainties about the validity of the entire process of revolution and change. There is a kind of shocked vulnerability about the poetic voice here, a realisation of helplessness as all the doubts flood in with the questions: Are they really dead? Was it necessary if England intended to grant home rule after the war? What if they were just confused and bewildered by an excess of patriotism? There is an awareness that some things cannot be answered, that some of this mysterious dynamic of change cannot be understood – 'That is Heaven's part.' And the poet adopts a soothing mother's voice and persona, murmuring 'As a mother names her child'.

But then he seems to shake off the uncertain and shocked voice and finds a new assurance for that very definite, confident ending. Why is this? Terence Brown believes it has to do with the magical significance of the poem, deliberately created by Yeats. He suggests that the poem is a 'numerological artefact', based on the date when the rising began: 24 April 1916. There are four movements or sections, with the following numbers of lines in each: 16, 24, 16, 24. It is suggested also that Yeats intended this to be a verse of power, a magical recitation, seen in for example 'I number him in the song'; 'I write it out in a verse'. Certainly there is a surge of powerful assurance in those final lines, whether we read them as a litany of respectful remembrance or an occult incantation.

> I write it out in a verse –
> MacDonagh and MacBride
> And Connolly and Pearse
> Now and in time to be,
> Wherever green is worn,
> Are changed, changed utterly:
> A terrible beauty is born.

The Second Coming
Text of poem: New Explorations Anthology page 66

This poem was finished in January 1919, to a background of great political upheaval in Europe: the disintegration of the Austro-Hungarian, German and Russian empires, and uprisings and revolution in Germany and Russia. The events in Europe are most likely to have prompted the speculation that 'mere anarchy is loosed upon the world'; but as the poem was not published for twenty-two months, in the *Dial* of November 1920, it came to be read as a reaction to the atrocities of the War of Independence in Ireland. It is included in the volume *Michael Robartes and the Dancer* (1921).

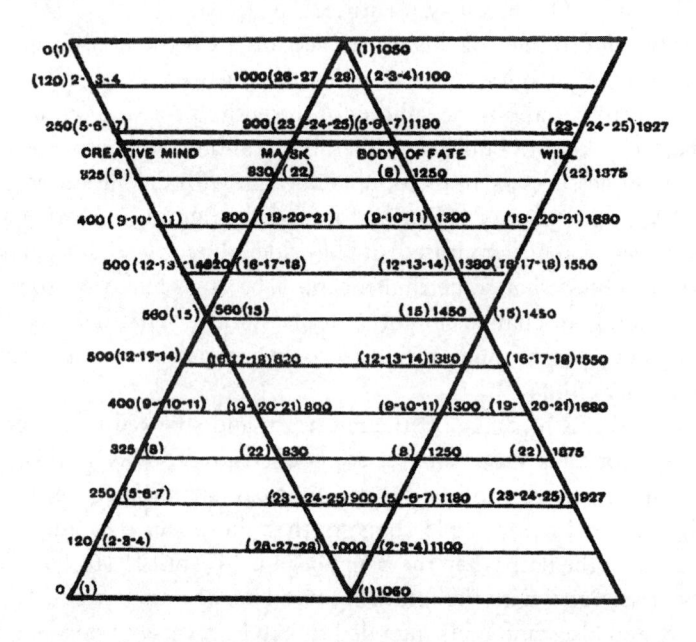

YEATS'S OCCULT PHILOSOPHY AND THEORIES OF HISTORY

Yeats was deeply interested in the patterns of history. He was also engaged in the study and practice of the occult and maintained regular contact with the spirits. These 'spirit communicators' helped him develop a cyclical theory of change in history, which is outlined in *A Vision* (1925). He used geometrical forms to express abstract ideas; and the concept of 'gyres' or cones representing time zones is one of these. In this poem the reference is to a single gyre or inverted cone. But the full representation of the gyres consists of two interpenetrating cones, expanding and contracting on a single axis. These represent the contrary forces, always changing, that determine the character of a person or the culture of a particular phase in history. There are particularly significant moments both for individuals and in historical time when the dominant influence passes from one gyre to its contrary. In history, he believed, this can happen every two thousand years. Hence the reference to 'twenty centuries of stony sleep' that preceded the Christian era, which is now waning and giving way to a new and antithetical era.

In its Christian interpretation, the 'Second Coming' refers to the prediction of the second coming of Christ; in Yeats's occult and magical philosophy it might also refer to the second birth of the Avatar or great antithetical spirit, which Yeats and his wife felt certain would be reincarnated as their baby son, whose birth was imminent. In fact the child turned out to be a girl, dashing that theory.

In this poem the hideous 'rough beast' that 'slouches towards Bethlehem to be born' is suggestive of the Anti-Christ, that legendary personal opponent of Christ and his kingdom expected to appear before the end of the world. See, for example, the Book of Revelations (chapter 13) on the portents for the end of the world:

> And I saw a beast rising out of the sea, with ten horns and seven heads, with ten diadems upon its horns and a blasphemous name upon its heads. And the beast that I saw was like a leopard, its feet were like a bear's, and its mouth was like a lion's mouth. And to it the dragon gave his power and his throne and great authority. One of its heads seemed to have a mortal wound, but its mortal wound was healed, and the whole earth followed the beast with wonder. Men worshipped the dragon, for he had given his authority to the beast, and they worshipped the beast, saying, 'Who is like the beast and who can fight against it?'

A READING OF THE POEM

This poem reflects Yeats's interest in historical change and his real fear that civilisation would break down and be replaced by an anti-civilisation or an era of anarchy. This was sparked off in part by his disgust and revulsion at what was happening in European politics and history around this time (1919). But, as we have seen, he was also preoccupied with patterns in history and immersed himself in the occult, with signs, portents, astrological charts and spirit communicators, and had developed a cyclical theory of change in history, which was represented graphically by the 'gyre' symbol.

So this poem deals with the turbulence of historical change; but what is particularly exciting is the enormous perspective that the poet takes. Time is not counted in years or decades but in millennia; and it is this vast perspective that is both exhilarating and terrifying.

First section

Essentially what is happening here is that Yeats is exploring the breakup of civilisation in metaphorical language. The falcon, that trained bird of prey, cannot hear the falconer and is reverting to its wild state. The falconer has also been interpreted as a representation of Christ, and so the image has been read as representing the movement of civilisation away from Christ. This dissipation is happening within the framework of its allotted time span, at a point within the gyre, representing the present. Yeats is bringing a critical philosophical viewpoint to bear on the social and political structures. He suggests that there is failure at the very heart of society, presumably in human beings themselves: 'Things fall apart; the centre cannot hold'. Instead of clear-sighted vision and forward progress there is this confusing circular movement, an out-of-control centrifugal force that threatens to send everything spinning away in disorder. In this chaos human beings are changing, becoming ignoble and destroying innocence: 'The ceremony of innocence is drowned.' People either have no convictions at all or are irrationally and passionately committed to causes; they have become either cynics or fanatics.

> The best lack all conviction, while the worst
> Are full of passionate intensity.

This first section embodies this very tension in its structure. Consider how the ideas are set up as opposites: centre – fall apart; falcon – falconer; indifference – intensity; innocence – anarchy. This polar oppositional tension is seen in the terrifying image of 'the blood-dimmed tide . . . loosed . . . innocence is drowned.' This sinister image has connotations of the great flood and its destruction of the world, but might also suggest a ruthless cleansing or purging. The repetition of 'loosed upon' and 'loosed' might suggest a savage wild animal, at the very least the 'dogs of war'. The circular imagery creates a sense of continuous swirling movement. Look at the repetition of -ing: 'turning, turning, widening'. There is a sense of a world out of control, of inevitable disaster.

Really it is the force of the imagery that carries the ideas in this section. Consider the falconry image. This was the pastime of kings and lords, so the image carries associations of an aristocratic life, civilised living, affluence. We know how much Yeats valued civilised living. Falconry was a 'noble' pastime, requiring skill and patience. Now this trained bird of prey is reverting to its wild state – a metaphor for the destruction of civilised living. It would also carry religious overtones and signal the breakdown of ordered religious systems. The falcon has also been interpreted as symbolic of the active or intellectual mind, so the breakdown of intellectual order might be signalled as well. Either way the image suggests dissolution in a number of different spheres and levels.

The second graphic image, of the 'blood-dimmed tide', has already been explored for its layers of suggestiveness. Its general impact is powerful, both visually and intellectually: innocence is drowned in a sea of blood. This is the ultimate nihilism, a world without justice, reason or order. Note Yeats's emphasis on the 'ceremony' of innocence. The rituals of civilised living will also be destroyed, of course.

The final image of the section, though somewhat ill defined, is a political one, suggesting that fanatical people have now got all the influence and are in power. The general impact of the imagery is one of frightening and irrational disorder and breakup in life and society.

Second section

Yeats begins by casting around for a reason for the breakdown of civilisation, and the possibility of a second coming together with the end of the world suggests itself as the only one great enough to cause this. 'Surely the Second Coming is at hand.' But it turns out not to be the Second Coming of Christ as foretold in the Gospels but rather the emergence of the Anti-Christ that Yeats imagines, an Anti-Christ who embodies the absolute reverse of the Christian era, which is now drawing to its end in the gyre of time. This rough beast, a nightmare symbol of the coming times, signals the end of this era, with its values and order.

Again, the image of this rough beast carries all the ideas about the new era. It is a 'vast image', overwhelming and troubling. It is a horrific hybrid of human and animal – suggesting unnatural times, such as foretold in the Book of Revelations. Its blank gaze suggests no intelligent sight or understanding; indeed it is as 'pitiless as the sun', incapable of empathy or feeling. The qualities it conjures up are gracelessness and brutishness: 'moving its slow thighs . . . Slouches towards Bethlehem to be born'. The final paradox is explained by the fact that its era has already begun, overlapping with the demise of the Christian era, so it is moving into position to initiate the new age or be born. The paradox further emphasises the antithetical nature of the coming age: how totally contradictory or opposite it is. There is something blasphemously shocking in the idea of the beast being born at Bethlehem. The nugget of insight gained by the poet out of this horrific vision concerns the nature of time and changing eras. He realises that eras have come and gone before, and that the advent of the Christian era must have been as troubling to the previous age.

> Now I know
> That twenty centuries of stony sleep
> Were vexed to nightmare by a rocking cradle.

Sailing to Byzantium
Text of poem: New Explorations Anthology page 68

This poem was written sometime in the autumn of 1926 and is the opening poem in the collection *The Tower* (1928).

A READING OF THE POEM

Writing for a radio programme in 1931, Yeats outlined some of the preoccupations of his poetry at that time, in particular the spiritual quest of 'Sailing to Byzantium':

> Now I am trying to write about the state of my soul, for it is right for an old man to make his soul [an expression meaning to prepare for death], and some of my thoughts upon that subject I have put into a poem called 'Sailing to Byzantium'. When Irishmen were illuminating the Book of Kells and making the jewelled crosiers of the National Museum, Byzantium was the centre of European civilisation and the source of its spiritual philosophy, so I symbolise the search for the spiritual life by a journey to that city.

So this poem is structured, as he says, in the shape of a journey – more of a quest, really – with a tightly argued personal commentary by the poet. The main theme surfaces immediately in the first stanza. With that strong, declamatory opening he renounces the world of the senses for that of the spirit and the intellect, the timeless.

> That is no country for old men. The young
> In one another's arms . . .

Notice the perspective ('that'): he has already departed and is looking back, not without a little nostalgic yearning for the sensuality of youth. The sensual imagery of lovers and the teeming rich life of trees and seas, the athletic vigour of the hyphenated words ('the salmon-falls, the mackerel-crowded seas') and the sensual 'f' and 's' sounds of 'fish, flesh or fowl' – all used to describe the cycle of life in the flesh – would strongly suggest that he does not renounce it easily. Indeed this ambiguity is carried in the paradox of 'those dying generations', with its linking of death and regeneration.

The importance of the spirit is re-emphasised in the second stanza as the poet asserts that it is the soul that gives meaning to a person: 'An aged man is but a paltry thing . . . unless | Soul clap its hands and sing.' And art enriches the soul, teaches it to sing: 'studying | Monuments of its own magnificence,' i.e.

works of art inspired by the spirit. Byzantium, as a centre of religion, philosophy and learning and also of a highly formalised art, is the ideal destination for the intellectual and spiritual person. In 'A Vision' (1925) Yeats wrote about the harmoniousness of life in fifth-century Byzantium: 'I think that in early Byzantium, maybe never before or since in recorded history, religious, aesthetic and practical life were one.' He had visited Ravenna in 1907 and when he composed the third stanza probably had in mind a mosaic on the wall of S. Apollinore Nuova showing martyrs being burnt in a fire.

Addressing these sages or martyrs directly in the third stanza, he entreats them to traverse history in the gyre of time, come to him and teach his soul to sing. He wants them to 'make' his soul, as he said, to purify it, separate it from emotions and desires and help it transcend the ageing physical body:

> Consume my heart away; sick with desire
> And fastened to a dying animal
> It knows not what it is . . .

These lines betray a seriously troubled state of mind. Central to the conflict is a dualist view of the human being as composed of two radically different and warring elements: body, and soul or spirit. Yeats values one element – the soul – imaged as singer and bird but is filled with self-disgust and loathing for his ageing body, imaged as a dying animal, not even dignified as human, that has entrapped the soul.

This confusion is evident even in the ambiguity of language here, in for example 'sick with desire'. Is he sick because of the desires of the flesh he cannot shake off, or does the desire refer to his spiritual aspiration, which continues to elude him? This acute existential conflict has led to a loss of spiritual identity: 'It knows not what it is'; hence his emotional entreaty to the sages to 'gather me | Into the artifice of eternity'.

It is worth exploring the richness of this ordinary language here. By using 'gather me' the poet is acknowledging how fragmented and scattered his condition is and how he needs both direction and comfort; it is as if he needs to be embraced, gathered in arms. Ironically, he wants to be gathered into the coherence and timelessness of art – 'the artifice of eternity'. It is through this transition that he will find immortality. But the language carries hints of ambiguity, even about this much-desired goal. 'Artifice' refers primarily to a work of art, but it can also mean 'artificiality'. Is this the first hint that this great quest might be flawed?

Still he begins the fourth stanza with great confidence that art holds the answer to the problem of mortality. 'Once out of nature' he will be transformed into the perfect work of art and so live on. The golden bird is ageless and incorruptible and will sing the song of the soul. The final irony, though, is that the song it sings is about the flux of time, 'what is past, or passing, or to come'. There is no perfect solution after all.

THEMES AND ISSUES

Discuss these and see if you can justify each from the evidence of the poem.
- Yeats in old age is attempting to develop his spiritual side. It is a poem about the values of the soul as against the world of the senses.
- It is an attempt to escape the harsh reality of old age and death through the immortality of spiritual things and of art.
- The view of the human being portrayed is that of a fractured, divided entity in an uncomfortable state of war between the spiritual and the physical.
- It is a meditation on the nature of art and its importance to humanity.
- It delivers fine insights into the nature of Byzantine imagination and culture.

STRUCTURE

As befits the theme of conflict, the ideas and images in this poem are developed in a series of *antinomies* or contrasts. In the very first line youth and age are set opposite each other: 'That is no country for old men . . .' While youth is imaged in those wonderful scenes of sensuous life in the first stanza, age is realised in the scarecrow image – 'a tattered coat upon a stick' – with all its suggestions of fake outward show, a grotesque parody of the human being and the sense of powerlessness and indignity. The body is imaged as a dying animal, while the soul is imaged as a priceless golden bird, singing.

The mortality of life is contrasted with the timelessness of art. The teeming sensuality of Ireland is set against the culture of Byzantium, with its religious ethos ('holy city'; 'God's holy fire'), its reputation for learning and philosophical thought ('O sages'), and its artistic achievement ('artifice'; 'a form as Grecian goldsmiths make | Of hammered gold and gold enamelling', etc.). These conflicts reflect the internal struggle, the yearnings and the reality within the poetic persona here.

Yet the struggle is smoothed over by the grace and elegance of the language used. There is a regular pattern of end-rhymes or sometimes half-rhymes, which gives the verses a musical ease. Yeats also uses a rhythmic phrasing, often grouping in lists of three, which has magical significance as well as producing a rhythmic rise and fall: 'fish, flesh, or fowl'; 'Whatever is begotten, born, and dies'; 'unless | Soul clap its hands and sing, and louder sing'; 'Of what is past, or passing, or to come'. We might also notice other rhetorical qualities, such as the strong, declamatory opening, the rhetorical plea to the sages, indeed the strong, confident, first-person voice of the poet all through. These sometimes belie the conflicts and uncertainties at the heart of the work.

The Stare's Nest By My Window
Text of poem: New Explorations Anthology page 72

FROM 'MEDITATIONS IN TIME OF CIVIL WAR'

'Meditations in Time of Civil War' is quite a lengthy poem, structured in seven sections. Apart from the first, composed in England in 1921, it was written in Ireland during the Civil War of 1922–23 and was first published in the *Dell* in January 1923. It is included in the volume *The Tower* (1928).

In the poem as a whole, Yeats explores aspects of the Anglo-Irish ascendancy tradition: its origins and heritage and his own sense of sharing in the values of that tradition, particularly those of continuity, culture and family line. Conflict too was a necessary element of that planter culture, and now he is brought face to face with the violence of the Civil War and must re-evaluate his own role in the continuing tradition of history.

Images of houses and building provide one of the unifying metaphors and themes throughout this poem. Yeats acknowledges the violence out of which the great Anglo-Irish culture was built:

> Some violent bitter man, some powerful man
> Called architect and artist in, that they,
> Bitter and violent men, might rear in stone
> The sweetness that all longed for night and day.

His own house in Co. Galway, Thoor Ballylee, was originally a defensive fifteenth-century tower. He acknowledges proudly that conflict is part of his tradition; he wishes that his descendants too will find 'befitting emblems of adversity'. So in section V, when a band of Irregulars calls to his door, he experiences a certain envy of the men of action. Perhaps it is the graphic details of that war in section VI that led to a reappraisal. The terrifying vision of the nightmarish destruction of civilisation in section VII throws him back to thinking on his own role as poet in his isolated tower.

Yeats wrote the following description of the genesis and context of section VI:

> I was in my Galway house during the first months of civil war, the railway bridges blown up and the roads blocked with stones and trees. For the first week there were no newspapers, no reliable news, we did

not know who had won nor who had lost, and even after newspapers came, one never knew what was happening on the other side of the hill or of the line of trees. Ford cars passed the house from time to time with coffins standing upon end between the seats, and sometimes at night we heard an explosion, and once by day saw the smoke made by the burning of a great neighbouring house. Men must have lived so through many tumultuous centuries. One felt an overmastering desire not to grow unhappy or embittered, not to lose all sense of the beauty of nature. A stare (our West of Ireland name for a starling) had built in a hole beside my window and I made these verses out of the feeling of the moment . . . [here he quoted from 'The bees build in the crevices' to 'Yet no clear fact to be discerned: come build in the empty house of the stare.'] . . . That is only the beginning but it runs on in the same mood. Presently a strange thing happened. I began to smell honey in places where honey could not be, at the end of a stone passage or at some windy turn of the road, and it came always with certain thoughts. When I got back to Dublin I was with angry people who argued over everything or were eager to know the exact facts: in the midst of the mood that makes realistic drama. (From *The Bounty of Sweden*)

A READING OF THE POEM

At one level, this poem is an attempt to balance the horrors of war with the healing sweetness and regenerative power of nature. As Yeats himself saw it, 'Men must have lived so through many tumultuous centuries. One felt an overmastering desire not to grow unhappy or embittered, not to lose all sense of the beauty of nature.' The brutality of war is graphically represented here:

> Last night they trundled down the road
> That dead young soldier in his blood . . .

The onomatopoeic sound of 'trundled' carries suggestions of some primitive war machine or evokes the tumbrels and savage excess of the French Revolution. There is none of the traditional respect for a dead enemy here, but rather the ferocity of civil war enmity in the indignity with which the dead solder was treated – 'trundled . . . in his blood'. The bees are evoked as an antidote to this savagery. They may symbolise patience and creative force, as opposed to the destructive forces round about. They bring sweetness, healing and the richness of life. These may also be a classical allusion to Pomphyry's bees, who visited the world to perform tasks for the gods. So the bees could be seen as a manifestation of the divine in the world. Whether they evoked for Yeats the simple beauty of nature or carried more complex connotations, his plea to them is a desperate, plaintive cry. That cry for healing and for natural regeneration of life echoes through that repeated refrain at the end of each stanza, culminating in the final direct personal address, 'O honey-bees'. There is honest emotion here.

But this is more than simply a reaction to a specific event. Taken in the context of the poem as a whole, we could read this section as a metaphor for Yeats's own life situation and that of his traditional class, the Anglo-Irish ascendancy. The tower-house, once a fortified planter house, used as a place of both safety and dominance, is now a place of 'loosening masonry'; the structures of that colonial past are crumbling. The Yeats' isolation in the tower during that particular fortnight is symptomatic of the isolation and uncertain future of the entire minority but once-powerful class.

> We are closed in, and the key is turned
> On our uncertainty.

This is not just physical imprisonment but a mental segregation, a way of viewing themselves as different, distinct and separate – a cultivated isolation. The key has been turned from the inside. The physical barriers of stone or wood accord with the mental barriers created by class and outlook, so that we are acutely aware of how introverted and cut off the poet is. Yet there is a hint in the first stanza that some sweetness can come with the ending of his self-isolation:

> My wall is loosening; honey-bees,
> Come build in the empty house of the stare,

Or is this just a vain hope?

In the final stanza he faces up to the illusions on which his philosophy is based and which are explored in the rest of the poem: that sweetness and beauty might grow out of bitter and violent conquest, that conflict and a life of adversity could be a glorious thing. These are the fantasies that sustain his class outlook and for which he now indicts himself. The consequence has not been beauty but self-brutalisation.

> The heart's grown brutal from the fare.

He strips away any delusions of superiority or righteousness as he admits that negative emotions are strongest.

> More substance in our enmities
> Than in our love.

It is as if the violence outside has forced him to confront the past violence of his own class, in an honest moment of shared guilt. This is a critical moment of bleak insight, yet one that he attempts to balance with the final plea: 'O honey-bees' – a plea for sweetness and healing at a time of pain, for order in a time of chaos.

Imagery

Images of houses and buildings dominate this poem; but they are either abandoned, like the house of stone, or destroyed by violence ('a house burned'), or are gradually crumbling away in time ('loosening masonry'; 'My wall is crumbling'). They are symbols of a way of life being destroyed; or else they are isolating and self-imprisoning:

> We are closed in, the key is turned
> On our uncertainty.

Any building done is for destructive and disorderly purpose: 'A barricade of stone or wood'. So the poet's plea, while romantic and positive in outlook, is rather pathetic in the context. Only the bees and birds may build where the once-powerful colonising class raised great edifices.

In Memory of Eva Gore-Booth and Con Markiewicz

Text of poem: New Explorations Anthology page 74

This poem was written in the autumn of 1927, was first published in 1929, and is included in *The Winding Stair and Other Poems* (1933). Constance Markievicz had died in August 1927, her sister Eva the previous year.

A reading of the poem

This is one of Yeats's poems of age, the reverie of an old man addressing the now-dead companions of his youth: 'Dear shadows . . .' It is very much a retrospective piece, viewing life from the perspective of the end. Yeats avoids sentimentality, opting instead for retrospective judgments, assessing the significance of their lives. He felt that they had wasted their lives. Constance Markievicz's years of political agitation for socialist and republican ideals he dismisses as dragging out lonely years – 'Conspiring among the ignorant' – while Eva's social and women's suffrage work is merely 'some vague Utopia'.

To understand this harsh condemnation of what to us seem idealistic and committed lives we need to take the poet's value system into account. His view was that the Anglo-Irish ascendancy class, with its wealth and great houses, had a duty to set an example of gracious and cultured living; this was its value for society. As the critic Alasdair MacRae says, 'The graciousness of accustomed affluence, the unostentatiousness of inherited furnishings and family traditions, what he saw culminating in courtesy, appealed to Yeats and he considered Eva and Con along with Maud Gonne as betraying something precious and feminine.' Yeats's idea of beauty is linked to the feminine. The image of feminine beauty he creates here is exotic. The silk kimonos give a hint of eastern mysteriousness, while the comparison with a gazelle suggests both a natural elegance and a certain wild, unknowable quality. And the two sisters are a decorative part of the big-house scene, a house that is elegant, imposing, a symbol of Anglo-Irish achievement and cultured way of life. It is primarily this image and what it symbolised that Yeats is nostalgic for: it is not the people he missed in the first instance, but the house and the cultured dinner-table conversation!

> Many a time I think to seek
> One or the other out and speak
> Of that old Georgian mansion, mix
> Pictures of the mind, recall
> That table and the talk of youth . . .

Yeats's negative retrospective judgments are not so much the bitter rantings of an old man, but rather what he saw as a failure to fulfil an inherited role in society.

But this has some of the more usual features of an 'age' poem – the contrast of youth and age. The 'two girls in silk kimonos . . . one a gazelle' become 'withered old and skeleton-gaunt'. It is interesting that old bodies are rarely beautiful for Yeats: he is repelled and disgusted by physical ageing. We are made aware of the ravages of time very early on in the poem, right after the first four lines of that beautiful limpid opening, and it comes as quite a shocking contrast:

> But a raving autumn shears
> Blossom from the summer's wreath.

Autumn is 'raving', mad, hysterical, out of control, and the sharp-edged onomatopoeic sound of 'shears' conveys its deadly potential. Even summer carries the seeds of death in its 'wreath'.

Out of this retrospection Yeats attempts to distil a certain wisdom about life. This philosophy he sets down in the second section. In a more kindly address to the 'dear shadows' he presumes they now agree with him about the vanity of all causes and all zeal, irrespective of rightness:

All the folly of a fight
With a common wrong or right.

And, secondly, he knows that the great quarrel is with time, destroyer of innocence and beauty. He reflects on the vanity of it all, as it will end in a great apocalyptic conflagration, which will consume not just all they've built – great houses or mere gazebos – but all the anguished decisions of their lives. All is vanity before the end.

Tone

At times he manages to be gently nostalgic, such as at the beginning and end of the first section. But he can be very censorious about lives wasted in political agitation. And he seems quite excited by the possibility of the great final conflagration. This is communicated by the energy and repetition of strong verbs (strike, strike, climb, run) and by the repetition of phrases ('strike a match').

Themes and issues

- What is a worthwhile way to live life?
- The vagaries of life, the imperfections
- Is it all vanity? What is the point of it all?
- The real enemy is time.
- Contrasting youth and age.

Rhymes and rhythms

Though Yeats imposes a quatrain rhyming scheme, *abba*, on the poem, he does not structure the thought in quatrains, apart from the first four lines. The first section, for instance, is structured periodically in groups of 4, 5, 4, 7. So the thought structure provides a sort of counter-rhythm to the rhyming structure and gives it a conversational naturalness.

This naturalness is emphasised by the use of off-rhymes rather than full rhymes, for example south – both, wreath – death, ignorant – gaunt, recall – gazelle. Some could argue that the imperfect rhyme befits the theme – the imperfections of life. The rhythmic quality of the language is achieved partly through repetitions: repetitions of phrases such as 'And bid me strike a match', but more obviously with the repetition of the well-known refrain 'Two girls . . .' However, the tone of the second repetition differs markedly from the first, because of the context, where it now carries all the bleak irony and the disappointment of hindsight.

Structure

The structure of this poem is almost unnoticed, so deftly is it done. It opens with

'The light of evening', proceeds to the darkness of 'Dear Shadows', and erupts again into the final apocalyptic inferno of the end of time. It begins with youth and ends with death; it opens with the great house of Lissadell and ends with a fragile gazebo.

Swift's Epitaph
Text of poem: New Explorations Anthology page 78

Begun in 1929 and finished in September 1930, this was first published in the *Dublin Magazine* in the winter of 1931. It is included in the volume *The Winding Stair and Other Poems* (1933). The poem is essentially a translation, with some alterations, of the Latin epitaph on Jonathan Swift's memorial in St Patrick's Cathedral, Dublin.

> Hic depositum est Corpus
> JONATHAN SWIFT S.T.D.
> Hujus Ecclesiae Cathedralis
> Decani,
> Ubi saeva Indignatio
> Ulterius
> Cor lacerare nequit.
> Abi Viator
> Et imitare, si poteris,
> Strenuum pro virili
> Libertatis vindicatorem.
> Obiit 19º Die Mensis Octobris
> A.D. 1745. Anno Aetatis 78º.

> Here is laid the body of
> JONATHAN SWIFT, doctor of sacred theology,
> dean of this cathedral church,
> where savage indignation
> can no longer
> rend his heart.
> Go, traveller,
> and imitate, if you can,
> an earnest and dedicated
> champion of liberty.
> He died on the nineteenth day of October
> AD 1745, in the year of his age 78.

Jonathan Swift (1667–1745) was dean of St Patrick's Cathedral, Dublin. Poet, political pamphleteer and satirist, he was the author of such famous works as *The Drapier's Letters, A Modest Proposal, A Tale of a Tub* and *Gulliver's Travels*. Politically conservative, Swift voiced the concerns and values of Protestant Ireland with an independence of spirit and a courage that Yeats admired greatly. Swift's writing made him enemies on all sides, but this isolation endeared him even further to Yeats, who often spoke admiringly of 'Anglo-Irish solitude'. Yeats thought of Swift as a heroic figure, an artist–philosopher who, despite the conflicts of his personal life, served liberty by speaking out in his writings and freeing the artist from the tyranny of the mob. He ranked Swift together with Berkeley, Goldsmith and Burke as one of the intellectual founders of the Anglo-Irish tradition.

Yeats's play *The Words upon the Window Pane* (1930) explores some of the conflicts of Swift's life.

A FREE TRANSLATION

Among the chief interests of the Yeats poem are the significance of the changes he made. For instance, 'Swift has sailed into his rest' is much more confident, energetic and vigorous than the original. It sounds more like a victorious progress, while being at the same time a gentle and graceful journey. There are also clearer overtones of a spiritual afterlife – 'his rest' – where the original merely notes the depositing of the body!

He retains the famous reference to *'saeva indignatio'* (savage indignation), which was the driving force of Swift's satirical work, and the reference to his capacity for empathy and for being affected by the injustices and miseries he encountered ('cannot lacerate his breast'). The challenge to the observer is stronger than in the original – to imitate him 'if you dare' rather than 'if you can'. And the traveller is described as 'world-besotted', worldly, lacking in spiritual values and outlook. The implication may be to enhance, by contrast, the unworldly qualities of Swift (which would be somewhat at variance with the facts). Yeats also retains the epithet noting Swift's defence of liberty, a philosophy they shared.

In general it might be said that Yeats has nudged the epitaph more in the direction of a eulogy. And there is more transparent emotion and admiration in the Yeats version.

An Acre of Grass

Text of poem: New Explorations Anthology page 80

This poem was written in November 1936 and first published in *New Poems* (1938).

A READING OF THE POEM

This poem is quite a remarkable response to old age and thoughts of death. The first stanza captures the shrinkage of an old person's physical world in the twilight years. With the ebbing of physical strength his world is reduced to the gardens of his house, 'an acre of green grass | For air and exercise'. The final two lines of the stanza are a marvellous evocation of the stillness, isolation and sense of emptiness that can be experienced at night by the wakeful elderly, a feeling carried in part by the broad vowel rhymes 'house – mouse':

> Midnight, an old house
> Where nothing stirs but a mouse.

He could easily resign himself to restfulness and silence. 'My temptation is quiet.'

But this old man, this poet, needs to write, to continue to find new truths, and he knows that neither a 'loose imagination' – an imagination that is not disciplined by the structure of writing – nor any ordinary observation of everyday occurrences will deliver up any significant truths.

> Nor the mill of the mind
> Consuming its rag and bone,
> Can make truth known.

Real creativity needs something more, like mystical insight; and that comes only through really passionate endeavour or frenzy. Hence his prayer, 'Grant me an old man's frenzy.' That frenzy or madness produced insight and truth for King Lear at the end of his life; and mystical visions, which some interpret as madness, produced the beautiful wisdom of William Blake's poetry. Even at the end of his life, Yeats knows the huge transforming energy necessary to forge new insights and truths, and he faces up to it.

> Myself I must remake

What courage for a person in his seventies!

Yeats had been reading Nietzsche's *The Dawn of Day*, about people of genius who can distance themselves from character and temperament and rise above the weight of personality like a winged creature. Yeats had used Nietzsche's ideas to develop his theory of the Mask: he felt the need to continually transform himself. And this is the ideology driving this poem – the need for transformation in order to achieve new insights and truths. So the poet must discard the persona of dignified old man and remake himself as a wild, mad prophet-like figure, such as Timon or Lear or Blake, and that will bring the searing vision, the 'eagle mind' 'that can pierce the clouds'. This is a poet's fighting response to old age and approaching death. It may remind us of Dylan Thomas's later 'Rage, rage against the dying of the light.'

THEMES AND ISSUES

Explore the following ideas, and expand on each with reference to what you find in the poem.
- A response to ageing: refusing to accept a quiet retirement; summoning reserves of energy to continue working; aware of the huge demands, yet praying for the chance.
- The process of creativity: the ordinary imagination processing or milling everyday events is not sufficient; a frenzy or madness is necessary in order to see things differently or see into things; the after-truths or insights are all-consuming; the power of that insight can 'pierce the clouds' and 'shake the dead'.
- The poet's need for continued transformation. Is it comfortable being a poet? Is it worth it?

Politics

Text of poem: New Explorations Anthology page 82

A READING OF THE POEM

We know that Yeats had intended that the volume *Last Poems* should end with 'Politics'. It is suggested that it was written as an answer to an article that had praised Yeats for his public language but suggested that he should use it more on political subjects. If so, then this is written as a mocking, ironic, tongue-in-cheek response. The speaker affects the pose of a distracted lover who is too preoccupied with the woman to give any attention to the political chaos of European politics of the mid-1930s: Franco, Mussolini, etc. He is little concerned for these earth-shattering events, dismissing them casually in a throw-away comment:

> And maybe what they say is true
> Of war and war's alarms . . .

We can almost see the shrug of indifference.

But the mask of the dispassionate observer slips in the final two lines as his passionate yearning breaks through and we realise that the 'she' is probably 'Caitlín Ní Uallacháin' – Ireland. So we understand Yeats's mocking response to those who have not understood one of his major poetical preoccupations.

The regularity of the four-stress lines alternating with three-stress lines and the simplicity of alternative end-line rhymes, together with the simplicity of the language, give the impression that this is lightweight verse. But, as with all good satire, we are lulled into a false sense of security until the final punch is thrown.

From 'Under Ben Bulben'

Text of poem: New Explorations Anthology page 84

SECTIONS V AND VI

The final draft of this poem is dated 4 September 1938, about five months before the poet's death. Parts of it were published in 1939.

BACKGROUND AND CONTEXT

Some acquaintance with the poem as a whole is necessary for an understanding of the context of sections V and VI. It is recommended that you read through all six sections.

'Under Ben Bulben' can be seen as Yeats's poetic testimony, an elegy for himself, defining his convictions and the poetical and social philosophies that motivated his life's work.

Section I incorporates the two main belief systems that informed his poetry: the occult philosophy, and folk beliefs and traditions.

Section II features another aspect of his belief system: reincarnation.

Section III suggests that poetic insight is born out of moments of violence; that violence and conflict can be invigorating.

Section IV outlines what he considers to be the great tradition in art, from Pythagoras through Egyptian and Greek sculpture to Michelangelo's Renaissance.

In Sections IV and V Yeats urges all artists, poets, painters and sculptors to do their work in this great tradition of art, to promote the necessary heroic images that nourish civilisation. Specifically, he had in mind the forms of the perfected human body as the necessary poetic inspiration, a concept linked to his ideas on eugenics (the pseudo-science of improving the human race through selective breeding). Yeats had joined the Eugenics Society in London in 1936 and became interested in research on intelligence testing. During 1938 he worked on a verse tract on this topic, published as *On the Boiler* (1939). Convinced that eugenics was crucial to the future of civilisation, he wrote: 'Sooner or later we must limit the families of the unintelligent classes and if our government cannot send them doctor and clinic it must, till it gets tired of it, send monk and confession box.'

Section VI of 'Under Ben Bulben' rounds his life to its close and moves from the mythologies associated with the top of Benbulbin to the real earth at its foot, in Drumcliff churchyard.

A READING OF THE POEM
Section V
This is Yeats's advice to Irish poets concerning the model or tradition they should follow. And the model he recommends is a new, composite one, attempting to fuse together two cultural traditions, those of peasant and aristocratic cultures.

> Sing the peasantry and then
> Hard-riding country gentlemen . . .

The former is the Irish tradition of folk and fairy tales and fantastical mythology; the latter is the Anglo-Irish cultural tradition, which Yeats traced back to the 'other days' referred to, the eighteenth century and the intellectual contribution of Swift, Berkeley, Goldsmith and Burke. He valued this tradition for its spirit of free enquiry, its sense of order and the example of gracious living it produced in Georgian mansions and fine estates. To this fusion he adds the religious tradition as worthy of celebration ('The holiness of monks'), followed immediately by 'Porter-drinkers' randy laughter', which rather devalues the former. Perhaps it's meant to be ironic. The Irish nobility are worthy of celebration, even though they 'were beaten into the clay | Through seven heroic centuries'. So heroic defeat is a fitting subject.

But once again Yeats scorns the present generation. Physically they do not conform to the traditional model of aesthetic beauty ('All out of shape from top to toe'). With an arrogance derived from the reprehensible theories of eugenics, he scorns their low intelligence and inferior lineage:

> Their unremembering hearts and heads
> Base-born products of base beds.

That arrogant tone continues, to end in that triumphant note – 'Still the indomitable Irishry.' The trouble with this poem is that it is so 'well made' – the rhythms of the language, the regular metre, the alliterative repetitions, the graphically grotesque imagery, etc. – that it can distract us from the seriously questionable class and racist attitudes.

Section VI
This section is beautifully structured, like a film shot. Opening with a long shot of the mountain, the camera draws back and focuses on the churchyard, panning by the church and the ancient cross until it finishes with a close-up of the epitaph cut in limestone. The effect is of a closing down of Yeats's life, a narrowing in to death. Many of the important elements of Yeats's life are here: the mythology and folklore associated with Benbulbin; the sense of ancestry, family and continuity provided by the rector; and the continuity of cultural

tradition in the 'ancient cross'. No ostentatious marble tomb or conventional, tired phrases are permitted, but rather a piece of indigenous material, local stone, to carry his epitaph.

This is a curiously impersonal epitaph, neither celebrating the person's virtues nor asking remembrance or recommending the soul to God: rather it is a stark piece of advice that the challenges of life and death should not be taken too seriously but should be regarded with a certain detachment. It is his final summation, that all the great issues merely come to this.

Developing a personal understanding

1. Select the poem by Yeats that made the greatest impact on you, and write about your reaction to it.
2. What issues raised by the poet did you think significant?
3. On reading this selection, what did you find surprising or interesting?
4. What impressions of Yeats as a person did you form?
5. What questions would you like to ask him?
6. Do you think it important for Irish pupils to study Yeats?
7. What do you find difficult about the poetry of Yeats?
8. What do you like about his poetry?

Overview

On each point, return to the poem for reference and further exploration.

Yeats and the national question

Among the issues explored by the poet under this heading are the following:

- the heroic past; patriots are risk-takers, rebels, self-sacrificing idealists who are capable of all that 'delirium of the brave' (see 'September 1913')
- how heroes are created, how ordinary people are changed ('Easter 1916')
- the place of violence in the process of political change; the paradox of the 'terrible beauty' (see 'September 1913', 'Easter 1916', and 'Meditations in Time of Civil War')
- the place of 'fanaticism' and the human effects of it – the 'stone of the heart' (see 'Easter 1916', 'September 1913', 'In Memory of Eva Gore-Booth and Con Markiewicz')
- the force of political passion (see 'Easter 1916', 'Politics').

Yeats's notions of the ideal society

- The vital contribution that both the aristocracy and artists make to society; the importance of the Anglo-Irish tradition in Irish society (see 'September 1913', 'In Memory of Eva Gore-Booth and Con Markiewicz', 'Meditations

in Time of Civil War', 'Swift's Epitaph', 'Under Ben Bulben')
- His contempt for the new middle class and the new materialism (see 'September 1913')
- Aesthetic values and the place of art in society (see 'Sailing to Byzantium', 'Under Ben Bulben')
- The yearnings for order and the fear of anarchy (see 'Meditations in Time of Civil War', 'The Second Coming')
- His views on the proper contribution of women to society (see 'In Memory of Eva Gore-Booth and Con Markiewicz', 'Easter 1916').

THEORIES OF HISTORY, TIME AND CHANGE
- His notion of thousand-year eras, 'gyres', etc. (see 'The Second Coming')
- The world and people in constant change and flux (see 'The Second Coming', 'Easter 1916')
- Personal ageing, the transience of humanity (see 'The Wild Swans at Coole', 'An Acre of Grass')
- The yearning for changelessness and immortality (see 'The Wild Swans at Coole', 'Sailing to Byzantium')
- The timelessness of art, or the possibility of it (see 'Sailing to Byzantium').

CONFLICTS AT THE CENTRE OF THE HUMAN BEING
- The conflict between physical desires and spiritual aspirations (see 'Sailing to Byzantium')
- The quest for aesthetic satisfaction (see 'Sailing to Byzantium')
- The search for wisdom and peace, which is not satisfied here (see 'The Lake Isle of Innisfree')
- A persistent sense of loss or failure; loss of youth and passion (see 'The Wild Swans at Coole'); the loss of poetic vision and insight (see 'An Acre of Grass').

General questions

1. Select any major theme explored by Yeats and outline his treatment of it.
2. Review critically any poem by Yeats that you considered interesting.
3. 'Yeats displayed great reverence for the past but little respect for his own time.' Consider the truth of this statement in the light of the poems you have examined.
4. 'W.B. Yeats explored complex issues of national identity with great honesty.' Discuss.
5. Having read his poetry, what do you think Yeats chiefly valued in life?
6. 'Yeats's poetry is fuelled by conflict – conflict between past and present, youth and age, mind and body.' Explore this view of his poetry.

Bibliography

Brown, Terence, *The Life of W.B. Yeats*, Dublin: Gill and Macmillan 1999.

Cullingford, Elizabeth Butler, *Yeats: Poems, 1919–1935* (Casebook Series), Basingstoke: Macmillan 1984.

Cullingford, Elizabeth Butler, *Gender and History in Yeats's Love Poetry*, Cambridge: Cambridge University Press 1993.

Donoghue, Denis (editor), *W.B. Yeats: Memoirs*, London: Macmillan 1972.

Ellman, Richard, *The Identity of Yeats*, London: Faber and Faber 1968.

Ellman, Richard, *Yeats: The Man and the Masks*, Oxford: Oxford University Press 1979.

Foster, R.F., *W.B. Yeats: A Life, vol. 1: The Apprentice Mage*, Oxford: Oxford University Press 1997.

Harwood, John, *Olivia Shakespear and W.B. Yeats*, Basingstoke: Macmillan 1989.

Hone, Joseph, *W.B. Yeats*, Harmondsworth (Middx): Pelican Books 1971.

Jeffares, A. Norman, *W.B. Yeats: Man and Poet*, London: Routledge and Kegan Paul 1966.

Jeffares, A. Norman, *W.B. Yeats: The Poems*, London: Edward Arnold 1979.

Jeffares, A. Norman, *W.B. Yeats: A New Biography*, London: Hutchinson 1988.

Jeffares, A. Norman (editor), *Yeats's Poems*, Basingstoke: Macmillan 1989.

Jeffares, A. Norman, and MacBride White, Anna (editors), *The Gonne–Yeats Letters, 1893–1938*, London: Hutchinson 1992.

Kelly, John (editor), *The Collected Letters of W.B. Yeats* (three vols), Oxford: Clarendon Press 1986, 1997, 1994.

Kinahan, Frank, *Yeats, Folklore and Occultism*, Boston: Unwin Hyman 1988.

MacRae, Alasdair, *W.B. Yeats: A Literary Life*, Dublin: Gill and Macmillan 1995.

Martin, Augustine, *W.B. Yeats*, Gerrards Cross (Bucks): Colin Smythe 1983.

Smith, Stan, *W.B. Yeats: A Critical Introduction*, Dublin: Gill and Macmillan 1990.

Tuohy, Frank, *Yeats*, London: Macmillan 1976.

Yeats, W.B., *A Vision* [1925], London: Macmillan 1937.

Yeats, W.B., *Autobiographies: Memoirs and Reflections*, London: Macmillan 1955.

Yeats, W.B., *Mythologies*, London: Macmillan 1959.

Yeats, W.B., *Essays and Introductions*, New York: Macmillan 1961.

3 Robert FROST

Marie Dunne

A literary life

Robert Lee Frost was born in San Francisco on 26 March 1874. He was a sickly child and received his early education at home. Though pampered by his protective mother, he was often harshly disciplined by his violent and drunken father. In 1885 his father died, following a long illness, leaving his family penniless. Robert moved with his younger sister, Jeannie, and his mother to Lawrence, Massachusetts, where his grandparents lived. His mother found employment in nearby schools, and the two children began their formal education in her class.

Robert entered Lawrence High School in 1888. He chose the classical curriculum: Latin, Greek, ancient and European history, and mathematics. During his final year he fell in love with a classmate, Elinor White. They married on 19 December 1895, when he was twenty-one and she was twenty-three. After finishing secondary school, Frost went to Dartmouth College, but he left in 1893, halfway through his first year. He taught his mother's senior class for several months until the term ended, then took a variety of low-paid jobs in a woollen mill, as a rural schoolteacher, and as a newspaper reporter. In September 1897 Frost entered Harvard University, but again left without a degree.

When he returned home he was encouraged by his doctor to become a farmer, in order to improve his health. At first in New Hampshire and later in Vermont he lived on small farms where the work – mowing, making hay, and apple-picking – was done by hand. He wrote his poems at night. Many years later he recalled his favourite activities as being 'mowing with a scythe, chopping with an axe, and writing with a pen.'

A WORKING LIFE

Neither farming nor poetry earned Frost enough money to support his wife and four children; so, at the age of thirty-two, he was forced to seek regular paid employment. A pastor of the First Congregational Church suggested to him that he should apply for a vacancy at Pinkerton Academy in Derry Village. A trustee of the academy told him he would be employed if one of his poems were read at the banquet of the Men's League of the Congregational Church. Frost submitted 'The Tuft of Flowers'. It was well received and secured him the position. He taught English, Latin, history and geometry, coached the debating team, advised the school newspaper and assisted with athletics. Exhausted by his workload, he moved from the academy in 1911 and became a lecturer in the teacher training college in New Hampshire.

A LITERARY EDUCATION

Frost devoted his free time to reading the major poets. He studied their diction, their imagery and their formal techniques in order to perfect his own writing. His work was heavily influenced by his classical education. The concise language, concentrated images and clarity of thought in his poems reflect this training, while his knowledge of strict classical metre allowed him to write with confidence in traditional forms. Biblical references reflect his early scripture studies.

Other influences on his work include Shakespeare, the English Romantics (Wordsworth, Keats and Shelley), and the Victorian poets (Hardy, Kipling and Browning). He followed the principles laid down in Wordsworth's 'Preface to the Lyrical Ballads' concerning the language, people, places and events appropriate to poetry. Like Wordsworth, he relied on incidents from 'common life' and discovered in them 'the primary laws of our nature'. He agreed with Wordsworth that these events should be described in 'language really used by men'. In his own poems he attempted to reproduce as accurately as possible the tone and modulations of the spoken word. 'Wordsworth was right,' he commented, 'in trying to reproduce in his poetry not only the words . . . actually used in common speech . . . but their sound.' He believed that rhymes should be unforced and natural, although, unlike many of his contemporaries, he refused to abandon the rules of poetry to achieve this effect. 'The most important thing about a poem . . . is how wilfully, gracefully, naturally, entertainingly and beautifully its rhymes are,' he wrote in 1939. He wanted the rhythm in his verse to spring from the tension that occurs when a strong rhythmic pattern based on iambic metre is played against the irregularity of ordinary speech. He repeatedly stressed the importance of the living voice, 'the rise and fall, the stressed pauses and little hurries, of spoken language', and insisted that the tone of voice added to the meaning of words in the poems.

Frost found modernist poetry unappealing and wrote instead about pre-industrial values, rural life, and nature. Yet there is nothing sentimental in his work: the world portrayed in his poetry can be bleak, lonely, chilled, blighted and deadly. Acknowledging this, Frost once said: 'There's plenty to be dark about, you know. It's full of darkness.'

First publications

For a long time Frost had difficulty finding a publisher. Partly as a result of this the Frost family decided to emigrate from America to England in 1912, and they settled at Beaconsfield, near London. Frost arranged his lyrical poems in book form and then sought a publisher. The collection called *A Boy's Will* appeared in April 1913; his second book, *North of Boston,* came out a year later. The books were widely praised, and Frost was quickly introduced into literary circles in London, where he met W. B. Yeats and Ezra Pound. He was very pleased when Yeats told Pound that *A Boy's Will* was 'the best thing that had come out of America for some time'.

A Boy's Will introduces the natural elements Frost would use in many future poems: stars, clouds, leaves, pools, brooks, flowers and birds. *North of Boston,* written between 1905 and 1913, saw a shift of emphasis from man as a solitary creature to man as a social being. Though he called it 'This Book of People', many characters in *North of Boston* experience a deep sense of loneliness. With his second publication Frost clearly indicated that, like the English poet Thomas Hardy, he would concentrate on the regional.

Frost is a New England poet. His previous experiences in low-paid jobs and on farms gave him an intimate knowledge of ordinary people living ordinary lives. His work expresses the value he placed on rural life, practical experience and the independence of the individual.

Return to America

Frost returned to America after the outbreak of the First World War; there he wrote his next book, *Mountain Interval,* which contains some of his best-known poems, including 'Birches', 'Out, Out –', and 'The Road Not Taken'. His characteristic themes of isolation, fear, sudden violence and death are all apparent here.

The favourable reviews *Mountain Interval* received strengthened Frost's reputation. He bought a farm in New Hampshire and supported his family by teaching, readings and lectures, as well as royalties from his books. In January 1917 he was made professor of English at Amherst College, Massachusetts. By 1920 he could afford to move to Vermont and devote himself to writing poetry and apple-farming. Following his fourth publication, *New Hampshire* (1923), Frost was awarded the Pulitzer Prize. He received the award four times in all: in 1924, 1931, 1937 and 1943. His fifth volume of poems, *West-Running Brook,* containing 'Spring Pools' and 'Acquainted with the Night', came out in 1928.

Sadly, Frost's personal life was as unhappy as his public life was successful. His sister Jeannie was committed to a mental hospital, where she remained until her death in 1929. His wife's health began to deteriorate rapidly. His eldest daughter, Lesley, who had dropped out of university and divorced her husband, angrily blamed her father for her problems. His favourite child, Marjorie, had a nervous breakdown and by 1930 developed tuberculosis; she died in 1934, aged twenty-nine, leaving a husband and baby girl. Irma, his third daughter, suffered from mental illness and, like Lesley, blamed all her problems on Frost.

Despite this turmoil, Frost produced *A Further Range* in 1936; it contains 'Provide, Provide' and 'Design'. Here he displayed his technical skills. Within this volume there is satire and comedy, the lyric, ballad, epigram, historical narrative and dramatic monologue.

Teaching, public appearances, interviews and readings kept him busy until tragedy struck again. On 20 March 1938 Elinor died from a heart attack. Unable to cope with her death, Frost left the funeral arrangements to Lesley; in a stormy scene she accused him of ruining her mother's life. Irma became permanently estranged from him, and his only surviving son, Carol, succumbed to deep depression. Frost was deeply upset. He turned to his friend, secretary and manager, Kay Morrison, for consolation. Disturbed by his mother's death and troubled by his father's relationship with Kay, worried by his wife's illness, a lack of money, and the belief that he was a failure, Carol committed suicide in 1940.

Frost looked to poetry to save him from despair. Many of his new poems were written for Kay, expressing his love for her. *A Witness Tree* (1942) won him his fourth Pulitzer Prize. His eighth volume, *Steeple Bush,* was published in May 1947 and is dedicated to his six grandchildren. Having held academic positions already in the University of Michigan, Harvard University and Dartmouth College, Frost returned to Amherst College from 1949 to 1963.

THE FINAL YEARS

In his final years Frost enjoyed public acclaim. He travelled as a celebrated visitor to Brazil, Peru, England, Israel, Greece, Russia and Ireland. He had paid his first visit to Dublin in 1928, when he spent five pleasant days in the company of his friends, the writers Pádraic Colum and George Russell. Colum and Russell took him to a reception where he met Yeats once again. He returned to Ireland in June 1957 to receive an honorary degree from the National University of Ireland, presented by the Taoiseach, Éamon de Valera, who was chancellor of the university. In 1961 he was invited to recite 'The Gift Outright' at the inauguration of President John F. Kennedy, watched on television by sixty million people. On his eighty-eighth birthday, in 1962, he was awarded the Congressional Gold Medal; in the same year he published his final volume, *In the Clearing*. On 29 January 1963, two months before his eighty-ninth birthday, Frost died in a Boston hospital.

PRINCIPAL VOLUMES OF POETRY
A Boy's Will (1913)
North of Boston (1914)

Mountain Interval (1916)

New Hampshire (1923)
West-Running Brook (1928)

A Further Range (1936)

A Witness Tree (1942)
Steeple Bush (1947)
In the Clearing (1962)

Poems for study
'The Tuft of Flowers'
'Mending Wall'
'After Apple-Picking'
'Birches'
'Out, Out –'
'The Road Not Taken'

'Spring Pools'
'Acquainted with the Night'
'Design'
'Provide, Provide'

The Tuft of Flowers

Text of poem: New Explorations Anthology page 90

A READING OF THE POEM

'The Tuft of Flowers' introduces the themes that dominate much of Frost's poetry. These themes, developed as the narrative unfolds, include the passage of time, loneliness, communication, and the power of the imagination. The use of a first-person narrator makes the poem a more immediate and realistic experience; the reader is drawn into the poet's world and explores the themes 'as with his aid'.

The poem opens with the narrator setting out to turn the cut grass so that it will dry in the sun. In a scene reminiscent of the Romantic era, the speaker is depicted as a figure of isolation in the landscape. He searches in vain for the mower; 'But he had gone his way, the grass all mown.' The narrator concludes sadly that loneliness is intrinsic to the human condition, whether people work 'together or apart.' This marks the end of the first movement of the poem.

The second movement begins with the arrival of the butterfly who, like the speaker, is searching for something he cannot find. He flutters in confusion around the withered flowers on the ground and then returns to the poet, who prepares to continue with his work. The butterfly, however, draws his attention to the tuft of flowers beside the stream.

This leads us into the third movement. Unlike the other flowers, these have been spared by the mower, because he loved them. He left them to flourish on the bank 'from sheer morning gladness'.

In the final movement the poet examines the effect of this discovery. The flowers connect the mower and the narrator, who sees in them a 'message from the dawn'. Through the power of the imagination he is transported back through time to the early morning, when the birds sang as the scythe cut through the tall grasses. The speaker recognises in the mower 'a spirit kindred to my own' and can reach out across time and space to touch the thoughts of the absent labourer. This connection forces the speaker to revise his earlier opinion that humans are destined to be lonely and alone. Now he can confidently declare: 'Men work together – whether they work together or apart.'

The turning-points in the poem are indicated by the use of the word 'but'. The speaker, who has eagerly sought the companionship of the mower, comes to the sad realisation

> But he had gone his way, the grass all mown,
> And I must be, as he had been, – alone.

Almost immediately he is joined by another creature.

> But as I said it, swift there passes me by
> On noiseless wings a bewildered butterfly.

He makes to turn away from the butterfly;

> But he turned first, and led my eye to look
> At a tall tuft of flowers beside a brook.

The narrator's mood undergoes a significant change as a result:

> But glad with him, I worked as with his aid.

A form of communication exists between the mower and the speaker; and the poem now ends with the consoling thought,

> Men work together – whether they work together or apart.

Imagery

The central image in the poem is the tuft of flowers called butterfly weed; Frost describes it as a 'leaping tongue of bloom'. The key word here is 'tongue', for the flowers 'speak' to him, bringing him a 'message from the dawn'. They enable him to hear the wakening birds and the whispering scythe. This message permits the speaker to commune imaginatively with the mower and hold 'brotherly speech' with him.

The mower with his long scythe is suggestive of the Grim Reaper. He cuts the grass, and possesses the power to kill the flowers or to spare them. He comes and goes silently and is never seen by mortal eyes. His power over life and death is contrasted with the helplessness of the butterfly on 'tremulous wing'. (Frost returned to the image of the flower, the moth and death in a later poem, 'Design'.) The mower should not be seen solely as a symbol of death: he is at the same time a farm labourer and a spiritual companion for the speaker, one with whom the speaker can communicate 'from the heart'.

Mending Wall
Text of poem: New Explorations Anthology page 94

This poem appeared in *North of Boston* (1914). During a reading, Frost explained that wall-mending was an occupation he used to follow. His neighbour was very particular every spring about repairing the boundary on their land. Frost never ceased to be amazed by the damage done to the wall during the winter; it reminded him of the line in St Matthew's gospel, 'There shall not be left here one stone upon another that shall not be thrown down.'

A READING OF THE POEM

In a note to the original edition of *North of Boston*, Frost stated that 'Mending Wall' considers the beliefs that separate men and takes up the theme where 'The Tuft of Flowers' laid it down. There are two characters in the poem, the narrator and his neighbour, who see the wall in very different ways. They are brought together to repair the damaged boundary in the spring. The poem opens on a mysterious note: some unidentified force exists that dislikes walls. The soft 's' sounds capture the sensation of the silently swelling ground that dislodges the stones. The broad vowels mimic the shape of the rounded boulders that roll off the wall, leaving 'o' and 'u'-shaped gaps behind.

Frost distinguishes between these unexplained gaps and those caused by the hunters. Of the gaps that he means, no-one 'has seen them made or heard them made . . .' In the spring the annual wall-repairing ritual occurs. Ironically, the narrator and his neighbour work together to maintain the boundary that separates them; they are unified by their divisions. It seems as if a magic formula is required to keep the stones in place. At first it is like a game. A more serious note is introduced when the need for the wall is questioned. Unable to provide a rational argument, the neighbour falls back on the proverb 'Good fences make good neighbours.' The narrator mischievously challenges this assumption. Borders wall things in, as well as blocking things out. They cause offence – a pun on the word 'fence'.

According to folklore, elves do not like walls or closed gates; but the speaker does not suggest this to his dourly practical neighbour. 'I'd rather he said it for himself.' The narrator wants the neighbour to reject the division, even imaginatively, for himself. He describes the man as 'an old-stone savage armed.' Not only is he working with stones but his attitudes are primitive, his beliefs have not evolved. He is as territorial as his Stone Age ancestors. He is armed not simply with stones but with dangerous, inflexible attitudes. His attitudes are unenlightened: 'he moves in darkness.' The neighbour, as dark and prickly as his pine trees, refuses to change sides. He sticks doggedly to 'his father's saying', repeating the proverb as proudly as if he had coined the phrase himself.

BALANCE

Frost always claimed he was not 'taking sides' in 'Mending Wall'. 'I've played exactly fair in it. Twice I say, "Good fences" and twice "Something there is" . . .' The tension between these two opposites is played out in the poem. With clear boundaries, each knows where his limits are, where he stands and what confines him; without a wall there is confusion and misunderstanding. Distance, like differences, can be good. This is one reason why the narrator informs the neighbour about the gaps, even though he later challenges him about the need to rebuild the wall.

The 'balancing act' Frost achieves between the arguments in the poem is mirrored in the image of the fallen stones

> To each the boulders have fallen to each.
> . . . We have to use a spell to make them balance.

Frost presents strong arguments on both sides. However, it is slightly disingenuous for him to claim that there is complete impartiality in the poem. The 'something' that dislodges the boulders and swells the ground beneath the wall is, of course, frost heaving.

THEMES

Frost explained that 'Mending Wall' is about boundaries. These boundaries can be physical, political, and psychological. The physical boundary in the poem is the stone wall. The two men repair the wall, working together to maintain their divisions.

> We meet to walk the line
> And set the wall between us once again.

Boundaries are often political in nature. In a discussion on 'Mending Wall' Frost once exclaimed: 'You can make it national or international.' Read in this way, the neighbours can be seen as representing different nationalities or cultures, separate yet coexisting peacefully, learning to respect their differences and co-operating to uphold them.

The psychological differences between the two men are perhaps the most striking. The narrator seems more open to change, willing to challenge accepted practices ('Why do they make good neighbours?'), humorous ('Spring is the mischief in me . . .'), more imaginative ('I could say "Elves" to him . . .') than his conservative neighbour. The narrator realises that sometimes 'we do not need a wall', but this notion meets with firm resistance: 'He will not go behind his father's saying.' His neighbour is a traditionalist and stands behind received wisdom with the same tenacity as he stands behind the stone wall.

STRUCTURE

The poem moves through three stages. The first phase is largely descriptive. Frost distinguishes between the gaps in the wall, those created by the unseen force and those made by hunters. In the second phase he introduces the neighbour and explains how the two men work to rebuild the wall. In the third and final phase he contrasts the attitudes of the men. The narrator is portrayed as mischievous, imaginative, progressive and questioning, while the neighbour is depicted as 'an old-stone savage armed,' conservative, lacking originality, staid, accepting and repetitive.

After Apple-Picking

Text of poem: New Explorations Anthology page 96

A READING OF THE POEM

'After Apple-Picking' is a complex poem. At a surface level it can be read as a nature poem, like Keats's 'Ode to Autumn' – a celebration of the natural abundance of the harvest. At the same time it dwells on the languor of the weary harvester and can be compared to 'Ode to a Nightingale', with its lethargic mood and sensuous imagery. At a deeper level it can be read as a study of the creative process.

The orchard is described at the outset. The harvest is over. The air, heavy with the scent of mature apples, has a sensual, almost narcotic effect on the apple-picker. The long vowel sounds, the irregular rhyming scheme, the slow tempo and incantatory rhythm suggest that the repetitive work has lulled him into a semi-conscious state. (The word 'sleep' appears six times in the poem.) The speaker, like Keats in 'Ode to a Nightingale', sinks into a drowsy numbness.

This suspension of consciousness releases his imagination. He enters a visionary state conducive to artistic creativity:

> I am drowsing off.
> I cannot rub the strangeness from my sight
> I got from looking through a pane of glass
> I skimmed this morning from the drinking trough.

In this dream-like state he evokes the sensuousness of the harvest. He can smell the 'scent of apples', see 'magnified apples appear and disappear,' feel 'the ladder sway' and hear the 'rumbling sound' of the fruit as it is loaded. The repeated sound patterns in the language used capture the sensuousness of the experience:

> There were ten thousand thousand fruit to touch,
> Cherish in hand, lift down, and not let fall.

Art cannot permanently transform life; the visionary state cannot be sustained for long. Frost accepts the transitory nature of the experience. Like the sheet of ice, 'it melted and I let it fall and break.' The creative effort has left him physically and mentally exhausted.

> I am overtired
> Of the great harvest I myself desired.

The creative mood disappears and he slips into sleep, long, dark and deep, as experienced by the hibernating woodchuck, or 'just some human sleep.' He has climbed down from the visionary heights, like the boy in 'Birches', and returned to earth.

Ways of seeing

Sight and insight are important issues in 'After Apple-Picking'. In the opening scene the speaker looks upwards towards Heaven and downwards to the barrel. This reflects the main movement in the poem, the ascent towards the visionary heights and the gradual descent to normality. The focus slips and becomes blurred when the speaker drowses off. He enters a semi-conscious state, neither awake nor asleep. Paradoxically, this releases his imagination and frees it from its sense-bound limitations. He now sees in a new way. The familiar becomes strange, transformed in a visionary world by his imagination. In this state his perspective changes, his perceptions intensify. The focus is sharpened and magnified. Even the smallest details on the apple are visible:

> And every fleck of russet showing clear.

In his heightened state of consciousness he is doubly aware of every sensation.

> My instep arch not only keeps the ache,
> It keeps the pressure of a ladder-round.

This in turn leads to new insights and understanding.

> One can see what will trouble this sleep of mine . . .

Finally, exhausted physically and mentally, he sinks into a long, natural sleep, his eyes closed, and he sees no more.

Mood

The poem describes the drift from consciousness to unconsciousness. The calm, peaceful mood in the opening lines is replaced by a sense of physical and mental exhaustion as the speaker becomes increasingly vague ('There may be,' 'upon some bough,' 'two or three'). The breakdown of the rhyming scheme and the repetition ('sleep' is mentioned six times, 'apple' or 'apples' seven times, 'I' sixteen times) reflect his weariness. It seems he is too tired to vary his vocabulary and maintain the discipline of a strict rhyming pattern.

The lethargic mood is reinforced through the use of long vowels and the slow, irregular rhythm. He enters a dream-like state, yet it is not without a feeling of unease. He is overtired and cannot escape the sensations of the day's work. There are moments of tension when he remembers the care required to prevent the fruit from falling:

> For all
> That struck the earth,
> No matter if not bruised or spiked with stubble,
> Went surely to the cider-apple heap
> As of no worth.

The languid mood is re-established in the final lines, where the speaker approaches complete loss of consciousness.

> The woodchuck could say whether it's like his
> Long sleep, as I describe its coming on,
> Or just some human sleep.

Birches

Text of poem: New Explorations Anthology page 99

A READING OF THE POEM

The poem begins with a description of the birches bending against a background of upright trees. Their movement inspires an imaginative response in the speaker: 'I like to think some boy's been swinging them.' These opening lines establish the tripartite structure of the poem: firstly there is the description of the trees, secondly there is the account of the young boy climbing the birches, and thirdly there is the speaker's response to this imagined scene.

The speaker describes the effect of the winter storms on the birches. He notes the noise they make as the ice-coated branches 'click', 'clack', and 'craze'. The hard *'cr'* sounds capture the tapping of the frozen twigs. The thaw causes them to shed their icy coverings. These 'crystal shells' litter the ground so thickly it seems that 'the inner dome of heaven had fallen.' This is a reference to mediaeval cosmology, which depicted the earth surrounded by crystal shells that held the sun, moon and stars in orbit. Shelley alluded to the same image in 'Adonais'. The great weight of ice bows down the trees. They never recover their original position but grow with their trunks arched and their branches trailing the ground. In a striking image, Frost compares them to girls, heads bent, drying their long hair in the sun.

The speaker departs from pure description to speculate about the cause of the trees' movement. He visualises a boy, alone in a natural setting, tempted from his chores by the trees. He imagines this boy to be independent and resourceful, someone who could 'play alone.' The boy challenges authority. He defiantly subdues his father's trees until 'not one was left | For him to conquer.' He flings outward, feet first, and rebelliously kicks his way to his destination. With practice, he combines caution with daring. Skilfully, like an artist, he learns the importance of maintaining his poise, until he reaches his point of departure; then he launches himself with carefree abandon through the air until he returns to earth. Similarly, a poet learns with practice 'over and over again' to take the 'stiffness' from his verse until he has mastered the poetic technique. A good poet, like a good climber, must not 'launch out too soon' but keep his poise and then, when the poem is completed, return to the prosaic world.

In the third section the speaker recalls that he was once a 'swinger of birches'. Now, when weary and troubled, he longs to recapture the freedom he knew in his youth. He would like to remove himself from the world for a short time and then return to begin afresh. This is not a death wish –

> May no fate wilfully misunderstand me . . .
> and snatch me away
> Not to return

– nor does he wish to escape from reality. 'Birches', Frost asserted, 'is not an escape poem. Anyone can see the difference between escape and retreat, and "Birches" is a retreat poem.' The speaker dreams of a temporary withdrawal from his worries. He describes this process as climbing towards, but never reaching, Heaven. He wishes to be set down gently again. Leaving and returning are both pleasant experiences. This leads him to conclude that 'one could do worse than be a swinger of birches.'

BALANCE

Frost's preoccupation with balance is evident from the opening line, where the birches 'bend to left and right'. The boy carefully climbs the trees until he is half-way between heaven and earth. He maintains his poise, 'not launching out too soon', and then at the right moment he kicks his way down through the air to the ground. Like the boy, the speaker in the poem wishes to get away and return. He believes in 'going and coming back'.

Frost balances the images in his poem: the sunlight and the ice, the straight trees and bent birches, the climbing boy and the 'girls on hands and knees', the black branches and snow-white trunk, heaven and earth, air and ground. The need to achieve a measure of balance or equilibrium is an underlying concern in much of Frost's poetry, including 'Mending Wall' and 'After Apple-Picking'.

LANGUAGE

The language in the poem is, for the most part, simple and colloquial. Frost addresses the reader directly ('Often you must have seen them . . .', 'You'd think . . .', 'When your face burns.') The conversational tone creates an intimacy between the poet and the reader ('But I was going to say . . .', 'I'd like to get away'). Using the language of ordinary people is a hallmark of Frost's work. He contrasted this flat, almost prosaic speech with formal patterns such as:

> So was I once myself a swinger of birches.
> And so I dream of going back to be . . .

or the impersonal:

> One could do worse than be a swinger of birches.

'Out, Out –'

Text of poem: New Explorations Anthology page 102
[Note: This poem is also prescribed for Ordinary Level 2007 exam]

'Out, Out –' is based on an event that took place in Bethlehem, New Hampshire, in March 1910. Raymond Fitzgerald, the son of Frost's friend, was cutting wood with a chain-saw when he accidentally hit the loose pulley and lacerated his hand. A doctor was called, but the young man died of shock. The incident made a deep impression on Frost. He wrote the poem between 1915 and 1916.

A READING OF THE POEM

The title of the poem is taken from Shakespeare's play *Macbeth*. When Macbeth is told of his wife's death he responds:

> Out, out, brief candle!
> Life's but a walking shadow, a poor player
> That struts and frets his hour upon the stage,
> And then is heard no more . . .

This poem, like Macbeth's speech, emphasises the brevity of human existence. The boy is depicted as a tragic hero, destined by forces beyond his control to meet an untimely and pointless death. The title may also refer to the blood flowing from the mutilated hand and the departure of life from the body.

The poem opens suddenly with the snarling machine cutting wood into sweet-smelling logs. The stove-length logs will be burnt for the life-supporting purposes of cooking and heating. However, the saw has the power to destroy as well as create. It reduces the wood to dust. The reader is reminded of the description of the body's decay after death: 'earth to earth, ashes to ashes, and dust to dust'. This image anticipates the fatal accident that will occur later in the poem. The mechanical noises, evocative of predatory animals and rattlesnakes, are suggestive of danger and death. The machine, a 'buzz-saw' (chain-saw), sounds like swarms of angry, stinging and biting insects.

These threatening images are contrasted immediately with the tranquil beauty of the natural world, as represented by the Vermont mountains. The effect is to heighten the menace of the saw. Significantly, the whole scene is enacted against the background of the setting sun. The fading light foreshadows the darkness that is shortly to fall upon the boy. As the sun sets, the brief candle of his existence will also be extinguished. His sister, homely in her apron, announces that supper is ready. Like the stove-logs, supper is life-sustaining. With cruel irony, the saw takes its cue, leaps to devour the boy's hand, and bites into the flesh.

The biblical overtones here of the Last Supper, flesh and blood, point towards the boy as an innocent victim, needlessly sacrificed, as the bystanders look on. In a double irony it appears as if he held out his hand to the saw:

> He must have given the hand. However it was,
> Neither refused the meeting.

The tragic hero always contributes to his own downfall. Betrayed by the embrace, he realises his fate.

> Don't let him cut my hand off –
> The doctor, when he comes.

The doctor, a figure traditionally associated with restoration and healing, unwittingly assists the malign forces operating against the young man, putting him in the 'dark of ether'. The boy dies. The final image of the living turning away from the corpse draws attention to the cold indifference operating in the universe that Frost frequently stressed in his work. Their attitude appears to concur with Shakespeare's conclusion that life is indeed a tale 'full of sound and fury, signifying nothing'.

SENTENCE STRUCTURE

The opening lines are long, flowing and descriptive lines that set the scene. The lines shorten when the accident occurs; this quickens the pace of the poem and heightens the tension.

> And then – the watcher at his pulse took fright.
> No-one believed. They listened at his heart.

The use of pauses and exclamation marks adds to the drama and further increases the tension.

> Don't let him cut my hand off –
> The doctor, when he comes. Don't let him, sister!

The multiple caesuras at the end slow down the pace in order to echo with three little words the last three heartbeats as the boy's life ebbs away.

> Little – less – nothing! – and that ended it.

The full stop refuses to admit any continuation of life or hope. The brisk, matter-of-fact attitude is summed up in the brief line

> No more to build on there.

The return to normality is indicated in the full-length closing line.

TONE

There are many shifts of tone throughout the poem. The anger evident in the opening line subsides into calmness with the descriptions of the sweet-scented logs and the peaceful sunset over the Vermont mountains, only to return with double force as

> the saw snarled and rattled, snarled and rattled.

The narrator wistfully comments:

> Call it a day, I wish they might have said
> To please the boy.

Unfortunately he continues with the work, and when the accident happens his reaction, ironically, is to laugh with shock. Fear and horror succeed rapidly as the terror-stricken boy pleads pathetically with his sister not to allow the doctor to amputate his hand. The irony here is that the doctor can save neither his hand nor his life. The coldly factual statement 'and that ended it' prevents any suggestion of sentimentality entering the poem. 'Out, Out –' ends on a bitter note:

> And they, since they
> Were not the one dead, turned to their affairs.

The Road Not Taken

Text of poem: New Explorations Anthology page 104
[Note: This poem is also prescribed for Ordinary Level 2007 exam]

When asked to list his likes and dislikes, Frost included 'The Road Not Taken' as his favourite poem. It was written for his friend Edward Thomas, killed in the First World War. In the film *Voices and Visions,* Frost stated that the poem was in part a gentle satire on Thomas's inability to make decisions. 'No matter which way he went he was always sorry he didn't go the other way. And he could go on like that until eternity.' One day Frost said to Thomas: 'No matter which road you take, you'll always sigh, and wish you'd taken another.' It seemed to Frost that there was a fundamental human dilemma here that could provide material for a poem.

In May 1915, before the poem was published, Frost revealed that the dilemma was his own as well as that of his friend. He went on to acknowledge that he had always taken the less practical, more poetic way: 'Every time I have taken the way it almost seemed as if I ought not to take, I have been justified somehow by the result.'

The poem was also partly inspired by an unnerving experience Frost had in 1912. While walking towards two lonely crossroads after a winter snowstorm he met a figure approaching him who seemed to be his double – 'my own image'. The figure came up to him and passed silently by while Frost 'stood in wonderment' at 'this other self'.

'The Road Not Taken' was published in the *Atlantic Monthly* in 1915 and in *Mountain Interval*.

A READING OF THE POEM

This poem suggests vast thematic issues through a simple narrative. The speaker stands in an autumnal wood at a point where two roads run off in different directions. Reluctantly he is forced to make a choice about which one he will take. Both roads seem 'about the same', so the focus is on the decision made and its consequences. The traveller cannot see where the first path will lead, as it bends in the undergrowth, so he chooses the other.

The grounds for his choice are unclear. While he states that this road had 'the better claim, | Because it was grassy and wanted wear', he goes on to admit that they were 'really about the same, | And both that morning equally lay' covered in leaves. He keeps the first for another day, knowing there is a finality inherent in his choice, and doubts he will ever return.

He conveys the sense of momentous, life-changing decisions in the final stanza when he predicts that in the future the speaker will look back on this moment 'with a sigh'. He knows he will regret losing the opportunity to investigate the other option. The choice he has made has serious consequences for him:

> I took the one less traveled by,
> And that has made all the difference.

IMAGERY

Frost uses imagery in an almost symbolic way to carry the meaning in the poem. The two roads in the yellow wood represent two different journeys through life. The narrator describes himself as a traveller who must choose which path to follow. One road bends in the undergrowth, making it impossible to see where it will lead, just as in life no one can foretell with certainty the outcome of a decision or what one's future will be like. Frost describes the woods as 'yellow' and the roads as covered 'in leaves no step had trodden black.' This suggests an autumn scene. Autumn is sometimes used in poetry to suggest maturity. The decision is being made at a time when the speaker is sufficiently experienced and wise to realise the implications of his choice; he knows 'how way leads on to way'. When he chooses, there is no turning back. He finally decides to take the road 'less traveled by,' and this changes his life completely.

Spring Pools

Text of poem: New Explorations Anthology page 106

This poem was written in 1925 in Ann Arbor, Michigan, where Frost lived while teaching at the university there. One spring evening, as he sat alone by a blazing fire, lonely and homesick, he thought of Vermont and New Hampshire, and the images that came into his mind prompted him to write 'Spring Pools'. The poem is influenced by the Romantic lyric 'To Jane: The Recollection' by Shelley and 'Ballad of Ladies of Olden Times' by Villons, which includes the line 'But where are the snows of yesteryear?'

A READING OF THE POEM

The title of this poem suggests fresh growth and renewal in the natural world when warm spring days return. The scene described in the first stanza, however, is bleak and wintry. The clear pools mirror the sky through the bare, leafless branches. In this icy-cold world the flowers and water 'chill and shiver' as if aware that their existence will be brief and they will soon perish. The pools will be absorbed by the roots of the trees, which will use the water to produce their dark leaves. The leaves will overshadow the flowers, denying them the sunlight they need to survive.

The second stanza emphasises the power of the great summer woods, whose immense strength can easily obliterate the still pools and the delicate flowers. Yet the dark trees are vulnerable, like the 'flowery waters and the watery flowers'. The pools were formed from the melted winter snows, only to be destroyed by the trees. The trees themselves will be destroyed by time.

IMAGERY

Frost uses nature images to elicit a range of responses in the reader. The scene itself generates conflicting emotions. The tranquil setting, the still pool mirroring the spring sky, the flowers and bare trees inspire awe at the beauty of the natural world. Yet it is a very cold scene, where the shivering flowers and chill water communicate a feeling of unease and fear.

The trees are a powerful and threatening presence in the poem. The warning that they should 'think twice' before they annihilate the pools and flowers reminds the reader that they are subject to an even more powerful force, which is time, the relentless destroyer.

The reversed adjectives and nouns in the 'flowery waters and watery flowers' evoke their frail beauty, yet the flowers feed on the pools and the pools were fed by the meltwaters from the snows destroyed 'only yesterday.' This final image of the brevity of existence does not permit a hopeful reading of the poem.

Rhyme and rhythms

A slow, steady pace is achieved through the use of long vowels, regular iambic pentameter, and a strict rhyming scheme, *aabcbc*. This suits the solemn tone of the poem:

> These pools that, though in forests, still reflect
>
> The total sky almost without defect . . .

The lines are long and sometimes run into each other in a conversational manner. Each of the stanzas is constructed around a single sentence. In the second stanza the lines flow almost without interruption, indicating the relentless processes operating in the natural world.

Themes

'Spring Pools' is more than a simple nature poem. It explores a number of themes found elsewhere in Frost's work.

Natural creation and destruction
The natural world destroys in order to create, and whatever is created is destined to be destroyed again. The snows melt into pools; pools water the flowers, and both are annihilated by the trees to produce foliage; the foliage will in its course be killed by the winter snows. The cycle of creation and destruction is incessant, inevitable and inescapable.

Indifference in the natural world
The natural world is an indifferent place. The seasons follow one another inexorably, producing and destroying: the winter snows, spring pools and summer woods. Nothing is spared, and existence is brief.

A bleak view of life
Time dominates creation. The massive trees, the small flowers, the deep snows and shallow pools are all doomed to destruction. The weak and strong alike will be swept away.

Natural beauty
The natural world is filled with beauty. This beauty should not blind us to the forces operating within it, nor shield us from the darkness that exists in nature.

Acquainted With the Night

Text of poem: New Explorations Anthology page 108

[Note: *This poem is also prescribed for Ordinary Level 2007 exam*]

Form

'Acquainted with the Night' is a meditative lyric composed in stanzas of *terza rima*. This form consists of linked groups of three rhymes following the pattern *aba, bcb, cdc, ded*, and so on. Frost was familiar with *terza rima* from his reading of Shelley's 'Ode to the West Wind'. Like Shelley's ode, this poem ends with a rhyming couplet.

A reading of the poem

This is one of Frost's darkest poems, where the mood is predominantly sombre, the tone unmistakably solemn. It expresses an overwhelming sense of anxiety, isolation and despair. The recurrence of the word 'acquainted' is an allusion to the passage in the Old Testament where the prophet Isaiah predicts the coming of one 'despised and rejected by men, a man of sorrows . . . acquainted with grief'. While the speaker is presented as a solitary figure walking at night through the city, the poem can be read as a psychological journey, where the townscape is coloured by the mental state of the speaker himself. The scenes portrayed are mental projections, reflecting the mood of the narrator. The world is covered in darkness and unrelieved gloom. The incessant rain is indicative of his depression as he travels through the blackness beyond hope and comfort, symbolised by the reassuring city lights.

In this 'saddest' of places he shuns human contact, refusing communication with any who might enquire. Jealously guarding his privacy, 'unwilling to explain', he retreats into his own silent world. The silence is punctured by a distant impersonal cry. The cry is 'interrupted', hinting at possible violence, repression, and suffering. The anonymity and impersonal nature of the incident deepens the fearful mood of the speaker. Yet he is not in immediate danger: the cry comes from far away, another street. These events occur beneath the 'luminary clock' – the moon, or perhaps a real clock – which marks the passage of time. This clock fails to offer guidance or comfort to those who look upon its face: it proclaims merely that 'the time was neither wrong nor right.'

In this short poem Frost explores his recurrent themes. He refers to darkness, isolation, the passage of time, sorrow, indifference, and an absence of communication between people. It is important to note, however, that the poem is set in the past. He writes that though he has 'walked . . . outwalked . . . looked . . . passed by . . . dropped his eyes . . . stood still and stopped the sound of feet', he has not escaped the night; instead he has undergone his ordeal alone ('I' is repeated seven times in fourteen lines), coped with it, and survived. 'I have been one acquainted with the night.'

IMAGERY

The poem is carefully crafted with images of darkness and rain overshadowing the first stanza, creating the bleak atmosphere that is sustained throughout. The images of light serve only to intensify the gloom. The city lights are distant, while the 'luminary clock' stands at an 'unearthly height . . . against the sky'. The second stanza is preoccupied with seeing and not seeing: 'looked', 'watchman', 'dropped my eyes'. The sounds accentuate the silences of the third stanza, reinforcing his isolation. The clock in the fourth stanza emphasises the impersonal nature of the world. The repetition of the opening line in the rhyming couplet is a reminder of the speaker's harrowing experience.

Design

Text of poem: New Explorations Anthology page 110

FORM

'Design' is a perfectly executed sonnet composed of fourteen lines, divided into an *octet* and a *sestet*. The octet is largely descriptive, with little comment. The sestet poses a series of questions raised by the scene described in the octet. The rhyming scheme is *abba, abba, acaa, cc*.

A READING OF THE POEM

The title refers to the idea that there is a design underlying the universe and that the one who created this design is a benign god. The concept, common in many religions, is supported by passages in the Bible. The poem challenges this belief, forcing the reader to face the dark side of the natural world and to confront the possibility that either evil is built into the universe as part of the design or there is no governing design in the first place.

In the poem, the normally blue flower and black spider have mutated into an unnatural colour for them: they are both white. White, the colour of innocence and purity, is here associated with treachery and death. The unsuspecting moth is lured by the heal-all, a medicinal flower, into the clutches of the predatory spider. The plump, well-fed spider is 'dimpled'; the coupling of this word with a spider creates a sense of evil triumphing over its hapless victim. The bloated, gloating spider has wrapped the moth in silken threads, thereby preserving the body so as to eat it later. The shroud-like case resembles a 'piece of rigid satin cloth'. Here the satin-like threads are woven into a sachet to cover the stiffened moth.

In the sestet Frost considers what malignant force corrupted the 'innocent' blue heal-all, making it white, what evil brought the albino spider to the very spot where it could ensnare the defenceless moth, what 'steered' the helpless creature to its ghastly end. One possible answer is that there is a 'design of darkness' woven into the very fabric of the universe. In the final line, however, a second possibility is proposed. The design, if one exists, may not affect 'things so small'; nature may be subject to a series of random incidents governed by chance.

The critic Lionel Trilling pointed out that Frost's poetry does not offer reassurances or affirmations of traditional beliefs; instead it presents the terrible actualities of life. Randall Jarrell also commented on the bleakness of Frost's vision, noting that his poems 'begin with a flat and terrible reproduction of evil in the world and end by saying: it's so, and there's nothing you can do about it.' If we accept and submit to the evil that befalls us, it should not be because of a religious acceptance that it is all for the best but simply because we, like the moth, are helpless to change the world. 'Design' offers little or no consolation to the reader.

IMAGERY

Frost presents the reader with two contrasting sets of images. The first consists of the spider, the blighted flower, the witches' broth, and death. The poet deliberately juxtaposes these images with beautiful and delicate objects – white satin, snowdrops, froth, and a paper kite – to contrast their innocent appearance with their deadly nature. The spider, plump and white, gorged, glutinous and murderous, has conspired with the blighted heal-all to kill the unsuspecting moth. The flower, moth and spider together form a horrific tableau representing death and disease. They appear to be the nauseating ingredients of a foul brew, prepared to begin the 'morning right' (a play on the word 'rite'). The scene, therefore, rehearses a daily ritual that casts an evil spell upon the universe. The effect is to 'appal' and to force the reader to examine the forces governing life and death.

Provide, Provide

Text of poem: New Explorations Anthology page 112

A READING OF THE POEM

In this poem the old woman washing the steps was once a young and beautiful actor in Hollywood. She did not realise that she would age, so she failed to provide for the future. Fallen on hard times, she is now reduced to being a charwoman. According to Frost, the opening lines were inspired by a strike of cleaning women at Harvard College.

The poet suggests a number of ways of avoiding this woman's fate. One could die young, or, if destined to live a long time, become rich. He observes satirically:

> If need be occupy a throne,
> Where nobody can call you crone.

The rich and powerful always inspire respect, no matter how old. Some people rely on their intellectual abilities for security, others on fidelity and loyalty. To escape degrading poverty in later life it is better to buy friendship than to have no friends at all. Frost strongly urges the reader: 'Provide, provide'. At public readings he usually added, 'Or somebody else'll provide for you! And how'll you like that?' He urges readers to avoid hardship and the need to buy friends by providing for themselves.

THEMES

This poem, written in seven triplets, deals with some of Frost's major themes.

The effect of time
Time destroys the 'picture pride of Hollywood', turning her into a 'witch . . . the withered hag'. It also impoverishes her; she must now 'wash the steps with pail and rag' to survive. Her fate is typical of many 'great and good'. Youthful success is soon eroded by time. The end is always hard, unless one learns to provide for old age.

The importance of independence
Frost admired those who could stand alone and fend for themselves. A central theme in the poem is that one should take control of one's own destiny, rather than be at the mercy of others. One should provide for oneself through accumulating wealth ('Make the stock exchange your own!'), power ('If need be occupy a throne'), knowledge ('Some have relied on what they knew'), or friendship.

Old age
Old age is seen as disfiguring, transforming beauty into ugliness. It is described as a descent, a going down into loneliness and misery. The old are subject to degrading poverty and derision. No memory of past successes can console them for their present plight or prevent 'the end from being hard.'

IMAGERY

The poem is structured around contrasting images of youth and old age, beauty and ugliness, wealth and poverty. These support the central theme: that youth and beauty eventually succumb to the ravages of time, and only those who provide for themselves will survive with dignity.

Frost uses images of witches, 'hags' and 'crones' to portray impoverished old age. These are contrasted with images of attractive, successful women. Frost chose Hollywood to represent a place where dreams and fantasies are brought to life. Dreams cannot survive in the real world; harsh reality explodes myths and fantasies. The screen goddess, the centre of attention, is now ignored as she scrubs the steps. But such hardships can be avoided. Political power and material wealth, symbolised by the throne and the stock exchange, are two ways of resisting the indignities of old age. Intellectual status, loyalty and 'boughten friendship' are means of surviving, ways of keeping the end from being hard.

An overview of Robert Frost

BACKGROUND INFLUENCES

Frost studied the classics, had a thorough knowledge of the Bible, and was well read in European and American literature. The Romantic and Victorian poets played an important role in shaping his poetic theory.

ROMANTIC POETRY (1798–1832)

Romantic poetry was written against a background of social, political, economic and religious change, not unlike the changes experienced by American society from the middle of the nineteenth century onwards. Frost was drawn towards aspects of their poetry when formulating his own distinctive poetic style.

- Wordsworth, Coleridge, Shelley and Keats, among other Romantic poets, believed that poetry should express the poet's own mind, imagination and feelings. His emotions, thoughts and experiences should form the central subject in his work.
- The lyric, written in the first person, became the preferred Romantic form. The 'I' is often the poet himself, not a persona created by the poet.
- The natural scene, accurately observed, is the primary poetic subject. Nature is not described for its own sake but as a thought-provoking stimulus for the poet, leading him to some insight or revelation.
- Romantic nature poems are usually meditative poems. The landscape is sometimes personified or imbued with human life. There is a reaction against a purely scientific view of nature. Humans are depicted as isolated figures in the landscape.
- The Romantics subscribed to Wordsworth's belief that poets should 'choose incidents and situations from common life' and write about them in 'language really spoken by men' who belong to 'humble and rustic life'.
- Wordsworth insisted the poet should use 'a certain colouring of imagination, whereby ordinary things should be presented to the mind in an unusual aspect.'
- The poet's visionary imagination rises above his limited, sense-bound understanding and enables him to see things in a new way. The Romantics

displayed a keen interest in visionary states of consciousness, dreams, nightmares and heightened or distorted perceptions.
• Romantic poetry is concerned with mystery and magic, folklore and superstition. The role of the imagination is related to the importance of instinct, intuition and the emotions or the 'heart' as the source of poetry, even though the 'heart' may be tempered by the 'head', the logical and rational faculty. According to Coleridge, 'Deep thinking is attainable only by a man of deep feeling.' The capacity to imagine permits the poet to enter a higher visionary state and regenerate the world.

Important romantic poets
William Blake (1757–1827)
William Wordsworth (1770–1850)
Samuel Taylor Coleridge (1772–1834)
George Byron (1788–1824)
Percy Bysshe Shelley (1792–1822)
John Keats (1795–1821)

VICTORIAN POETRY

Frost studied Victorian poetry in great detail. He cited Thomas Hardy and Robert Browning among his favourite poets. Three features of this poetry made a particular impression on him:
• the use of traditional forms, such as the sonnet
• the revival of the narrative poem, prosaic in style and casually colloquial in tone
• an abiding awareness of time and its effect on humans.

Robert Browning (1812–1889)
Browning turned the dramatic monologue into a major art form. Many of his best-known poems are dramatic monologues. Frost saw the potential of this form for his own work. Browning experimented with diction and syntax, creating a harshly discordant style in some poems. Frost was intrigued by the possibilities of playing discordant sounds off one another in a poem.

Thomas Hardy (1840–1928)
In his poetry, as in his novels, Hardy shows natural forces shaping human destiny. He portrays his characters at the mercy of indifferent forces, victims of fate in a world governed by chance. Like Frost, Hardy did not believe in a universe ruled by a benevolent god. Frost felt Hardy came closest to his own perception of life.

American Writers

Frost was familiar with the works of such American writers as Ralph Waldo Emerson (1803–1882), Walt Whitman (1819–1892) and Henry David Thoreau (1817–1862).

Emerson was a philosopher and poet. He founded the Transcendentalist movement, which revered nature, and, like Frost, had been influenced by the Romantic movement. He encouraged writers and poets to make ordinary life the subject matter of their works.

Walt Whitman produced *Leaves of Grass* in 1855. This volume contained poems that were distinctly American in their setting and subject matter.

Thoreau wrote extensively about his experiments in self-sufficiency. The concept of the individual struggling to survive in rural America appealed to Frost.

Poetry and the Historical Tradition

Poets are part of a wider literary community, and their works belong to the historical tradition. Each poet can look back at the works of previous poets, while at the same time providing new material for the next generation. Frost believed the works of earlier poets provided a treasury of images and ideas available to all writers. He drew on the ideas and images, disguising and subtly altering his allusions, thereby enriching and deepening his poetry. The Bible, the classics, Shakespeare, metaphysical poetry, Romantic poetry, Emerson, Victorian poetry, popular ballads, even nursery rhymes, provided him with material for his poetry.

Some Themes and Issues

The natural world

Frost was a keen observer of the natural world. Plants, insects, geographical features and the seasons have their place in his poetry.

- Creatures: dimpled spiders, trapped moths, bewildered butterflies.
- Plants: butterfly weed, blue or white heal-all, yellow leaves, dark pines, apple trees, birches, russet apples, summer forests.
- The physical world: spring pools, winter snows, the sky, brooks, Vermont mountains.
- The seasons: autumn and winter are the dominant seasons, with falling leaves, bare trees, snow, ice, chill winds and rain.

The natural world is rarely described for its own sake or as a background against which the action of the poem takes place. Instead nature leads the poet to an insight or revelation. Often a comparison emerges between the natural scene and the psyche, what Frost called 'inner and outer weather'.

Frost's descriptions of nature are not sentimental. He describes a world that is bleak, empty and cold, where creatures suffer in silence and humans feel isolated. His natural world contains blight, darkness and death and therefore can be threatening, hostile or indifferent.

Isolation and communication
Humans are depicted as figures of isolation in the landscape. Not only are they isolated but they represent loneliness, and thereby acquire symbolic status. Loneliness can be seen as a human condition. Efforts to communicate effectively are at best difficult ('The Tuft of Flowers') and frequently fail ('Mending Wall'), are sometimes rebuffed ('Acquainted with the Night'), and can have unforeseen consequences ('Out, Out –').

Frost shared with Emerson and Thoreau the belief that individuality and the independence of the individual were very important. Frost in particular felt that people should stand alone and make their own choices. Note the repetition of 'I' in his poems.

The role of fate and chance
Frost is far less affirmative about the universe than the American Transcendentalists. Looking at nature, they discerned a benign creator, whereas he saw 'no expression, nothing to express'. In Frost's world, God is either hostile or indifferent to the plight of helpless creatures, who, like humans, are victims of fate or chance. His poetry records an ever-present, underlying darkness that erupts in a random manner with tragic consequences.

Mutability – the effect of time on people and nature
Time is perceived as being destructive:
- yesterday's flowers wither
- winter snows melt, spring pools are drained by trees, trees lose their leaves in autumn
- the boy dies at the end of the day
- time destroys beauty, impoverishes the elderly.

The effect of time can be overcome to some extent by the power of memories and the imagination ('The Tuft of Flowers').

The role of the imagination
The imagination enables the poet to see the world in a new way. In brief, intense moments he may enter a higher, visionary state. This allows him to regenerate his imaginative and creative capability and provides him with fresh insights and new inspiration for his poetry. This state cannot be sustained for long, however, and he must return to the real world.

Style and technique: some points

Language
From his study of Hardy's writing, Frost learnt how to achieve simplicity in poetry through the use of a few well-chosen words. He made a conscious effort to use ordinary language in his poems and captured the full range of human emotions, from joy to sorrow and from exaltation to fear, through the use of plain, monosyllabic speech. He stressed the importance of colloquial language, as it was appropriate to the subject matter in his verse and made his poetry accessible to a wide audience. Frost played the colloquial rhythms against the formal patterns of line and verse and constrained them within traditional forms, such as the sonnet or dramatic monologue. The plain diction, natural speech rhythms and simplicity of images contrive to make the poems seem natural and unplanned.

Frost used repetition for effect, to emphasise, and to add to the musical quality of his verse. He described sound in the poem as 'the gold in the ore', and added that 'the object in writing poetry is to make all poems sound as different as possible from each other.'

Rhyme
Unlike many American poets in the twentieth century, Frost upheld formal poetic values during the Modernist era, when formal practices were widely abandoned. He emphasised the importance of rhyme and metrical variety, observed traditional forms and developed his technical skills. He could claim without fear of contradiction that 'I am one of the notable craftsmen of my time.' His poetry is written so that the rhyming 'will not seem the tiniest bit strained'. He used *terza rima*, end-of-line rhymes, full and half rhyme. He also wrote in blank verse.

Verse forms
Frost used a wide variety of verse forms, including the sonnet, dramatic monologue, narrative and lyric. His preferred metre was based on the strict or loose *iambic*, as it echoed ordinary speech. The verse derives its energy from the tension that evolves when a rhythmic pattern based on strict or loose iambic metre is set against the irregular variations of colloquial speech.

Imagery
The imagery in Frost's poems is deceptively simple. There are images from the natural and the human worlds. Some are everyday and ordinary, some are grotesque and macabre. In a number of poems, such as 'Spring Pools', the imagery carries the meaning. Frost uses precise details to re-create the colour, texture and sounds of the world within the poem. This makes his poetry richly

sensuous. Yet, using the same technique, he can paint a cold, bleak scene that is chillingly realistic.

His use of similes and metaphors creates layers of meaning in his poems. In 'Mending Walls', for example, the wall can be understood to be something that unites or divides, something that should be maintained or cast down. It can be physical, political, cultural or psychological.

Tone
The tone of voice used is vital to the meaning in Frost's poems. His poetry displays a great range of tone, and it may vary considerably within a particular poem. It can be precise and matter-of-fact, sympathetic, sad, relieved, strong and confident, despairing, humorous, dark and ironic, wistful or weary.

First-person narrative
Frost frequently used the first person for his narrative. The reader is permitted a glimpse into the speaker's life at a specific moment, often during a crisis. The use of the first person creates a feeling of reliability: the reader is given a first-hand account of an event, and trusts the accuracy of the narrator. The authenticity of the story is never doubted in 'Out, Out –', for example.

Dramatic stories
A strong narrative structure is apparent in many of Frost's poems. The narrator takes the reader through a series of events and actions, which lead to a dramatic conclusion. These events are often thought-provoking or provide an insight into life.

'The figure a poem makes'

(An essay by Frost published as an introduction to *The Collected Poems of Robert Frost*, 1939.)

Abstraction is an old story with the philosophers, but it has been like a new toy in the hands of the artists of our day. Why can't we have any one quality of poetry we choose by itself? We can have in thought. Then it will go hard if we can't in practice. Our lives for it.

Granted no-one but a humanist much cares how sound a poem is if it is only a sound. The sound is the gold in the ore. Then we will have the sound out alone and dispense with the inessential. We do till we make the discovery that the object in writing poetry is to make all poems sound as different as possible from each other, and the resources for that of vowels, consonants, punctuation, syntax, words, sentences, metre are not enough. We need the help of context – meaning – subject matter. That is the greatest help towards variety. All that can be done with words is soon told. So also with metres – particularly in our language where there are virtually but two, strict iambic and loose iambic. The ancients with many were still poor if they depended on metres for all tune. It is painful to watch our sprung-rhythmists straining at the point of omitting one short from a foot for relief from monotony. The possibilities for tune from the dramatic tones of meaning struck across the rigidity of a limited metre are endless. And we are back in poetry as merely one more art of having something to say, sound or unsound. Probably better if sound, because deeper and from wider experience.

Then there is this wildness whereof it is spoken. Granted again that it has an equal claim with sound to being a poem's better half. If it is a wild tune, it is a poem. Our problem then is, as modern abstractionists, to have the wildness pure; to be wild with nothing to be wild about. We bring up as aberrationists, giving way to undirected associations and kicking ourselves from one chance suggestion to another in all directions as of a hot afternoon in the life of a grasshopper. Theme alone can steady us down. Just as the first mystery was how a poem could have a tune in such a straightness as metre, so the second mystery is how a poem can have wildness and at the same time a subject that shall be fulfilled.

It should be of the pleasure of a poem itself to tell how it can. The figure a poem makes. It begins in delight and ends in wisdom. The figure is the same as for love. No one can really hold that the ecstasy should be static and stand still in one place. It begins in delight, it inclines to the impulse, it assumes direction with the first line laid down, it runs a course of lucky events, and ends in a clarification of life – not necessarily a great clarification, such as sects and cults are founded on, but in a momentary stay against confusion. It has denouement. It has an outcome that though unforeseen was predestined from the first image of the original mood – and indeed from the very mood. It is but a trick poem and no poem at all if the best of it was thought of first and saved for the last. It finds its own name as it goes and discovers the best waiting for it in some final phrase at once wise and sad – the happy-sad blend of the drinking song.

No tears in the writer, no tears in the reader. No surprise for the writer, no surprise for the reader. For me the initial delight is in the surprise of remembering something I didn't know I knew. I am in a place, in a situation, as if I had materialised from cloud or risen out of the ground. There is a glad recognition of the long lost and the rest follows. Step by step the wonder of unexpected supply keeps growing. The impressions most useful to my purpose seem always those I was unaware of and so made no note of at the time when taken, and the conclusion is come to that like giants we are always hurling experience ahead of us to pave the future with against the day when we may want to strike a line of purpose across it for somewhere. The line will have the more charm for not being mechanically straight. We enjoy the straight crookedness of a good walking stick. Modern instruments of precision are being used to make things crooked as if by eye and hand in the old days.

I tell how there may be a better wildness of logic than of inconsequence. But the logic is backward, in retrospect, after the act. It must be more felt than seen ahead like prophecy. It must be a revelation, or a series of revelations, as much for the poet as for the reader. For it to be that there must have been the greatest freedom of the material to move about in it and to establish relations in it regardless of time and space, previous relation, and everything but affinity. We prate of freedom. We call our schools free because we are not free to stay away from them till we are sixteen years of age. I have given up my democratic prejudices and now willingly set the lower classes free to be completely taken care of by the upper classes. Political freedom is nothing to me. I bestow it right and left. All I would keep for myself is the freedom of my material – the condition of body and mind now and then to summon aptly from the vast chaos of all I have lived through.

Scholars and artists thrown together are often annoyed at the puzzle of where they differ. Both work from knowledge; but I suspect they differ most importantly in the way their knowledge is come by. Scholars get theirs with conscientious thoroughness along projected lines of logic; poets theirs cavalierly and as it happens in and out of books. They stick to nothing deliberately, but let what will stick to them like burrs where they walk in the fields. No acquirement is on assignment, or even self-assignment. Knowledge of the second kind is much more available in the wild free ways of wit and art. A school boy may be defined as one who can tell you what he knows in the order in which he learned it. The artist must value himself as he snatches a thing from some previous order in time and space into a new order with not so much as a ligature clinging to it of the old place where it was organic.

More than once I should have lost my soul to radicalism if it had been the originality it was mistaken for by its young converts. Originality and initiative are what I ask for my country. For myself the originality need be no more than the freshness of a poem run in the way I have described: from delight to wisdom. The figure is the same as for love. Like a piece of ice on a hot stove the poem must ride on its own melting. A poem may be worked over once it is in being, but may not be worried into being. Its most precious quality will remain its having run itself and carried away the poet with it. Read it a hundred times: it will forever keep its freshness as a petal keeps its fragrance. It can never lose its sense of a meaning that once unfolded by surprise as it went.

Questions

1. 'The human being, lonely, helpless, and in crisis, is the main concern in much of Frost's poetry.' Discuss this statement with reference to three or more poems you have read.
2. 'Poetry begins in delight and ends in wisdom.' Consider Frost's poetry in the light of this statement.
3. 'Frost's poems are a celebration of the ordinary.' Discuss this opinion, with reference to three or more poems you have read.
4. 'The local and the universal are seamlessly woven together in the poetry of Robert Frost.' Is this statement justified? Explain your answer, referring to four poems by Frost.
5. 'Frost's poetry depicts the world as dark, dangerous, and ultimately indifferent.' Discuss this statement, with suitable reference to the poems on your course.
6. 'Natural images are used to convey human emotions and moods in the poems of Robert Frost.' Examine four poems by Frost in the light of this statement.
7. 'Frost takes a pessimistic view of life, unrelieved by any gleam of hope.' Discuss.
8. 'Frost's poems are deeply sensual.' Comment on Frost's use of language and imagery in the light of this statement, referring to at least four poems you have studied.
9. 'Universal truths plainly expressed are a feature of Frost's poetry.' Discuss.
10. 'Frost's poems are strangely beautiful, unbearably bleak.' Consider this statement, referring to at least four poems in your answer.
11. 'Sound is the gold in the ore.' Examine the importance of sound in Frost's poetry.
12. 'A wide range of tone and mood is found in Frost's poetry.' Discuss, referring to at least four poems in your answer.

Bibliography

Baym, Nina, et al. (editors), *The Norton Anthology of American Literature*, New York: Norton 1994.

Cook, Reginald, *Robert Frost: A Living Voice*, Amherst (Mass.): University of Massachusetts Press 1974.

Cook, Reginald, 'Robert Frost's asides on his poetry,' in *On Frost: The Best from American Literature* (E. Cady and Louis Budd, editors), Durham (NC): Duke University Press 1991.

Frost, Robert, 'The figure a poem makes,' in *The Collected Poems of Robert Frost*, Harcourt 1939.

Jarrell, Randall, 'The other Frost' and 'To the Laodiceans,' in *Poetry and the Age*, New York: Knopf 1955.

Meyers, Jeffrey, *Robert Frost: A Biography*, London: Constable 1996.

Pritchard, William H., *Frost: A Literary Life Reconsidered*, New York: Oxford University Press 1984.

Thompson, Lawrence (editor), *Robert Frost: Selected Letters*, New York: Holt, Rinehart and Winston 1964.

Thompson, Lawrence, *Robert Frost, vol. 1: The Early Years, 1874–1915*, New York: Holt, Rinehart and Winston 1966.

Thompson, Lawrence, *Robert Frost, vol. 2: The Years of Triumph, 1915–1938*, New York: Holt, Rinehart and Winston 1970.

van Doren, Mark, 'Robert Frost's America', in *Atlantic Monthly*, 1951.

Wordsworth, William, Preface to *Lyrical Ballads*, London: Arch 1802.

4   *Thomas Stearns* ELIOT

Sean Scully

Timeline

September 26, 1888	Thomas Stearns Eliot is born in St Louis, Missouri.
1906–1909	Undergraduate at Harvard. Becomes interested in the symbolists and Laforgue.
1909–1910	Graduate student at Harvard. Studies in France and Germany. 'Prufrock' is completed but not published.
1911–1914	Graduate student at Harvard. Begins work on the philosophy of Francis Herbert Bradley.
1914–1915	Study in Germany stopped by war. Moves to Oxford. Short satiric poems. 'Prufrock' is published in Chicago, June 1915. Marriage to Vivienne Haigh-Wood, July 1915.
1915	Eliot moves to London.
1915–1916	Teaching and doing book reviews in London. Bradley thesis is finished.
1915–1919	Eliot has many different jobs, including teaching, bank clerk and assistant editor of the literary magazine *Egoist*.
June 1917	*Prufrock and Other Observations* is published.
1917–1920	Works in Lloyd's Bank. Many editorials and reviews. Writing of French poems, quatrain poems.
1921–1922	London correspondent for *The Dial*.
1922–1939	Founder and editor of *The Criterion*.
1922	'The Waste Land'. Eliot wins Dial Award for *The Waste Land*. London correspondent for *Revue Française*.
1925	Senior position with publisher Faber & Faber.
1927	Eliot is confirmed in the Church of England and becomes a British citizen.
1927–1930	*Ariel Poems*.

1940–1942	'East Coker', 'The Dry Salvages' and 'Little Gidding'.
1943	'The Four Quartets'.
1947	Death of Eliot's first wife, Vivienne Haigh-Wood, after long illness.
1948	King George VI awards the Order of Merit to T.S. Eliot. Eliot is awarded the Nobel Prize in Literature.
1957	Marries Valerie Fletcher.
1958	*The Elder Statesman.*
January 4, 1965	T.S. Eliot dies.

The Love Song of J. Alfred Prufrock (1917)
Text of poem: New Explorations Anthology page 116

THEMES/ISSUES AND IMAGERY

Title

This is, perhaps, one of Eliot's most striking titles. Yet the poem is neither a song nor a traditional, conventional expression of love. Neither is J. Alfred Prufrock a conventional name for a love poet. It is more evocative of a respectable small-town businessman. (In fact, there was a furniture dealer named Prufrock in St Louis when Eliot lived there.)

The name can be seen as mock-heroic, if not comically ridiculous, in the circumstances of the poem. Indeed 'Prufrockian' has entered the language as an adjective indicative of a kind of archaic idealism which is paralysed by self-consciousness. The rather self-conscious 'J.' before Alfred recalls Mark Twain's distrust of men who 'part their names in the middle'.

Overall the incongruity of associations between the two halves of the title prepares us for the tension developed in the poem.

Epigraph

A literal translation of the epigraph reads:

> *'If I thought that my answer were to one who might ever return to the world, this flame should shake no more; but since no-one ever did return from this depth alive, if what I hear is true, without fear of infamy I answer you.'*

The passage is from Dante's *Inferno*, XXVII, lines 61–66, in which Guido de Montefeltro, tortured in hell for the sin of fraud, is willing to expose himself to Dante because he believes that the poet can never return from the pit of hell to the world. In Eliot's poem, too, the speaker tells of himself, because he feels his audience is also trapped in a hell of its own making. This is so since he is speaking to himself.

The use of the extract from Dante's *Inferno* also suggests that the lovesong is not sung in the real world, but in a 'hell' which is the consequence of being divided between passion and timidity.

Lines 1–12

Most critics agree that the 'you and I' of the first line are two sides of the same personality, the ego and alter ego, as it were. Thus the poem is an interior monologue, an exposure of the self to the self. However, the reader is, of course, free to think that it is he who is being addressed, as the self he addresses may be in all of us.

At any rate, the character Prufrock is struggling with the idea of asking the 'overwhelming question' of line 10.

The poem opens with a command to accompany him, presumably to the room of line 13. However the air of decisiveness collapses immediately with the simile of describing the evening (line 3). This image may be quite striking but it does not give us an immediate visual image. Rather, it reveals a great deal about Prufrock's psychological state. He is helpless – 'etherised'.

The setting of these opening lines is evening or twilight – a sort of halfway period, neither night nor day. This enhances the theme of indecision.

The description of what appears to be the seedy side of the city in the next four lines is presented in a series of quite sordid images. They may indicate the pointlessness of Prufrock's search. His emotional numbness would appear to have led him to unsatisfactory, sordid sexual relations in the past, in 'one-night cheap hotels'. The image of the 'sawdust restaurants with oyster-shells' suggests the vulgarity of these encounters, while also introducing sea imagery, which is a feature of the poem.

These seedy retreats show the tiresome, weary nature of city life. So the streets are compared to 'a tedious argument | Of insidious intent'. Thus Prufrock's encounters and perhaps life itself are seen as mechanical and repetitive and characteristic of an inner sickness. Such an area and such a lifestyle naturally lead to 'an overwhelming question'.

Prufrock is unwilling to face this question. It remains isolated and hidden within, and the 'you' is told not to ask. Thus we are beginning to see the depiction of a melancholic character who cannot satisfy his desires.

Lines 13–14

This room would appear to be Prufrock's destination. The women are satirised and seen as quite pretentious. Their 'talking of Michelangelo' as they 'come and go' is made to seem quite trivial and empty-headed. This is suggested by the jingling rhythm and rhyme.

The subject of their conversation, Michelangelo, is the great sculptor of heroic figures. This is a figure to whose magnanimity and greatness Prufrock could not possibly aspire. So how could the women find him (Prufrock) interesting, even if their knowledge is limited and their talk pretentious? Prufrock is a most unheroic figure.

Lines 15–22

There is a fusion of imagery here. The fog which surrounds the house (presumably the house which contains the room) is described in terms of a cat. This essentially metaphysical concept suggests the theme of unfulfilled promise. This is seen in particular by the fact that the action leads to sleep.

Cats, it must be noted, have been traditionally associated with sexuality and so much of the imagery here may also suggest unsatisfied desire.

The image of the fog serves another purpose. It may convey blurred consciousness or vision, a constant theme in Eliot's poetry. Thus on a wider note, through the imagery of the poem and the character of Prufrock, Eliot is speaking of the degenerated vision and soul of humanity in the twentieth century.

Lines 23–34

Time is one of the important themes, not only of this poem, but also of Eliot's poetry generally. Prufrock takes great comfort in time, repeating rather hypnotically, 'there will be time'.

There will be time to 'prepare a face' against the exposure of the true self, or 'To prepare a face' to make small talk over 'a toast and tea', and to 'murder and create' reputations or characters in a gossipy fashion, perhaps.

This unexciting prospect, with its mundane 'works and days of hands' merely leads him back to the question, which he puts off because of his timidity and hesitancy. The sarcasm of lines 32–33 emphasises the avoidance of decision. The play on the words 'vision' and 'revision' adds further emphasis to this.

And all this anxiety and procrastination doesn't lead to some momentous event, but merely to taking 'toast and tea'. The element of mock-heroic is clear.

Lines 35–36

The repetition of lines 13–14 here underscores the tediousness of the women's talk. It further emphasises Prufrock's limitations and how he is inhibited and perhaps intimidated by so-called social discourse. It, together with the reference to Hamlet later, represents the greatness of the past in contrast to the modern world.

Lines 37–48
Here Prufrock speculates on the women's view of his physical self. The 'prepared face' is no protection against the pitiless gaze of the women. The time for decisive action may be at hand, yet he wonders if he dares. He fears a rebuff and even if he retreats – 'turn back and descend the stair' – he may still seem absurd. He is aware of his unheroic appearance. He is growing bald and 'his arms and legs are thin!' He dresses well – albeit in a very conventional manner – possibly to compensate for these physical shortcomings, and indeed his attractive clothes may be part of his mask – his need to make an appearance.

His doubts are expressed in obvious hyperbole – 'Do I dare | Disturb the universe?' How could *he* possibly disturb the universe? The possibility may lie in the immediate sense of the 'universe' of his own world or in his realisation that even trivial human actions may have immeasurable consequences. This self-conscious awareness precludes his taking any decisive action. Emotionally, at least, Prufrock is impotent.

Lines 49–54
Here Prufrock puts forward the first of three arguments against deciding the overwhelming question. Again, Prufrock is hesitant to act due to the limitations of his inner self. He lacks self-confidence due to the sterility and meaninglessness of his life – which is merely an endless round of 'evenings, mornings, afternoons'. The line 'I have measured out my life with coffee spoons' not only epitomises the repetitive tedium of his everyday existence, but may also suggest a desire to escape the pain of living via the use of a stimulant.

How could he, Prufrock, challenge the meaninglessness of such a life? Such a challenge would be presumptuous.

Lines 55–61
His second argument is presented here. He is afraid of being classified and stereotyped 'in a formulated phrase' by the perhaps contemptuous looks of the women. He recoils from the absolute horror of being pinned down and dissected like an insect in some biological experiment. He has a phobia of being restricted, linked perhaps to a fear of emasculation. So how could a man with such fears risk, or presume, to expose himself to further ridicule? The image of the 'butt-end' of a cigarette to which he compares his life suggests further self-disgust.

Lines 62–69
His third argument against deciding the overwhelming question is presented here. He cannot ask the question because he is simultaneously attracted and revolted by the physicality of women.

The ideal perfection of 'Arms that are braceleted and white and bare' develops into the physicality of '(But in the lamplight, downed with light brown hair!).' The sense of the ideal becoming real reflects his being overwhelmed at the prospect of turning desire into action.

The altered but effectively repeated question of 'And should I then presume?', reflecting his insecurity, suggests an apparent increase in tension towards a sense of impending climax. Yet he cannot conceive any formula for his proposal – 'And how should I begin?'

Lines 70–74

Prufrock offers a possible preface or preamble to his question. He wonders if he should mention that he is aware of a different type of world from that known by the women in the room – the seedy world of lines 4–9 recalled in the imagery here. This awareness may be his justification for asking the question. He knows more, but the fact that he poses the preamble in the form of a question suggests uncertainty as to its relevance.

Again the imagery suggests he is a passive observer, not an active participant. Failure to address the overwhelming question leads, as in line 10, to a trailing off into silence indicated by the three dots.

This section ends with his wish to be something like a crab. This sea imagery in fact is reduced to 'claws'. Thus Prufrock seems to wish to dehumanise himself completely, to become a thing of pure action without self-awareness – living, yet mentally inanimate; to be in a place where he can survive in the depths and yet avoid the pain of living. Obviously this is the very opposite of Prufrock's true situation.

Lines 75–88

This section must be seen as a form of reverie. It is also the turning point of the poem.

Having previously seen the fog as a cat (lines 15–22), Prufrock now sees the afternoon as such. All the tensions up to now are resolved, not in action but in images of inaction and weakness. The afternoon/evening/cat 'sleeps', 'malingers', 'Stretched on the floor'. The sense of being etherised (line 3) is recalled.

The triviality of Prufrock's existence is seen in the mock-heroic rhyming of 'ices' and 'crisis'. This prepares us for Prufrock's efforts to put himself in a heroic perspective. However, his greater sense of personal inadequacy won't permit him to sustain the comparison with St John the Baptist. The ironic discrepancy between John the Baptist and Prufrock is heightened by the self-mockery of '(grown slightly bald)'. Prufrock's head would simply look absurd. He is aware of this and immediately denies the possibility of heroic status for himself – 'I am no prophet' (line 84). The continuation of this line can be read as 'it doesn't really matter' or 'I'm not important.' Either way it is an acknowledgement of his own inadequacy.

The final image in this section is of the eternal Footman. This is Death personified. Even death is laughing at him, but the image also suggests that the servants of the polite society hosts whom he visits do not take him seriously. He feels he is the butt of their jokes. To both death and the ridicule of servants, the profound and the trivial, Prufrock admits his fear. It is too late for him to act. Fear is his reality.

Lines 89–115

Prufrock's speculation on whether forcing the crisis, asking the overwhelming question, would have been worthwhile reads like an excuse for inaction. He is rationalising his failure.

He names again the trivial aspects of his polite environment, recalling earlier lines (49–51, 79). However, now the 'you and I' of line 1 are very much part of the trivia of this environment. They are 'Among the porcelain, among some talk of you and me'. Perhaps he cannot accept that any significant action can take place in this type of environment. He is afraid of being misunderstood. What would he do if his 'overwhelming question' should meet with an offhand rejection like:

> 'That is not what I meant at all.
> That is not it, at all.'

The fact that these lines are repeated shows the extent of his fear.

Two references in this section suggest that Prufrock continues to compare himself to those of heroic status.

Line 94 is a reference to Andrew Marvell's poem 'To His Coy Mistress' in which the poet urges his beloved to enjoy immediate sexual union with him as a sort of victory over time. Prufrock's inaction is the antithesis of this.

Both men by the name of Lazarus in the Gospels were figures of triumph over death: one, the brother of Martha and Mary, by being recalled to life by Jesus; the other, a poor man, by gaining Heaven – unlike the rich man, Dives.

Prufrock fears that even the most profound knowledge may be decorously, but casually, rejected.

Essentially Prufrock's fear here is of never being able to connect emotionally with another person. The gulf between human beings' inner selves cannot be bridged. This has him cry out in frustration:

> It is impossible to say just what I mean!
> (line 108)

The possibility of the insensitive comprehension of the other exposes his own sensitivity. It is 'as if a magic lantern threw the nerves in patterns on a screen' (lines 109–110). Thus throughout this section women again appear as catalysts to Prufrock's inadequacy and inferiority.

Lines 116–124

Here Prufrock settles for a less than heroic version of himself. He recognises that any further heroic action would be absurd. He may have something in common with Shakespeare's Prince Hamlet, for he too was indecisive, but any direct identification would be ridiculous.

Rather, he sees himself as a Polonius figure – an advisor to kings – or even a lesser person. The theatrical imagery of lines 117–119 suggests a bit player. Prufrock has become consciously unheroic. In lines 119–124 he is quite self-deprecating, reducing himself eventually to the level of a wise Fool. A passage that begins with 'Hamlet' ends with 'the Fool'.

However, there is the possibility, with the capitalisation of 'the Fool', that Prufrock does not see himself as any old fool, but perhaps akin to the Fool in Shakespeare's *King Lear* – a wise fool who utters uncomfortable truths, which powerful people would prefer not to hear. Maybe this is Prufrock's final fantasy.

Lines 125–136

A world-weariness introduces this section. This in effect becomes a process of dying, until 'we drown' in the last line.

He does, however, make a decision in line 126 – to 'wear the bottoms of my trousers rolled'. The triviality of the decision, in contrast to the 'overwhelming question', suggests his resignation to a trivial existence. This decision is followed by two further trivial questions, which underscore the point. Parting his hair may hide his bald spot. Eating a peach may be the riskiest behaviour he will ever again indulge in.

This hopeless, empty existence has him resort to the beach. Sea imagery throughout the poem (lines 7, 73–74) has suggested some alternative lifestyle – some hope of avoiding the pain of consciousness.

The mermaids of line 129 symbolise a sort of idealised erotic beauty similar to the arms in line 63. But Prufrock realises that this is only a fantasy, a dream. He has been deluding himself. His realisation of this is expressed in the simple bathos of line 130: 'I do not think that they will sing to me.'

Yet delusions are hard to let go and he asserts the existence of the mermaids, of the erotic ideal, in a defiant final cry (lines 131–133).

But he has 'lingered in the chambers' of his world of ideal relationships and heroic actions for too long, perhaps. The dream is unattainable. The use of 'we' here is not just the 'you and I' of line 1, but also the universal plural. All of us can get lost in our reveries, until we are called to reality by other human voices – a reality where 'we drown'. All struggle is ended and we accept the death of our inner selves.

LANGUAGE, TONE AND MOOD

The irony inherent in the title has already been described. It is the self-irony of Laforgue, adapted to a dreadful seriousness. The poem is a tragic comedy, the epitaph sets the mood.

The lyricism of the opening is appropriate to a love-song, but it collapses almost immediately in the simile of Line 3. The simile is quite comically inappropriate for a love-song but is tragically appropriate for the hapless Prufrock and his situation.

The repetition of 'Let us go' suggests that he is already faltering.

The sibilant sounds which dominate the opening sequence underscore the seedy imagery and the sense of being 'etherised'. This is continued into the simile of 'like a tedious argument'. These sounds combined with the rhyming couplets do give a lyrical or musical effect, but also enhance the sense of ennui.

The dramatic pause indicated by the three dots in line 10 emphasises Prufrock's tragic flow and reinforces the bathos.

This bathos is further felt in the jingling rhythm and rhyme of lines 13–14: 'In the room the women come and go | Talking of Michelangelo.'

The fog/cat passage (lines 15–22) is also dominated by sibilant sounds which enhance the tone. These sounds are in contrast with the more cacophonous lines 23–34 which follow.

The fog/cat metaphor is in effect a metaphysical conceit. It is a flight of fancy, a sort of *jeu d'esprit*. Adding to the sensual sibilant sounds is the use of the letter 'L', often seen as the liquid letter, enhancing the sinuous movement of the fog.

The solemn incantatory tone of lines 23–34, echoing the Old Testament speaker in Ecclesiastes, contributes to the mock-heroic element of the poem, which is further added to by the pun on 'revisions' (lines 34 and 48).

Unlike the contrasts in the Book of Ecclesiastes, the opposing forces here do not show a sense of balance or equilibrium, but add to the confusion. The repetition of lines 13–14, which are in danger of becoming a refrain, emphasises the sterility and shallowness of the modern human condition, as mentioned above.

The constant repetition of rhetorical questions is a feature of the next several sections:

> 'Do I dare?'
> So how should I presume?
> And how should I begin?

These suggest a tone of uncertainty and underscore the sense of inaction.

The dominant verbs of lines 58–61 – 'formulated', 'sprawling', 'pinned', 'wriggling' – suggest not only the fear of individual inadequacy, but also a sense of being a victim.

His self-contempt, and possibly anger, are seen in the mixture of sibilants and cacophonous consonants in lines 73–74:

> I should have been a pair of ragged claws
> Scuttling across the floors of silent seas.

The ridiculous rhyming of 'ices' and 'crisis' (lines 79–80) has already been alluded to for its mock-heroic, satiric effect. The same effect is achieved with the rhyming of 'flicker' and 'snicker' in lines 85 and 87. The pathetic admission of:

> I am no prophet – and here's no great matter;
> I have seen the moment of my greatness flicker,

is reduced to a snort of mockery with the word 'snicker'.

The note of tragic satire is also in the bathetic joke on his 'head (grown slightly bald)' and the prophetic Biblical echoes of:

> 'I am Lazarus, come from the dead,
> Come back to tell you all, I shall tell you all' –
> (lines 96–97)

The broad vowels here remind us of one crying in the wilderness and being ignored.

The tone changes in the last section. Now that he acknowledges that 'It is impossible to say just what I mean!', and the 'overwhelming question' is gone, the poem settles down to a lyricism which merely flickered earlier. The use of alliteration, assonance and onomatopoeia in lines 131–136 both intensifies the description and underscores the tone and mood:

> I have seen them riding seaward on the waves
> Combing the white hair of the waves blown back
> When the wind blows the water white and black.
>
> We have lingered in the chambers of the sea
> By sea-girls wreathed with seaweed red and brown
> Till human voices wake us, and we drown.

The reference to Prince Hamlet does not seem pedantic, given the tone of this section. The rather comic bewilderment of:

> Shall I part my hair behind? Do I dare to eat a peach?

helps to raise our sympathy for him. Thus both the 'serious' references and the mocking tone serve to emphasise the comic-tragedy of Prufrock's situation.

Overall, the poem is quite fragmented, full of quickly changing images – aural, visual and tactile – presented in a cinematic, stream-of-consciousness style, reflecting both his character and situation.

THE CHARACTER OF PRUFROCK
- He is consciously unheroic.
- Melancholic and contemplative
- Feels inferior, inadequate and inhibited
- Fears rejection
- Both attracted to and threatened by women
- Women fall short of his idealised vision.
- Cannot find a language in which to express himself
- Indulges in escapist fantasies to avoid despair
- Indecisive, self-contemptuous and sees himself as a victim
- In a 'hell' – the consequence of being divided between passion and timidity – his tragic flaw
- A sensitive man in a psychological impasse
- An ageing romantic, incapable of action
- Tormented by unsatisfied desire
- A comic figure made tragic by his acute self-awareness
- The poem gives us not only the thoughts and feelings of Prufrock, but also the actual experience of his feeling and thinking.

PRUFROCK'S PROBLEMS WITH LANGUAGE
- Much of the meaning of the poem arises from its form: the digressions, hesitations, references, all suggest Prufrock's inability to express himself.
- Language regularly fails him. The first section never arrives at the question.
- Prufrock struggles with his own inarticulateness – 'Shall I say?' 'It is impossible to say just what I mean!'
- The failure of his love-song is also a failure to find a language in which to express himself.
- The fragments that make up the poem are essentially a collection of potential poems, which collapse because Prufrock cannot express his 'overwhelming question'.
- He is not included in the mermaids' song.
- Human voices suffocate and drown him.

MAIN THEMES
- Indecision
- Confronting the difficulty of action
- Time
- Emotional impotence
- The obduracy of language

- Superficiality and emptiness
- The hidden and isolated inner self
- The limitations of the real world
- Dying – spiritually, mentally, physically – death in life
- The movement in the mind.

MAIN IMAGES
- Sordid, seedy city life
- Fog/cat
- The room of pseudo-gentility
- Sea imagery – shells, crab, mermaids
- Cultural imagery – Michelangelo, John the Baptist, Lazarus, Hamlet
- Hair, clothes
- Coffee, tea, cakes and ices.

Preludes (1917)

Text of poem: New Explorations Anthology page 124
[Note: *This poem is also prescribed for Ordinary Level 2007 exam*]

INTRODUCTION

The 'Preludes' present us with urban scenes where what is seen reflects a particular state of mind. For the deeply disillusioned young poet they illustrate the ugliness, decline, emptiness and boredom of modern life.

The city here is effectively the same as that described by Prufrock in the 'Love Song of J. Alfred Prufrock'. It is a sordid world of deadening monotony and empty routine. The time-sets of the poem – evening, morning, night and day – reinforce the feeling of tedious monotony.

The title 'Preludes' can be seen as a reference to this sequence of evening, morning, night and day. They, as it were, are a 'prelude' to more sameness in the purposeless cycle of life.

'Preludes' could also point to the musical or lyrical effects in the poems.

As is usual with Eliot the poetry here is fragmented, full of quickly changing images – visual, aural, tactile and olfactory – in what is often described as a cinematic style. In what is essentially also a stream-of-consciousness style, Eliot takes us on a journey through the senses and the minds of his observers.

A READING OF THE POEM

Section I
Here the 'winter evening' is personified as it 'settles down' in a way reminiscent of the fog/cat in 'The Love Song of J. Alfred Prufrock'.

Olfactory images and tactile images abound – 'smell of steaks', 'burnt-out', 'smoky', 'grimy', 'withered leaves about your feet', the showers 'wrap' and 'beat' – leaving a sense of staleness and decay. This is compounded by the image of cramped apartments in 'passageways'.

'The burnt-out ends of smoky days' is a visual image that reminds us of Prufrock's 'butt-ends of my days and ways' and also evokes a sense of weariness and disgust.

Adjectives such as 'withered', 'broken', 'lonely' and 'vacant' suggest the decay and isolation of city life, while the insistent beating of the rain adds to the misery. The visual image of the uncomfortable and impatient cab-horse completes the picture of dreariness.

The isolated last line of this section: 'And then the lighting of the lamps', suggests that something dramatic might be about to happen. But nothing does. The opening words 'And then' are not a prelude to drama, but rather a closing in of the night.

Thus the imagery of the section evokes the speaker's mood. The reader can imagine him trudging home through the wet misery of a winter's evening, surrounded by withered leaves and discarded newspapers and inhaling the burnt and musty smells of his living quarters. What else could he be but depressed by it all? The feeling of a numb, aimless, struggle in an ugly, sterile environment suggests a mood of spiritual and mental decay.

Section II

Like 'evening' in the first section, 'morning' is here personified. It is as if the monotonous time-sets were living an independent life from the actors in this tedious drama of life.

Olfactory and tactile images – 'smells of beer', 'sawdust-trampled street', 'muddy feet that press', 'coffee-stands' – again suggest a sense of staleness and decay. Words such as 'trampled' and 'press' add to the mood of oppressiveness.

Individual life is submerged in the city and by the onward march of time and what emerges is a mass conformity and uniformity:

> One thinks of all the hands
> That are raising dingy shades
> In a thousand furnished rooms.

This sense of sameness and monotony is also suggested by:

> all its muddy feet that press
> To early coffee-stands.

Eliot regularly depersonalises the character of individuals to show the mechanical nature of their lives. Here people are reduced to 'hands' and 'feet', invoking something living yet spiritually inanimate. Life has become an enslavement to pressure – the pressure of time, crowds and gulped-down coffee.

For Eliot this morning rush to work is a masquerade. It is an act put on by all the 'feet' and 'hands' to give their lives some meaning. The poet is suggesting that behind all the mad masquerade of activity there is a paralysis of the metaphysical, as people's lives are constituted solely by their mundane masquerades.

Section III

The third section illustrates physical inaction as a woman (the 'you' of the poem) struggles to wake and sluggishly prepares to get out of bed, where during the night she fitfully dozed.

Her uncomfortable, sleepless night is caught in the verbs of the first three lines – 'tossed', 'lay', 'waited', 'dozed', 'watched'. She is trapped between sleep and wakefulness which allows her imagination to wander randomly:

> . . . revealing
> The thousand sordid images
> Of which your soul was constituted;

Thus her paralysis, just like the city's, is also a paralysis of the metaphysical. She is quite inert, apart from throwing the blanket from her bed.

As is typical of Eliot, we are again presented with a character's state of mind. The woman cannot sleep and when she dozes her semi-conscious mind projects, like a film on a screen, her interior self which 'flickered against the ceiling'. These 'sordid' images reflect not only her degradation, but are symbolic of the degenerated consciousness and spirit of mankind in the twentieth century. As a projection of the twentieth century she is more passive and vulgar than the woman in 'A Game of Chess'.

When morning arrived, its light 'crept up between the shutters', almost as if it were an unwelcome intruder, while the sparrows are stripped of all beauty by being heard 'in the gutters'. Her vision of the street is not clarified. It is again blurred – a vision that is hardly understood. Both woman and street appear earthbound – she is supine in bed, while the personified street is 'trampled' in both Sections II and IV.

The feeling of degradation and disgust is continued in the last four lines of this section. Eliot again depersonalises the character of the woman to portray this. She is dehumanised into bodily parts – 'hair', 'feet', 'hands' – to evoke the image of a living person who is spiritually inanimate, just as in Section II.

The sense of disgust is more intense here, however. Her hair is artificially curled with paper, her feet are unhealthily 'yellow' and her hands are 'soiled'. This is quite unlike the meticulous image of Prufrock in the 'Love Song of J. Alfred Prufrock'. He may be ridiculous. She is repulsive. The capacity for spiritual growth is non-existent.

Section IV

This final section in this poetic sequence reveals the speaker more fully. Like the woman in Section III whose soul's images are 'flickered against the ceiling', his soul is also mirrored upwards. But the skies on which it is stretched are not attractive. They 'fade behind a city block'. Indeed, the image is rather tortured – 'His soul [is] stretched tight', reflecting the tension and strain of urban life. The passing of the hours – 'At four and five and six o'clock' – merely reflects the tense tedium and emptiness of his existence.

Eliot again dehumanises and depersonalises individuals to show the mechanical nature of city life – 'trampled . . . feet', 'short square fingers', 'and eyes'. Their daily routine consists of 'newspapers' and 'pipes' and being 'Assured of certain certainties'. Thus the human reality of the street reveals itself as neither conscious nor aware of its own insecurities and sordid dilapidation. The poet sees these people as living lives of drudgery, whose 'conscience' has been 'blackened'. This is a valueless, dreary society, which is now menacingly seen as being 'Impatient to assume the world.'

In one of those abrupt shifts for which he is famous, Eliot suddenly reveals himself in a moving, pathos-filled quatrain:

> I am moved by fancies that are curled
> Around these images, and cling:
> The notion of some infinitely gentle
> Infinitely suffering thing.

What saves the poet from being swamped by his disgust for modern life is his clinging to a belief in 'some infinitely gentle | Infinitely suffering thing.' This is, perhaps, indicating his move towards Christianity as a source of order and veneration.

However, in an equally abrupt shift he returns to cynicism and encourages us to laugh at, and not sympathise with, the human condition:

> Wipe your hand across your mouth, and laugh

The emptiness in life and the struggle for survival are suggested in a simile which underscores the horrific drudgery of deprivation:

> The worlds revolve like ancient women
> Gathering fuel in vacant lots.

The process of dying, which is prevalent among most, if not all, of the characters in Eliot's poetry, is dramatically evident here also.

LANGUAGE AND MOOD

Lyrical devices are common throughout.

The monotonous metre of the first section emphasises the drudgery and oppression of these mean streets. Most lines have four iambic stresses, while the others have two. This is in keeping with the image of trampling feet in Sections II and III and, matched by the inexorable flow of time, emphasises the general weariness of moods.

The emphatic rhymes equally convey the sense of oppression. This is particularly the case with the rhyming couplets – 'wraps – scraps' and 'stamps – lamps'.

The insistent beating of the rain is further emphasised by the use of alliteration:

> The showers beat
> On broken blinds . . .

while the impatience of the horse is intensified by alliteration and the strong iambic rhythm:

> And at the corner of the street
> A lonely cab-horse steams and stamps.

Earlier in this section the use of alliteration and consonance furthers the sense of decay and staleness. The use of sibilant 's' sounds is particularly effective in this:

> The winter evening settles down
> With smell of steaks in passageways.

Thus, in keeping with the musical note of its title, the poet uses lyrical devices to emphasise his themes and underscore imagery and mood.

While Section I is generally composed of end-stopped lines, Section II is composed of lines which run on. This use of enjambment serves to convey a sense of movement – the movement of 'muddy feet' on a 'trampled street'. It also emphasises the pressure of time.

The use of synecdoche, in which a part is substituted for the whole, has been alluded to earlier for the way in which it depersonalises individuals and emphasises monotonous conformity:

> One thinks of all the hands
> That are raising dingy shades
> In a thousand furnished rooms.

While Eliot favoured *'vers libre'*, he does use rhyme to draw attention to or satirise a situation, as we saw in Section I. The rhyming of 'consciousness' with 'press' and 'masquerades' with 'shades' here underscores the theme of pretence; the desire to put on an act to give life some meaning. It also intensifies the mood of oppression.

Overall in this section there is a strong sense of contrast between the descriptions of movement and the sense of spiritual paralysis.

The essentially passive nature of the verbs used at the beginning of Section III reflects her supine state and degenerated consciousness.

The repetition of 'And', which introduces three lines, intensifies the experience of dull monotony, while the almost onomatopoeic effect of the rhyming couplet, 'shutters . . . gutters', reflects the lack of lyricism in the perceived sound of the sparrows. The result is particularly satiric.

The monotonous metre evident in the earlier part of Section IV emphasises the drudgery and oppression of this city's life, just as in Section I. The movement of these first nine lines underscores the repetitive routine. They go on and on.

The abrupt shift from the third to the first person in the tenth line dramatises the poet's revelation of himself and his feelings. The strong iambic metre is also relaxed, suggesting a sense of release from tension and strain.

The sense of pathos inherent in these lines is lost in another abrupt shift in the last three lines to a mood of deep cynicism. The simile is intensified by the word choice – 'ancient', 'vacant' – and the slowing down of the rhythm.

MAIN THEMES
- Incessant toil and suffering
- The decay and isolation of twentieth-century life
- Time
- Death-in-life
- Life is mundane, monotonous, repetitive, mechanical.
- Paralysis of the soul/consciousness
- A journey through the mind and senses.

MAIN IMAGES
- The street
- The woman
- Food and drink
- Body parts
- The detritus of the street
- Masquerades
- Rapidly changing images – visual, oral, tactile, olfactory – cinematic style.

Aunt Helen (1915)

Text of poem: New Explorations Anthology page 128
[*Note: This poem is also prescribed for Ordinary Level 2007 exam*]

INTRODUCTION

This is one of those poems in which Eliot outlines his impressions of genteel society in Boston, to the inner circle of which he was introduced through his uncle.

What the philosopher Santayana referred to as its cultural deadness and smug righteousness left this society open to satire. In this poem Eliot comments on its manners and mores, while also suggesting the emotional and spiritual shallowness behind its conventional beliefs and culture. Aunt Helen is a symbol of a world that ought to be mocked. Eliot himself called it a world 'quite uncivilised, but refined beyond the point of civilisation'.

A READING OF THE POEM

The poem is written in the imagist style. The satiric meaning of the poem, therefore, has to be inferred from the few concise detailed images.

The personal note of the first line is quickly dropped in favour of Eliot's usual device of the detached observer. The banal tone borders on that of a newspaper reporter as a series of apparently objective details are given.

She lived 'in a small house' – a large one would have been vulgar. 'Near a fashionable square' further suggests a genteel refinement. Living *in* the square would be too ostentatious.

The rather contrived and archaic-sounding line 3 conveys the fastidious nature of Miss Helen Slingsby and her self-contained little world: 'Cared for by servants to the number of four.'

Lines 4 and 5 have a satiric edge, which is devastating in its implications. The 'silence at her end of the street' is what is expected out of respect for the dead person. However, the 'silence in heaven' conveys the full contempt of the poet for Aunt Helen's self-serving lifestyle. Faced with this, Heaven has nothing to say. Eliot's contempt is not surprising when one considers how he was raised in a religious environment that promoted unselfish service to the wider community's needs.

The observance of conventions that indicate respect for the dead is also seen in line 6: 'The shutters were drawn and the undertaker wiped his feet –'

However, the dash at the end of the line is almost a challenge to the reader to see the gesture as one of rejection. The reader is reminded of Christ's advice to followers concerning those who reject His and their values – to shake the dust of their towns from their sandals.

The deadpan sarcasm of line 7:

> He was aware that this sort of thing had occurred before

reduces the death of this privileged lady to the commonplace. Aunt Helen's death is being dismissed as 'this sort of thing'.

Her decorous but distorted sense of values is seen in the next line:

> The dogs were handsomely provided for,

The implied criticism of such values controls our response to line 9, which evokes laughter rather than sympathy. Perhaps the poet is also implying that her values don't survive her any longer than the life of a parrot.

The lifeless, artificial, materialistic world in which she lived is seen in:

> The Dresden clock continued ticking on the mantelpiece,

and when we read that the servants resort to behaviour which Aunt Helen would not have tolerated, disregarding both her property and her values, laughter entirely replaces sympathy. The servants' behaviour is not a perversion of ancient values, but a release from their artificial confines.

However, even though we do laugh at and reject Aunt Helen's self-centred values, we are also left with a slight sense of distaste at the vulgarity of the final lines. Satire has not entirely reversed our sense of pathos.

The student may wish to compare Miss Helen Slingsby with the portrayal of women in 'A Game of Chess' and in 'Preludes'.

Language and tone

The flat, banal tone has been alluded to already. This banal style of narration undermines the seriousness with which Aunt Helen viewed herself and the trivialities that surrounded her.

However, the reader might declare the ultimate tone of the narrator to be quite serious and reject its apparent levity; but, as F.R. Leavis has pointed out, 'It is as necessary to revise the traditional idea of the distinction between seriousness and levity in approaching this poetry as in approaching the metaphysical poetry of the seventeenth century.'

A few random rhymes do little but emphasise the overall absence of lyricism, thus reflecting the general dullness of Aunt Helen's life. Indeed, some lines read almost as prose. This is particularly so of lines 6 and 7. This adds to the sense of boredom and staleness.

The reader could not be blamed for believing initially that this poem is a sonnet. It has the general appearance of one. However, if it does then Eliot is perhaps mocking the attitudes and expectations of the reader, for this is a very distorted 'sonnet', being 13 lines long, with little rhyme and varying rhythm patterns. Thus, this distortion may reflect not only Aunt Helen's distorted values but the reader's also. Satire works in a number of ways.

The contrast between the behaviour of the footman and housemaid and that of Aunt Helen might also be said to add to the humour and introduces a slightly risqué, if not entirely vulgar element.

Finally, Eliot the dramatist is very much in evidence in this poem. Apart from his ability to create a comic type with a few strokes of his pen, he has also created a time and place and most especially, perhaps, he has mimicked the pompous tone of Aunt Helen. Thus quite ordinary words and phrases, such as 'a fashionable square', and 'this sort of thing' echo the bourgeois speech of Miss Helen Slingsby.

The reader will have to decide whether Aunt Helen's life was a tragedy or a comedy.

MAIN THEMES
- Criticism of cultural deadness and self-righteousness
- Emotional and spiritual shallowness
- Distorted values
- Time.

MAIN IMAGES
- Silence
- The undertaker
- The dog and the parrot
- The Dresden clock
- The servants.

A Game of Chess (extract from The Waste Land II, 1922)

Text of poem: New Explorations Anthology page 130

THEMES, ISSUES AND IMAGERY

'A Game of Chess' is section II of Eliot's best-known long poem, 'The Waste Land'. This was first published in 1922 and quickly and enduringly became synonymous with the poet himself.

Just like the full poem, 'A Game of Chess' can be read on the level of a narrative or in its more complicated form, when an understanding of the many references helps to universalise the themes and issues. This use of references concurs with Eliot's belief, expressed in an essay published in 1919 called 'Tradition and the Individual Talent', that literary tradition does not just belong to the past but should be used by the poet to express himself more completely.

This allows Eliot to overtly contrast the marvels of the past with the squalid nature of the present. 'A Game of Chess' is an example of this, where the first 33 lines describe, amongst other things, past grandeur, while the rest of the poem depicts the present.

'A Game of Chess' describes the stunting effects of improperly directed love or of lust confused with love. The poem is constructed as an apparent contrast between the class, wealth and education of the characters in the first part and the lower-class female characters in a pub at closing time. A closer reading will suggest that the differences are superficial in comparison with the fundamental similarities.

The title of the poem is taken from a play by Thomas Middleton (1580–1627), where the action is played out like moves in a game of chess. This play is a political satire which created a furore at the time and which Eliot has described as 'a perfect piece of literary political art'. Middleton's greatest tragedy, *Women beware Women*, is also in Eliot's mind here. In this play a young woman is raped while her mother, downstairs and quite unaware of what is happening, plays a game of chess. The allusion to the rape of Philomel by Tereus, as told in Greek legend, is symbolised later in the poem. All of this is related to the principal theme of the section: the theme of lust without love.

The opening lines place a woman in a room that has been described as full of 'splendid clutter'. This room, or more precisely a rich lady's boudoir, is surrounded by symbols of our cultural heritage. The extreme lavishness of the boudoir is stressed by evoking the opulence of legendary queens like Cleopatra, Cassiopeia, Dido and Philomel.

These opening lines also reflect Enoborbus's description of Cleopatra's ceremonial barge in Shakespeare's *Antony and Cleopatra*. Cleopatra is famous for her love affairs with powerful Roman generals such as Julius Caesar and Mark Antony. However, Eliot substitutes 'chair' for 'barge', thus evoking the Andromeda legend and the story of Cassiopeia, which are also 'waste-land' tales. Lavish wealth is suggested by 'burnished throne', 'marble', 'golden'. The carved Cupidons on the glass standards suggest possible shameful love affairs.

The 'sevenbranched candelabra' (line 6) adds to the richness of the room while evoking further historical and cultural references. The seven-branched candelabra suggests the Jewish Menorah, which in turn reflects a religious sanctuary and the laying waste of much of Judaic culture over the centuries. The candelabra may also be a reference to the constellation of the Seven Sisters (the Pleiades), which is next to the Cassiopeia constellation. Thus the richness of description also becomes a richness of reference.

This superabundance of rich visual details continues. There are glittering jewels, 'satin cases', 'ivory and coloured glass'. However, the greater the accumulation, the greater the confusion in the reader and the less sure we are of what we are seeing or sensing. The woman's perfumes are strange and synthetic (line 11) and they 'lurked' in her vials, suggesting perhaps something illicit or at least decadent. Words such as 'unstoppered' and 'unguent' add to the sense of decadence, as does a phrase like 'drowned the sense in odours' (line 13) and thus the reader also is left 'troubled, confused'.

'The air | That freshened from the window' (line 13–14) doesn't really freshen the room, but stirs the odours into 'fattening the prolonged candle-flames'. Thus the sense of a stifling, decadent sensuality, or indeed sexuality, is further enhanced.

The 'laquearia' (line 16), which is a panelled ceiling, also holds a reference to Virgil's Aeneid, to the scene in Carthage where Queen Dido gives a banquet for her beloved Aeneas. He will eventually desert her. This reinforces the theme of misplaced love.

The patterns on the ceiling continue the notion of almost divine decadence. The colours are rich; the scale is huge and the associations are deliberate. The 'sea-wood' can be linked with the dolphin, which in early Christian times was a symbol of diligence in love, and the word 'framed' prepares us for the pictorial representation of the Philomel story. Even as he introduces the story, Eliot reinforces the theme and tone with a reference to Milton's 'Paradise Lost'. The picture was like a window opening upon 'a sylvan scene', but this sylvan scene is the one which lay before Satan when he first arrived at the Garden of Eden. Thus sexual corruption is introduced in a deceptively beautiful scene. 'The change of Philomel' is a euphemism for what really happens – the violent rape of this girl. The reader is troubled by such violence occurring in such a beautiful place. The story of Philomel, which Eliot takes from Ovid's *Metamorphoses*, is continued in lines 24–27. The barbarity of the sexual violence done to Philomel by King Tereus of Thrace (who was married to Philomel's sister Procne) is compounded by the cutting off of her tongue. Zeus, the king of the gods, took pity on Philomel and turned her into a nightingale – the 'nightingale' of line 24. This classic tragic story is given further voice in this room of the present. The theme of rape, the most immoral and improperly directed love/lust, forces us to react and to see its significance in the 'present' of the poem.

The violated Philomel, her tongue cut out, still manages to express her sorrow in inviolable voice when, as the nightingale, she fills all the desert with song. Perhaps this expresses Eliot's own wish to fill the wasteland, or desert, with song.

However, this may not be possible, for even the sound of the nightingale – the 'Jug Jug' of line 27 was a conventional Elizabethan method of expressing birdsong – becomes merely salacious in the modern world 'to dirty ears'. The move in line 26 from the past tense 'cried' to the present tense of 'pursues' underscores this more prurient perspective.

Lines 28–31 return to a description of the room. The other decorations, presumably outlining scenes from our cultural inheritance, are dismissed as 'withered stumps of time'. The poet is scornful of those who possess but do not appreciate such riches. This further suggests modern people's failure to come to terms with this same cultural inheritance. These 'stumps of time' then, ironically, no longer speak to us, despite being 'told upon the walls'. Perhaps, the 'stumps of time' may also evoke Philomel's stump of a tongue.

The image of the woman brushing her hair in lines 32–34 suggests a nervous person under considerable emotional strain. The rather surreal image of her hair glowing into words suggests her hypersensitivity and her tense speech, while 'savagely still' suggests a truly neurotic silence.

Lines 35–62 are made up of a dialogue between this woman and a male protagonist. The lines between the quotation marks represent the woman's words. The man's are not given quotation marks. Perhaps he is silent, his answers to her questions being unspoken thoughts. Thus the episode is not, perhaps, a full dialogue: just an exchange of sorts, indicating an emotional and communicative stalemate.

While the staccato rhythm of the woman's utterances reveals her nervous tension, the substance suggests her state of purposelessness. The dialogue, if such it be, pivots around aimless questions and nervous imperatives. The answers of the protagonist indicate that his is as desperate a situation as hers is. However, his is a calmer, more resigned despair. He may be in a psychological Hell ('rats' alley') but he is aware of alternatives. He quotes from Shakespeare's *Tempest*: 'Those are pearls that were his eyes.' This suggests the possibility of transformation. Indeed, in *The Tempest* two lovers play a game of chess that may be linked with genuine love.

However, the sardonic counter-perspective immediately intrudes with 'that Shakespeherian Rag' of line 52, an American hit tune of 1912. The words 'elegant' and 'intelligent' deny in this context both true elegance and true intelligence, and perhaps the possibility of finding the true nature of either in this room with these people, despite the grandeur of the room itself.

The overall sense of purposelessness is reinforced by the woman's final questions and the answers to them. Water, which is normally a symbol of life giving, is here without potency. In fact it must be avoided by using a closed car.

The pub scene, apparently set in a working-class urban area from the tone of the narrative, opens in line 63. Much of the essential nature of this scene is its vocalness. We, the readers, have the experience of eavesdropping on a barside monologue. The speaker of the narrative is a woman. The difference in class between her and the woman of the earlier lines is quite apparent. There is a sense of immediacy in the setting, with the woman recounting a dialogue between herself and another woman, Lil, some time earlier. The barman's words, in capitals, break into the narrative contributing meanings to the narrative not recognised by its narrator.

The theme of the past haunting the present is again immediately identifiable, as are those of sterility, lust without love, spiritual/emotional illness and emptiness and intimations of mortality and the role of women. The sense of a Waste Land is acute: not the waste of war's destruction, but the emotional and spiritual sterility of modern man.

In a society where appearance means everything, Lil is told to smarten herself up for her husband Albert, who is returning from war. Lil is criticised for looking old before her time (line 82). Indeed Albert had criticised her some time earlier, presumably when he was on leave, and had given her money to get a new set of teeth. She, however, had used the money to procure an abortion (line 85).

The sympathy of the narrator lies with Albert – the 'poor Albert' of line 73 who will want 'a good time' after his four years in the army. Albert may even 'make off' with those who will give him a good time if Lil doesn't.

Lil, meanwhile, is told to smarten up; that she 'ought to be ashamed . . . to look so antique' and that she is 'a proper fool'. Little sympathy is had for her nearly dying in pregnancy (line 86) and a fatalistic attitude is held towards the sexual demands of her husband (lines 90–91). The vulgar insensitivity of it all can be compared to the fate of Philomel in the first section, while the use of the word 'antique' (line 82) also reminds us of the imagery of the first section. In this outline of Lil's life, social satire is in effect evoking sympathy.

The narrative is not concluded. It is disrupted by closing time and there is the suggestion of the speaker leaving the pub (line 98). Time is running out for the characters in the narrative, reinforced by the urgent, constant calling of 'Hurry Up Please It's Time'. Their farewells fade into the Shakespearian final line, drawing us back to one of those stumps of time – Ophelia's madness and her drowning. This reference adds a sense of dignity to the narrative, while also universalising the themes of misplaced love and destruction.

Language, tone and mood

As said, Eliot's poetry is essentially dramatic – from conflict to characterisation, from action to dialogue, from plot to imagery. The student may be well advised to search for examples of these dramatic elements.

The language in 'A Game of Chess' both reflects and is part of the essential drama of the poem. The diction and syntax of the first section reflect the description of the room. Thus words used to describe the 'props' of the dramatic setting could well describe the style also – words such as 'burnished', 'synthetic', or 'rich profusion'. Archaic and artificial-sounding words such as 'Cupidon', 'unguent' and 'laquearia' add to this sense of an urgent, forced style. Overall, the feeling is one of claustrophobia, a sense of being trapped, or 'prolonged' in this gorgeous, cluttered room. The long sentences add to this feeling. (The first sentence is nine lines long.) Similarly, the various subordinate clauses within these long sentences contribute to the sense of being 'troubled, confused'. The lavish opulence of the room and the language in which it is described thus create a feeling of unease.

In the same way there is a glut of active verbs and participles from lines 14–34, almost hypnotising the reader and stifling a response.

At times, however, the language is wonderfully economic. 'Sad light' (line 20) and 'And still she cried, and still the world pursues' beautifully combine both description and emotion.

However, on other occasions the deliberate literariness of the lines hides the brutal reality. This is the case with the description of the rape of Philomel. The rather lofty, Miltonic tone of:

> Above the antique mantel was displayed
> As though a window gave upon the sylvan scene

tends to obscure what is actually happening in the picture. The euphemisms used, 'The change of Philomel' and 'So rudely forced', tend to lessen the enormity of the sexual violence. Thus the sense of sexual decadence is evoked.

The poet's scornful reaction to such opulent decadence is seen in lines 28–29:

> And other withered stumps of time,
> Were told upon the walls . . .

The cold brevity of these lines is in sharp contrast to the aureate earlier descriptions. This economy of expression continues in line 30:

> Leaned out, leaning, hushing the room enclosed.

Here the strained repetitiveness of the line prepares us for the strained emotions of the woman introduced in line 35, while the word 'enclosed' confirms for us the claustrophobia of the room.

The woman's speech reflects her neurotic state. The repetition of one word from earlier on in the line at the end of three of the lines – 'Speak.' 'What?' 'Think.' – emphasises the neurotic state.

The repetition of 'nothing' from lines 44–50 reflects not only the emotional vacancy of the man, but also suggests that this vacancy reverberates in her mind as well. An emotional stalemate is the result.

The unnaturalistic rhythm of the woman's speech, with its deadening, repetitive, nervous questioning, is counterpointed by the smooth rhythm of the quotation from Shakespeare's *Tempest* (line 49). However, the irony here is further compounded by the vulgar ragtime rhythm of 'that Shakespeherian Rag –'

The diction and syntax of the speaker in the pub scene is essentially that of urban English working class. In tone it is an abrupt shift from that of the woman in the room. The word 'said' is repeated some fifteen times in a gossipy fashion.

This not only realistically reflects the rhythms and patterns of speech of the working class, but also adds a certain prayer-like intonation.

The barman's sonorous 'HURRY UP PLEASE IT'S TIME' both breaks into and breaks up the speaker's narrative, adding levels of meaning not intended by the speaker. Its repetition contributes to the urgency of the narrative, even introducing a comic, quasi-apocalyptic tone.

The quotation from Shakespeare's *Hamlet*, which ends the passage, has Ophelia's lingering farewell remind us that the time is indeed out of joint. Ophelia's words, which rise out of the mêlée of farewells in lines 100–101, enhance the pathos of these people's lives and remind us again that the past does indeed haunt the present and that music may be made out of suffering.

MAIN THEMES
- The marvels of the past contrast with the squalid nature of the present.
- The past haunts the present.
- The stunting effect of improperly directed love/lust
- Lust without love
- Sexual corruption may be deceptively beautiful.
- The desire to fill the wasteland with song
- Modern people's failure to come to terms with their cultural heritage
- The emotional strain of modern life
- Sense of purposelessness in modern life
- Intimations of mortality.

MAIN IMAGES
- Opulent luxury of the room
- Rape of Philomel
- Nervous gestures of the woman
- The story of Lil and Albert
- The landlord crying 'Time'.

Journey of the Magi (1927)

Text of poem: New Explorations Anthology page 136

This is the first of the Ariel Poems, a set of poems which, beginning in 1927, the year in which Eliot joined the Anglican church, were published by Faber & Faber as a sort of Christmas card. Both this poem and 'A Song for Simeon' (1928) refer specifically to the birth of Christ.

The Magi were the three wise men or kings – commonly, but not scripturally, known as Balthazar, Caspar and Melchior – who journeyed from the east to pay homage to the newly born baby Jesus, according to the gospel of

St Matthew 11: 1–12. However, Eliot's inspiration comes not from this well-known gospel story alone but also from a sermon preached by Lancelot Andrews, Bishop in Winchester, on Christmas Day 1622, which Eliot quotes in his 'Selected Essays'. The first five lines of the poem are a direct quotation from this sermon by Lancelot Andrews.

The poem is essentially a dramatic monologue spoken by one of the magi, who is now an old man, recalling and reminiscing on the journey he and his companions made to witness a Birth. Thus the poem is concerned with a quest and those travelling must traverse a type of wasteland to reach the promised land. The Magi's journey is challenging, painful and difficult. It involved giving up old comforts, certainties and beliefs so that it became a 'Hard and bitter agony for us'. Reaching their destination doesn't lead to any great sense of achievement or celebration. Instead the narrator is unsure of the significance of what he has seen. 'It was (you may say) satisfactory.' The narrator remains disturbed and bewildered as he returns to the 'old dispensation' which he and his companions now find strange. He longs for death now, so that he can achieve new life.

The poem can be seen as an analogy of Eliot's own agonising spiritual journey. The quest for a new spiritual life involves rejecting the old life with its many attractions. Thus, the Birth also includes a death; the death of the old way of life. Such a journey involves doubt, regrets and lack of conviction. Maybe 'this was all folly.' This tone of uncertainty leads us to appreciate that rather than asserting his beliefs Eliot is expressing his willingness to believe, which is his present spiritual condition.

THEMES AND ISSUES

The poem is a dramatic monologue in which the magus, the narrator, tells of his and his companions' experiences in their journey to the birth of Christ. The opening five lines are an abbreviation of Andrew's sermon as mentioned above, which Eliot includes as part of the magus's narration.

The journey undertaken is one from death to life. It begins in 'The very dead of winter.' The hardships endured represent the sacrifice the magi must make in order to achieve new birth. Also, before there is a birth there must be a death of the old life.

The hardships undergone include not only the weather and trouble with their camels, but also major regrets for what is left behind:

> The summer palaces . . . the silken girls bringing sherbet.
> (lines 9–10)

These real attractions cannot be easily overcome.

Exactly how tough the journey was is seen in the sequence from line 11 to line 16. The increasing torment outlined in the matter-of-fact, descriptive statements here is made all the more effective by the repetition of 'And . . . ' The hostility of various communities, symbolic of a disbelieving world, leads them 'to travel all night'. Adding to their discomfort is the realisation that the hostile unbelievers may be right – 'That this was all folly.' (line 20)

The next section, beginning at line 21, seems at first to confirm the death-to-life theme. It is 'dawn'; there is 'a temperate valley', 'a running stream and a water-mill beating the darkness' – all of which can be seen as birth images. However, ambiguity and uncertainty quickly return. The 'three trees' are reminders of the Crucifixion of Christ, as are the 'Six hands . . . dicing for pieces of silver' (line 28). These, coupled with the negativity of the horse galloping away, 'the empty wine-skins' and 'no information', can be seen as furthering the theme of death. However they may also suggest the interrelation between death and birth. Christ's incarnation leads inexorably to His Crucifixion, just as His Crucifixion leads to eternal life.

Ambiguity can also be seen in what should be the joyful climax of the journey and confirmation of belief. However, this is not so. The intense anticipation and anxiety of 'not a moment too soon' is immediately followed by the uncertain reticence of

> it was (you may say) satisfactory. (line 32)

No description of the Birth or the One who was born is given.

This sense of uncertainty turns to a degree of confusion in the last section, as the magus tries to work out the meaning of what he saw. Maybe like the knight meeting the Fisher King in the Holy Grail legend, he has failed to ask the right question. While he is convinced that it was significant – 'And I would do it again' (line 34) – and is anxious that no part of his narrative should be overlooked:

> . . . but set down
> This set down
> This: . . .
>   (lines 34–36)

the Birth doesn't seem to have been what he expected. He 'had thought they [birth and death] were different', but 'this Birth was . . . like Death, our death.' (lines 39–40).

So the Magi return to their kingdoms but feel alienated among their own people. They must continue to live amidst the old way of life – 'the old dispensation' (line 42) – while not believing in it. So their Birth remains a bitter agony while they wait for 'another death' (line 44). Another death is required – the magus's own, or perhaps Christ's – before he can enter a new life.

IMAGERY AND SYMBOLISM

The whole poem is structured around a journey, both real and symbolic. The journey as recalled by the magus is one from death to birth, the imagery of which suggests the inner struggles of the narrator and his companions.

The journey begins at 'the worst time of year' with 'The ways deep and the weather sharp' and ends in 'a temperate valley . . . smelling of vegetation'. The symbolic movement from death to life is clear. Paradoxically, however, there is also a movement from life to death. Here 'The summer palaces . . . And the silken girls bringing sherbet' represent the old life. The travellers make their way through a wasteland of 'cities hostile and the towns unfriendly', until in the valley there is a symbolic death of the old life as the 'old white horse galloped away'. Some critics have seen references to the Fisher King myth in the journey and its symbols.

The second stanza contains a series of death and birth images. 'Dawn', 'temperate valley', 'vegetation' can be seen as birth images, while water is universally acknowledged as symbolising life. However, a flowing river or stream is also a traditional poetic symbol of the passing of time. The action of the 'water-mill' can be seen as beating the darkness of time.* There then follow a series of images foreshadowing the well-known imagery surrounding Christ's death. The 'three trees on the low sky' reflect the three crosses on the Hill of Calvary. The 'hands dicing' suggest the Roman soldiers dicing for Christ's clothes and the 'pieces of silver' remind us of the thirty pieces of silver that Judas was paid for his treachery.

The 'white horse' can be seen as an ambiguous image. It may symbolise the life-giving, triumphant Christ of the Book of Revelations (VI: 2, 19:11). However, as the horse is said to be 'old' and since it 'galloped away' it may also represent the collapse of paganism, 'the old dispensation' of line 42.

LANGUAGE AND TONE

As befits a dramatic monologue the language reflects not only natural speech patterns, which catch the rhythms of speech, but also a particular voice – the voice of the magus, at times both reminiscent and complaining:

> Then the camel men cursing and grumbling
> And running away, and wanting their liquor and women.

Here the emphasis falls into a natural pattern of speech and voice inflection. The prayer-like, incantatory tone also befits both the speaker and the theme. The strong repetition of 'And' in the first two sections reflects this. Overall the purposefully ambiguous symbols and images introduce a tone of uncertainty.

The opening paraphrased uncertainty of Lancelot Andrews' sermon sets the tone of desolation and the bitter environment of the first stanza. The quotation also serves a second purpose for Eliot. It incorporates the poem into a particular tradition. Thus it serves a similar function to the quotation from Dante at the beginning of 'Prufrock' and is part of his efforts to create a synthesis between past and present.

The remainder of the first stanza is quite vitriolic in tone, as the magus criticises both his predicament and his previous life. This criticism is coupled with a tone of regret,

> The summer palaces on slopes, the terraces,
> And the silken girls bringing sherbet.

The sensual sibilant 's' sounds of these lines underscore what is being regretted. A tone of contempt can be seen in the ever-expanding criticism of the remainder of the first stanza.

The second stanza suggests a tone of nostalgia as the magus remembers his arrival at 'a temperate valley'. Then the last three lines of this stanza culminate in an understatement: 'it was (you may say) satisfactory.'

The word 'satisfactory' as seen, reflects the ambiguity and uncertainty of the magi's reaction. Perhaps, they are not completely aware of its relevance. The word is given particular emphasis by the expression in parentheses preceding it and by its irregularity with the set rhythm of the line.

This tone of uncertainty is continued in the next stanza and develops into a tone of anxiety and of urgency:

> ... but set down
> This set down
> This: ...

The dislocation and repetition of these lines emphasise this residual tone of uncertainty and urgency. The run-on line:

> ... this Birth was
> Hard and bitter agony for us, ...

creates a similar tone of anxiety and perhaps even of self-pity.

The poem ends in a conditioned statement:

> 'I should be glad of another death',

perhaps expressing a tone of resignation.

MAIN THEMES

- The Birth of Jesus Christ
- A quest/journey as an analogy of spiritual searching
- Lack of conviction/uncertainty/alienation
- Birth entails death

- The need for suffering in order to attain a new Birth.

Main images
- A journey
- A wasteland of 'cities hostile'
- Death and birth images
- Biblical images.

Usk (extract from Landscapes III, *1935)*
Text of poem: New Explorations Anthology page 138

Introduction
This is one of Eliot's five 'Landscape poems', three of which are based in America, one in Wales and one in Scotland.

This poem resulted from a ten-day holiday taken by Eliot in Wales in 1935.

In keeping with the term 'Landscape', the poem is a suggestive or evocative sketch in which the poet can be seen as an artist/painter. Like the other 'Landscape' poems, this poem consists of scenes and perceptions of deep significance in the development of Eliot's thinking. In particular, the 'Landscape' poems are definitive pointers in terms of Eliot's developing religious and poetic sensibilities, which are further explored in the 'Four Quartets'.

In this sense, although listed under *Minor Poems*, there is nothing minor about the significance of these poems. Indeed, taken as a sequence of five poems, we can see that Eliot is again evoking drama here, as he did in 'The Wasteland' and in the individual quartets of 'Four Quartets'. The sequence of five is in keeping with the number of acts required by Aristotle for tragic drama. Shakespeare also adhered to this. So both 'Usk' and 'Rannoch' can be seen as two acts in a drama outlining the relationship between human beings and the natural world. As number III, Usk marks a climax in the sequence.

A reading of the poem
'Usk' is a pastoral poem in both senses of the word, i.e. it is descriptive of the countryside and is also spiritually instructive.

The opening of the poem is abrupt, sudden and in the imperative mood. The reader is being instructed:

> Do not suddenly break . . . or
> Hope to find . . .
> . . . do not spell

We are being told *not* to seek images such as 'the white hart', 'the white well', the 'lance'. These are evocative of the classical Arthurian/Celtic legends. As such they are also evocative of the countryside.

Thus Eliot is suggesting that in such a landscape we should not conjure up the past or any notion of romantic fantasy. This he dismisses as 'Old enchantments.' He tells us to 'Let them sleep.' As a sort of second thought he allows us to '"Gently dip, but not too deep"'.

However, having been instructed *against* something, we are now instructed *towards* something. Our relationship with the landscape should not be escapist or full of romantic fantasy, but should be such as to lead us *towards* the spiritual.

In a prayer-like incantation, he tells us to 'Lift your eyes'. We are being sent on a more active spiritual journey – a pilgrimage – 'Where the roads dip and where the roads rise'.

Here we are to seek 'The hermit's chapel, the pilgrim's prayer' which, although conventional images of the spiritual, will not be found in any conventional setting but 'Where the grey light meets the green air'.

A spiritual home will be found in something that is neither human nor animal. Indeed it may not be found in the natural landscape at all, but in the eternal continuum of light and space, i.e. 'Where the grey light meets the green air'.

There is a note of hope here that is not found in 'The Love Song of J. Alfred Prufrock', 'Preludes' or 'A Game of Chess'. It echoes that tiny note of hope, which is to be found in 'The Journey of the Magi' and marks a shift towards a spiritual solution for Eliot in the face of life's difficulties.

USE OF LANGUAGE

The language suggests a certain sense of detachment on the part of the poet. The poem reads as advice to others from someone who has already reached a conclusion or discovered a position with which he is happy. Even though this is a description of a place, the poet is not part of the place. This can be seen as a type of metaphysical detachment.

The negative imperatives and the cacophonous alliterative sounds of the first line introduce us to the poet's attitudes towards the 'Old enchantments.'

These same imperatives also evoke that sense of self-assured, commanding authority we associate with metaphysical poets such as the seventeenth-century poet, John Donne.

In keeping with this robust style the rhythm is quick and irregular. This lively, almost bounding style is furthered by the use of alliteration and repetition in many of the lines. The rhythm, like the road, dips and rises. The use of enjambment, or run-on lines, in the second part of the poem in particular, and the quite intense rhyme, also add to the sense of insistent energy.

The incantatory tones of some of the imperatives have been alluded to already. In fact the tone of the whole poem can be found in the three dimeter lines:

> Hope to find . . .
> Lift your eyes . . .
> Seek only there . . .

The dramatic exhortational tone of an Old Testament prophet is clear and in keeping with one aspect of the pastoral theme.

Finally, the choice of colours in this landscape 'painting' suggests both a sense of peace and invigoration. 'White' is bright, while 'grey light' evokes images of a chill, bracing wind, and 'green' is traditionally seen as a natural, soothing colour. The sense of peace is also evoked by the choice of individual words such as 'sleep', 'gently', 'dip' and 'prayer'.

MAIN THEMES
- A pastoral poem in both senses
- Avoid the 'old enchantments'
- Seek the spiritual
- A journey.

MAIN IMAGES
- Medieval romantic fantasies – 'hart', 'well', 'lance'
- The road
- 'The hermit's chapel'
- 'Grey light', 'green air'.

Rannoch, by Glencoe (extract from Landscapes IV, 1935*)*
Text of poem: New Explorations Anthology page 140

'Rannoch' is the fourth in the five-poem sequence, 'Landscapes'. (See Introduction on 'Usk'.)

A READING OF THE POEM
The poem explores the relationship between human beings and the natural world. Like 'Usk' it is a pastoral, in the sense of being both a description of a countryside and also containing a message. It may suggest elements of a pastoral elegy to some readers.

In many ways this poem is a stripping away of the idyllic, idealised Golden

Age pastoral to reveal a landscape of famine and war.

The poem opens with two death-in-life images – 'the crow starves', 'the patient stag | Breeds for the rifle.'

They are the distressing results of the capacity of humans to condition the landscape. This is a barren landscape full of death. Here all creatures feel constricted and oppressed:

> . . . Between the soft moor
> And the soft sky, scarcely room
> To leap or soar.

The softness here is not of ease or comfort, but a reflection of the sense of oppression. Sky and moor practically meet. If all relationships need space and time, then failure is inevitable here due to a distinct lack of space. This landscape is a burden.

Erosion is the norm here – 'Substance crumbles'; everything is suspended 'in the thin air' of the inexorable movement of time – 'Moon cold or moon hot.'

This psychological topography allows no means of escape. 'The road winds' without apparent purpose. Instead we are offered a journey through 'listlessness', 'languor' and 'clamour'. The sense of direction and invigorating movement evident in 'Usk' is totally absent here. We are stuck in the wretchedness of history and its endless cycles: 'ancient war', 'broken steel', 'confused wrong'. These are the relics of embattled lives, before which the only appropriate response is silence. These old rivalries will not be resolved because 'Memory is strong | Beyond the bone.'

In this landscape of memory where 'Pride snapped', the 'Shadow of pride is long'. In 'the long pass' of a lifetime, there will be no resolution, no reconciliation – 'No concurrence of bone.' This is because even though pride is humiliated (snapped), it holds onto its shadow.

Unlike 'Usk' this poem offers no religious perspective, no sense of hope and direction between life and death – only a sense of 'betweenness', where we are biologically fated to evoke old rivalries. They are of the bone and 'Beyond the bone'.

Living in a state of betweenness, the rational aspect of ourselves is lost amidst the 'Clamour of confused wrong', almost indifferent to suffering, including our own. As is common in Eliot's poetry, the human in its non-rational state is symbolised in animal imagery. Here the human is seen as 'crow' and 'the patient stag' awaiting their fate. They are as unable to understand what they had been reduced to as are the inhabitants of the city street in the 'Preludes'.

The existentialist awareness and its agony are to be found in the speakers and the readers of these poems.

The tragedy of 'Rannoch' may be alleviated by the hope of 'Usk'. However, 'Usk' is not a solution but an indication of the journey that must be taken. But

'Rannoch' is the tragedy that may prevent 'Usk'.

The use of language

This is a dysfunctional landscape and the poet's use of language reflects that.

The end-of-line neatness of strong rhyme and natural pauses in 'Usk' is absent. Instead we are presented with a rather discordant structure. A line or lines run on, only to finish abruptly in the middle of the next line.

There is an emphasis on alliteration, in keeping with Eliot's admiration of medieval English.

This, however, does nothing to even out or smooth the lines. Rather the effect is insistent, if not altogether frenzied when combined with the stutter-like rhythm. This nervous, stutter-like effect is added to by actual close word repetition. All of this creates an unease and a tension in the reader.

Rhyme, where it does exist, is internal or slightly off end – e.g. 'wrong', 'strong' and 'long' and 'sour', 'war'. Again this adds to the sense of a discordant structure.

The sense of constriction explored in the imagery of the first four lines is also present in the language. In the second sentence:

> Between the soft moor
> And the soft sky, scarcely room
> To leap or soar.

there appears to be no room for a main verb.

We are also presented with an anagram as a type of rhyme, i.e. 'moor' and 'room'. The 'moor' turns on itself to become 'room', emphasising the constriction and oppression and becoming an analogy for the retracing and restating of grievances in a closed system of confused wrongs and strong memories.

Main themes

- Death in life
- Time
- Impact of human beings on the natural world
- War, destruction and erosion
- Unresolved rivalries.

Main images

- The crow and the stag
- Moor and sky
- Winding road

- (Images of) war
- Bone.

East Coker IV (extract from The Four Quartets, 1940)

Text of poem: New Explorations Anthology page 142

INTRODUCTION

This short piece is part of 'East Coker', the second of 'The Four Quartets'.

'The Four Quartets' is seen by many critics as the most important work of Eliot's career. Helen Gardner has called them Eliot's masterpiece. The new forms and ideas with which he experimented in the 'Landscape' poems ('Usk', 'Rannoch') are developed fully in 'The Four Quartets'.

In keeping with the musical title, the structure of the 'Quartets' is symphonic and thus extraordinarily complex – a complexity which need not trouble the student here.

Time is again one of the central themes – in particular its constant change in contrast with unchanging eternity. The philosophical considerations of the contrast between the real and the ideal, the human and the spiritual, explored in his earlier poetry, are again evident here.

'East Coker' takes its name from the village in Somerset, England, from which Eliot's ancestors emigrated to America. 'East Coker' is concerned with the place of mankind in the natural order of things and with the notion of renewal. This theme of rebirth, which is also found in the 'Journey of the Magi', is part of the spiritual progress of the soul. The soul must yield itself to God's hands and die in order to be born again. Indeed the soul must first suffer in order to be capable of responding fully to God's love. St John of the Cross calls this 'the dark night of the soul'. The saint's writing on this has influenced Eliot here.

A READING OF THE POEM

The poem, written for Good Friday 1940, sees Eliot at his most symbolic and a reading of the poem is, in effect, an interpretation of this symbolism.

The poem is a metaphysical one, structured around metaphysical conceits and paradoxes similar to those which may be found in the poetry of the seventeenth-century poet, John Donne. It lies in the tradition of seventeenth-century devotional verse, such as that of Donne, Herbert and Vaughan.

The 'wounded surgeon' is Jesus Christ, whose suffering and death on the Cross, and whose subsequent Resurrection, ensured mankind's redemption.

The 'wounded surgeon' will cure the soul of its sickness: 'the distempered part'. The surgeon's knife, 'the steel', which operates, or 'questions', is God's love. This is in keeping with St John of the Cross's 'The Dark Night of the Soul', which has influenced Eliot here.

The soul is not unaware of God's love operating on it. It feels 'The sharp compassion of the healer's art'.

The oxymoron that is 'sharp compassion' suggests the idea of a necessary evil, i.e. in order to be cured the soul must suffer first. Suffering is a means of grace. This is 'the enigma of the fever chart'. A physical evil can be seen as a spiritual good. Thus the metaphysical paradox is 'resolved'.

The beginning of the second verse continues this notion of suffering as a means of grace. Thus, 'Our only health is the disease'.

The conceit of a hospital is continued with the image of 'the dying nurse'.

'The dying nurse' is the Church – 'dying' in the sense of the common fate of mankind. The Church's role is not to placate or please us, but to remind us firstly of 'Adam's curse', which is never-ending toil and suffering, similar to the vision of mankind's daily life in the 'Preludes'. The Church's second role is to remind us that, 'to be restored, our sickness must grow worse', meaning that it is only through the fullest suffering that we can be fully cleansed or cleared of our sickness/evil.

The 'hospital' conceit is continued in the third stanza. 'The whole earth is our hospital' in the sense that it is here we can learn the value of suffering and can be cured of our sickness. The 'ruined millionaire' is Adam, whose endowment brought sin into the world – Adam's sin is Original Sin in Christian belief. The 'paternal care' is that of God, under Whose care we would be privileged to die, if we do well as 'patients' in this world. The word 'prevents' is used in its seventeenth-century sense, meaning to go before us with spiritual guidance. God will help us by guiding us towards repentance. The second and modern meaning of 'prevents', that is to stop or frustrate, is also appropriate. God stops our lives everywhere through death.

The notion of cure is continued in the fourth stanza. The cure is a fever one – because 'to be restored, our sickness must grow worse', as stated in the second stanza. The purgation, or cure, must move from a purgation of the flesh, burning away all the sickness and impurities of the flesh, until it ascends to a purgation of the mind:

> If to be warmed, then I must freeze
> And quake in frigid purgatorial fires

The essence of a breaking cold/hot fever, the body shivering and sweating as it rids itself of disease, is achieved here.

The flames of purgation Eliot calls roses, the symbol of both human and divine love. Roses and thorns are also the emblem of martyrdom. So suffering is seen as the basis of the cure – a thorough penitential suffering.

The fifth stanza opens with an image of the 'wounded surgeon' again. It is

Jesus Christ on the Cross, whose suffering leads to our Redemption. The image also evokes the Eucharist, the central act of worship for Christians. It may also evoke the need for suffering in ourselves, so that we too will be cured.

The image of flesh and blood is continued in the next two lines in Eliot's criticism of our blindness. We like to think that there is no need for humility and penance with our ideas of our own importance – 'we are sound, substantial flesh and blood'.

The adjectives 'sound, substantial' suggest that we rely too much on the physical, the materialistic.

However, Eliot recognises that behind our materialism, we innately acknowledge our need for repentance and the grace of God. This is why 'we call this Friday good.'

USE OF LANGUAGE

In this poem Eliot has revived the metaphysical poem. He uses many of the features we associate with the seventeenth-century poetry of Donne, Herbert and Vaughan.

In line with metaphysical poetry there is a strong sense of argument throughout the poem. The argument, as outlined above in the READING OF THE POEM, is that we need to reject the demands of the body and achieve redemption through curing its ills. Pain and suffering are means towards achieving redemptive grace or enlightenment.

This argument is presented throughout a series of metaphysical paradoxes, e.g.

> The 'wounded surgeon' will cure us
> 'sharp compassion'
> 'the enigma of the fever chart'
> 'Our only health is the disease'
> 'to be restored, our sickness must grow worse.'
> 'if we do well, we shall | Die'
> 'If to be warmed, then I must freeze'
> 'frigid purgatorial fires'
> 'in spite of that, we call this Friday good.'

Many of these are examples of what is known as metaphysical wit, which is renowned for its clever but serious, incisive, challenging and intelligent puns and paradoxes. The wit of the last stanza in particular removes any sense of emotional religiosity and serves to intensify the devotional mood.

A conceit is an elaborate, sustained comparison. These were much used by the seventeenth-century metaphysical poets. Eliot, in keeping with this, uses conceits in this poem. The 'wounded surgeon' is an example, as are seeing the earth as a hospital and the notion of the fever cure.

The meaning of symbols used is explored above in READING OF THE POEM. However the student should be aware that symbolism is as much a use of language as it is an exploration of meaning. Such usage invigorates both language and meaning.

Similarly, Eliot's precision of language adds depth to the meaning of both individual words and the poem as a whole. His use of the word 'prevents' in the third stanza is an example of this.

Examples of metaphysical wit are seen in the last stanza, in the evocative fused imagery of the first two lines in particular.

Eliot 'reinvented' the alliterated four-stress line commonly found in medieval English. This poem generally follows that pattern, with quite strong medial pauses: e.g. 'The **wound**ed **surg**eon **plies** the **steel**' or 'Be**neath** the **bleed**ing **hands** we **feel**'.

However, this kind of verse can become monotonous. Eliot's genius was to apply the pattern with sufficient flexibility to avoid monotonous rigidity.

W.B. Yeats once said that rhythm in poetry should be used 'to prolong the moment of contemplation'. Perhaps we can say this of both the rhythm and the strong, definite rhyme patterns in this poem.

MAIN THEMES

- The idea of necessary evil – a physical evil may be a spiritual good.
- Suffering as a means of attaining grace/redemption
- The purgation of evil
- The caring love of God
- Growth towards a new life.

MAIN IMAGES

- The wounded surgeon
- Conceit of a hospital
- The nurse
- The ruined millionaire – Adam
- Play of opposites – 'frigid fires'
- The Cross
- The Eucharist.

T.S. Eliot – An Overview

Not even the most learned critic has said that Eliot's poetry makes easy reading. Yet of all twentieth-century poets he is perhaps the most rewarding. No other poet has better expressed the social condition and psychological state of modern man.

While Eliot's poetry can be read with pleasure at first sight, a full understanding will not come immediately. This is so because quite often, instead of the regular evocative images other poets use, Eliot presents us with a series of literary and historical references. Eliot himself insisted that the reader must be prepared to answer the call for knowledge which poetry demands. Indeed if the reader does persevere, then he/she will be rewarded with a use of symbolism and allusion, and an experimenting with the language and form of poetry, which deepen and intensify the experience of reading it. He/she will feel what Eliot himself called the 'direct shock of poetic intensity'.

Influences and the 'Modern Movement'

The 'Modern Movement' is that which effected a revolution in English literature between 1910 and 1930. As the leading poet in the movement, Eliot brought about the break from the poetic tradition of the nineteenth century. Apart from some notable exceptions, such as Hopkins and Hardy, poetry in English had become degenerate in both taste and theme. It appealed to the imperialist prejudices of a smug, self-complacent audience, convinced of its own superiority in just about everything. Poetry flattered rather than educated.

Eliot's achievement, in both his poetry and his critical essays, was in founding new criteria of judgement on what constitutes poetry.

Similar revolutions were happening in the other arts. James Joyce revolutionised prose writing, as did Pablo Picasso painting and Igor Stravinsky music. The First World War (1914–1918) also helped. At first poetry was used for propaganda. Rupert Brooke's saccharine war sonnets were enthusiastically received. However, as the war dragged on public perception was forced to change, as Wilfred Owen and Siegfried Sassoon wrote of the revolting horrors of war. Owen insisted that poetry need not be beautiful, but it must be truthful.

One aspect of the revolution that Eliot effected was the introduction to English of a style of poetry that is known as 'Symbolism'. When he arrived at Oxford in 1914, Eliot brought with him a deep love and admiration for the French nineteenth-century symbolist poets. These included Charles Baudelaire and Jules Laforgue. Eliot's debt to these poets is extensive – from diction to creative remodelling of subject matter, from tone to phrasing.

Eliot adapted from Charles Baudelaire (1821–1867) the poetical possibilities of addressing 'the more sordid aspects of the modern metropolis'. Examples of these are seen in 'Preludes' and in 'The Love Song of J. Alfred Prufrock'.

From Laforgue (1860–1887) he adopted a tone of mocking irony and despair. Eliot said he owed more to Laforgue 'than to any poet in any language'. Laforgue was a technical innovator. He pioneered *'vers libre'*, or free verse, which Eliot also adopted. *'Vers libre'* is verse freed from rigid, conventional forms of regular rhyme and rhythm. Instead Laforgue, and Eliot, use odd or irregular rhyme with varying rhythms to enhance both the theme and tone of the verse. Examples of these can be found throughout Eliot's poetry.

Laforgue also developed a sort of dramatic monologue, a stream-of-consciousness or interior monologue, as it is better known. Eliot adapted this method also, as can be seen in 'The Love Song of J. Alfred Prufrock' and 'Journey of the Magi'. However, Eliot developed the method to a further degree in the distancing and the self-mockery of the dramatic personae of his poems.

Eliot also admired many of the seventeenth-century English poets, seeing in them the emotional intensity and intellectual precision he found in the French Symbolists. Eliot saw a similarity between the seventeenth and twentieth centuries, in that both centuries experienced the disintegration of old traditions and the arrival of new learning. He particularly admired what came to be known as the Metaphysical Poets and felt that John Donne was closer to him in spirit than most other English poets. Eliot shares with Donne an often robust style, with colloquial language mingling with intellectual language. Like Donne, Eliot's poems contain a sense of argument, unexpected juxtapositions and eclectic references, demanding an intelligent attention from the reader. Even a cursory glance at 'A Game of Chess' or 'The Four Quartets' will confirm this.

However, it was the Italian poet Dante (1265–1321) who was the greatest influence upon Eliot. He saw Dante as greater even than Shakespeare, seeing the Italian poet expressing 'deeper degrees of degradation and higher degrees of exaltation'. The presence of Dante in Eliot's verse extends beyond the epigraph in 'The Love Song of J. Alfred Prufrock' to a recreation of the whole experience of his verse. The hell or purgatory in which both Prufrock and the women in 'A Game of Chess' live reflects this.

Eliot first met Ezra Pound in 1915, another great American poet and critic, who subsequently had a profound influence on Eliot's development both as a poet and as a literary critic. It was through Pound that Eliot came to be influenced by the so-called imagist school of poetry. Imagism promoted the use of common speech in poetry, a complete freedom in subject choice, accuracy, concentration and precise description. The reader need only look at the 'Preludes', 'Rannoch, by Glencoe' or 'Aunt Helen' to see how true all of this is of Eliot's poetry.

THEMES

As said above, Eliot lived in a period that saw the disintegration of old traditions and beliefs and the arrival of new learning and new experiences. As a poet then, he had to find a different way of addressing the new. Pound's famous phrase 'Make it new' was a rallying cry to those who wished to tackle themes relevant to their own experience. For Eliot, this was as much a recovery of a lost tradition in poetry as it was a revolution. Thus we find in Eliot's poetry a *contemplation of the past and an examination of the new* in relation to the past. 'Journey of the Magi' is one such poem.

While Eliot made poetry new, it didn't mean that he approved of everything that was new in contemporary life. On the contrary, there was his belief that much in modern life was a betrayal of civilised values. His poetry is full of his sense of disgust for urban society. 'The Love Song of J. Alfred Prufrock' and 'Preludes' are two such poems. *Modern urban life*, for Eliot, *is an emotional and cultural wasteland*, a world of thoughtless self-gratification and deadening purposelessness. The modern city is a symbol of the nightmare of human decadence. This view is explored in particular in 'Preludes' and 'A Game of Chess'.

This particular notion of *meaningless existence* expands into the wider theme of *death-in-life* and *life-in-death*. Twentieth-century man may be condemned to a living death, but redemption can be achieved. For Eliot this is the answer to how we should live: that is, we need to die to the old life in order to be born into the new. Humanity needs to *journey in search of its spiritual well-being*. This may involve *suffering*, but the cure is at hand. The 'Journey of the Magi', 'Usk' and 'East Coker IV' explore these themes. To redeem itself and construct a new life for itself, humanity must face a painful readjustment of its values and attitudes. Death accompanies a new Birth. Joy follows.

Much of the above reflects Eliot's own *spiritual journey* and his conversion to Anglicanism in 1927. Anglicanism, or more particularly Anglo-Catholicism, appealed to his need for orthodox theological dogma and for an emotional, mystical spirituality.

His conversion to Anglicanism was also a consolation to him during the nightmare that was his first marriage. This too was a living death. His marriage with Vivienne Haigh-Wood may explain the most persistent *personal theme* underlying Eliot's poetry i.e. the *sexual*, whose erotic note is as often as not linked with regret, disappointment, frustration and longing. 'The Love Song of J. Alfred Prufrock' explores this theme most strongly. At the centre of Prufrock's purgatory is a *confusion between love and sexual gratification*. Prufrock is both attracted to and repulsed by women. The theme of *appearance and reality*, or the *real and the ideal*, is explored in Prufrock's love-song, where his fear of women who 'fix you with a formulated phrase' is contrasted with his idealised vision of womanhood as 'sea-girls wreathed with seaweed red and brown'.

Eliot's *portrayal of women* is said to be critically and tortuously realistic, reflecting his attitude towards *human relationships* in general. The girl in the 'Preludes' is physically repulsive and, while the woman in the first part of 'A Game of Chess' may be attractive, she is an emotional wreck. The second part of 'A Game of Chess' explores the tragedy resulting from casual relationships. Miss Helen Slingsby, in 'Aunt Helen', is his 'maiden aunt', whose social foibles suggest a fastidious but repressed character and whose mores are flamboyantly rejected by the behaviour of the footman and maid after her death.

For Eliot, though, it is only the *beauty of divine love* that makes sense of all human relationships. In the 'Preludes' he declares:

> I am moved by fancies . . .
> The notion of some infinitely gentle,
> Infinitely suffering thing.

'The Journey of the Magi' too can be seen as an exploration of divine love or as a struggle to understand the Incarnation of Christ, that moment when divine love made itself manifest.

This theme of *divine love* is made all the more clear in 'East Coker IV', where Christ himself is seen as suffering and dying in order to be reborn. Divine love is linked inextricably with the theme of a journey through suffering to a rebirth.

The Incarnation took place in a moment of time, a moment when historical time and the timelessness of God's eternity met. Eliot's exploration of *time* is central to his poems. It is part of his effort to make sense of life. This is seen in 'Journey of the Magi'.

In 'The Love Song of J. Alfred Prufrock', time is seen as inexorably repetitive, a process which leads ultimately to decay. In the 'Preludes' time is a burden, whose rhythmic patterns beat out the tedium of urban life. Time destroys 'Aunt Helen's' passion for order and restraint, while the result of man's behaviour in times past is seen in 'Rannoch, by Glencoe', where both man and animals are stuck in the wretchedness of history.

IMAGERY, SYMBOLISM AND ALLUSION

While all of the above are dealt with in specific detail in the discussion of the individual poems, a few general points may be useful for the student also.

Eliot's use of *imagery is eclectic*, that is he drew inspiration from a wide tableau of human experience and did not limit himself to nature as a source, something which had become so much a part of the later Romantics. Under French influence and his admiration for seventeenth-century English poets, Eliot trawled widely to ensure an intellectual sharpness and an emotional intensity in his poems.

Much of the meaning and the power of Eliot's poetry lie in his use of images and symbols. *Sordid, seedy images of city life* appear again and again, from 'The

Love Song of J. Alfred Prufrock' to 'Preludes' to 'A Game of Chess'. Even in 'Journey of the Magi', cities are seen as 'hostile'. Such use of significant imagery becomes, with repetition, a symbol. It evokes particular ideas and emotions. This is in keeping with Eliot's rather notorious view that poetry communicates before it is understood. Thus the suggestiveness of imagery and symbolism become part of the excitement of discovery when reading Eliot's poetry.

Similarly *journeys, a street or road are common images* throughout Eliot's poetry. These are seen in 'Journey of the Magi', 'Preludes', 'Usk' and 'Rannoch, by Glencoe', for example. These images also become symbolic, evoking Eliot's search or quest for meaning in life, culminating in his achievement of a satisfactory religious perspective.

However, individual images can also be symbolic. Eliot, for example, uses *animal imagery* to reflect the human in its non-thinking, non-rational state. Hence the use of the crab image/symbol in 'The Love Song of J. Alfred Prufrock'. The 'crow' and 'the patient stag' play similar roles in 'Rannoch, by Glencoe'.

Similarly, Eliot's use of *body parts as images*, as in 'Preludes', 'The Love Song of J. Alfred Prufrock' and 'A Game of Chess' becomes symbolic of the depersonalisation, stereotyping and conformity of modern urban society.

Similarly also, the *images of clocks* and the references to *time*, from 'Aunt Helen' to 'Preludes' to 'A Game of Chess' and 'The Love Song of J. Alfred Prufrock', can become a symbol of individual transience and the urgency for renewal.

The student should be particularly aware of Eliot's abrupt transitions in imagery and of his use of images other than visual ones. 'Preludes', for example, explores *aural, tactile and olfactory images* in quickly changing, cinematic-style sequences.

Eliot is the most erudite of poets. He was widely read in *everything from literature to history, from psychology to anthropology, from psychology to philosophy*. This is in keeping with his passion not only for self-discovery, but also for discovering the nature of twentieth-century man. Hence his use of allusion is his way of exploring intellectual traditions and expressing himself more precisely.

In this way, his use of allusion is not just an ostentatious *reference to literary history*, for example, but is a way of making a tradition alive again, while also focusing the present situation in that tradition. So, his epigraph in 'The Love Song of J. Alfred Prufrock' both recalls Dante's work and places Prufrock in an urban Hell. Thus, his allusions universalise his themes and the situations in which his characters' personae exist.

Sometimes his allusions come in the form of more *indirect quotation*, as in his reference in 'The Love Song of J. Alfred Prufrock' to Andrew Marvell's poem

'To His Coy Mistress', or in his references to Hamlet and Lazarus. *Direct quotation* of Shakespeare also takes place in 'A Game of Chess', while indirectly Thomas Middleton, Virgil and Milton are alluded to. All such references and allusions help to build up the picture which tells us some universal truth.

The detailed notes on each poem explain the significance of these allusions and references.

VERSE STRUCTURE

In keeping with the French Symbolists' *'vers libre'*, or free verse, Eliot broke with the regular forms and structures of his immediate predecessors. The suggestiveness of his imagery and symbols demanded that the structures of his verse should be equally suggestive.

If Eliot's imagery often consists of *abrupt transitions*, so also does his verse structure. The structure often reflects both themes and imagery. Thus the *irregular juxtaposition of lines of different length* in 'The Love Song of J. Alfred Prufrock' reflects the agitated nature of Prufrock, while the regularity of lines 23–34 reflects the incantatory tone of the lines. Similarly, the *short lines 33–35* in 'Journey of the Magi' reflect the anxiety of the magus that no part of his narrative should be overlooked.

Eliot also composes his lines to suggest *the natural speech patterns and rhythms of contemporary speech*. This is particularly true of the pub scene, which opens in line 139 of 'A Game of Chess'. The direct speech rhythms of the female narrator give a sense of immediacy to the tone and themes. Into these speech patterns Eliot introduces *colloquialisms and even slang*. The lines do indeed reflect speech patterns, but they also satisfy a metrical pattern.

At times Eliot *repeats particular words and phrases to give a prayer-like or incantatory tone*. This may also effect a reflective mood. This is seen in 'Journey of the Magi' with the strong repetition of 'And'. The strained repetitiveness of lines in 'A Game of Chess' and in 'The Love Song of J. Alfred Prufrock' reflects the nervous tension of the speakers.

Rhyme is used for particular effects in Eliot's poetry. The jingling rhyme of the couplet referring to Michelangelo in 'The Love Song of J. Alfred Prufrock' reflects the shallowness of the women and the mock-heroic tone. Rhyme is used in the 'Preludes' to create a *lyrical effect* in keeping with its title. Both the rhythm and rhyme use in 'East Coker IV' are 'reinventions' of Medieval English verse, which W.B. Yeats, for one, believed helped 'to prolong the moment of contemplation'.

Eliot's interest in music is seen not only in many of the titles of his poems – e.g. 'The Love Song of J. Alfred Prufrock', 'Preludes', 'The Four Quartets' – but *in the very structures of the poems and his use of language*. Some of the verses of 'The Love Song of J. Alfred Prufrock' are composed of single sentences, whose repetitiveness not only reflects the tedium of Prufrock's life but gives a symphonic effect. The heavy stressed *rhythm* of the 'Preludes' suggests the fatigue of the city's inhabitants, while the lyrical sibilant 'S' sounds of lines 9 and 10 of 'Journey of the Magi' evoke the sensuality of the life being left behind. The robust rhythm of 'Usk' suggests the invigorating landscape and underscores the commanding authority of the imperative verbs. The musicality of 'East Coker IV' has been referred to already.

Eliot – a dramatic poet

As can be seen in his poems, Eliot excels in creating characters whose situations reflect the universal condition of man.

Eliot's greatest *verse drama* is, without doubt, 'Murder in the Cathedral', but many of his poems are verse dramas in themselves. The use of *internal monologue*, or stream-of-consciousness speech, is a particularly effective device in *creating drama* in verse.

'The Love Song of J. Alfred Prufrock' has all the elements of drama. The main character is in *conflict*, within himself and with society in general. In his monologue he develops his conflict and demonstrates his *character*, while also creating both the characters and speech of others. Characters are placed in *particular times and places* where the drama unfolds. A *plot*, or storyline, is developed and comes to a conclusion. The reader (or audience) becomes interested in the fate of this character – one who reflects the reader's own predicament, perhaps. Overall, *dialogue* is either direct or implied, advancing the plot and enhancing the reader's understanding of the character.

In this way, 'Aunt Helen', 'Preludes', 'A Game of Chess' and 'Journey of the Magi' are also verse dramas. The pub scene in 'A Game of Chess' is a dramatic reflection of the world in miniature. The student may enjoy reading it out loud in 'an appropriate accent'.

Many of Eliot's poems are 'spoken' by created personae or else detached observers. The latter, as in 'Preludes', has been called a cinematic style. For the student interested in film these may prove especially rewarding. It may also be worth noting how many of Eliot's characters are grotesque in the literary sense. In Prufrock, Miss Helen Slingsby and the women in 'A Game of Chess', Eliot has created characters as memorable as those of Shakespeare or Dickens.

Questions

1. Write a personal response to the poetry of T.S. Eliot. Support your answer by reference to the poetry of Eliot that you have studied.
2. 'The poetry of T.S. Eliot appeals to modern readers for various reasons.' Write an introduction to Eliot's poetry in which you suggest what these reasons might be.

3. Imagine you have been asked to give a reading of T.S. Eliot's poetry to your class. What poems would you choose and why would you choose them?
4. Suppose someone told you that he/she found T.S. Eliot's poetry too obscure. Write a response to this person in which you outline your understanding of Eliot's poetry.
5. What impression did the poetry of T.S. Eliot make on you as a reader? In your answer you may wish to address the following:
   - your sense of the poet's personality
   - his major themes
   - the poet's use of imagery and language
   - the poem/poems that appealed to you most.
6. 'Eliot's major achievement is as a verse dramatist.'
   Write out a speech you would make to your class on the above topic.

Bibliography

Gardner, Helen, *The Art of T.S. Eliot*, Faber and Faber: London 1985.

Moody, A.David, (editor), *The Cambridge Companion to T.S. Eliot*, Cambridge: Cambridge University Press 1994.

Braybrooke, Neville, (editor), *T.S. A Symposium for His Seventieth Birthday*, London: Garnstone Press 1958.

Donoghue, Denis, *Words Alone: The Poet T.S. Eliot*, Yale University Press 2000.

Steed, C.K., *The New Poetic: Yeats to Eliot*, Pelican Books 1967.

Herbert, Michael, *T.S. Eliot Selected Poems*, York Notes, Longman York Press 1982.

Southam, B.C., *A Student's Guide to The Selected Poems of T.S. Eliot*, London: Faber and Faber 1968.

Press, John, *The Chequer'd Shade: Reflections on Obscurity in Poetry*, London: Oxford University Press 1963.

Leavis, F.R., *New Bearings in English Poetry*, Pelican Books 1972.

---

* If the 'water-mill' represents Christ then 'darkness' could represent death, which Christ conquers by the Resurrection. On the other hand the water-mill could represent the superior forces of those in the world who put Christ to death.

5   Patrick KAVANAGH

John McCarthy

Kavanagh Overview

Kavanagh was born on 21 October 1904, in the village of Inniskeen, Co. Monaghan. His father was a shoemaker and had a small farm of land. Kavanagh received only primary school education and at the age of thirteen, he became an apprentice shoemaker. He gave it up 15 months later, admitting that he didn't make one wearable pair of boots. For the next 20 years Kavanagh would work on the family farm, before moving to Dublin in 1939. From his early years on, he was a man who was out of place. When in Monaghan Kavanagh was a dreamer in a world of realists who were concerned with what seemed to him to be the mundanities of life. In Dublin he stood out as the man up from the bog, who didn't understand the complexities of city life. He was seen as gauche and unrefined. Ironically in Monaghan he was seen as effeminate for having an interest in poetry.

Kavanagh's interest in literature and poetry marked him out as different from other people in his local place. In a society that was insular and agricultural, a man's worth was measured by the straightness of the furrow he could plough, rather than the lines of poetry he could write. Kavanagh's first attempts to become a published poet resulted in the publication of some poems in a local newspaper in the early 1930s, and in the publishing of his autobiographical novel, *Tarry Flynn*, in 1939. Urged by his brother Peter, who was a Dublin-based teacher, Kavanagh moved to the city to establish himself as a writer. At that time, the Dublin Literary Society was dominated by an educated Anglo-Irish group with whom Kavanagh had nothing in common; among them were Oliver St John Gogarty and Douglas Wylie. They saw Kavanagh as a country bumpkin and referred to him as 'that Monaghan boy'.

Kavanagh's early years in Dublin were unproductive as he struggled for recognition. In 1947 his first major collection, 'A Soul for Sale', was published. These poems were the product of his Monaghan youth. In the early 1950s Kavanagh and his brother Peter published a weekly newspaper called 'Kavanagh's Weekly'; it failed because the editorial viewpoint was too narrow. In 1954 Kavanagh became embroiled in an infamous court case. He accused 'The Leader' newspaper of slander. The newspaper decided to contest the case and employed the former Taoiseach, John A. Costello, as their defence counsel;

Kavanagh decided to prosecute the case himself, and he was destroyed by Costello. The court case dragged on for over a year and Kavanagh's health began to fail. In 1955 he was diagnosed as having lung cancer and had a lung removed; he survived, and the event was a major turning point in his life and career. In 1958 he published 'Come Dance with me Kitty Stobling'. In 1959 he was appointed by John A. Costello to the faculty of English in UCD. His lectures were popular, but often irrelevant to the course. In the early 1960s he visited Britain and the USA; in 1965 he married Katherine Maloney. He died in 1967 from an attack of bronchitis. Kavanagh's reputation as a poet is based on the lyrical quality of his work, his mastery of language and form and his ability to transform the ordinary and the banal into something of significance. He is an acute observer of things and situations, and this allows him to make things that may seem ordinary and unimportant into something deserving of a place in poetry.

He is constantly using his work to make sense of the natural world, be it in Dublin or Monaghan. More importantly, Kavanagh is always trying to assess his own place in this world. He often approaches a poem from a point of doubt, where he is unsure about where he belongs, and uses the poem to come to a resolution. The best example of this is in the poem 'Epic'. He is also trying to praise God and Nature in his poems. Indeed his Monaghan poems are not so much about the area, but about how it affects him and his work. It would not be unfair to say that Kavanagh is very self-obsessed. But on the other hand, he is writing about what he knows best.

Technique and Style

LANGUAGE

In attempting to create a sense of the mystery and magic of a child's mind, Kavanagh's use of language is a vital ingredient in his work. He uses words in a new fashion. He fuses words together, such as 'clay-minted' and most famously 'leafy-with-love'. These phrases and words give extra energy to his poetry and provide it with vigour.

IMAGERY

Kavanagh's use of imagery is a very important aspect of his language. In 'Advent' he alludes to the Nativity: '. . . old stables where Time begins'. In 'Inniskeen Road' he refers to Alexander Selkirk. Colloquial language is an intrinsic element of Kavanagh's style. His phraseology is conversational and many of his phrases owe their origin to his Monaghan background: 'Among simple decent men too who barrow dung . . .'; 'he stared at me half eyed'; '. . . every blooming thing'.

Structure – Form

The poems on the course display Kavanagh's ability in the sonnet form, which is a structural feature of 'Inniskeen Road', 'Advent', 'Lines Written . . .' and Canal Bank Walk'. In 'Inniskeen Road', Kavanagh combines features of the Petrarchan and Shakespearean forms. Stanzaic pattern reflects the Petrarchan subdivision of a sonnet into an octet and a sestet. In the octet a picture is painted by the poet and the problems are posed. The poet's own personal response is contained in the sestet. The opening stanza can be subdivided into two quatrains, each containing a separate picture of Monaghan life. The sestet also can be divided into a quatrain and couplet, therefore mirroring the Shakespearean division into three quatrains followed by a rhyming couplet. The rhyme scheme of the poem is also Shakespearean: *abab, cdcd, efef, gg*. 'Advent' represents Kavanagh's particular use of the sonnet form. The poem is an amalgam of two sonnets, and the stanzaic pattern is neither Petrarchan nor Shakespearean. The opening two stanzas each contain seven lines, with the third stanza representing an entire sonnet. The division of the sonnet into two septets is unusual and Kavanagh formulates a rhyme scheme to parallel this: *aabbccbd, aab, aacc*. Stanza three is again different as Kavanagh reverts to the Shakespearean rhyming technique: *abab, cded, fgfg, hh*. The thought pattern of the third stanza follows that set out by the opening two stanzas, with a natural pause occurring at the end of the seventeenth line. The reason why Kavanagh does not create a fourth stanza is that the rhythm of the third one reflects the excitement that he associates with having rediscovered '. . . the luxury of a child's soul'. The three stanzas in the poem reflect the three stages in Kavanagh's bid to regain this position – penance, forgiveness, grace.

'Canal Bank Walk' is written in the traditional 14-line sonnet form with no stanzaic separation. In this poem, Kavanagh combines both the Petrarchan and Shakespearean sonnets, using the same methods as in 'Inniskeen Road'.

'Lines Written . . .' is fashioned completely in the Petrarchan style. Both the thought pattern and the rhyming scheme follow an octet–sestet sublimation.

'Memory . . .' and 'On Raglan Road' are reminiscent of ballad technique in that they each feature four-line stanzas; however, Kavanagh doesn't stick rigidly to the rhyming schemes of the ballad, displaying again his ability to individualise a fashion or feature.

Religion

Religion is a dominant feature in Kavanagh's poetry, both as a theme and as a source of imagery. Religion features thematically in 'Advent', 'Canal Bank Walk' and in a minor way in 'Stony Grey Soil'. 'Advent' derives from religion in both its theme and its main source of imagery. The theme of the poem is penance–forgiveness–grace, which reflects the Catholic church's seasons of

Advent, the Nativity and the beginning of the new church year. Kavanagh formulates his wish to return to the state of innocence as a child within the imagery of religion, using original sin to represent acquired knowledge, penance as a main act of contrition and the grace of the forgiven soul as the newly required state of innocence. In 'Canal Bank Walk' the theme is one of redemption reflecting baptism, as Kavanagh draws analogies between the waters of the baptismal font and the water of the canal.

Rural and urban

Although Kavanagh arrived in Dublin in 1939, leaving behind his sixteen acres of stony grey soil, it was not until the mid-1950s that his adopted city provided the environmental background to his work. The summer of 1955 and the banks of the Grand Canal in Dublin are the time and place which moved Kavanagh to write 'Canal Bank Walk' and 'Lines Written . . .'.

Kavanagh's attitude to the environment changed dramatically following his operation for lung cancer. He said, 'As a poet I was born in or about 1955, the place of my birth being the banks of the Grand Canal.' This new appreciation of the environment, his vision of Eden, is evident in his novel *Tarry Flynn*, where he wrote: 'O the rich beauty of the weeds in the ditches, Tarry's heart cried: the lush Nettles and Docks and tuffs of grass. Life pouring out in critical abundance.' In the novel he also wrote, 'Without ambition, without desire, the beauty of the world pared in thought his unresting mind.' These two sentences describe exactly the moods of Kavanagh in 'Canal Bank Walk' and 'Lines Written . . .' Here the environment is glorified in a pantheistic manner. Kavanagh uses hyperbole and many neologisms in an attempt to demonstrate the magnificence of Nature, as experienced by the innocent mind of a child or of the poet reformed to the state of grace. The opposing attitudes expressed by Kavanagh to the environments of Monaghan and Dublin reflect more on his state of mind than on the environments themselves. In 1963 he did recognise the beauty of the Monaghan countryside:

> Thirty-years before, Shank Duff's water-fill could of done the trick for me, but I was too thick to realise it.

Bibliography

Primary sources

Ploughman and other poems	1936
The Green Fool	1938
The Great Hunger	1942

A Soul for Sale	1947
Tarry Flynn	1948
Recent Poems	1958
Come Dance with me Kitty Stobling	1960
Self Portrait	1964
The Complete Poems	1972 (Posthumous)

SECONDARY SOURCES

John Nemo	*Patrick Kavanagh*
Alan Warner	*Clay is the Word*
Antoinette Quinn	*Patrick Kavanagh: Born Again Romantic*
Peter Kavanagh	*Sacred Keeper*
Anthony Cronin	*Dead as Doornails*

Inniskeen Road: July Evening

Text of poem: New Explorations Anthology page 146

Kavanagh self-visualises himself in this poem. The poem is all about him, even though he spends over half the poem appearing to be concerned with others. In the poem Kavanagh attempts to describe where he sees his position in society; this question is central to all of his work. His position is at best on the fringes of the society he chooses, and at worst completely outside it and isolated. Another question central to Kavanagh's work is: where does he want to be? Is this role, as the outsider looking in, one that he has decided suits him? Does he need the tension of being different to stimulate his work?

The poem may or may not be based on a real event, but the first thing that Kavanagh does is make everything seem real. He does this by giving us real places and time. The poem's title presupposes a reality. It is 'Inniskeen Road', not a road in Monaghan. It is a 'July Evening', not some time in his youth. Kavanagh seems to be looking for sympathy in this poem, and by making things real he adds to this emotional appeal. He even mention's 'Billy Brennan's barn', which is a real place owned by a real person. The premise is that if Kavanagh is using fact here, then everything else that he says must also be true.

In fact the truth may matter little, and what may be most important in this poem is how Kavanagh sees himself and how he wants to be seen.

This part is simple. To Kavanagh, he is '*l'étranger*'. He is the outsider who can observe his own community's actions from the inside, yet still look objectively. The major question for a reader is, 'Is Kavanagh objective enough?' The answer to this question must be 'no'. Even when he's outside the action of the poem, his observing is still central to the poem.

WHAT DOES KAVANAGH SEE?

He sees society passing him by. He sees local people passing him by on the way to a dance. They don't look at him or stop to talk to him. They are in 'twos and threes'; he is on his own. They are on their way to something too important. This is a regular occurrence.

> There's a dance in Billy Brennan's barn tonight.

This is not *the* dance. It's just *a* dance. It is a regular thing that he takes no part of. It appears he never will. The alliteration in this line suggests optimism and a childlike sense of fun, and these sit uneasily with Kavanagh. The alliteration of the B's is inapposite with the spat-out sounds of desperation that come in the final stanza.

Kavanagh sees a means of communication that he does not understand. He hears 'half-talk' and 'wink and elbow language'. This frustrates him. He is not allowed to be part of this society. There is even a hint of knowingness and sexuality in this way that people are communicating.

As full of people and life and communication as the first quatrain was, the second quatrain is quickly depopulated. Kavanagh spends four lines telling us that there is nobody to be seen. Even the coded language he complained about in lines three and four is gone for there is:

> . . . not
> A footfall tapping secrecies of stone.

As much as he complained about the people passing him by, he seems to feel that it was better than the silence.

This quatrain is full of the language of spy movies. It is almost like a scene from the movie *The Third Man*, with its silence and secrets and footfalls and shadows. Again there is a frustrated isolation evident here. Kavanagh is convinced that he is incapable of decoding the language and the nuances that these people use.

In the sestet, Kavanagh gets to the nub of the matter. The people that populated the octet are gone and now he turns to himself. He addresses his audience in an aggressive and prosaic manner. He is direct and uncompromising in the first two lines. He then makes direct reference to a much older poem by William Cowper, 'Verses supposed to be written by Alexander Selkirk'. Cowper's Selkirk has the following to say:

> I am monarch of all I survey.
> My right there is none to dispute;
> From the centre all round to the sea,
> I am lord of the fowl and the brute.
> O solitude! Where are the charms

> That sages have seen in thy face?
> Better dwell in the midst of alarms
> Than reign in this horrible place.

Kavanagh takes these sentiments and adapts them to his own situation. He is more concerned with the bogs and farms of county Monaghan than with a deserted island where Selkirk was supposed to have been abandoned. He nevertheless shares the sentiment that his 'gift' brings bitter fruits with it. Is this too extreme a metaphor? Selkirk was abandoned and left on a deserted island. In circumstances beyond his control, he had to live the life of a hermit on a deserted island, with no hope of communicating with anybody for years. Kavanagh is in self-enforced exile, unless you submit to his own theory that he has no choice but to be a poet, and to be a poet meant exiling himself from the society that he felt closest to. The irony is that he still needs to write about these people and include them in his poetry. There is a complete contradiction between trying to stay away from these people and still writing about them centrally.

He finishes his rant with the wonderful pun on the curse 'blooming thing'. The double meanings are a euphemism for 'bloody' and another word for 'growing'. If he says 'bloody', you can understand this: he is angry at his exile. If he is talking about 'growth', then he is saying that there is room for growth in a land where there should not be hope for any type of growth, an area 'Of banks and stones . . . '; maybe this is like his poetry, an area were he sees little of hope, but that little amount of hope is enough for a poem to grow.

Language, Structure and Sounds

Kavanagh works within the confines of the sonnet and this seems to suit his purpose well. The structure moves from the first quartet, which is well populated, to the second quartet where everybody is now off the road and in the barn, presumably enjoying themselves. The sestet brings us Kavanagh and allows him to pontificate on what all this means to him.

The rhyming sequence is *abab cdcd efefgg*. The effect of this is a highly exalted poetic sense. By working with a Shakespearean structure, he seems to imply a sense of accuracy and truth, that everything that is reported is correct.

The sonnet's sense of false balance is also used well. There is no 'I' in the first eight lines, yet it dominates the sestet.

The prominent sounds in the poem suggest anger and bitterness. The heavily prominent 'B' sound at the beginning is spat out like an unwanted taste by his use of alliteration. Importantly, he brings this sound back right at the end of the poem, when he writes about '. . . every blooming thing.'

Epic

Text of poem: New Explorations Anthology page 148

This poem has a grandiose title, a grandiose first line and an even more grandiose last sentence. Kavanagh's favourite poetic theme has always been poetry and the role of the poet. He is constantly self-conscious. Often in his poetry he will use a specific real event from his own life or the lives of the people who surrounded him in order to make a more direct point about poetry, the job of the poet or aesthetics.

In this poem he uses a real incident: a row between two families over a plot of land. In the notes to the collected poems, Kavanagh's brother Peter gives the background to the incident:

> I recall the row over the half a rood of rock in 1938. The row was temporarily settled when the contestants agreed to arbitration by the local schoolmaster who was also unofficial surveyor. Neither side was fully satisfied and the row smouldered for some years. Today all the surrounding farms including the disputed rock are owned by the same farmer.

Kavanagh starts the poem in what might seem to be an ironic mood. Words such as 'important places' and 'great events' can hardly be appropriate when referring to something as trivial as a dispute between two families over a 'half a rood of rock' or 'iron stones'. But when relativity kicks in, then these retrospectively trivial occurrences can seem gigantic to the protagonists. This, according to Kavanagh, is the stuff of poetry. This is where his concerns are, because this is where his people's concerns are. The 'Munich Bother' might as well have been happening on another planet as far as the Duffys and the McCabes were concerned. It would be easy for Kavanagh to mock or patronise these people, but he doesn't. Or at least he doesn't any more. Kavanagh admits that he was:

> . . . inclined
> To lose my faith in Ballyrush and Gortin

But he was inspired by a fellow artist, the great Greek poet Homer, whose 'Ghost came whispering to my mind'. Kavanagh says that if it was good enough for Homer and Greece, then it must be good enough for himself and the parishes of County Monaghan.

In the action of the poem, Kavanagh sets up a drama between the two sides and reports about it directly to us. He even tells us what each side said. The fierceness of the dispute is typified by the warlike declaration of 'Damn your soul'.

He shows us one of the protagonists stepping on the disputed land and declaring a new border between the families – the iron stones being like Hitler's Iron Cross.

It then looks as if he is delving into farce, as he compares this dispute with one of the twentieth century's most important events, the beginning of World War Two. He even dismisses this event as 'the Munich bother'.

When he finally decides on which one was more important, he says he has changed his mind. He tells us that once he dismissed the local matter, but then after he did some reading of Homer's 'Iliad' (and more importantly, E.V. Rieu's biography of Homer), he came to change his mind.

In Kavanagh's poem 'On Looking into E.V. Rieu's Homer' he describes the Greek poet's vision:

> For only the half-god can see
> The Immortal in things mortal.

And later he observes of Homer:

> The intensity that radiated from
> The Far Field Rock – you afterwards denied –
> Was the half-god seeing his half-brothers
> Joking on the fabulous mountain-side.

In 'Epic' he is talking to Homer to justify the idea that nothing is beyond a poet's telling of it. A literary classic may begin in a simple local event, but it is the poet's telling of it that makes it immortal. It is not the event but the reporting of the event that gives immortality. By proposing this thesis Kavanagh makes this not a poem about a local dispute, but a poem about poetry itself.

Kavanagh's ego comes through twice. First of all he shows no shyness in comparing himself with Homer. Remember that this poem was published in the early 1940s, before Kavanagh's reputation was in any way established in the way it is today. To compare himself with one of the most important poets of all time seems incredibly presumptuous. He also seems to compare a poet with a God in this poem and in the other Homer poem. He says that a poet is a creator of worlds. There may be some sense to this; a poet does have control of the world that he reports on. He is allowed to influence his readers' thoughts. It seems that Kavanagh is acknowledging the importance of this role. He is saying that what a poet reports on will last and become important.

At the end of the poem the reader is left to wonder whether the events are important or not, because Kavanagh uses those events to make a point about poetry itself, rather than the events the poem is describing.

Shancoduff

Text of poem: New Explorations Anthology page 150

[Note: This poem is also prescribed for Ordinary Level 2007 exam]

According to the critic Antoinette Quinn, 'Shancoduff is a north-facing hill farm depicted at its wintry worst, frostbound, starved of grass, swept by sleety winds.' Yet this is a love poem to it.

Kavanagh had a love–hate relationship with the countryside of his youth. One of his most famous poems is 'Stony Grey Soil'. In that poem the poet accused the area where he was reared of burgling 'his bank of youth'. He describes the area as being one that is lifeless and soulless, and he questions how he managed to survive in a place where even plant life struggled to maintain an existence. Yet in this poem his attitude is different; he is more interested in finding the good in his 'black hills'. He turns any notion of something negative into something positive. He transforms the faults of Shancoduff in the same way that a lover transforms his partner's faults into something to be loved. The immediate question that must be asked is: Why would anybody write a love-poem to Shancoduff?

The answer must be because the hills are his. He claims ownership four times. He calls them '*My* black hills' twice in the first verse, and then '*My* hills' and '*my* Alps' in the second. Possession of this land is obviously very important to Kavanagh. After all, they are 'eternal'. Shancoduff will last long after he has gone and more importantly, they will still be there after the people who sneer at them are gone. He also personifies them. They are given a personality like a lover would have. The hills can 'look', they are 'incurious', they are 'happy', they 'hoard'.

Kavanagh relishes their drabness. Anything that might be confused as being something negative can be construed into a positive: for example, the fact that the hills are so incurious or inactive that they can't even be bothered to look at the sun. This is seen as a good thing when Kavanagh compares it with the fate of Lot's wife, who was turned into a pillar of salt for looking back as she left Sodom and Gomorrah.

Kavanagh puts a lot of emphasis on the local place names. He lists them with pride: Glassdrummond, Rocksavage, Featherna Bush; these are as important as the Alps. The names themselves have mythic qualities. They sound tough and treacherous. They have a resonance of something from an action movie, in which a hero stands proud above the hills. They all have a grandness granted to them by being multisyllabic.

Kavanagh's own importance in the poem is also highlighted here as the person who has:

>   . . . climbed the Matterhorn
> with a sheaf of hay for three perishing calves.

This act itself seems heroic, as if he had climbed the most dangerous mountain face in the world – whereas all he has done is walk up a hill to feed the cows. This use of hyperbole shows the love that Kavanagh has for this place. The rebellious nature of the hills is also shown as they refuse to conform to the usual structures of nature. They are oblivious to the changes in the seasons and the weather. Their immortality is stressed by the fact that they are unchanged by the travails of time Springtime cannot catch up with them as his

> . . . hills hoard the bright shillings of March
> While the sun searches in every pocket.

The poem turns at this point; the poet has come to the realisation, albeit after being told, that his mountains are not the glorious thing of beauty that he may have thought they were. The farmers who are in a more sheltered, wealthier place sneer at him. Even though his hills are personified with their 'rushy beards', nobody else declares them worth looking after. When he is acknowledged as a poet, it is almost done as a form of derision. A poet may be someone who is seen as poor.

Kavanagh departs with a rhetorical question that is forced on him by the comments of the other men. This affects him deeply, just as if his wife or lover were to be described as ugly or disgusting. He asks himself: 'Is my heart not badly shaken?' The love that he felt for the hills is broken by the piece of reality forced on him.

The Great Hunger

Text of poem: New Explorations Anthology page 152

'The Great Hunger' could well be Kavanagh's most important work; the format of the poem is certainly the most unique and ambitious. One of Kavanagh's biggest influences (although their subject matter was often completely different) was the English poet W.H. Auden. Auden was one of the best and most frequent practitioners of the long poem. 'The Great Hunger' is quite different from Auden's dramatic poems, or his 'Letter to Lord Byron' or 'New Year Letter', which are meditations on a specific time. Even poets who were in turn influenced by Kavanagh, like John Montague and Seamus Heaney, knitted together a series of poems to make up 'The Rough Field' and 'Station Island' respectively. This long poem is almost divided as a novelist would divide a book into chapters, with different parts coming together to give us a more rounded view of the life, times and opinions of Patrick Maguire.

Kavanagh takes on a narrative structure in this poem. The narrative allows him to use a cinematic technique to develop the central character in the poem. 'The Great Hunger' is focalised completely around the character of Patrick Maguire. It allows us to see what he sees, feel what he feels and hear what he says and hears. However, it also allows us some time to look at Maguire objectively.

Kavanagh seems to be on a voyage of discovery in this poem, and he seems to be enjoying bringing his reader with him. He uses a 'cinematic technique' to do this, by helping the reader to visualise what's going on as it happens. He is always shifting the angle, even though we are constantly viewing the character of Maguire. In the middle of the first section he reaffirms this by imploring the reader to:

> Watch him, watch him, that man on a hill whose spirit
> Is a wet sack flapping about the knees of time,

This poem sees Kavanagh with his most negative attitude towards his own background. The poem begins with lifelessness and a sense of biblical foreboding where the Word is not made Flesh, a symbol of the beginning of Life. Instead all is turned to where Death exists. We are pointed to where the dead go; in Kavanagh's landscape we begin with a lack of life.

> Clay is the word and clay is the flesh.

It is already obvious that this terrain that Kavanagh is about to map out is one that sees little chance for hope. When we see the

> ... potato-gatherers like mechanised scare-crows move
> Along the side-fall of the hill –

it feels like being stuck in a purgatorial vision from Dante. Then Kavanagh gives his instruction and his despair as he asks:

> If we watch them an hour is there anything we can prove
> Of life as it is broken-backed over the Book
> Of Death?

There appears to be no hope in this landscape at all. There appears to be no sympathy between the inhabitants of the landscape, between wind and worms and frogs and seagulls. And then he gets to the question that must be asked: why write this poem? What is the point in examining this seemingly desolate terrain? He tells us that he is searching for the 'light of imagination'. He is searching for something worth searching for.

He finds what he is looking for in a character who seems different from the other bleak people who live on the terrain. The rest of this first section of the poem attempts to show us Patrick Maguire. Kavanagh promises us a view of his life:

> Till the last soul passively like a bag of wet clay
> Rolls down the side of the hill,

This life is in a terrain where accuracy and intent are dismissed, things seem to happen with routine – but if they don't, it doesn't seem to matter too much. Kavanagh litters this early part of the poem with places where the plough missed, dogs lie lazily and horses pull rusty ploughs. This languorous air seems to suit Maguire, or at least that's the impression that he likes to give. He shrugs off the idea that experience of a broader life would be preferable – but the narrator of the poem tells us differently when he tells us that Maguire 'pretended to his soul'. Maguire convinces himself that children would only get in his way and be a nuisance even more than crows are. There is a sense here of regret; that something is missing from his life.

Central to this is the idea that Maguire is married to the land. The land dominates his life: he is in love with it and he hates it. He is committed to it, but the commitment may be too much. It is causing a deficit in other areas of his life. The narrator shows us Maguire bent among the potato fields, turning over the clumps of root. He asks *the* most important question: 'What is he looking for there?' The answer tells us that Maguire is a man lost; a man who thinks he is in control of his own life and destiny, but isn't. We know this from his answer: 'He thinks it is a potato, but we know better . . .' This seems like condescension from the omniscient narrator, but we now get a chance to examine Maguire in his own voice. The narrator is almost saying to us, 'If you don't believe what I'm saying, then listen for yourself.'

At this point the narration changes to allow us to listen to Maguire. When we hear him speak, he sounds like a man in charge of his own affairs. He is giving instruction to his workers, he is ordering people to 'move', 'balance', 'pull', 'straddle'. He is a man in touch with Nature:

> The wind's over Brannagan's, now that means rain.

He is capable of planning for the future:

> And that's a job we'll have to do in December,

and capable of getting angry when he sees 'Cassidy's ass'.

So perhaps he is not the solitary stand-still figure that we saw in the first 40 lines. But if we believed that thesis, then the narrator brings us back to earth by putting Maguire back in the 'cloud-swung wind'. He is married to the land: a man who is living his life for the future not of his children, but of the crops that will grow in his fields even when he:

> Is spread in the bottom of a ditch under two coulters
> crossed in Christ's Name.

This poignant vision of his own future, as no future at all, is even more depressing with the symbol of the Cross being represented by two parts of a plough. There is also the element of martyrdom here. He has sacrificed his own life for the good of others.

We are shown his distance from a regular youth by the way he sees girls of his own age. If they laughed, they laughed at him. When they screamed, he regarded them as animals. He knew that life was showing him a difficult path ahead, and it seems that perhaps he was aiming for it.

The next piece, from lines 67 to 79, is probably the most harrowing of the poem. Maguire seems depressingly regretful here; he is not able to shake 'a knowing head | And pretend to his soul'. He acknowledges that he is trapped by his undying commitment to the land; he knows that there is no easy way out from here, but that perhaps there was a time when a way out was possible. He sighs in despair twice: 'O God if I had been wiser!' The only thing that lifts him temporarily from his despair is the knowledge that he could be part of a bigger picture, that he and his life are part of Nature and God's will, because 'God's truth is life', even the hardship that he has to endure. The trick that Maguire has learned is to find ways of coping with Nature. He has taught himself compensatory skills, such as when to avoid life's obstacles, when to avoid climbing over boulders that will make him bleed.

The poem begins its end with universal natural images – the sun, rain, wind, light – blending in with more local, specific images like Donaghmoyne and Brady's farm, reinforcing the earlier thesis that 'God's truth is life,' no matter where it is.

Finally an invitation is issued to look at the beginnings of this story (we have already seen the end). The narrator asks us to detach ourselves and listen to the grim story that he wants to tell.

It must be remembered that this poem is part of a larger piece. There are dominant themes in the poem of self-sacrifice and of the relationship between man and Nature, and more specifically of the relationship between man and The Land. It would be wrong, however, to see this poem as one of Kavanagh's lyric poems, that have an exact structure and a single dominant theme. It is more wide ranging in its scope and aspirations. It genuinely attempts to provide a truthful, honest and – most importantly – full picture of a man at a particular time. By doing that Kavanagh gives us an insight into a whole society. He is presenting a vivid portrait of rural Ireland in the prewar years by focusing us on the character of Patrick Maguire.

A Christmas Childhood

Text of poem: New Explorations Anthology page 157

[*Note: this poem is also prescribed for 2007 Ordinary level exam*]

In 'A Christmas Childhood', Kavanagh seems to be very conscious of his voice and the voice that he is using in the poem. Kavanagh adopts an innocent, naïve attitude in this poem and that seems to be central to both the style and the substance. It is the merging of what he is saying and how he is saying it that gives the poem real quality. It uses simple, direct language and this simplicity is also important in what the poet is attempting to say. It is, however, in this reader's eyes a poem of two halves, to use the football cliché. Indeed it was originally published as two separate pieces, the first part being published in 1943, and what is now the second part a full three years earlier. This reader feels that the later addition was unnecessary.

Part I

The poem begins with a simple description of a potato field, where one side was in the sun and was beginning to thaw out. The other side was still frozen over and 'white with frost'. Nature dominates everything; it takes over and liberates inanimate objects. The paling-post that was once merely supporting a fence now sends music out through it:

> And when we put our ears to the paling-post
> The music that came out was magical.

The way that Nature attacks all the senses is important to Kavanagh. He goes through sight, taste and hearing in order to give us a holistic vision of how the Christmas spirit invades everything.

He then inserts an 'over-the-top' repetition of his emotions. Hyperbole pervades this part, with even the fence providing 'magical' music. He continues with this mixture of the simple and the marvellous when comparing a gap of light with 'a hole in Heaven's gable.' Even an apple tree reminds him of the temptation of Adam.

The death of innocence, and a longing to return to innocence, is a familiar theme in Kavanagh's poetry and it is reinforced here. The world has taken him, like Eve took Adam from what he supposed was a better life:

> O you, Eve, were the world that tempted me
> To eat the knowledge that grew in clay
> And death the germ within it!

He then sets up the second part of the poem by leaving us tranquil symbols of the 'gay garden that was childhood's', the most important being the final image: 'Of a beauty that the world did not touch.'

There is a longing here to return to a better time for himself. That time is when people were more dependent on Nature. This closer interaction with Nature is epitomised and made clearer by the amount of religious imagery that runs through the first section. There is plenty of religious imagery present, such as 'Heaven's gable' and Eve and the apple. The time was more sacred to Kavanagh; he saw it as a time that was also good and holy.

PART II

The second part of the poem continues with the religious imagery, making striking comparisons between an Irish town and Bethlehem with its 'stars in the morning east'. There is a genuine excitement pervading this part and it is less diluted by adult knowingness than the first part was. There are simple descriptions of what was going on in his childhood, and this allows him to retain an attitude of childlike wonder. The voice in the second half of the poem is certainly more full of clarity.

The setting for the second half of the poem is almost completely outdoors, and this natural open setting allows him to go from the local to the universal – or even biblical – with ease. There is a seamless intertwining of the personal and the public. Again, the significance of the fact that the father was playing his music outdoors cannot be underplayed. He finds harmony with Nature and allows it to influence his playing. The stars manage to recognise his father's music and are so captivated that they decide to dance to it.

Rapidly Kavanagh brings us back to his own townland and remarks on the unspoken signs between the families. Where in 'Epic' he describes local rivalries, here the unspoken language of music is a uniting force as 'his melodion called | To Lennons and Callans.' Kavanagh remarks that he 'knew some strange thing had happened.' The harmonising power of his father's music is highly significant when one reflects on the first verse, where the music from the paling-post is described as magical.

His mother's daily ritual of milking the cows becomes inspired by 'the frost of Bethlehem'. The religious imagery continues here. Bethlehem brought new hope to Christians, and this time of year, with its sense of a new start, also suggests rebirth. Nature in the form of ice and wind and the water-hen is recalled. It is the sense of 'wonder of a Christmas townland', where even the dawn is personified and winks, which makes this poem one of the most beautiful that Kavanagh wrote. Yet again he tries to show how the senses are affected: sight with the 'child-poet (who) picked out letters'; the sound of the melodion and of when:

> A water-hen screeched on the bog,
> Mass-going feet
> Crunched the wafer-ice on the potholes,

In the sixth verse he shows exquisite skill at mixing the northern constellation Cassiopeia with 'Cassidy's hanging hill', using run-through lines with clever use of alliteration to expose the child's sense of awe at Christmas. This also introduces the religious notion again and suggests the Eastern Star that guided the Three Wise Men towards the birth of Christ; instead, the stars guide people towards his father's house.

There is one wise man who proves his intelligence by commenting on the poet's father's fiddle playing. His father is working just like Nature, when the inanimate is brought to life as the man says, 'Can't he make it talk.'

Pleasant childhood memories of Christmas are exposed graciously throughout the poem: his father's way of making the melodion talk, his mother's commitment to the daily work on the farm, his presents, and an overall satisfaction that Nature had provided all of these things.

Advent

Text of poem: New Explorations Anthology page 160

'Advent' is a poem made up of two sonnets. The sonnet itself is a structure that gives way to easy division. It is usually divided into an octet followed by a sestet. Kavanagh abandons this convention in the first sonnet, dividing his sonnet into two even halves of seven lines each. It is no coincidence that in this poem he seeks an equality. (That initial octet is often divided into two quatrains.) So the idea of stitching two separate sonnets together should immediately suggest some sort of linear progression of ideas. Kavanagh does that in this poem. The journey that he decides to adopt is a peculiar one; he sets out his new poetic manifesto in this poem. To do so, he decides that in order to go forwards, he must first go back. The poem was originally called 'Renewal', and to this reader that title was certainly a more direct approach.

The poem starts with a world-weary reminiscence to somebody familiar:

> We have tested and tasted too much, lover

He then returns to an earlier poem, 'A Christmas Childhood'. In that poem he states:

> The light between the ricks of hay and straw
> Was a hole in Heaven's gable.

Here he points out that you can overexpose yourself. He decides that it is more worthwhile to search for the minutiae of life than for true wonderment. So he has to go back to real basics in a genuine and ascetic way, because 'Through a chink too wide there comes no wonder.'

He advocates returning to simple sustenance, because he feels that this will garner a truer sense of spiritual purity. When he talks about penance he attributes no negativity to it, but rather sees it as part of a process towards self-fulfilment. He promises himself that he will give back the negativity of useless knowledge. Experience for its own sake is not enough for him now – just as it wasn't when he was younger. Back then he did not appreciate it:

> The knowledge we stole but could not use.

In the second half of the first sonnet he spells out his own poetic manifesto. He needs to return to a state where he finds wonder in simple things. He makes a list of the lifestyle he has abandoned, and he obviously feels that he has suffered from being without this feeling. He wants to have his spirit shocked; he needs to feel a 'prophetic astonishment'. If he can find these things again, then he will have a poetic rebirth.

It is all very well Kavanagh talking about these things; the proof will come in whether or not he puts them into practice.

> And the newness that was in every stale thing
> When we looked at it as children.

Kavanagh uses hyperbole again and again in his poems, to great effect. So when he talks about 'the spirit-shocking | Wonder in a black slanting Ulster hill', the sense of uniqueness is certainly very heightened, even though it seems mundane now. He is longing for a time when these hills were comparable to the Alps. It is perception that is important here, and the ability to see things as though for the first time. Again Kavanagh is never content with dealing with one of the senses, just in case we might think that sight is the only sensation that is allowed to be heightened. To a child, even what is heard seems different. What can seem now to an adult like 'the tedious talking | Of an old fool' can be relayed to the child as 'prophetic astonishment'.

The imagery that he uses in the poem is one clear indication that he is capable of doing this. He uses apparent opposites to achieve it. When he breaks a paradox he sets out his poetic philosophy, so he can reconcile 'newness in every stale thing', 'astonishment in the tedious talking of an old fool . . .', and he can find 'old stables where Time begins'. This brings to mind a connection reminding us that Jesus himself was born in a an 'old stable'. There is a strong note of caution here: don't take things like 'bog-holes, cart-tracks, old stables' for granted.

The second sonnet allows Kavanagh to say what he's going to do about all of this. He is saying that the poetry is dependent on his attitude. If he opens himself to a new way of reacting to Nature, then the poetry will come to him. There is a lot of emphasis on faith and fate in the second verse; he seems determined to change his ways now. He says, 'We'll have no need to go searching', or he insists we don't have to listen for it: 'We'll hear it . . . .' It is almost as if the hearing is enough and that the hearing will come naturally, too. If he gives way to God.

Where this new inspiration comes from is an important element. It will be in simple places and from simple people doing simple things, such as:

> . . . in the whispered argument of a churning
> Or in the streets where the village boys are lurching.

And especially:

> Wherever life pours ordinary plenty.

This shall be reward in itself. The inspiration will come to him. Indeed, too much analysis by him could destroy the beauty of the act. He makes this clear when he insists to his lover:

> Won't we be rich, my love and I, and please
> God we shall not ask for reason's payment,
> The why of heart-breaking strangeness . . .
> Nor analyse God's breath in common statement.

This is a Catholic poem, accepting without question God's goodness and simplicity, and Kavanagh insists that 'pleasure, knowledge and the conscious hour' should be 'thrown in the dust-bin'. He must open himself to the glory of God and constantly praise the vision that he has been given.

The poem is partly an obituary for the past, and partly an incantation to a new celebratory aesthetic. Kavanagh says that by learning the lessons of self-sacrifice and rebirth that are taught during Advent, he will re-emerge reinvigorated and more in understanding with Christ, like a 'January flower.'

On Raglan Road

Text of poem: New Explorations Anthology page 162
[Note: *this poem is also prescribed for 2007 Ordinary level exam*]

Note: *This poem is better known as a song, made most famous by Luke Kelly of the Dubliners. It is worth the reader's effort to hear a recorded version of this song.*

This is a love poem. In itself this is rare in Kavanagh's poetry. It is a love poem tinged with regret. Kavanagh sometimes prided himself on his innocence in his poems; indeed, in a number of them he advocated a sensibility that encouraged it. In this poem he expects the reader to see him as completely naïve.

He begins the poem with a specific place. This is very similar to many of his poems. Of the poems in this anthology, however, this is the first poem set in Dublin rather than in Monaghan. When Kavanagh names a place he does so not only because

> Naming these things is the love act,
> ['The Hospital']

but also because the naming of these places helps to ground the poems. It allows the reader to believe them and him. The perception may be that if this is a real place and time ('an autumn day'), then it must be true.

From the beginning of the poem, Kavanagh puts himself in the place of an innocent who has been dragged into a situation that he did not want but could not avoid. Kavanagh sees the inevitable pitfalls ahead but cannot resist. He admits that he

> ... knew
> That her dark hair would weave a snare that I might one day rue;

He acknowledges that he 'saw the danger', yet still walked into her path. Indeed, the image created by Kavanagh of himself is of an innocent hypnotised by a Medusa-like creature who forces him to do her will. Kavanagh admits to giving in to temptation, but like Othello he only admits in his own way that he 'did not love too wisely but too well'. He says that he '. . . loved too much and by such and such is happiness thrown away.'

The Queen of Hearts image is a curious one. There is an element here that suggests Kavanagh was gambling and it didn't pay off. He certainly didn't end up 'making hay'. He seems to be complaining that the woman was too quiet and spent her time doing homely things, rather than making hay with him.

In the third verse he declares that he gave and she took. This may seem like an arrogant attitude to a contemporary reader:

> I gave her gifts of the mind I gave her the secret sign that's known
> To the artists who have known the true gods of sound and stone
> And word and tint.

He declares that he has brought her to Parnassus and has given her that which every intelligent person would want: an insight into his mind. He was even gracious enough to name her in some of his poems. What more could any woman want?:

> I did not stint for I gave her poems to say
> With her own name there ...

He does this even though she may have ruined his talent and killed the sunshine that should have fallen on him:

> ... her own dark hair like clouds over fields of May.

In the fourth verse Kavanagh sees his 'ex' and rationalises why she would turn away from him. He comes to the final damning conclusion that she did not deserve his love. He describes himself as an angel and his ex as a gargoyle. The angel made too much of a sacrifice, by trying to love somebody so base that they are made of clay. The net result of this encounter has been inevitable; the angel was injured:

> ... I had wooed not as I should a creature made of clay –
> When the angel woos he'd lose his wings at the dawn of day.

As a poem, 'On Raglan Road' is certainly presented from the poet's point of view. Should he be expected to give more balance? He is not writing a piece of journalism. Poetic licence with the truth is allowable, but it is important to see that this is one side of the argument and maybe Kavanagh loses some of the impact that he might have had.

Some of the imagery that Kavanagh uses is worth remarking upon. He seems to be referring to himself in a passive mode and as somebody who is angelic and taken by Nature, whereas the woman in the poem is associated with darkness: 'her dark hair', 'a deep ravine', 'Clouds over fields of May', 'made of clay'.

The long, winding lines of the poem are often associated with poetry written *as gaeilge* and they fit in with many of the poems written in the bardic tradition. Many of these poems were also about women, but saw a woman in a vision poem and as someone who was pure, representing Ireland to the poet and encouraging him to eulogise rather than lament (although Kavanagh's lament seems to be more for himself). These long lines fit into the pattern of the song-line; they flow dreamily and sweetly.

He uses a lot of mid-line rhyme in this poem, too, which also encourages a lament-like atmosphere. There are examples of this all the way through the poem. In the first verse: 'hair' and 'snare' and 'grief' and 'leaf'. In the second verse he uses 'ravine' and 'seen', 'hearts' and 'tarts' and 'much' and 'such'. The third verse has 'mind' and 'sign', 'tint' and 'stint' and 'there' and 'hair'; while finally the fourth has 'street' and 'meet', 'me' and 'hurriedly', 'wooed' and 'should' and 'woos' and 'lose'.

The Hospital
Text of poem: New Explorations Anthology page 164

This is yet another sonnet, obviously Kavanagh's favourite form; yet again its content is what makes this sonnet different from other poets' versions of the same form. This is a love poem. That must be clear from the fact that he uses the word 'love' or 'lover' five times in the space of the five sentences that make up the poem. The main question that should be going through the reader's mind is: why would anybody want to write a love poem to a building? For it is the building that he is in love with, not what has been done to him within the building. He does not seem to be writing a poem about being grateful for being cured. He seems to be referring in this paean to just the hospital itself. Or is he yet again writing a poem about poetry?

The octet begins in a matter-of-fact manner. There is nothing austere or profound about this place. It is not a miraculous healing place; it is a 'functional ward'. It seems incredibly uniform and without personality:

> . . . square cubicles in a row
> Plain concrete, wash basins –

Immediately it is dismissed as 'an art lover's woe'. Surely a poet should know something about art. Is his dismissal a contradiction, or does he hate art? Not only is the room drab, but also the other occupants are not exactly people to be revered. Rather than populate his hospital with healing angels, Kavanagh inserts a 'fellow in the next bed (who) snored'.

Kavanagh uses that first quatrain to describe the place. The next two lines explain the motivation for his love. There is nothing that cannot be loved. He reassures himself that by loving something:

> The common and banal her heat can know.

There is nothing that cannot be used as a subject for poetry; this is the essence of much of Kavanagh's work. The same theme is directed at us in 'Epic' or in 'Shancoduff'. It is not enough just to write about them, however. It must be done well and in a proper poetic genre. Therefore it is also not enough to 'just love' the Hospital: it must be done with passion, as he tells us about 'her heat'.

This poem was written during a period of transition for Kavanagh. It is one of the first of his poems that was written during what is known as his Canal Period. It is appropriate, therefore, that just as his period of illness led him to a new period of poetic freedom, then he should also point out that the hospital is not just the building itself, but outside there is 'the inexhaustible adventure of a gravelled yard.' He doesn't tell us what the adventure is, but he tells us some of the things that go on there.

He then goes on to tell us what type of things have not just happened, but have existed. Kavanagh, by naming them in his poem, has now given them immortality. They exist outside themselves now. They exist in his poem; this is the love that he can give to them. Indeed he sees it as his duty to name them. The naming is an act of love; it is personal and intimate between Kavanagh and the hospital.

He is giving it a life 'out of time'. He feels it is important to give immortality to that which has affected him. Because he has been affected by a particular place or situation, he feels that he has a duty to explain about it and to give it life. Places are the lifeblood of his poetry; he always names them. The venues of his life make up the different stages of his life – his time in Monaghan, his illness in the hospital, and afterwards his time at the Grand Canal.

The time that he spent in the Rialto Hospital was obviously a very important time for him. It did mark a turnaround in his poetic oeuvre. This poem is important for him because it is a time when he began to have a self-realisation about his own future, and about the direction in which his poetry should go.

Canal Bank Walk

Text of poem: New Explorations Anthology page 166

If in 'Advent' Kavanagh was looking for a renewal of his way of looking at things, he seems to have found it in this sonnet. He found his spiritual renewal, or rather it found him, when he fell ill in 1955. This poem was written during his convalescence. As his health was improving, Kavanagh became more and more grateful for his gifts and for life itself. This poem is a clear celebration; indeed, one critic has described it as a hymn. It is not perhaps a hymn to God, but to the world that God has created. This is important in the overall context of Kavanagh's new poetic philosophy. He felt that poetry was a gift, and he believed that poets had a duty to use that gift.

The predominant images in the poem are natural ones, and he starts with a beautifully crafted neologism: 'leafy-with-love' gets the mood of the poem right almost immediately. This place, after all, is a little piece of the country in a city setting. The area and the canal are inspiring him to do the 'will of God'. When the poet says that God would wish him to wallow, he does not mean that he should lie and do nothing, but rather that he should cherish and enjoy the glory of being with Nature and that he should celebrate it fervently.

Kavanagh sees redemption coming with water and he wishes to grow 'as before'. The image of the stick represents himself 'immobilised and helpless, but radiant'. His new way of living will be populated by romance and he wants to feel comfortable with Nature, as the couple on the bench do. He wants to use the energy of moments such as these and to add 'a third | Party to the couple kissing on the old seat'. But he wants to be infused with the knowledge that Nature will have a controlling influence. His poetry will take off into a different sphere of thought and it will be 'Eloquently new and abandoned to its delirious beat.'

The sestet is a prayer that reaches out for inspiration and like 'Lines written . . .', it reaches out with a poetic invocation to Nature to allow him to become a better poet and to envelop his senses. It is when surrounded by Nature that he can paradoxically be most free. Kavanagh wants to be both enraptured and encaptured. He expects Nature to do this to him; all he has to do is to submit to it.

What he desires is to abandon himself to another power which will allow him to become a medium for the glory of Nature:

> Feed the gaping need of my senses, give me ad lib
> To pray unselfconsciously with overflowing speech

Kavanagh has needs in this poem, just like a baby might have. The 'new dress woven' is like a baptismal gown that will bring him and his poetry to a place where his spiritual and poetic rebirth can take place.

The rhythm and structure of the poem suggest fluidity and use enjambment or 'run-on lines', subtle rhyme and assonance to produce an incantation that flows like the canal which he describes.

There are a lot of differences between this poem and 'Advent'. They are both about the importance of being grateful to God; the difference between them is simple. 'Advent' urges a sense of solemn ascetic devotion, whereas 'Canal Bank Walk' is in favour of a more glorious outpouring of emotion where the poet is urging himself to praise God in a more open and vigorous manner. The verbs that Kavanagh uses are much more aggressive: 'enrapture', 'encapture', 'gaping'. He wants to lose control here, rather than keep things under control like he did in 'Advent'. He feels that the qualities of the water can have an invigorating effect on him, just as they did on Jesus when he met John the Baptist.

Lines Written on a Seat on the Grand Canal, Dublin
'Erected to the Memory of Mrs Dermot O'Brien'

Text of poem: New Explorations Anthology page 168

'Lines Written . . .' is the second of the Canal poems, and is a plea from the heart for poetry to be given the tribute that he feels it deserves. There are some questions raised by the idea of such a poem in the first place. The first one is:

does a poet deserve commemoration in the first place? To answer this we must understand Kavanagh's ideas behind the role of a poet. The second obvious question is: why set the poem on a seat overlooking a canal? The third is: why does he leave the subtitle in?

A READING OF THE POEM

To answer the last point first, he seems to admire the idea of having a seat as a memorial. He thinks it is a good idea, so he includes it in his poem. He also includes it perhaps to instigate an idea of mortality in the reader of the poem. This poem may be seen as the poet's requiem for himself. It is worth it, at this point, for the reader to reread the poem in that context.

The poem begins in a gloriously poetic manner; the first word is the declaring 'O'. The 'O' sets up an intensely poetic mood. If it is left out, what difference does it make? One of the effects it definitely has is that it sets up the poem as a grand exercise. We have seen in Kavanagh's poems up to this point that he likes using simple, even colloquial language, but this declaration is something new and unusual for him. There is also a sense of death in this opening phrase, and Dr Antoinette Quinn has remarked that the opening and its mirror phrase at the end 'frame the sonnet like a black mourning border'. This introduces an element of finality in the poem again and goes back to the inscription on the seat.

So Kavanagh continues through the poem and reflects that the place for people to remember him should be where there is water. Water suggests life, but it also suggests birth and in the Christian tradition it suggests rebirth. A rebirth of the imagination was important to Kavanagh's poetic thesis. He felt that a poet should not just accept what he could see, but should constantly re-inspect his perception of what was seen to be present.

It is Kavanagh's belief that a poet should seek out the wonder of the ordinary that brings him to see the water as something that was capable of many lives: and perhaps so, too, a poem can have many different readings for its readers. The idea of a simple lock in Dublin roaring like Niagara Falls is a use of hyperbole that backs up Kavanagh's belief that perception and attitude are everything. If you wish to see the Niagara Falls, you can. The inspiration that comes from this sight is what is important to him. Kavanagh also wants this attitude to be his legacy to other poets:

> No one will speak in prose
> Who finds his way to these Parnassian islands.

Nature and the seemingly banal as muse is an important theme in Kavanagh's work. He uses an image that was previously used in 'Advent' and 'Shancoduff', where light can find its way through any hole and bring life to a place where previously it was thought that there was none. In 'Advent' we are told:

Through a chink too wide there comes in no wonder.

Here we are reminded that:

Fantastic light looks through the eyes of bridges –

Hyperbole is used throughout this poem. His references to Parnassus, Niagara and 'fantastic light' are in an exaggerated manner, and now Athy is a place where mythologies are born.

He siphons this hyperbole by coming back at the end of the poem with a simple, modest, heartfelt plea that we would not commemorate him with a 'hero-courageous | Tomb – just a canal-bank seat for the passer-by.'

This poem is Kavanagh's last great poem, and it is entirely appropriate that in it he tries to find a place for himself in the whole scheme of the world. He desperately seeks a return to the natural world of his youth – the difference being that he is now in a position to enjoy what he sees and what goes on around him. He has found modesty in this poem, not just with God, because he had found that already; he has found his place among regular people and seems to be much more aware that this is where life is at its most vibrant. Seeing things becomes very important to him here. He wants to acknowledge the greatness and majesty of the ordinary things that go on around him. By recognising them, he makes things seem far more magnificent. He transforms the Grand Canal into Parnassus quite naturally, because this is the place that transforms him and gives him his inspiration. This inspiration to his art is awe-inspiring to him, and it is for that reason that he feels free to make the comparison.

Again it is the sense of place that influences Kavanagh. In the Gaelic tradition 'Dinnseanchas' is the term given to the poetry written about a sense of place. In this tradition, the act of describing a place left behind was very important to the poets. In Kavanagh's case, he tries to bring his craft a bit further. He has already acknowledged the influence that County Monaghan and the past have had on him, for better or for worse; now he wants to pay tribute to his present.

6 Elizabeth BISHOP

John G. Fahy

A literary life

Elizabeth Bishop was born on 8 February 1911 in Worcester, Massachusetts. Her parents, William Bishop and Gertrude Bulmer (the family name was variously spelt Bulmer, with a silent l, and Boomer), were both of Canadian origin.

Her father died when she was eight months old; her mother never recovered from the shock and for the next five years was in and out of mental hospitals, moving between Boston, Worcester, and her home town of Great Village in Nova Scotia, Canada. In 1916 Gertrude Bulmer's insanity was diagnosed as permanent and she was institutionalised and separated from her daughter, whom she was never to see again. She died in 1934. Elizabeth was reared for the most part by the Boomer grandparents in Great Village, with occasional long stays with the wealthy Bishop household in Worcester, which she did not enjoy. As a child she suffered severe lung illnesses, often having to spend almost entire winters in bed, reading. Chronic asthma became a problem for her all her life.

She describes her early days in Nova Scotia from a child's point of view in the autobiographical short story 'In the Village'. The elegy 'First Death in Nova Scotia' also draws on some childhood memories. 'Sestina' too evokes the sadness of this period. These, and snippets from unpublished poems and papers, point to an unsatisfactory relationship with an ill and transient mother. Yet in spite of these difficulties her recollections of her Nova Scotia childhood were essentially positive, and she had great affection for her maternal grandparents, aunts and uncles in this small agricultural village.

In 1927 she went to Walnut Hill School for girls, a boarding school in Natick, Massachusetts. From 1930 to 1934 she attended Vassar College, an exclusive private university in Poughkeepsie, New York, where her fees were paid at first by the Bishop family and then by the income from a legacy left by her father. She graduated in English literature but also studied Greek and music, and she always retained a particular appreciation for Renaissance lyric poetry and for the works of Gerard Manley Hopkins. It was at Vassar that she first began to publish stories and poems in national magazines and where she met the poet Marianne Moore, who became an important influence on her career as a poet and with whom she maintained a lifelong friendship and correspondence. It was also at Vassar that she formed her first lesbian relationship, and here too, on her own admission, that the lifelong problem with alcohol addiction began.

Between 1935 and 1938 she made a number of trips to Europe, travelling to England, Ireland, France, North Africa, Spain and Italy in the company of her friends Louise Crane and Margaret Miller, the latter losing an arm in a road accident on the trip. Bishop dedicated the poem 'Quai d'Orléans' to Miller.

In 1939 she moved to Key West, Florida, a place she had fallen in love with over the previous years. 'The Fish' reflects her enjoyment of the sport of fishing at that time. She and Louise Crane bought a house there, now called the Elizabeth Bishop House. Later she lived with Marjorie Carr Stevens, to whom 'Anaphora' was dedicated posthumously after Stevens's death in 1959. Key West became a sort of refuge and base for Bishop over the next fifteen years.

In 1945 she won the Houghton Mifflin Poetry Award. In 1946 her first book of poetry, *North and South*, was published and was well received by the critics. 'The Fish' is among its thirty poems. At this time she met and began a lifelong friendship and correspondence with the poet Robert Lowell.

In 1948 she won a Guggenheim Fellowship, and in 1949–50 she was poetry consultant to the Library of Congress, supervising its stock of poetry, acquiring new works, and providing opinions and advice. The income from this work was important to her, as she had dedicated herself exclusively to her poetry, at which she was a slow and often erratic worker.

The years 1945 to 1951, when her life was centred on New York, were very unsettled. She felt under extreme pressure in a very competitive literary circle and drank heavily. 'The Bight' and 'The Prodigal' reflect this dissolute period of her life. In 1947 she began receiving medical support for her chronic depression, asthma, and alcoholism.

In 1951 she left for South America on the first stage of a trip around the world. She stopped first in Brazil, where she went to visit her old acquaintances Mary Morse and Maria Carlota Costellar de Macedo Soares. She was fascinated by the country and by Lota Soares, with whom she began a relationship that was to last until Soares's death in 1967. They lived in a new house in the luxurious Brazilian countryside at Petrópolis. 'Questions of Travel' and 'The Armadillo' reflect this period of her life.

A Cold Spring, her second volume of poetry, was published in 1955. It contains 'The Bight', 'At the Fishhouses', and 'The Prodigal'.

In 1956 she won the Pulitzer Prize. In 1957 *The Diary of Helena Morley* was published. This was a translation by Bishop of the diary of a girl aged between thirteen and fifteen who lived in the Brazilian village of Diamantina in the 1890s. In 1965 *Questions of Travel*, her third volume, was published. Among this selection, as well as the title poem, were 'Sestina', 'First Death in Nova Scotia' and 'Filling Station'.

In 1966–67 she was poet in residence at the University of Washington in Seattle, where she met Suzanne Bowen, who became her secretary, human caretaker and, after Soares's death, lover. They lived in San Francisco (1968–69), where Bishop found the new culture bewildering, and then in Brazil, until the tempestuous ending of the relationship in 1970.

In 1969 the *Complete Poems* was published. In 1970 Bishop won the National Book Award for Poetry. She was appointed poet in residence at Harvard University, where she taught advanced verse writing and studies in modern poetry for her first year and, later, poets and their letters. She described herself as 'a scared elderly amateur prof'. It was here she met Alice Methfessel, an administrative assistant who became her minder and companion for the remainder of her life. She began to do a good many public readings of her poetry to make a living, as she had not been able to get much of her money out of Brazil. She continued to teach courses for the remainder of her years, though she found the work draining and it interfered with her already slow production of poetry. But she needed the money to maintain her style of life and travel.

In the summer of 1972 she went on a cruise through Scandinavia to the Soviet Union. From 1973 to 1977 she secured a four-year contract from Harvard to teach a term each year, until her retirement in May 1977. She continued to do public readings, punctuated by spells in hospital caused by asthma, alcohol and depression. She managed to visit Mexico in 1975 and went on a trip to Europe in 1976.

In 1976 *Geography III* was published. Among this slim collection of nine or ten poems are 'In the Waiting Room' and 'The Moose'. The poems in this volume show a new, more directly personal style and a return to her past and her sense of self in search of themes. Competing with failing health, including a bleeding hiatus hernia, she continued her usual round of readings, travel and some writing. She died suddenly of a brain aneurysm on 6 October 1979.

The Fish
Text of poem: New Explorations Anthology page 173
[Note: This poem is also prescribed for Ordinary Level 2007 exam]

In the late 1930s, Bishop discovered Florida and a love of fishing. Based on real fishing experiences, her notebooks of the time show images and line fragments that were later developed in 'The Fish'. She worked on the poem during the winter of 1939 and sent a finished draft to Marianne Moore in January 1940, and the poem was first published in the *Partisan Review* in March 1940. It is included in her first published collection of 1946, *North and South*.

THE SPEAKER: THE I AND THE EYE
The poem is narrated in the first person, so we get to meet the poet – the 'I' in the poem – directly, as we do in quite a few of Bishop's poems. This gives the

experience of the poem an immediacy and an intimacy for the reader. But while the reader may feel closely involved in the drama, there is a hint that the speaker herself is something of an outsider, not a native of the place, the inhabitant of a 'rented boat'. Perhaps this lends a certain objectivity to the drama and the description of it.

We are also introduced here to the famous Bishop 'eye', which sees both the beautiful and the grimy, describes not only surface detail but even imagines the interior:

> the dramatic reds and blacks
> of his shiny entrails,
> and the pink swim-bladder
> like a big peony.

Minute descriptions and calculated use of detail are a feature of Bishop's poetry. This is how she apprehends the world and comes to grips with experience: through aesthetic re-creation. Detail is important as a basis for understanding.

Bishop re-creates the fish in minute detail. This is how she 'interiorises' it, comprehends it. At first she domesticates it in the imagery, making it familiar by linking it to details of faded everyday living (he is 'homely', 'brown skin hung in strips like ancient wallpaper,' 'shapes like full-blown roses', 'rags of green weed'). Yet something of its essential wildness, the otherness of its creative being, is retained in some of the descriptions:

> – the frightening gills,
> fresh and crisp with blood,
> that can cut so badly . . .

This is also rendered in war imagery:

> . . . from his lower lip . . .
> grim, wet, and weaponlike,
> hung five old pieces of fish-line . . .
> Like medals with their ribbons
> frayed and wavering . . .

But perhaps the most crucial moment in the poet's comprehension of the fish is when she examines the eyes,

> which were far larger than mine
> but shallower, and yellowed,

> the irises backed and packed
> with tarnished tinfoil
> seen through the lenses
> of old scratched isinglass.

The detail is re-created poetically, using all the echoes and sound effects of alliteration and assonance reminiscent of a Hopkins 'inscaping', re-creating in words the essence of the thing observed ('shallower', 'yellowed', 'backed and packed', 'tarnished tinfoil'). The detailed re-creation leads to the poet's realisation that these eyes are unresponsive: the fish is oblivious to her, there is no real sentient contact between human and animal.

> They shifted a little, but not
> to return my stare.

There is no question here of humankind's heroic struggle against Nature, such as we find in Hemingway's *The Old Man and the Sea*. The experience is not glorified or mythologised, but rather rendered as she saw it. She is reported as saying to her students (quoted by Wesley Wehr):

> I always tell the truth in my poems. With 'The Fish', that's exactly how it happened. It was in Key West, and I did catch it, just as the poem says. That was in 1938. Oh, but I did change one thing: the poem says he had five hooks hanging from his mouth, but actually he only had three. Sometimes a poem makes its own demands. But I always try to stick as much as possible to what really happened when I describe something in a poem.

We notice that, even as she is asserting the absolute integrity of her eye and the accuracy of the descriptive process, she is also aware of the creative demands of the poetic process. The poem is an accurate record, but only up to a point.

A DRAMATIC POEM

The critic Willard Spiegelman, reflecting on the dramatic quality of Bishop's poetry, said: 'We do not normally think of Bishop as a poet of struggle; the tension in her poems is mostly internalised, and confrontations, when they occur, are between the self, travelling, moving or simply seeing, and the landscape it experiences.' This is particularly applicable to this poem. The first and last lines ('I caught a tremendous fish' and 'and I let the fish go') frame this drama. There is little external conflict, though there are hints of military antagonism and danger from the fish. The confrontation framed by these lines is mainly internal.

So why does she release the fish? Was it because of the lack of heroic struggle?

> He didn't fight.
> He hadn't fought at all.

Does the lack of contact in the eyes disappoint her? Or does she release him out of respect for his history of previous successful encounters, a record emblazoned on his lip ('a five-haired beard of wisdom trailing from his aching jaw')? Perhaps these are part of the decision, but the real moment of truth occurs because of the sudden appearance of the accidental industrial rainbow when the bilge oil gleams in the sun ('where oil had spread a rainbow around the rusted engine'). Fortuitous this may be – a grim parody of natural beauty, an ironic comment on humankind's relationship with nature – but it provides for the poet a moment of aesthetic unity with the grandeur of the world, and everything is transformed ('everything was rainbow, rainbow, rainbow!'). It is a moment of revelation, in which this new image of the fish colours the environment and alters her relationship with nature. No longer antagonistic, confrontational, she has metaphorically tamed, re-created and understood the fish.

The ending of the poem is very similar to a Wordsworth nature poem such as 'The Daffodils': the hypnotic vision ('I stared and stared'), the wealth accruing to the viewer ('victory filled up the little rented boat'), and feelings of inspiration and joy through creating a connection with the world, a world that has been transformed by the vision, this moment of epiphany,

> where oil had spread a rainbow
> around the rusted engine
> to the bailer rusted orange,
> . . . until everything
> was rainbow, rainbow, rainbow!

The Bight

Text of poem: New Explorations Anthology page 176

GENESIS OF THE POEM

'The Bight' was probably written in early 1948. In a letter to Robert Lowell dated January of that year Bishop tells of the excavations at Garrison Bight, Key West. 'The water looks like blue gas – the harbor is always a mess here, junky little boats are piled up, some hung with sponges and always a few half sunk or splintered up from the most recent hurricane – it reminds me a little of my desk'

(Brett Millier, *Elizabeth Bishop: Life and the Memory of It*). She wrote to Lowell again the following month, saying that she was trying to finish two poems about Key West, 'and then I hope I won't have to write about the place any more.'

Bishop's idiosyncratic descriptions

This is a typical example of the poet's technique of description, minutely detailed and accurate yet coloured in a personal way, either by her wit or by the view implicit in the imagery. The extraordinary quality of the water is emphasised by the poet wittily turning the accepted view of things on its head. It is made to look strange, so that we look at it afresh.

> Absorbing, rather than being absorbed,
> the water in the bight doesn't wet anything.

She presents the water to us through a number of sense perspectives: touch, sight, smell, and sound:

> the color of the gas flame turned as low as possible.
> One can smell it turning to gas; if one were Baudelaire
> one could probably hear it turning to marimba music.

To Bishop, the world of the bay seems predominantly mechanical – not just the dredge at work, but 'pelicans crash . . . like pickaxes,' 'man-of-war birds' have 'tails like scissors,' and 'glinting like little plowshares, the blue-gray shark tails'. There is even a hint that the scene is dangerous, potentially explosive ('the pilings dry as matches' and the water 'the color of the gas flame'). The helpless, ineffectual aspect of creatures and things is displayed (pelicans 'rarely coming up with anything to show for it,' boats 'stove in, and not yet salvaged, if they ever will be'). Altogether there is presented a detailed picture of life chugging along in the midst of disorder and ineffectuality.

View of the world

Bishop's world here is a tired, run-down, worn-out one, her view completely unromantic. It is a world of mechanical reactions, of trained responses.

> The frowsy sponge boats keep coming in
> with the obliging air of retrievers.

There may be routine, but there is little sense of spirit, of wholeness or of perspective in the picture. The usual mechanical, monotonous pulse of life goes on ('Click. Click. Goes the dredge') but against a background of 'untidy activity', 'unanswered letters', 'old correspondences' and a general lack of cohesion. This atmosphere is created, at least partly, by the disparate nature of the imagery: picture follows unconnected picture, and there is no sense of any linkage or pattern (water, dredge, birds, frowsy sponge-boats, fence of sharks' tails for the Chinese-restaurant trade, little white boats stove in, and again the dredge). Yet the prevailing attitude is one of stoicism: life goes on, 'awful but cheerful'.

A PERSONAL POEM?

The subtitle 'On my birthday' really colours the entire poem. Despite the absence of the first-person voice, the sub-title forces us to acknowledge the shadowy presence of the poet, like the ghost at the feast. Why does she mark her birthday in this unusual way, viewing this particular scene? What special significance has the scene for her?

It has been suggested that the 'disorder and latent violence in the vehicles convey the disorder in Elizabeth's mind' (Millier) as she thinks about her own life. 'Thirty-seven and far from heaven,' she noted. The comparison between the confusion in the bay and the clutter of her own desk, as recorded in her letter to Lowell, together with the extraordinary simile or conceit of the 'little white boats . . . like torn-open, unanswered letters', would indicate a high degree of personal meaning in the poem, even though the description of the bay has been universalised. Indeed, often in Bishop's poems, private significance is revealed out of apparently objective description.

Does she identify with the frowsy sponge-boats, the little white boats piled up against each other, or the wrecked ones 'not yet salvaged'? Perhaps she is celebrating the survival against the storms of many small craft, as much of her own life was spent at the mercy of the tides of alcohol and depression. It is difficult not to read 'awful but cheerful' as a personal statement.

At the Fishhouses

Text of poem: New Explorations Anthology page 178

GENESIS OF THE POEM

Elizabeth Bishop travelled to Nova Scotia in the summer of 1946. It has been suggested that she undertook the trip in order to be out of the way when her first collection, *North and South*, was published. At any rate, it was her first visit to Great Village in fifteen years. She had spent the previous two years undergoing counselling, trying to understand the origins of her alcoholism and bouts of depression. Now she was returning to her physical origins, the scenes of her less-than-idyllic childhood.

From her notebook entries of the time we know that the trip was disturbing, but it gave rise to a number of poems. 'At the Fishhouses' was published in the *New Yorker* on 9 August 1947.

SUBJECT MATTER AND THEMES

This poem could be read as a meditation on the significance of the sea and its influence on humanity and landscape.

The poem is set at the convergence of sea and shore and at a place of important interaction between humankind and the sea. Human enterprise depends on the sea and is subservient to it. Symbolically, the 'cleated gangplanks' lead up out of the water to the storerooms, but the 'long ramp' also descends into the water, 'down and down'. This symbiotic relationship is also alluded to in the 'talk of the decline in the population | and of codfish and herring'. The sea's influence permeates and colours everything, having the power to transform magically ('all is silver . . . the silver of the benches, | the lobster pots, and masts, scattered | among the wild jagged rocks, | is of an apparent translucence'), or to bring decay and ruin ('an ancient wooden capstan . . . where the ironwork has rusted'). Humankind is surrounded by the sea and dwarfed by it. One has the sense of the sea as some forbidding power encircling humanity ('element bearable to no mortal'), indeed indifferent to humanity's fate, as suggested in the incantatory evocation of the tides:

> the same sea, the same,
> slightly, indifferently swinging above the stones

Yet the sea provides that crucial moment of epiphany for the poet, when she gains insight into the nature of knowledge: that it is temporal and transient.

Our knowledge is historical, flowing, and flown.

THE POET'S METHOD

The speaker slowly draws us into the picture in the opening sequence, with vivid details of sight (the 'old man . . . a dark purple-brown,' the description of the fish-houses: 'all is silver'), sense ('a cold evening', 'the air smells'), and sound (the talk, the presumed sounds of wheelbarrow and scraping). The specific detail augments this sense of realism in the opening (five fish-houses, steeply peaked roofs, narrow, cleated gangplanks, etc.) The present tense of the narrative gives it immediacy.

The reader is invited to share in the speaker's 'total immersion' in both the uncomfortable reality ('it makes one's nose run and one's eyes water') and the mesmeric fantasy ('if you should dip your hand in . . . your hand would burn | as if the water were a transmutation of fire').

Once again the poet uses detail as a way of possessing. Only by describing and imagining the mysterious movements and powers of the sea does the speaker win some control over them.

Through total immersion and conjuring up, she finally wins some insight and understanding. Her method, as usual, is a combination of straightforward description and poetic imagining. In the latter, she often transforms the scene or the object in the retelling: she deliberately makes it strange in order to force us to see it afresh ('your hand would burn | as if the water were a transmutation of fire | that feeds on stones and burns with a dark gray flame').

The process of winning through to her final visionary insight is marked by fits and starts, reflecting perhaps the difficulty of achieving any kind of self-knowledge. The poetic contemplation of the silvering of the landscape is interrupted by the mundane conversation on population decline. The renewed contemplation of the sea in the third section ('cold dark deep') is interrupted by the humorous episode with the seal.

> He was interested in music;
> like me a believer in total immersion,
> so I used to sing him Baptist hymns.

But it finally manages to build to that rhythmic incantation of the climax ('indifferently swinging above the stones . . .').

This stop-start method employed in the narrative is also used by Bishop in the rhythm of the language, in order to control the emotion in the poem. She uses the metre, and repetition of words and phrases (*anaphora*), to convey the hypnotic power of the sea.

> I have seen it over and over, the same sea, the same,
> slightly, indifferently swinging above the stones,
> icily free above the stones,
> above the stones, and then the world.

But she breaks this atmosphere with the everyday language of the conditional clause ('if you should dip your hand in'). The flow of the verse builds again, and is again brought down to earth by 'if you tasted it, it would first taste bitter,' before it is allowed to build to that intense and rhythmic conclusion.

THE VISIONARY INSIGHT EXPERIENCED BY THE POET

This entire poem is devoted to the strange and inexplicable power of the sea, a subject revealing Bishop's romantic impulses. The sea in this poem takes on qualities of the other elements, particularly of air and fire, thereby establishing itself as the primal force in nature. More significantly for the poet, the sea is equated with knowledge, and it is the realisation of this, achieved gradually through her total immersion and re-creation process of poetry, that forms the climax of the poem.

Knowledge is broken down into its elements ('dark, salt, clear, moving, utterly free'). Could these epithets be translated as disturbing, preserving, transparent, ever-changing, and outside our control? The description of knowledge might be read as a view of human knowledge in general, but it is difficult not to read it also as personal. The reference to its darker side, as well as to its objectivity and transparency, could be seen as a personal note, in view of Bishop's psychological search and journey back to the roots of her depression and alcohol problems. The nature of the knowledge in the poem is overtly sexual, with maternal overtones:

> drawn from the cold hard mouth
> of the world, derived from the rocky
> breasts . . .

This hard, forbidding maternal image might be taken as a reference to her unsatisfactory relationship with her mother and to the human and genetic knowledge derived from her. This knowledge is temporal and transient, no lasting inheritance, rather 'flowing, and flown' – quite a bleak view of life, with its suggestion of the isolated individual, unconnected to the past, at the mercy of the tide.

The Prodigal

Text of poem: New Explorations Anthology page 182

GENESIS OF THE POEM

Elizabeth Bishop said that this poem originated from her thoughts when one of her aunt's stepsons offered her a drink of rum in the pigsty at about nine o'clock in the morning during her trip to Nova Scotia in 1946. Perhaps that was the final spark that engendered the poem, but the theme could never have been far from her thoughts, as she herself struggled with alcoholism all her life.

About the time of her thirty-eighth birthday, on 8 February 1949, she fell into a deep trough of depression. In an effort to rally out of it she went on a holiday to Haïti, from where she wrote to Marianne Moore to say that she had finished some poems, including 'The Prodigal'. Ironically, on her return from Haïti she went into a long and heavy drinking bout.

'The Prodigal' was published in the *New Yorker* on 13 March 1951.

Theme and development

This poem deals with the exile of the alcoholic. Like all good poetry, it functions at the level of the individual in the narrative but also at a universal level, exploring the metaphorical exile of alcoholism: the isolation, the skulking, the deception and hiding, the lack of control, aspirations rather than action. (Where do these feature in this poem?)

There is enormous human understanding in this poem. Despite the physical dirt of odour and ordure, the heart can still lift to the religious impulse ('the lantern – like the sun, going away – I laid on the mud a pacing aureole') or thrill to the romantic beauty of nature ('the sunrise glazed the barnyard mud with red; I the burning puddles seemed to reassure'). In fact the prodigal seems to retain a particularly benign relationship with nature, appreciating the delicacy of even these animals ('light-lashed . . . a cheerful stare') and maintaining a comfortable domesticity between animal and human ('The pigs stuck out their little feet and snored'). Nature here is a bringer of wisdom. The bats' 'uncertain staggering flight' is the spur to his self-awareness, his moment of 'shuddering insights', and so his eventual turning back.

The poem is depressingly realistic in its evocation of filth and human abasement:

> even to the sow that always ate her young –
> till, sickening, he leaned to scratch her head.

But it is noble and uplifting in its awareness of the spark of soul that still flickers even in the most abject circumstances.

Form

The poem is structured as two sonnets of a rather loose nature. They each have the requisite fourteen lines, and the first one maintains the conventional octave–sestet division, but the rhyming schemes are eccentric, if not absent altogether. The rhythm is a mixture of iambic pentameter and four-stress lines.

Questions of Travel

Text of poem: New Explorations Anthology page 184

Genesis of the poem

In 1951 Bishop left for an intended journey around the world, travelling via South America. But she stopped off in Brazil, where she remained, with brief intervals, for the next fifteen years or so. This poem reflects her fascination with travel and with Brazil in particular. 'Questions of Travel' is the title poem of her third volume of poetry, published in 1965, though it had been worked on for a good while before that. There are at least seven earlier drafts in existence.

SOME OBSERVATIONS ON THEMES

- This is a travel poem with a difference. True, it features the expected descriptions of the unusual and the exotic, as Bishop views, with a traveller's curiosity, 'the crowded streams', 'the trees . . . like noble pantomimists, robed in pink', 'the sad, two-noted, wooden tune of disparate wooden clogs', the 'music of the fat brown bird', the 'bamboo church of Jesuit baroque', the 'calligraphy of songbirds' cages', and the silence after rain – all the elements of a superior imaginative letter home.

- Her observations are given a particularly temporal significance as they are made against the great dwarfing background of the ages of time. But it is a time that, with typical Bishop quirkiness, has a disorderly aspect:

    – For if those streaks . . .
    aren't waterfalls yet,
    in a quick age or so, as ages go here,
    they probably will be.

- Bishop goes deeper than the postcard façade in order to acknowledge the limitations of our knowledge and understanding of a foreign culture.

    To stare at some inexplicable old stonework,
    inexplicable and impenetrable . . .

    She really doesn't expect it all to add up in the visitor's mind ('to have pondered, | blurr'dly and inconclusively').

- Even more basically, Bishop examines and questions the very need to travel. Partly motivated by traveller's exhaustion ('think of the long trip home'), she rises above this to engage the question at a philosophical level.

    What childishness is it that while there's a breath of life
    in our bodies, we are determined to rush
    to see the sun the other way around?

Is it lack of imagination? she wonders. She presents the idea as a philosophical debate between movement and travel ('Should we have stayed at home and thought of here?' and 'could Pascal have been not entirely right | about just sitting quietly in one's room?'). She seems to attribute the travel urge to the human need to achieve our dreams.

> Oh, must we dream our dreams
> and have them, too?

- The conclusion of her musings, expressed at the end of the poem, is that the human being is not absolutely free to choose: the necessity for travel is often forced upon a person ('the choice is never wide and never free'). She seems to see travel or homelessness as part of the condition of humankind ('should we have stayed at home, I wherever that may be?').

SETTING

The setting is the interior, away from the coast, the more usual scene of Bishop's conflicts. But even here she is ever-mindful of the sea, and her geographical mind-frame continues to make connections ('the crowded streams I hurry too rapidly down to the sea'), as if the sea is associated with oblivion and annihilation, and even the beauty here is threatened and transient.

POETIC METHOD

- She uses the now familiar method, combining precise observation with her idiosyncratic descriptions, where objects are made to look entirely strange so that we view them in a new light. She draws the reader in with detail and then challenges us visually to look hard and understand.

We can see this at work in the first section of the poem. Using all the conventional poetic devices of alliteration, assonance and sibilance, she re-creates the fluid continuity of the waterfalls as they 'spill over the sides in soft slow-motion'. With graphic, clever imagery she evokes the gigantic scale of the scene, giving it an aura of sadness ('those streaks, those mile-long, shiny, tearstains'). Then, shockingly, we are invited to this upside-down view of the mountains:

> the mountains look like the hulls of capsized ships,
> slime-hung and barnacled.

She has domesticated them by reference to human machinery, yet allowed them to retain their strangeness by the imagery associations with the secret depths of the earth.
- The poem is structured as a dramatic monologue, a dialogue with herself, which is an appropriate form given the philosophical approach to the subject. Having asked if it would not have been better to stay at home, she proceeds,

by a series of negative questions, to reach that indefinite conclusion.
- The poem is written in free verse.
- Flashes of humour sparkle here and there, as a welcome relief from the gentle complaining and insistent questioning. We notice the comparison of equatorial rain with politicians' speeches ('two hours of unrelenting oratory | and then a sudden golden silence').

> And have we room
> for one more folded sunset, still quite warm?

Should this be read as a genuinely Romantic urge or as a sardonic swipe at acquisitive and sentimental tourists?

The Armadillo

Text of poem: New Explorations Anthology page 188

GENESIS OF THE POEM

This poem was published in the *New Yorker* on 22 June 1957 and falls among the later of the first batch of poems about Brazil that Bishop published. She had been working on various components of it – imagery etc. – for a number of months, if not years. The fire balloons, the armadillo, the owls and the rabbit feature in her letters of the previous year.

DEDICATION TO ROBERT LOWELL

Lowell had said that his famous poem 'Skunk Hour' was indebted to 'The Armadillo'. So, when she finally published it, Bishop dedicated the poem to him. But there may be more significance than just personal sentiment in the dedication, as Lowell had become a conscientious objector to the Second World War when the Allies fire-bombed German cities. The gesture of defiance of destruction from the skies finds an echo in the last stanza of the poem.

A PHILOSOPHICAL READING OF THE POEM

What view of humanity informs this poem? Does she see humankind as deliberately destructive? No; but unthinking and primitive, yes. The balloons are a manifestation of primitive worship. They are also illegal and dangerous. But they are beautiful, romantic – likened to hearts, stars, and planets, with the planets developed as the main association in the poem. There is also a hint of the fickleness of the human heart ('light that comes and goes, like hearts'). Humankind aspires to the beautiful and to a religious spirit but is unthinking, and the consequences of our actions bring destruction on human beings and the environment, threatening the balance of nature.

So it is really an ecological outlook of Bishop's that is at play here. Lacking a religious outlook on life, what is the big question for humanity? It must be, how do we best preserve for the future what exists here? One of the options is to return to a world that existed before man began to 'impose his egotistical will' on it, to try to recover childhood's innocence, structure and security. It might be suggested that this is what Bishop is attempting in 'First Death in Nova Scotia' and 'Sestina'; but here all she can do is make an uncertain gesture of defiance, as in the last stanza.

POETIC METHOD

- The usual detailed observation is evident, accurately catching, for example, the frantic movement of the owls, or the stance of the armadillo. Sometimes the descriptions are poetic ('It splattered like an egg of fire').
- Bishop's eye is that of the observer rather than the expert. 'The pale green one,' she says of a star. Rather like 'the fat brown bird' of 'Questions of Travel', this creates an easy familiarity with the reader.
- She is adept at leisurely, detailed portraiture, as when describing the balloons that take up the first five stanzas. But she is good also at swift drawing that catches the essential image – of the armadillo, for example.

> a glistening armadillo left the scene,
> rose-flecked, head down, tail down . . .

- But she is no longer able to dupe herself into believing that her descriptions are accurate. She does realise that she has re-created the scene poetically.

> Too pretty, dreamlike mimicry!

In this final stanza she stands outside the poem, reflecting on the poetic process and on the opposition of her two modes: accurate description versus poetic re-creation in order to understand.

TONE: HOW BISHOP CONTROLS FEELINGS

The last stanza provides what is for Bishop a most unusual emotional outburst. The critical cry 'too pretty, dreamlike mimicry!' can be read as aimed at the poetic method but also at the fire balloons' imitation of the destructiveness of war. The gesture of defiance is vulnerable, for all its posturing ('weak', 'ignorant'). It is little better than a hopeless, passionate, vain gesture, which further emphasises the poet's emotional involvement.

> a weak mailed fist
> clenched ignorant against the sky!

This is an unusual outburst from Bishop, whose poetry is tightly controlled even when dealing with an emotive subject. This technical control over her verse keeps it from sentimentality and gives it 'an elegant, muted, modernist quality', as Penelope Laurans put it (in *Elizabeth Bishop: Modern Critical Views*, edited by Harold Bloom). Laurans examines in detail how the poet shapes the reader's response to this beautiful and cruel event:

(1) **by a factual presentation,** as we have seen;

(2) **by metrical variation** – in other words, continually changing rhythm so as not to allow the reader to become lost in the lyrical music, stopping the momentum of the verse. A detailed study of the first four stanzas will show how this operates. Stanzas 1 and 2 have a regular metrical pattern: lines 1, 2 and 4 are all of three stresses, with the five-stress third line emphasising the descriptions of the balloons, their frailty, beauty and flashing romanticism. Then stanzas 3 and 4 change to varying three-stress and four-stress lines. Even in the first two regular stanzas there are irregularities. For example, the first sentence of stanza 1 ends in the third line, so the sense is against the flow of the metre. The *abab* rhyme of the first stanza changes in the second. The rest of the poem has three-stress and four-stress lines, but they vary from stanza to stanza. Technically, the overall effect is to arrest any flow or musical momentum that might allow the verse to become sentimental;

(3) **by using metre and other technical strategies** to draw back from moments of emotional intensity, just at the point where a Romantic poet would let it flow. Stanzas 6 to 9 provide a good example of this. In particular, the flow and enjambment from the end of stanza 6 to 7 conjure up the fright of the owls.

> We saw the pair
> of owls who nest there flying up
> and up, their whirling black-and-white
> stained bright pink underneath, until
> they shrieked up out of sight.

But this moment of intensity is broken up by a change in the metre from tetrameter to irregular three-, four- or five-stress lines. We also find single-unit end-stopped lines, which break the flow:

> The ancient owls' nest must have burned.

The poet now focuses on the detailed description of the animals – the armadillo and the baby rabbit. We are caught up in this and brought back to reality.

Sestina
Text of poem: New Explorations Anthology page 190

Four poems from *Questions of Travel* – 'Manners', 'Sunday 4 a.m.', 'First Death in Nova Scotia' and 'Sestina' – deal with Bishop's return to her origins. 'Sestina' (originally entitled 'Early Sorrow') works on all the significant elements of her childhood. The poem probably evokes the time and atmosphere after her mother's last departure from Great Village to the mental hospital. It also reflects a great deal of thinking and reading about child psychology. In reality, despite the privations and tensions reflected in the poem, Elizabeth Bishop always maintained that she was happy in Great Village.

The sestina form

A *sestina* is a poem of six, six-line stanzas in which the line endings of the first stanza are repeated, but in different order, in the other five. The poem concludes with an *envoy*, which is a short address to the reader (or the person to whom the poem is addressed). So the elements here are: house, grandmother, child, stove, almanac and tears; and they are rearranged in the other stanzas like a sort of moving collage.

Some of the elements carry greater symbolic weight, such as the almanac, which has been construed as representing the poet's lifelong anxiety about the passing of time. The house is a pictorial representation of her childhood, and the little Marvel stove seems to provide a counterbalance of domesticity, heat and comfort.

A psychological reading of the poem

The poem deals with memories of childhood uncertainty, loss and a pervasive sense of sorrow. Interesting psychological readings of the poem have been offered by Helen Vendler (in *Elizabeth Bishop: Modern Critical Views*, edited by Harold Bloom), among others. Her reading focuses on tears as the strange and crucial component of this childhood collage. The grandmother hides her tears. The child senses the unshed tears and displaces them elsewhere: in the kettle, the rain, the teacup. The child must translate the tears she has felt, so she transfers them to the 'man with buttons like tears'.

The absence of parents is the cause of all these tears. By the end of the poem, in the tercet that draws together all the essential elements, tears are planted, or sorrow implanted, in the child's life cycle.

The drawing of the house also attracts the interest of psychologists. Its rigid form is taken to represent the insecurity of the young child's makeshift home, her path and flowerbed seen as an attempt to domesticate and put her own stamp on it and so give her some tenuous grasp on security. Helen Vendler asserts: 'The blank center stands for the definitive presence of the unnatural in the child's domestic experience.' Of all things, one's house should not be inscrutable, otherwise there is a great void at the centre of one's life. This becomes one of Elizabeth Bishop's recurring themes: that nothing is more enigmatic than the heart of the domestic scene.

The tercet achieves a resolution of sorts, offering a more balanced view of the human condition. It asserts that grief, song, the marvellous and the inscrutable are present, perhaps necessarily, together in life. But we are left with the impression that the inscrutable, the strange, is the most powerful element in human development.

First Death in Nova Scotia
Text of poem: New Explorations Anthology page 192

BACKGROUND NOTE

Apart from her short story 'In the Village', the poem is one of the few published memoirs of Bishop's childhood. It is also the only time her mother is featured in a published poem. The elegy is based on an actual funeral, probably in 1914, of a cousin named Frank. 'First Death in Nova Scotia' was published in the *New Yorker* on 10 March 1962.

POINT OF VIEW

This is another of Bishop's poems in which she attempts to recover her childhood. With an astute and sensitive psychological understanding, she is very successful at re-creating the consciousness of a child and establishing the point of view of the very young.

She manages to suggest the feelings of confusion through the blurring of colour distinctions. Red and white, the national colours, seem to permeate the entire scene, or at least colour the meaning of it. As well as of the national flag, they become the colours of little Arthur, of the dead bird, of the royal robes, and even of the coffin timbers. The child has held on to just one set of familiar colours.

Also, the child's memory seizes and holds objects (the chromographs, the stuffed loon, the lily of the valley). The child's memory recalls desires, desires for objects ('his breast ... caressable', 'his eyes were red glass, | much to be desired').

The child has difficulty coping with the difference of death, so the 'reality hold' slips. The familiar becomes unreal, the bird is alive again, just uncommunicative (he 'kept his own counsel | on his white, frozen lake'). There is an effort to make the unfamiliar – death – real in the child's terms, with surreal consequences.

> Arthur's coffin was
> a little frosted cake.

The adults too cope with death by participating in a sort of fantasy:

> 'Come,' said my mother,
> 'Come and say good-bye
> to your little cousin Arthur.'

The child fantasises that the 'cold, cold parlor' is the territory of Jack Frost and that the royal couple have 'invited Arthur to be | the smallest page at court.' The child has created a fantasy world in which reality and fantasy, present, past and future, and the national colours all fuse together. But the strain of credibility is too great, and doubt begins to enter her head. The doubt is not an adult doubt about Arthur's ultimate destiny but, in typical child fashion, a doubt about the means of transport.

> But how could Arthur go,
> clutching his tiny lily,
> with his eyes shut up so tight
> and the roads deep in snow?

The use of the child's point of view has allowed a very dispassionate treatment of death. Emotion does not get in the way, and the entire focus is on the unknowable strangeness of death.

THEMES AND ISSUES

- **Memories of childhood.** If this poem can be taken to reflect Bishop's recollections of childhood as a whole, then it is a bleak view. It encompasses death, both of people and creatures; a confused inability to comprehend the reality of the world; a world lacking in warmth or the normal human comforts of childhood ('cold, cold parlor', 'marble-topped table'); a world devoid of emotion; and a shadowy mother figure who is associated with the rituals of death rather than any maternal comfort.
- **A child's first exposure to death and her attempts to comprehend it** ('domesticate' it, in Bishop's terms).
- **Death – its unknowable strangeness.**
- **A secular view of death** (Arthur goes to court rather than Heaven!) – yet not completely secular, as it recognises another reality beyond this.
- **The frailty of life** ('he was all white, like a doll | that hadn't been painted yet').

Filling Station

Text of poem: New Explorations Anthology page 194
[Note: *This poem is also prescribed for Ordinary Level 2007 exam*]

A CELEBRATION OF THE ORDINARY

Many of Elizabeth Bishop's poems show a fascination with the exotic: with travel, with the mysterious forces in nature, and with the extremes of human experience; but she is also a poet of the ordinary, the everyday, the mundane and banal. She is interested in both the extraordinary and the ordinary.

And the scene we are introduced to at the beginning of this poem is not just the antithesis of beauty, it is unmitigated 'grot': 'oil-soaked, oil-permeated', 'crushed and grease- | impregnated wickerwork,' 'a dirty dog,' etc. What Bishop does is focus her well-known curiosity on this everyday dull scene and probe its uniqueness and mystery. She finds its meaning through her usual poetic method: accumulation of detail and a probing beneath the surface of the seen.

THE DOMESTIC GIVES MEANING TO LIFE

What is revealed as the details pile up is evidence of domesticity, even in this greasy, grimy world of oil and toil: the flower, the 'taboret | (part of the set)', the embroidered doily; and even the dirty dog is 'quite comfy'. In a parody of metaphysical questioning,

> Why the extraneous plant?
> Why the taboret?
> Why, oh why, the doily?

the poem searches for answers, for reasons why things are so, for some harmony or coherence at the heart of this grimy scene. The answer appears in the last stanza, where there are indications of an anonymous domestic presence:

> Somebody embroidered the doily.
> Somebody waters the plant.

For Bishop, domesticity is the greatest good, and establishing domestic tranquillity is what gives meaning to life. She has elevated this into a philosophy of life in place of a religious outlook. Indeed this last stanza has been read as a parody of the great theological Argument from Design used as an indication of the existence of God.

In Bishop's 'theology', is the Great Designer feminine? Certainly we could argue that the world of work described here operates on the male principle. The 'several quick and saucy | and greasy sons' and even the 'big hirsute begonia' all evoke a male world of inelegant, rude and crude health. In contrast, the domesticity is achieved mainly through the female principle:

> Embroidered in daisy stitch
> With marguerites, I think,

and it is this principle that provides order and coherence and meaning ('arranges the rows of cans') and is a proof of love ('somebody loves us all').

TONE

There are some complicated and subtle shifts of tone throughout this poem. From the somewhat offhand tone of the opening line ('Oh, but it is dirty!') she first takes refuge in descriptive detail. Some critics have read the beginning of the poem as condescending ('little filling station,' 'all quite thoroughly dirty'). The flashes of wit may give some credence to that interpretation ('Be careful with that match!' and the comic book of 'certain color').

But the poet is gradually drawn into the scene and becomes involved. The stance of detached observer no longer provides complete protection for her. She is engaged intellectually at first ('why, oh why, the doily?'), and, as she uncovers what gives coherence and meaning to the scene, an emotional empathy is revealed ('Somebody loves us all'). Perhaps this is as much a *cri de cœur* of personal need as it is an observation. But the wit saves the poem from any hint of sentimentality:

> Somebody waters the plant,
> or oils it, maybe.

Could we describe the tone of the poem as wryly affectionate? Or do you read the tone of the ending as bemused, as the poet is left contemplating the final irony that love is a row of oil cans?

In the Waiting Room

Text of poem: New Explorations Anthology page 197

A READING OF THE POEM

This poem depicts a traumatic moment of awareness in the child's development. It occurs when the young girl first experiences the separateness of her own identity and simultaneously becomes aware of the strangeness of the world of which she is a part. She fails to find a satisfactory, intelligible relationship between her now conscious 'self' and this 'other' world, a failure so emotional for her that it causes a momentary loss of consciousness, a temporary retreat into that black abyss.

At the beginning of the poem the child sees the world as safe, domestic, familiar: the world of her aunt, a waiting-room, overcoats, lamps and magazines. But the magazines expose her to the primal power of the earth, volcanic passion erupting out of control, the primitive destructive urges of humans (cannibalism), and the barbarous decorations of the naked women. Clearly this newly revealed primitive and exotic world is frighteningly 'other' to the child, and she can comprehend it only by domesticating it through a household simile:

> black, naked women with necks
> wound round and round with wire
> like the necks of light bulbs.

The unfamiliarity of this broader world is shocking to the child ('Their breasts were horrifying'.) Yet it is a world she shares, as she empathises with her aunt's cry of pain.

> What took me
> completely by surprise
> was that it was *me*:
> my voice, in my mouth.

The conflicting claims of self and of the world are cleverly conveyed by Bishop through a constantly changing inside–outside perspective maintained throughout the poem. At first we are in Worcester but outside the room, then inside the room ('sat') while it grew dark outside. Next we are back in the waiting-room while the aunt is further inside. The child looks inside a volcano but outside the cannibals and the naked women. The cry ('from inside, I came an oh! of pain') first drives the child inside herself ('my voice, in my mouth'). This sends her into a fainting dive ('I – we – were falling, falling'), until she is driven right off the world, and the perspective changes radically to a view from space ('cold, blue-black space').

These radical changes in perspective – from the people in the waiting-room to inside herself, to the African women, from inside to outside the waiting-room and the world, from 'I' to 'them' and back again – convey the child's confused apprehension of this widening world and bring on the fainting spell.

And it is in this atmosphere of shifting perspectives that she asserts her individuality, naming herself for the first time in a poem ('you are an *I*, | you are an *Elizabeth*'), yet immediately the claims of the 'other' world are manifest ('you are one of them'). She has great difficulty integrating the recently discovered elements of this world, unifying the exotic and the familiar, the naked women with the aunt and the people in the waiting-room in the familiar trousers and skirts and boots. She has even greater difficulty accepting any kind of personal unity with this other world, particularly at a time when she feels most alone, having just discovered herself.

> What similarities –
> boots, hands, the family voice
> I felt in my throat, or even
> the *National Geographic*
> and those awful hanging breasts –
> held us all together
> or made us all just one?

Even though the fainting spell passes, the moment of visionary insight fades and the child is relocated in actual time and place, the issue is not resolved ('the War was on'). This war is both political and personal for the child. Outside, the world is hostile ('night and slush and cold'), and her uneasy relationship with it continues.

These twin realisations of being an individual and yet somehow being uneasily connected to this strange and varied world form the central wisdom of this poem, what her biographer Brett Millier has described as 'the simultaneous realisation of selfhood and the awful otherness of the inevitable world'. It is interesting that Bishop chooses the age of seven to mark this onset of adult awareness, an age traditionally seen as initiating moral responsibility. She herself has dated the onset of many of her own most important attitudes from the age of six or seven, including a feeling of strangeness or alienation from the world. She also dates the beginnings of her feminist philosophy from that age.

ELIZABETH BISHOP AND CONSCIOUSNESS OF SEX ROLES

'In the Waiting Room' describes the poet's first encounter with consciousness of sex roles. Through the magazine the child learns, though perhaps at a sub-rational level, that women practise mutilations on themselves and their babies to make them more sexually attractive. They themselves perpetuate their role as sex objects, encourage this vanity, accept this type of slavery. Aunt Consuelo's 'oh! of pain' suggests the weakness and vulnerability of women. And Bishop identifies with woman's pain.

Yet her attitude to women is somewhat ambivalent. While she identifies with the cry, she is disparaging about the woman's weakness.

> even then I knew she was
> a foolish, timid woman.
> I might have been embarrassed,
> but wasn't.

She recoils in horror from female sexuality, from 'those awful hanging breasts.' This ambivalence about the value of femininity affected her view of herself, her sexual orientation, and gave rise to a complicated treatment of questions of sex roles in her poetry.

Poetic style: some comments

A private poem

'In the Waiting Room' is somewhat unusual in that it is such a self-contained poem. Usually in Bishop's poems the private experience described mushrooms into a universal truth. While we might draw some universal conclusions about childhood and the development of self-awareness, the truths this poem essentially conveys reflect idiosyncratic Bishop attitudes to life: the estrangement, the pain, the confusions of life, the view of woman, etc.

Descriptive accuracy

The fabled truth of Bishop's descriptions lets her down here. Research has shown that there are no naked people in the *National Geographic* of February 1918, and Osa and Martin Johnson had not yet become famous at that time. So for once her realism is a product of poetic licence!

Use of metre

The poem is written in very short, sometimes two-stress but more often three-stress lines. Trimeters are quite a limiting line formation, not often used for the communication of complicated ideas or deep emotions (though Yeats manages to convey deep irony and anger through the regular thumping trimeter beat of 'The Fisherman'). The use of trimeters here by Bishop is probably deliberate, to limit the reader's emotional engagement with the poem. Not that the poem is devoid of emotional impact: the moments of revelation are intensely felt. But, as the critic Penelope Laurans (in *Elizabeth Bishop: Modern Critical Views*, edited by Harold Bloom) demonstrates in her scanning of some passages, Bishop deliberately varies the metre to prevent a lyrical build-up that might invite an emotional investment by the reader. Instead, the reader is forced to think and reflect, in this example on the word 'stranger', which is stressed both by its placement and by the metre:

I knew | that nothing | stranger

had ever | happened, | that nothing

stranger | could ever | happen

The less usual *amphibrach* foot (˘ ‾ ˘) creates a certain ponderousness, which forces the reader to reflect on, rather than be caught up in, the experience.

At another key moment, the variation of feet is used to create the effect of puzzlement.

    How – | I didn't | know any

    word for it | – how 'un|likely' . . .

    How had I | come to | be here

Again, the effect is to limit the emotional appeal. Bishop uses her technical skills to keep the reader at bay, at a safe distance.

An overview of Elizabeth Bishop

The purpose of this section is to assist the reader in forming an overview of the poet's work. For this reason the material is structured as a series of 'thinking points', grouped under general headings. These cover the poet's main preoccupations and methods, but they are not exhaustive. Neither are they 'carved in stone', to be memorised: they should be altered, added to or deleted as the reader makes his or her own notes.

These thinking points should send the reader back to the poems, to reflect, to reassess, to find supporting quotations, etc.

THEMES OF BISHOP'S POETRY

Childhood
- Many of her poems have their roots in childhood memories, indeed are based on her own childhood ('Sestina', 'First Death in Nova Scotia', 'In the Waiting Room').
- The perspective is mostly that of adult reminiscence ('Sestina', 'In the Waiting Room'), but occasionally the child's viewpoint is used ('First Death in Nova Scotia').
- The lessons of childhood are chiefly about pain and loss ('Sestina', 'First Death in Nova Scotia', 'In the Waiting Room') and about alienation from the world ('In the Waiting Room'), but there is also the comfort of grandparents ('Sestina').
- There is a strong tension between the need to return to childhood and the need to escape from that childhood ('In the Waiting Room', 'At the Fishhouses', 'The Moose'); she even returns in dreams in a poem called 'The Moose'.
- Perhaps this is based on the notion of childhood as the completion of the self, and the poems are a search for the self?

- We know that she attended counselling to find the origins of her alcoholism and depression. Yet her reconstructions of childhood do not seem to function as Freudian psychoanalytical therapy. She doesn't seem to alter her direction or attitudes as a result of drawing her past into the conscious, though she does seem to find a deal of comfort and a greater acceptance in the later poem, 'The Moose'. She is not trying to apportion blame, neither is she trying to be forgiving or sympathetic. In general she seems neutral and detached ('First Death in Nova Scotia', 'Sestina').
- She also deals with the end of childhood and the awakening to adulthood ('In the Waiting Room').

Her life was her subject matter
Bishop was 'a poet of deep subjectivity', as Harold Bloom said. She wrote out of her own experience, dealing with such topics as:
- her incompleteness ('Sestina', 'In the Waiting Room')
- her disordered life and depression ('The Bight')
- alcoholism ('The Prodigal')
- her childhood – of loss, sorrow and tears ('Sestina'), absence of parents ('Sestina'), balanced by grandparents' sympathy and support ('Sestina')
- achieving adulthood and the confusion of that ('In the Waiting Room')
- travel, her wanderlust ('Questions of Travel'), her favourite places ('At the Fishhouses')
- even her hobbies, such as fishing ('The Fish').

The poet and travel
- As her own wanderings show, she was a restless spirit, constantly on the move: Nova Scotia, Florida, Brazil, Europe, New York, San Francisco, Harvard.
- Many of the places she visited (Nova Scotia, the Straits of Magellan, the Amazon Estuary, Key West, Florida) stand at the boundary between land and sea. There is a tension between land and sea in her poems ('At the Fishhouses', 'Questions of Travel'), with the sea viewed as a strange, indifferent, encircling power ('At the Fishhouses'). Perhaps this is a metaphor for the conflict between the artist and life. Quite a few of her poems are set at this juncture between land and sea ('The Fish', 'The Bight', 'At the Fishhouses').
- She seemed to be fascinated by geographical extremities: straits, peninsulas, wharves; mountains, jungle, outback ('Questions of Travel', 'The Armadillo', 'At the Fishhouses', 'The Bight'). Perhaps she was attracted to the near-isolation of these places. They are almost isolated in her poems. One critic viewed these as the sensual organs of a living earth, 'fingers of water or land that are the sensory receptors of a large mass'. The poet is seen as making sensuous contact with the living earth.

- Bishop has an eye for the exotic and the unusual ('Questions of Travel', 'The Armadillo') but also for the ordinary ('Filling Station').
- She dwells on the difficulty of ever really knowing another culture ('Questions of Travel'), but this did not prevent her trying.
- Travel and journeying can be seen as a metaphor for the discovery of truth in some poems ('Questions of Travel').
- Could this preoccupation with travel be seen as exile from the self?

Bishop and the natural world
- Nature is central to her poetry, either as an active element central to the experience of the poem or by making an intrusion into the domestic scene (in a minority of poems such as 'Filling Station', 'Sestina', 'First Death in Nova Scotia', 'In the Waiting Room').
- An ecological world view is at the core of her philosophy – replacing religion, some would say ('The Armadillo'). Her view of humankind's relationship with nature involves a dialectical process of interdependence rather than humankind dominating or subjugating nature. But we see both extremes in the poems: humankind's destructiveness ('The Armadillo') but also the achievement of a comfortable domesticity with nature, even at the primitive animal level ('The Prodigal').
- The experience of really looking at and encountering the natural is central to her poetic process ('The Fish', 'Questions of Travel').
- Our ability to understand the natural is sometimes limited, yet there are great moments of awe and insight in our encounters with the other-worldly spirit of nature ('The Fish').
- Bishop is always aware of the sheer beauty of nature ('The Bight', 'Questions of Travel', 'The Armadillo').
- This is tied in with her fascination with travel and her interest in the exotic ('The Armadillo', 'Questions of Travel').
- She attempts to domesticate the strangeness of nature through language and description.
- Consider also some points already discussed, such as how geographical extremes fascinate her, her beloved places, and the significance of journeys for her.

The domestic and the strange
- The importance of the domestic is also a central ground in her poetry. Domesticity is one of the unifying principles of life. It gives meaning to our existence ('Filling Station').
- The comfort of people, of domestic affections, is important ('Filling Station', 'Sestina').

- Yet the heart of the domestic scene can sometimes be enigmatic. This strangeness, even at the centre of the domestic, is a powerful element in human life ('Sestina', 'First Death in Nova Scotia', 'In the Waiting Room'). One can be ambushed by the strange at any time, even in the security of the domestic scene ('In the Waiting Room').
- The process of domesticating is a central activity of humanity: domesticating the land, domesticating affections, domesticating the non-human world.

Bishop's philosophy as revealed in the poems
- Bishop's is a secular (non-religious) world-view: there is no sense of ultimate purpose, and in this she relates to modernist American poets like Frost and Stevens.
- Hers is very much a here-and-now, existential philosophy: the experience is everything. There is some sense of tradition or linear movement in her life view, but tradition is just an accumulation of experience. The transience of knowledge ('At the Fishhouses') and the limits to our knowing ('Questions of Travel') contribute to this outlook.
- Her ecological outlook is at the basis of her philosophy, as we have seen: humankind in dialectical action with nature, discovering, encountering, not domineering ('The Fish').
- She demonstrates the importance of the domestic ('Filling Station').
- Her view of the human being is as fractured and incomplete ('Chemin de Fer'). This duality has been described by Anne Newman (in *Elizabeth Bishop: Modern Critical Views*, edited by Harold Bloom) as follows: 'She sees the ideal and the real, permanence and decay, affirmation and denial in both man and nature'; a sort of 'fractured but balanced' view of humanity. Examine 'Filling Station' and 'In the Waiting Room' for signs of this.
- A person may not always be entirely free to choose her location ('Questions of Travel'), yet she can make a choice about how her life is spent. Life is not totally determined ('The Prodigal').
- The bleaker side of life is often stressed, the pain, loss and trauma ('The Prodigal', 'Sestina', 'First Death in Nova Scotia', 'In the Waiting Room'), yet she is not without humour ('At the Fishhouses', 'Filling Station').
- She believes we need to experience our dreams ('Questions of Travel').
- Is the overall view of humankind that of the eternal traveller, journeying? And is the journey all? Would you agree with Jerome Mazzaro's view (in *Elizabeth Bishop: Modern Critical Views*, edited by Harold Bloom): 'Like Baudelaire's voyagers she seems instead to be accepting the conditions of voyaging as the process of a life which itself will arrive meaninglessly at death with perhaps a few poems as a dividend'?
- She expresses the unknowable strangeness of death ('First Death in Nova Scotia').

- Yet there is a sort of heroism evident in her poems. Many of the poems feature a crisis or conflict of some sort, with which the narrator deals courageously, often learning in the process ('The Fish', 'In the Waiting Room').

Bishop and women's writing
- Are you conscious of the femininity of the speaker in Bishop's poems? Some critics have argued that the importance of the domestic principle in her philosophy ('Filling Station') and the attitudes of care and sympathy in the poems (for the fish, the prodigal, the animals and birds) and even the occupational metaphors, for example of housemaking ('Filling Station', 'Sestina') and dressmaking and map colouring in other poems, all indicate a strong feminine point of view in her poetry. Other critics have argued that her rhetoric is completely asexual, that the poet's persona is neutral, the Bishop 'I' is the eye of the traveller or the child recapturing an innocence that avoids sex roles altogether, an asexual self that frees her from any sex-determined role. Examine 'Questions of Travel' and 'First Death in Nova Scotia' in this regard.
- We have already encountered something of her treatment of her own sexuality and her attitude as a child to female sexuality ('In the Waiting Room'). She also deals with sexuality in other poems, such as 'Crusoe in England', 'Santarém', 'Exchanging Hats', and 'Pink Dog'.

Bishop's links to the Romantics
The following are some of the distinguishing features of Romanticism. Consider Elizabeth Bishop's poetry in the light of some or all of these statements.
1. Romanticism stressed the importance of the solitary individual voice, often in rebellion against tradition and social conventions.
2. The subjective vision is of great value in society.
3. In place of orthodox religious values the individual looks for value and guidance in intense private experience.
4. Nature often provides such intense experience, hence the notion of nature as the great teacher and moral guide.
5. Romanticism can show a divided view of the individual. The individual is often pulled in opposite directions – for example solitariness versus sociability, lonely pursuit of an ideal versus community fellowship.
6. It is anti-rational. Feelings, instinctive responses, unconscious wisdom and passionate living are valued more than rational thought.
7. Dreams and drug-enhanced experiences are especially valued. Children, primitive people, outcasts, even the odd eccentric figure are regarded as having special insight and wisdom.
- 'Bishop explored typical Romantic themes, such as problems of isolation, loss, and the desire for union beyond the self.' Explore the poetry in the light of this statement.

- It has been said that Bishop's practice of poetry follows Wordsworth's advice that poetry should embody controlled passion, should deal with powerful feelings but with the restraint of hindsight: 'spontaneous overflow of powerful feelings', 'emotion recollected in tranquillity'. Would you agree?
- Examine 'At the Fishhouses' as a great Romantic poem.

STYLE AND TECHNIQUE

Variety of verse forms
- Though she was not often attracted to formal patterns, a variety of verse forms is found in Bishop's poetry: sonnet, sestina, villanelle, etc. ('The Prodigal', 'Sestina').
- She used a variety of metres, but often favoured trimeter lines ('The Armadillo'). This sometimes resulted in those long, thin poems.
- She was happiest using free verse ('Questions of Travel', 'The Bight', 'At the Fishhouses', etc.).

Her descriptions
- The surface of a Bishop poem is often deceptively simple.
- A favourite technique is 'making the familiar strange' ('The Bight', 'Questions of Travel').
- Her detailed descriptions function as repossession or domestication of the object by the artist. This is how she gradually apprehends her subject, through the accumulation of detail ('The Fish').
- Bishop often insisted on the truth of her descriptions, but the reality is more complex than that. Her descriptions are both re-creation and creation, creating veracity but also using poetic licence ('The Armadillo'; also 'In the Waiting Room').
- Her similes and metaphors are often surprising, like conceits. They can be both exciting and exact.

Control of feeling
- Many of her poems deal with emotive subjects ('In the Waiting Room').
- There is an element of spontaneity and naturalness in the tone. Consider the opening of 'In the Waiting Room' and 'Filling Station'. 'The sense of the mind actively encountering reality, giving off the impression of involved immediate discovery, is one of Bishop's links to the Romantics,' as the critic Penelope Laurans put it.
- Yet spontaneity and feelings are firmly controlled by technique, in particular by variation of metre (see critical commentary on 'The Armadillo', among others). 'It is sometimes assumed that the cool surfaces of Bishop's poems reveal their lack of emotional depth; in fact Bishop often uses such reticence

as a strategy to make a deeper, more complex emotional appeal to the reader' (Penelope Laurans). (Examine 'The Armadillo' and 'In the Waiting Room' and their critical commentaries.)
- The matter-of-fact tone avoids sentimentality. The use of understatement controls feeling ('In the Waiting Room').

The absence of moralising
- Her dislike of didacticism is well documented. She disliked 'modern religiosity and moral superiority', and so she avoids overt moralising in her poems. The scenes offer up their wisdom gradually, as the descriptions help us to understand the object or place ('At the Fishhouses', 'Questions of Travel').

Bishop as a dramatic poet
Consider:
- scenes of conflict or danger
- moments of dramatic encounter
- dramatic monologue structure in many of the poems.

Making the strange familiar: forging a personal understanding of Bishop's poetry

Think about the following points, and make notes for yourself or discuss them in groups.
- Which poems made the deepest impression on you? Why?
- Which passages would you wish to read and reread? Why?
- In the selection you have read, what were the principal issues that preoccupied the poet? What did you like or dislike about the way she treated these issues?
- Did you find that reading Bishop gave you any insights into human beings or the world? What did you discover?
- From your reading of the poems, what impression did you form about the personality of the poet herself? What do you think made her happy or sad? What did she enjoy or fear? What values or beliefs did she have? Or is it difficult to answer these questions? If so, what does that tell you about the voice of the poet in these poems?
- Think about the landscapes and places that attracted her. What do they suggest about the poet and poetry?
- Think about the people featured in her poetry. What do you notice about them?
- Describe your overall response to reading her poetry: did you find her voice disturbing, frightening, challenging, enlightening, comforting, or what? Refer to particular poems or passages to illustrate your conclusions.
- What do you like or dislike about the style of her poetry?

- Do you find her poetry different in any way from other poetry you have read? Explain.
- Why should we read Bishop? Attempt to convince another pupil of the importance of her poetry, in a letter, speech, or other form.
- What questions would you like to ask her about her poetry?

Questions

1. 'The human being at a moment of crisis is the central concern of much of Bishop's poetry.' Discuss this statement, with reference to two or more poems you have read.
2. The child's relationship with the world is a major theme in Bishop's poetry. What aspects of this theme do you find developed in the poems?
3. 'Bishop's poems may be set in particular places, but the discoveries made are universal.' Discuss this statement, with reference to any two poems.
4. 'The real focus of Bishop's poetry is inside herself. Her poems are primarily psychological explorations.' Discuss.
5. 'The view of the poet that comes across from these poems is of an isolated eccentric who nevertheless has a keen interest in human beings.' Discuss.
6. 'A keen eye for detail and a fascination with the ordinary are distinguishing features of Elizabeth Bishop's poetry.' Discuss.
7. 'A deep sense of interior anguish lies at the heart of many of her poems.' Discuss this view, with reference to at least four of the poems you have read.
8. 'She is a poet who lives in a painter's world in which shapes and colours are enormously significant' (Anne Stevenson). Discuss, with reference to a selection of her poems.
9. 'For all the unhappiness of the themes she deals with, we often find a note of humour, even of fun, in Bishop's poems.' Discuss.
10. 'Bishop has the oddest way of describing things; she sometimes makes the ordinary appear strange.' Explore the effects of this technique in at least two of the poems you have studied.
11. 'We find a distinct lack of emotion in Bishop's poetry.' (*a*) How does she achieve this? (*b*) Is it always true of her poetry? Explain.
12. 'Man, for her, appears as a figure in a landscape, flawed, helpless, tragic, but capable also of love and even of happiness' (Anne Stevenson). Discuss this aspect of Bishop's poetry, with reference to the poems you have studied.

Bishop's writings

Complete Poems, London: Chatto and Windus 1991.
Collected Prose (Robert Giroux, editor), London: Chatto and Windus 1994.
One Art: The Selected Letters (Robert Giroux, editor), London: Chatto and Windus 1994.
Exchanging Hats: Paintings, Manchester: Carcanet 1997.

Bibliography

Bloom, Harold (editor), *Elizabeth Bishop: Modern Critical Views,* New York: Chelsea House 1985.
Harrison, Victoria, *Elizabeth Bishop's Poetics of Intimacy,* Cambridge: Cambridge University Press 1993.
McCabe, Susan, *Elizabeth Bishop: Her Poetics of Loss,* Pittsburgh: Pennsylvania State University Press 1994.
Millier, Brett, *Elizabeth Bishop: Life and the Memory of It,* Berkeley: University of California Press 1993.
Spiegelman, Willard, 'Elizabeth Bishop's natural heroism' in *Centennial Review,* no. 22, winter 1978, reprinted in *Elizabeth Bishop: Modern Critical Views,* edited by Harold Bloom.
Stevenson, Anne, *Elizabeth Bishop,* New York: Twayne 1966.
Wehr, Wesley, 'Elizabeth Bishop: conversations and class notes' in *Antioch Review,* no. 39, summer 1981.

7 John MONTAGUE

Carole Scully

Praising the burden

EARLY LIFE

> 'Brooklyn born, Tyrone-reared, Dublin-educated, constituted a tangle, a turmoil of contradictory allegiance it would take a lifetime to unravel.'

This is how John Montague describes his own life and it is important for us to be aware of his life if we are to develop an understanding of his poetry, because Montague's life is the starting point for his writing. This is not to suggest that he writes a poetic diary. Rather, in his poetry he takes his own 'tangle' of experiences and observations and draws out of them lessons and Truths that are universally relevant. Thus, by reading Montague's poetry we may also begin to reflect on the 'tangle' that lies within each of us.

Montague has described his life as being 'a burden', and there is no doubt that his early life was a difficult one. He was born on 28 February 1929 in St Catherine's Hospital, Brooklyn. His parents had only recently been reunited after a separation lasting for three years. This separation had come about because of his father's political activities in Northern Ireland. Montague's father, James, had come from a comfortable Catholic family in Co. Tyrone; however, he had become actively involved in Nationalist activities after the Easter Rising in 1916. When Ireland was partitioned and Northern Ireland was established, James found it impossible to find employment. As a married man with two small sons, James decided that he had no choice but to travel to America, while his wife Molly and the children stayed behind in Co. Tyrone.

Unfortunately, when the family were reunited in New York life was still hard for them. John's mother found it difficult to bond with her new son, and this rejection proved to be a major issue in Montague's life and writing. When the American stock market collapsed in 1929 John's father, along with many others, lost his job. To make matters worse, his mother became ill with tuberculosis. The family lived in a 'speakeasy', an illegal drinking den, owned by John's uncle. But when John's uncle died the decision was made to send John and his two older brothers back to Northern Ireland, while James and Molly remained in New York.

For the two older boys it was a return to their 'home'. But for the four-year-old John it was an expedition into the unknown. Later he was to write, 'Losing a family and a country in one sweep must not have been easy, although for long I suppressed my earlier memories.' The effects of this early disruption on his environment are evident in Montague's search for a sense of identity in his writing, where he tries to work out who he is and where he belongs.

When the three boys arrived back in Co. Tyrone, John was separated from his two brothers. While they went to live with their maternal grandmother in Fintona, John was taken to live with his father's two unmarried sisters in the Montague family home in Garvaghey. The reasons behind this surprising decision were complicated. John's grandmother was an old lady who was reluctant to take on the rearing of a small child. Also, his father wanted one of his sons to grow up in the Montague environment.

So John lost his last remaining certainty, the presence of the two brothers that he had lived with constantly for the first four years of his young life. He found himself living with strangers, in an unknown house, set in an unknown landscape far away from the teeming streets of Brooklyn.

Education

John's aunts were two kind women, with his Aunt Brigid, in particular, providing great support for John. They made the sensitive decision to let John stay at home for a year before sending him to school. It was during this time that he began to explore the wide, open landscape of Co. Tyrone and to develop a love and appreciation of nature. This early interaction with the natural world was to have a positive influence on Montague: not only did it help him to begin to develop a sense of his own identity, but it also provided him with a wealth of experiences. As an adult poet, Montague frequently taps into this storehouse of childhood memories to produce the most wonderfully vivid pieces of writing, as in 'The Trout' and 'Killing the Pig'.

Montague has said that the 'few years from four to eleven' were 'a blessing and a healing'. He went to the local school and proved to be a bright pupil. However, this was not a completely happy time for him. When John was seven years old his mother returned home to Co. Tyrone, leaving his father in Brooklyn. However, she made no attempt to bring John to live with her. Perhaps she did not want to disrupt John's life by taking him from his aunts' home; or, perhaps, she had been so worn down by the disappointments of her life in America that she was unable to take on the responsibility of a young child. Whatever the reason, Molly went to live some eight miles away from her son, in her family home at Fintona, and they met only occasionally. The trauma of this second rejection was a major contributory factor to the little boy developing a stutter, as Montague suggests himself:

'I have no doubt that the separation from my mother, whatever the reasons for the decision, is at the center of my emotional life, affecting my relationships with women, shadowing my powers of speech . . .'.

In 'The Locket' Montague traces, with brutal honesty, his boyhood attempts to establish some type of relationship with his mother.

His mother was not the only female figure who exerted a negative influence on his development. The treatment that John received at the hands of a local teacher, who seemed to dislike the Montague family, may also have added to his speech difficulties. John was particularly good at reading, and one day he was sent to this teacher to read a passage aloud. Owing to the content of the passage, a description of a young, naked girl dancing under the moon, John became somewhat unsettled. In response, the teacher began to mock him and his accent, which still bore traces of his early years in Brooklyn. Indeed, Brooklyn continued to feature in young John's life, for his father was still living there and would do so until he returned to Northern Ireland in 1952, when John was in his twenties. In his poem 'The Cage' Montague confronts his relationship with his father, presenting an honest representation of their situation.

At the age of eleven Montague won a scholarship to St Patrick's College, Armagh. He found it an unhappy experience: 'Those five years in Armagh were the most cramped of my childhood.' His aunts were hopeful that he might discover a religious vocation. John, however, was less sure. Although he was impressed by the ceremony and rituals of the Catholic Church, he found something even more interesting – girls!

In 1946 Montague won a scholarship to attend University College Dublin, where he studied English and History. Initially he found it difficult to settle into college life. Then he noticed that the 'intellectuals', a group of students who controlled the English Literature Society and a literary magazine, were very popular with 'the brighter girls, who were often the more pretty'. John decided to become part of this group, and it was here that he discovered that he 'might possibly be able to write something like the kind of poetry I admired'. The connection between women and poetry persisted for Montague. In 'All Legendary Obstacles' Montague describes his feelings as he waits for his girlfriend to arrive on the train; while in 'The Same Gesture' he considers the nature of the love that he and his lover share.

Montague's involvement with the 'intellectuals' led him into the Dublin poetic scene, where he met such poets as Austin Clarke and Patrick Kavanagh. He was hopeful that engaging with this group might help him to develop his writing skills, so that he would be better able to understand and shoulder the burden of his life. Disappointingly, Montague found that, 'The poetic world of Dublin was acrimony and insult: a poem was to be kicked, not examined; the begrudgers ruled.'

However, his connection with this group did have two major effects on his development as a writer. He was horrified by the financial poverty and lack of recognition that both Clarke and Kavanagh endured, and he worked hard to gain recognition and financial support for the two men. As a result, Montague vowed that he would never rely on poetry for his income. He has stuck to this decision throughout his life and has worked in such areas as journalism and lecturing while continuing to write poetry. In addition, because of his negative experiences as a young poet, Montague has always been immensely supportive of other writers, commenting 'I would not wish anyone to go through what I endured as a young writer.'

THE WIDER WORLD

By the time Montague had completed his final exams in 1952, gaining a double First in English and History, he was very frustrated by his life in Ireland. Luckily, he received a scholarship to study in America. This not only gave him the opportunity to break away from the negativity of the Dublin poetic scene; it also offered him the chance to escape from the claustrophobic and inward-looking attitude that pervaded Ireland in the 1950s. He had long felt that Ireland was a country that existed on the fringes of the world. As a schoolboy during the Second World War he had followed the theatre of wartime actions, conscious that he was 'just a boy living on the edge of a giant historical drama'. In his poem 'A Welcoming Party', Montague expresses his sense of Ireland's peripheral position and the effects that it had on both himself and the Irish people.

He also developed the belief – one that he holds to this day – that for his writing to develop to its full potential he must engage with literary influences from all over the world. This is not to suggest that he is rejecting all that is Irish; on the contrary, he feels that 'The wider an Irishman's experience, the more likely he is to understand his native country.'

Montague landed in a very different world in America. He discovered the literary world that he had yearned for: 'a literary world filled with writers revelling in the creation of living, breathing poetry'. He embraced the opportunity to encounter new ideas and to develop deep friendships with other writers. His writing blossomed and he began to find some easiness in his shouldering of the burden of his life.

Having met his first wife in America, Montague returned to Ireland for some time before travelling to his wife's native country, France. There he met writers such as Samuel Beckett. Indeed, no matter where Montague has lived, be it in Ireland, America or France, he has always sought the company of other writers and artists because he sees the 'idea of a fertile community' as being of great benefit to the creative process. Furthermore, by being part of such groups, Montague developed a feeling of belonging that has contributed to his sense of identity. Finally, it was through these opportunities for open companionship and the enthusiastic pooling of ideas that Montague constructed and refined his view that writing in the twentieth century was a 'shared adventure': an adventure that both he and Northern Ireland had to become part of.

A MODERN FORM OF NORTHERN IRISH POETRY

In his evolution of a poetic style Montague has consistently had a double purpose: to develop a personal writing style, and to initiate a new form of writing for Northern Irish poetry. So, through his writing, he has acted as a kind of trailblazer, or as he describes himself, 'the missing link of Ulster poetry', because 'There had not been a poet of Ulster Catholic background since the Gaelic poets of the eighteenth century.'

This style rests on two foundations: first, Montague's awareness of the relationship between Ireland's past and the present; and second, his belief that for poetic progress to occur there must be an investigation and inclusion of influences from the international world of modern poetry.

Through his exploration of the connection between Ireland's past and present, Montague not only contributed to his writing style, but he also added to his own sense of identity. His awareness of his life being related to past lives gave him a sense of belonging to a living inheritance that was held within the Northern Irish countryside and further eased the burden of his living. The danger, as Montague sees it, is that modern life has taken the people away from their land and destroyed their sense of connection to the past:

> The whole landscape a manuscript
> We had lost the skill to read,

So in his poetry Montague frequently tries to highlight and emphasise this connection between the past and the present. In 'Like Dolmens Round my Childhood . . .' he examines his relationship with the past, as represented by the old people and the dolmens, and comes to an understanding that they are indeed very much a part of his own being and the present; while in 'The Wild Dog Rose' he uses the story of the attempted rape of one woman as a representation of the history of the political relationship between Ireland and England. For Montague's view of the past is no idealised vision: he confronts the violence, the harshness of the struggle and the determined endurance that lie within the past.

Allied to this emphasis on the relevance of the past is his drive to incorporate elements from modern writing, known as Modernism, into his own work and Northern Irish literature. From his earliest years in America Montague developed a close bond with writers who were at the forefront of poetic experimentation, such as Gary Snyder and William Carlos Williams, and he embraced and refined some features of Modernist writing in his poetry. In order to provide a stylistic context for our consideration of Montague's work we will briefly discuss four of these features: the Artist-centred View; Nature; Imagery; and Poetic Form and Language.

The Artist-centred View
Modernists emphasise the importance of the artist in the creative process. In poetry, this means that a poet examines experiences from his own life and the way in which he responds to his world, with a view to uncovering the universal Truths of life that have a relevance to all people. Therefore by reading a poem we, as readers, can come to a deeper understanding of the workings of our own lives and the world that we live in. This approach is closely connected to the Modernists' fondness for the Lyric poem. A Lyric poem is one in which the poet seeks to express an individual state of mind, mood or attitude. Poets usually write from a personal point of view, using the personal pronoun 'I' in their writing. Occasionally a poet might create an imaginary character, a persona, to express this personal point of view. Montague uses the Lyric form in many of his poems – for example in 'The Cage', 'All Legendary Obstacles' and 'A Welcoming Party' – and he has described how, as a young writer, he modified the form so that he would be able 'to express himself in a compressed, more direct, yet still clearly lyrical form'.

Nature
In Modernist writing, nature is used as a trigger to stimulate the imagination. Unlike Wordsworth and the Romantic poets, Modernists are not mainly concerned with trying to recreate the wonder of nature in words, although they do produce extremely vivid descriptions. Instead, Modernist writers place the emphasis on their imaginative responses to nature. For them, it is the way the individual processes what he/she experiences that is important. We can see this approach in Montague's poem 'Windharp'. As we noted previously, Montague developed his great love of nature when he was a child. For a time he felt a connection with the great Romantic poet William Wordsworth. However, Montague was uneasy with the way that Wordsworth tended to idealise nature. He developed a much more honest and uncompromising view of the natural world, evident in his imagery in 'Killing the Pig' and 'The Trout'.

Imagery
Modernists use imagery to achieve realisation. Realisation means that the poet conveys more than just the sensory realism of an object. Therefore it is not enough for them to do as the Romantics did and appeal to the reader's five senses. Modernist poets do use sensory-based images, but they also seek to

create images that allow the reader to be fully 'there' with the object: to be completely aware of it and to understand clearly the nature of its being. In addition, because Modernist poetry frequently uses the artist-centred view, the images that are used in this realisation are connected together by 'a stream of consciousness'. This means that the poet tries to retain the immediacy and the energy of the way his thoughts and feelings blend and merge within him, rather like an internalised 'Lava Lamp'. This can prove to be both the pleasure and the pain of Modernist poetry. Sometimes the connections between the images mesh and we, as readers, experience an insightful understanding of the realisation that the poet seeks to convey. But there are occasions when, try as we might, the links remain unclear and all we are left with is a feeling of bewilderment. Although Modernists do accept bewilderment as a valid response, in such instances it is often helpful to simply allow the images to 'float' around 'inside your head' until the link reveals itself.

Poetic Form and Language

In an effort to give their realisations an undiluted vividness and accessibility for the reader, the Modernists firmly rejected traditional poetic forms and language. Rhyme was no longer considered essential, neither was the rigour of the fourteen-line sonnet. Instead blank or unrhymed verse, rhythm and short verse lines, sometimes consisting of only a few words, allowed the poet to grapple directly and intensely with the essential qualities of his topics and themes.

Such a method can be viewed as a kind of verbal paring back to the very core. In fact, one could compare this approach to the way in which 'text messaging' has caused the simplification of spellings and grammar so that we can communicate the essence of what we want to say as briefly as possible. Modernists use similar methods in their work, as they too alter the type of grammar and language used in poetic expression: make punctuation less rigid; do not have lines of poetry necessarily beginning with a capital letter; no longer cluster lines into stanzas; and replace obviously poetic words such as 'oft' and 'hence' with the everyday vocabulary of real life, as in the phrases 'the Clark Street I.R.T.' and 'work, phone, drive'. Montague summed up his approach to this abandonment of traditional poetic rules in a typically succinct phrase: 'I never strain a line to gain a rhyme.' This does not imply that any less work is put into the writing; rather that the work goes into different, and what could be regarded as more important, areas. Indeed, John Montague's work with words has an elegance and finesse that can be achieved only with a great deal of thought and effort.

The Modernist poets also took a new approach to the appearance of the printed poem on the page, and Montague urges a more experimental approach to layout, commenting:

> It is only a habit of mind which makes us expect a poem to march as docile as a herd of sheep between the fences of white margins.

Poems such as 'Killing the Pig' and 'The Wild Dog Rose' are good examples of his desire to break down the traditional methods of poetic presentation.

Praising the Burden

There is a long distance to be travelled between Montague's discovering ways to ease his view of life as a burden and his developing the strength to praise that burden; and yet, it seems to me, that this is precisely the journey that he makes in his poetry.

We have seen how the young Montague's search for a sense of identity, to find out who he was and where he belonged, was impaired by a number of factors: the disruption of his childhood environment caused by his early move from America to Ireland; his father's absence; and, perhaps the most significant of all, his mother's rejection of him. Yet through his poetry Montague has found a way to come to terms with all of these life issues. He can now welcome the duality of his American/Irish background as a positive influence on his writing in that it provided him with a unique view. Of the many honours that he received in America he wrote:

> ... destiny seems to have decided to give me back my lost childhood in America.... But ... I am grateful to have explored Ireland so intimately.

He can even accept the damaged humanity of his parents, because of his muscular determination to view them in an honest and uncompromising way.

Indeed, it is evident from our consideration of John Montague's life and work that it is this same determined, uncompromising honesty that lies at the heart of his poetry. His exploration of Love confronts the reality rather than the dreams of romantic novels. His writing on Nature recognises and accepts the brutality of the survival instinct. His view of the past acknowledges the violence and harshness that are part of it and the influences, both positive and negative, that it can have on the present. He has questioned the accepted traditions of Irish poetry and turned to worldwide literary influences to develop his own style, which would reflect contemporary Ireland while at the same time initiating the rebirth of Northern Irish poetry.

John Montague has spent time travelling and living in France, America and Ireland, teaching in such universities as Berkeley, UCD and UCC. When he retired from teaching in 1988 he continued with his writing and now divides his time between France and Ireland. As the following passage suggests it seems that, finally, Montague has succeeded in finding the key to ease his sense of burden:

> . . . I approach my future with energy of gratitude: what were once obstacles are becoming miracles, and after years of ploughing rough ground I might be allowed a period of harvesting. For a rearing can be too drastic, despite Kavanagh's theory about all art being 'life squeezed through a repression'. . . . That dolorous discord, that forlorn note, still calls but something sustained me through those harsh, uncomprehending years. My amphibian position between North and South, my natural complicity in three cultures, American, Irish and French, with darts aside to Mexico, India, Italy or Canada, should seem natural enough in the late-twentieth century as man strives to reconcile local allegiances with the absolute necessity of developing a world consciousness to save us from the abyss. Earthed in Ireland, at ease in the world, weave the strands you are given.

It seems to me that this is why Montague's poetry is relevant and has something to offer to all those who read it. It tells of the recognition of what it is to feel lost and alone in a confusing world; the understanding that this is part of all human existence; the determination to accept the reality of one's own living, and from this to discover the strength to praise and celebrate the contribution that each one of us can make to the ebb and flow of humanity. He shows us the tangled strands of his life so that we may see our own tangled life strands and, with him, learn how to 'weave the strands you're given'.

Seamus Heaney once described John Montague as the 'whin bush of Irish Poetry'. Although I am most reluctant to disagree with Mr Heaney, I have to say that I find the image of a yellow gorse bush a little too fixed, too statically stoic for Montague. While I was writing this piece on Montague one image kept forcing its way into my mind. It was an image that I initially found surprising, yet one that steadily gained a relevance to my view of him. It was the image of a Gaelic footballer, managing the burden of the football with finesse and discipline as he powers towards his opponents, forging his way with an uncompromising strength and determination towards the goal. So it is with Montague. The refinement and elegance of his poetry are underpinned by a muscularity of focus and a determined and powerful honesty. Like Montague, the footballer is fully aware of the imminent presence of pain, suffering and defeat in what he is doing, and it is this awareness that makes the commitment of both breathtaking, their courage admirable, their engagement with life elemental. Montague once said, 'But though to understand, however dimly, is to begin to forgive, a writer should never forget.' It is Montague's unyielding resolve to understand, to forgive and most importantly of all, never to forget the 'human pain' involved in living, that enables him not merely to manage the burden of his life but to welcome it and, finally, to celebrate and praise it.

Killing the Pig

Text of poem: New Explorations Anthology page 234

The Appearance of the Poem

Montague uses the layout of this poem to increase the impact of the content. By clustering connected lines together, by separating others and by a skilful use of punctuation, he controls the pace of reading. As a result, we are compelled to linger over certain descriptions, as with lines 5–10, while other lines interrupt the pace in an abrupt manner, as in lines 17–18.

A reading of the poem

Montague opens the poem with two words that are filled with such drama that they irresistibly attract attention, 'The noise.' The full stop that follows the two words forces the reader to a sudden stop, just as the real noise halts the farmyard activities. 'The noise' can penetrate walls and doors, so that even before the pig comes into view, it is the 'noise' that signals what is about to happen. The natural question that occurs in response to these two words is 'What noise?' So, Montague sets out to convey in vivid images the source and quality of the noise that has the power to stop the world in its tracks.

The image of the source of the noise, a pig being dragged to the slaughter, is brutally real. Montague does not shy away from the horror of the pig's situation, the 'iron cleek sunk in the roof | of his mouth.' Once again, a full stop forces the reader to pause, prevents a quick gliding over of this unpleasant description.

The parenthesis, the comment that occurs in the brackets in lines 5–10, has a disturbingly conversational tone about it. It is as if we are engaged in a chat about the weather. But the sense of horror is increased: not only is the pig suffering physically, with an iron hook through the roof of its mouth, it is also suffering mentally because it is aware of what the future holds: 'they know the hour has come'. The line 'they dig in their little trotters' emphasises the futility of the pig's resistance and has a kind of black comedy about it. We can visualise the large, fat pig pushing hard on four incongruously small trotters. It would be so much easier if the pig were cooperative, silently unaware, 'dumb', or even happily unaware, 'singing'. But this pig behaves in neither of these ways.

Suddenly, the 'noise' interrupts our 'cosy' conversation. Montague launches into a series of images in lines 13–16, to convey the nature of the 'noise', because 'no single sound could match it –'. Each of the four images has been condensed, reduced to its very essence, in order to vividly suggest the piercing, unsettling nature of the 'sound'. It has the qualities of a plane taking off; a lady opera singer hitting a high note; an electric saw cutting and scrap metal being crushed.

All of these sounds are difficult to cope with because they push the human sense of hearing to its limits. There is also the suggestion that they are noises that occur as a result of great exertion. In a similar way, the pig's squeals represent his 'high pitched final effort' to resist his slaughter.

Once again, Montague reinforces the 'Piercing' quality of the sound. It is 'absolute' in that it is unconditional and unlimited. The pig puts his whole being into making this noise, so that his squeals fill the surroundings. Montague has worked very hard on his realisation of this sound, in the last eighteen lines, so that we comprehend both sensually and intellectually the qualities of the 'noise'. Then, without any warning, the noise stops.

With four words 'Then a full stop', he pivots the poem towards a completely different focus. The sound alters to a brief 'solid thump' and then the quietly squeamish squelches of knives at work. Unlike the persistent squealing, these noises occur 'swiftly', until the pig is hung up silently 'shining and eviscerated'. The image of the 'surgeon's coat', in line 27, at first appears clinical and sterile. But there is something deeply disturbing about the bloodied, shining, folded whiteness that it conveys. Both the pig's 'carcass' and the 'surgeon's coat' are inextricably linked with a detached attitude towards a living body. Mickey Boyle slaughters and butchers the pig with an unemotional efficiency. Similarly, the surgeon must remain independent from his patients' humanity while he works in order to operate as effectively as possible.

In the final five lines of the poem, Montague presents us with an immensely dramatic image that highlights the themes underlying the piece. The 'child', representing innocence and life, is given the pig's bladder and, in an unthinking acceptance of what has happened, happily plays with it. Yet surrounding this lively energy are 'the walls of the farmyard'. The walls that shelter the child and echo to his happy shouts are the same walls that were penetrated by the pig's death squeals. These walls have been built to house those who are engaged in the ending of life. The child in all his youthfulness lives in the moment, while the walls are suffused with past deaths. Thus Montague leads us to thoughts of the connections between Life and Death; Construction and Destruction; and the Present and the Past.

STRUCTURE

With this poem, Montague takes the Lyric form and gives it a leaner, more concentrated structure. The main concern of the lyric poem is to express an individual state of mind, mood or attitude in order to share the poet's feelings and thoughts with his reader. Montague certainly does this here, but his expression is trimmed of any niceties, so that it conveys the uncompromising reality of the situation. We encounter images such as 'an iron cleek sunk in the roof | of his mouth'.

In addition, Montague moves away from the standardised length for a line of poetry, instead adjusting the length of his line to reinforce meaning. For instance, when he describes the protracted sound of the electric saw he uses a long line: 'the brain-chilling persistence of an electric saw'; whereas when he writes of the sudden death blow inflicted on the pig, the lines are much shorter 'a solid thump of the mallet | flat between the ears.'

Language

It would be a mistake to think that because Montague uses language in a lean and condensed form his writing requires less effort. Similarly, because he uses the language of everyday conversational speech, one might fall into the trap of underestimating the amount of skill required to shape his writing. Consider the following lines:

> they dig in their little trotters,
> will not go dumb or singing
> to the slaughter.

The leanness and apparent simplicity of these lines is deceptive, since each word carries a wealth of suggestion and meaning.

Similarly, the use of everyday speech challenges the poet to initiate new word combinations and connections, as with the lines:

> But the walls of the farmyard
> still hold that scream,
> are built around it.

Here, Montague succeeds in conveying his theme by harnessing ordinary words in an extraordinary sequence.

Our appreciation of Montague's use of language becomes even greater when we notice his ability to incorporate such poetic devices as metaphor, assonance, alliteration and onomatopoeia into such a compact form of language. His use of the four metaphors in lines 13–16 is particularly disciplined, in that each makes a contribution to our understanding of the quality of the pig's squealing. Rather than losing the point in a cascade of metaphors, Montague ensures that there is a clear connection between the noise and the four metaphors.

Montague uses alliteration and assonance in an equally effective manner. Indeed, his use of such 'musical' poetic devices not only adds to the depth of sound in the poem, but it also increases the 'reality' of the images. Simply put, alliteration is where two or more words, close together, begin with the same letter. Thus the letter 's' in the following line suggests the sound of the knife slicing into the pig's flesh: 'Swiftly the knife seeks the throat'. Assonance is where two or more words, close together, have the same vowel sound. So the 'a' sound in 'a solid thump of the mallet | flat between the ears' conveys the force and action of the mallet hitting the pig's head. Onomatopoeia is also present in this quotation with the word 'thump', as this is a word that is made up of the sound that is created. By using 'thump', Montague recreates the hollow sound of the mallet hitting the pig's head. In this way, Montague appeals to the reader's sense of hearing as well as sight, in order to make the images seem more real and vivid.

Perhaps it is with his use of rhythm that Montague's consummate skill becomes particularly evident. As we have seen, he connects poetic line length to line meaning. This connection is reinforced by his mastery of rhythm. Montague is able to control line rhythm without disrupting the natural rhythm that suggests everyday speech, as can be seen in the following quotation:

> (Don't say they are not intelligent:
> they know the hour has come
> and they want none of it;
> they dig in their little trotters,

There is an obvious alteration in rhythm between the first three lines and the fourth line. The fourth line has a much quicker rhythm, in order to suggest the pig's determined resistance and the little steps that he is forced to make. This rhythm helps the reader to 'feel' the pig's legs stiffly stretched, locking his trotters into the ground.

The Trout

Text of poem: New Explorations Anthology page 236

A READING OF THE POEM

From the opening lines of this poem, Montague creates a vivid scene that involves his reader directly in the experience that is being described. So we are instantly lying on the bank with him, pushing back the rushes and sliding our hands gently into the river. His ability to convey this sense of immediacy is one of the key aspects that make Montague's poetry so accessible. This is largely due to his ability to construct images that appeal to a number of senses. Thus, in the first four lines we see and feel the solidity of the river-bank, the papery stalks of the rushes and the cool liquidity of the river water.

The image of the trout, in lines 5–6, is packed with sensory information. Not only can we see him suspended in a 'sensual dream', we can also feel the easy pulse of his relaxation. Montague's joining of the two words 'tendril' and 'light' creates a vivid image: 'tendril' suggests an almost erotic sensuality in that it calls up pictures of a slender, smooth shoot of a plant, like a fine shining curl of soft hair; while 'light' suggests a feeling of weightlessness, a brightness and a warmth. Montague's realisation of the trout enables us to become one with him; we too are held in the 'fluid sensual dream.'

In the second stanza, Montague sweeps us out of the water and back onto the bank. We are there with the 'I', poised above the trout, suspended not in water this time, but in a kind of all-powerful, airy expectation. The hunter watches, while his prey has no knowledge of the hunter's existence. But the hunter–prey relationship is deeper than this in that the hunter almost becomes part of the prey, so focused is his attention. The hunter feels his identity vanish and is left 'Savouring my own absence'. Again, there is an erotic element in this deep-level connection, where the hunter feels his 'Senses expanding'.

The third stanza plunges us back into the river again, but this time the focus is on the hunter stealthily moving to capture the trout. The slight disturbance caused in the water strokes the trout pleasurably. Again, the hunter is totally focused on the prey: 'I could count every stipple'. But this fascination does change the hunter's objective. He wants to trap the fish, and so he is very careful to 'cast no shadow', since this would alert the fish to his presence.

This lack of sympathy on the hunter's part continues into the final stanza, where we feel the hunter close his hands around the trout, still unsuspectingly motionless apart from his erotically 'lightly pulsing gills'. Suddenly, Montague quickens the pace of the poem and the moment of capture happens with the shock of 'I gripped.' It is at this point that Montague's accomplishment as a poet becomes evident. In the final lines of the poem he completely reverses the balance of power. Up until now, the hunter has been portrayed as powerful and in control, determined to catch the fish irrespective of the effect that this will have on the creature. But in lines 23–24 the hunter understands what his actions mean for the trout. The trout's 'terror' is communicated so vividly that the hunter can actually taste it. This tasting reference is extremely effective, since the hunter will eat the fish, but it also suggests his gut-wrenching response to the fish's panic. The hunter's unshakeable desire to trap the fish has unleashed responses that he never expected, not only in the fish, but also in himself.

THEMES

Once again with Montague, apparent simplicity dissolves to reveal a complexity of thinking. Initially 'The Trout' seems to be an extremely vivid description of the capture of a fish; a masterly use of words to 'paint' a stunning picture. Gradually, however, the compacted density of Montague's imagery creates intellectual connections that go far beyond the scene at the centre of the poem.

The relationship between the hunter and prey is explored. We feel the hunter's obsessive attentiveness and his sense of power. Similarly, we experience the trout's oblivious relaxation. Montague conveys the intense intimacy that the two share. Then he alters the poem's perspective, so that we confront another aspect of this relationship; the hunter's loss of control in the face of the shock of his prey's terrified response.

There is a sensual aspect to this relationship. Indeed, it is no accident that human pairings are often seen in hunter-and-prey terms. This balance of control, desire, fascination and fear are all present in male-and-female relationships. Indeed, there is a heightened level of sensuality in the poem, with a physical intensity in his use of the senses of sight, touch and taste that is suggestive of eroticism.

John Montague has frequently used the image of fishing to illustrate his view of the act of writing poetry. Thus, this poem could also be seen as an examination of the creative process. The effort to capture something that is 'slippery' and difficult to hold; the feeling of being 'lord of creation'; the obsessive fascination; and the shock of finally trapping something that is not quite what was expected, could all be applied to an artist's struggle to create.

STRUCTURE

In appearance 'The Trout' seems to have a more traditional format than 'Killing the Pig', having four stanzas of six lines with each line beginning with a capital letter. However, the lines do not end in a definite rhyme scheme, although there are occasional subtle end rhymes:

> And tilt them slowly down**stream**
> To where he lay, tendril-light,
> In his fluid sensual **dream**.

Montague makes other adjustments to the traditional format in order to create a more effective vehicle for his thoughts. His use of punctuation departs from the usual end-of-line method. Instead he uses punctuation sparingly, to control the rhythm of his lines and to reflect the actual meaning and movement expressed in his writing. So the first stanza has no punctuation until the fifth line, where commas initiate a brief pause before moving on to a full stop at the end of the sixth line. This absence of punctuation serves to reinforce the smooth continuity of movement in the parting of the rushes, the hands sliding into the river and moving under water. The commas cause the reader to pause over the brilliant pairing of the words 'tendril-light', so that the image is absorbed and our sense of the trout is heightened. If we compare this first stanza with the final one of the poem, the differing effects of his use of punctuation become evident. In the fourth stanza the increased punctuation serves to reflect the breathless mixture of excitement and fear, the sudden movements and the shock of the moment.

Language

Montague skilfully uses assonance, alliteration and rhythm to cause his reader to feel a part of the experience. Assonance, where two or more words close together have the same vowel sound, appears in the very first line, 'Flat on the bank I parted'. This repetition of the 'a' sound conveys the sensation of lying stretched at full length, totally grounded, on the river bank. Alliteration, where two or more words close together begin with the same letter, is used in an equally effective way, as for instance in the final line of the poem, 'Taste his terror on my hands.' The 't' sounds make the reader move his tongue as if to spit out something unpleasant, thereby reinforcing the sensory appreciation of the moment.

In addition, Montague's use of 's' and 'l' sounds is particularly successful, as with the papery, dry whispering of the 'Rushes to ease my hands' and the smooth liquidity of 'And tilt them slowly downstream'.

Montague controls the rhythm of this piece with the skill of a composer. In lines 13–14, for example, he uses assonance and rhythm to convey the hunter's actions:

> As the curve of my hands
> Swung under his body

Similarly, his use of assonance and 'l' sounds in 'Under the lightly pulsing gills' initiates a rhythm that reflects the fish's movements.

In his use of such poetic devices, Montague is continuing the work that was begun in early Irish poetry and rediscovered by Austin Clarke. His appreciation of the musicality of language and his ability to marry sound, rhythm and meaning enable Montague to realise scenes and experiences vibrating with life and reality.

The Locket

Text of poem: New Explorations Anthology page 240

[Note: *This poem is also prescribed for Ordinary Level 2007 exam*]

A reading of the poem

The first two lines of this poem have a nursery-rhyme or songlike quality about them: 'Sing a last song | for the lady who has gone'. The sing-song rhythm of these lines reinforces this impression. Interestingly, Montague has commented that one particular folk-song, 'The Tri-coloured Ribbon', was in his head when he wrote this poem. However, it quickly becomes clear that this is no nursery rhyme, no light-hearted ballad. Rather than being a queen or a maid, this lady is in fact a much darker character, a 'fertile source of guilt and pain.' The following lines are filled with palpable distress and, at the same time, a deliberate attempt to be rather dismissive about that distress:

> *The worst birth in the annals of Brooklyn,*
> that was my cue to come on
> my first claim to fame.

The line in italics is the phrase that Montague's mother frequently repeated in connection with his birth. His use of italics may be simply to indicate that this is, indeed, a quotation. But the change in the type-face has additional effects: it serves to emphasise the phrase in that it stands out visually from the rest of the poem; it also calls up inscriptions on tombstones or memorials, as if to indicate that Montague, despite all his adult achievements, feels that this will always sum up his role in life. Finally, it acts as a kind of emotional distancing mechanism because, unlike the rest of the poem, it highlights the fact that these are not Montague's words, neither are they his feelings.

There is a definite attempt to create an emotional distance between Montague and what he is describing, as with his use of the word 'cue', which conjures up images of actors and plays; and also in the apparently throwaway remark, 'my first claim to fame.' Montague seems to be trying very hard to minimise his reaction to his mother's comment. Nevertheless, despite all his effort, it is his 'pain' that comes through.

This brittle veneer of glibness continues into the second stanza and hangs on the word 'Naturally', as Montague tries desperately to accept and justify his mother's treatment of him as natural. His mother's longing for a girl is presented as a valid reason for her behaviour. Yet once again the veneer cracks, and we see the damage that lies beneath it. The image of the 'infant curls of brown' is very moving. It conveys the vulnerability of the baby and is suggestive of the young Montague's efforts to win his mother's affection by being an attractive baby with a head of brown hair. But it was all in vain, for he had made the 'double blunder': the lumbering heaviness of these two words emphasises the weight of the 'awful sins' that this small, attractive, vulnerable baby had committed by 'coming out, both the wrong sex, | and the wrong way around.' These, then, were the 'sins' that Montague had committed in his mother's eyes: he was not a girl and he was a breech birth, that is he came bottom first rather than head first.

Clearly the baby had absolutely no control over either of these situations, and yet he feels 'guilt' and justifies his mother's reaction with the phrase 'Not readily forgiven'.

As the brittle veneer of glibness hung on the word 'Naturally' in the second stanza, it pivots on the word 'So' in the third stanza. 'So' suggests a logical, cause-and-effect relationship, that all his previous explanations make his mother's rejection of him perfectly understandable: 'So you never nursed me'. It is a simple line, but the heartbreak is clear in his change of address from 'she' to 'you' for his mother. Montague sweeps on to another of his mother's phrases, notably not in italics this time: '"when poverty comes through the door | love flies up the chimney"'. Thus we encounter another excuse offered as a justification for her behaviour: being poor had destroyed her capacity to love. This may well have a degree of truth about it, but it seems immensely sad that the two quotations that Montague remembers from his mother are so negative.

In the fourth stanza, Montague maintains this cause-and-effect connection by beginning it with the word 'Then'. However, this poem is not outlining a scientific procedure, it is the description of a profoundly affecting series of actions that culminate in the horribly simple line, 'Then you gave me away'. So, we can see that with the first lines of the second, third and fourth stanzas Montague works hard to clothe an emotionally charged situation in a quasi-logical sequence. But despite his efforts it is evident that, try as he might, Montague knows that this logic is only apparent and not real at all.

Montague's reaction to his mother's 'giving away' of him is deeply moving. Rather than withdrawing entirely from her and meeting her rejection with one of his own, he goes to great lengths to try to establish some form of relationship with her. He cycles the eight miles to see his mother, knowing full well that if he did not she 'might never have known' him. Once there, he cannot expect to be treated as a son, to be fussed over, asked all those 'irritating' questions that mothers ask their children because they love them dearly. Instead, Montague has to 'court' his mother 'like a young man'. His use of the word 'court' links back to his use of the word 'lady' in line 2 of the poem: these words are suggestive of Courtly Love, that is, the type of love that features in the stories about King Arthur and his Knights of the Round Table. Films such as 'A Knight's Tale' and 'First Knight' give some idea about the way that Courtly Love worked. The knight was expected to woo, or try to win, the lady by giving her gifts or performing heroic deeds. All his efforts were designed to prove his loyalty and devotion to her. Frequently the knight went through all of this without any real hope of the lady returning his devotion. Clearly, this idea of love tells us a great deal about Montague's approach to his mother. He 'teasingly' unties her apron and persuades her to sit 'drinking by the fire'. But the focus of their conversation is very definitely on the mother and the 'wild, young days' of her youth.

Montague's genuine sympathy for his mother is revealed in his recognition of the brief time that she lived a happy and carefree life. Her life quickly deteriorated, until she 'landed up mournful and chill'. His sympathy is particularly evident in his use of the word 'wound' in line 30, where he deliberately plays upon the two ways in which this word can be read: wound as in 'to wind,' meaning 'to wrap', and wound as in 'to injure'. By doing this, Montague increases the layers of suggestion in his writing in order to convey the depth of his mother's emotional injuries.

The fifth stanza captures the moment of his departure, to cycle the eight miles back to his home with his aunts. It is a dramatic snapshot that vibrates with lost opportunities and damaged souls. Despite all Montague's wooing there is no sense of positive warmth from his mother. Instead, she can only signal her emotional response in her customary negative terms: '"Don't come again," you say, roughly, | "I start to get fond of you, John,"'. Once again, the young Montague responds with a generosity of spirit to yet another rejection, understanding that these words are simply 'the harsh logic of a forlorn woman'.

At this point in the poem, the reader could be forgiven for believing that Montague has reached the heart of what he is trying to reconcile within himself. He has been brutally honest in confronting the nature of his relationship with his mother, and seems to have arrived at a point where he can make allowances for her. But Montague's writing has a muscularity about it that prevents him from avoiding the true reality of a situation. He cannot complete the poem until he has expressed all the aspects of this problematic relationship. Thus in the final stanza he tells us how, after his mother's death, he discovered that she wore 'an oval locket'. Heartbreakingly, enclosed within this locket, like a precious moment frozen in time, was 'an old picture', not of her husband, nor a lost love from her carefree youth, but 'of a child in Brooklyn', Montague himself.

So how can Montague call this a 'mysterious blessing'? Surely it is no more than the ultimate lost opportunity, the final rejection out of so many? Yet, it seems to me that if we relate the locket back to the Courtly Love imagery that he used previously, his attitude begins to make sense. His mother wore the locket 'always', in the secret gesture of a woman who wants to cherish and to protect, to hold close and to nurture. For him, it represents the unspoken words of love that the lady gives to her knight when she presents him with her colours before he enters the tournament. It holds the promise that the love that Montague offered was, finally and wondrously, returned. While the lady of the Courtly Love stories is prevented from openly responding by the customs of the time, Montague's mother is trapped within the 'cocoon of pain' that life has wound around her. Thus, for Montague, the locket is indeed a 'mysterious blessing'.

DEPICTION OF CHARACTER

Montague has the remarkable ability to convey character vividly by using a series of condensed phrases that highlight key personality traits. So, in this poem, he does not give us any physical description of his mother. The most we learn about her appearance is that she used an apron, she was pretty when she was young and she wore a locket. What Montague does instead is to concentrate on her words and actions. He tells us some of her comments:

> *The worst birth in the annals of Brooklyn,*
> 'when poverty comes through the door
> love flies up the chimney',
> 'Don't come again,'. . .
> 'I start to get fond of you, John,
> and then you are up and gone';

All these words carry a terrible feeling of negativity. They express the lost hopes of a woman who was deeply wounded by a life that she found disappointing and painful; who was afraid to unwind her protective but imprisoning 'cocoon of pain' because she expected more wounds and was 'resigned to being alone.'

Her actions largely reinforce this 'harsh logic'. She longs for a girl baby and then cannot accept the baby boy who arrives after a difficult birth. Nowadays, such behaviour would be seen as being indicative of post-natal depression, but in the 1920s this condition was unknown. She avoids the emotional and physical contact of nursing her baby. Finally, she gives him away. Then, in later years, when he is no longer a baby and cycles some eight miles to see her, she has to be teased and persuaded to spend some time with him. There is the suggestion that in allowing Montague to untie her apron she is permitting him some small level of closeness and intimacy. But in the final analysis she is utterly unable to allow him or herself to untie her 'cocoon of pain'. She speaks to him 'roughly' and all her behaviour is indicative of 'a forlorn woman'. The only positive action is, of course, her constant wearing of the locket. Her tragedy was that the 'cocoon of pain' would not allow her to wear her locket openly, nor to display what was in her poor, battered heart.

THEMES

On a first reading the theme of this poem seems to be Montague's relationship with his mother. He tells of her rejection of him, his attempts to win her round, her inability to respond in any major way, and then her death. Finally, after her death, he discovers the locket and he takes this to be a sign that she did, indeed, love him.

Although this is the main theme of the poem, there are other themes that lie alongside it. Montague's writing often begins with his individual experience of life and then expands outwards to embrace wider issues. Thus, a second theme in this poem is that of Life having the potential to be a negative force. It can destroy human hopes and batter human hearts into a condition in which love and positive human feelings cannot be expressed openly. Through this poem, Montague finds it possible to face and acknowledge this possibility.

Allied to this is the third theme – that of the dehumanising and brutalising effects that have arisen out of the political situation in Northern Ireland. His parents were forced by this turmoil to move to poverty and disappointment in America, which led to the break-up of the Montague family. Thus the dysfunctional nature of his family reflects the dysfunctional nature of the society of Northern Ireland.

Language

Montague's management of rhythm and tone is extremely successful in 'The Locket'. As we have seen, Montague had the song 'The Tri-coloured Ribbon' in mind when he wrote this poem and the opening stanza has a strong sing-song rhythm and tone. Try reading the highlighted words louder than the others in the following two lines:

> **Sing** a **last** song,
> **For** the lady **who** has **gone**,

This not only produces the sing-song effect, it also sounds rather like a church bell tolling at the funeral of Montague's mother.

Rhythm and tone are part of everyday speech. We each have a particular rhythm in our way of talking: some may have a fast rhythm, while others are much slower. Our tone changes to match the feeling behind our words. When Montague quotes his mother's comments, he does not try to shape them into a poetic form; instead he leaves them with her own distinct rhythm and tone:

> 'when poverty comes through the door
> love flies up the chimney',
> 'Don't come again,'. . .
> I start to get fond of you, John,
> And then you are up and gone';

If we listen to these words, we can hear something of what Montague's mother was really like, just as we heard the bell tolling in the first two lines of the poem. The rhythm of these lines is neither as regular nor as smooth as in lines 1–2. It is as if his mother's unhappiness is strangling the words that she speaks, so that they come out in a staccato, broken-up manner. There is a roughness about their tone that hints at a woman who has become tougher because of her hard life: a woman who is afraid to be gentle or loving because she has been deeply hurt.

This is in marked contrast to the rhythm and tone of the final stanza. Here, Montague discovers that his mother always wore his picture in a locket. The rhythm is much slower than that of his mother's speech. Montague achieves this effect by using commas to introduce pauses in the way that we read the lines. Similarly, the tone is much gentler. The overall impression is of Montague speaking quietly because he is amazed by what he has discovered, and because he realises that his mother was not as tough as her speech had suggested.

The Cage

Text of poem: New Explorations Anthology page 244

[*Note: This poem is also prescribed for Ordinary Level 2007 exam*]

A READING OF THE POEM

'My father, the least happy man I have known.' The opening sentence of this poem is a perfect example of Montague's ability to condense a lot of information into a few significant words fastened together in a taut structure. By using simple, straightforward words, Montague makes the poem accessible and easily understood. But it is the way that he connects the words together that lifts them into the realm of poetry. So, we meet the first two words 'My father' followed by a comma. We have seen previously how Montague uses punctuation to control the rhythm of the poem and the impact of his words. Here, his use of the comma forces the reader to pause, to linger on the idea of Montague's father. It is as if we are in conversation with Montague and he has said 'My father', then stopped. We have to wait for him to go on, to choose the words that will sum up this man in an appropriate manner. The wait is worthwhile, because Montague comes out with a character summary that is stunningly descriptive despite its brevity: 'the least happy | man I have known.' The phrase says it all, paints a picture of a man who lived life largely in the absence of joy and humour, whose main impact on his son's existence was that he was 'the least happy man' that Montague had ever encountered. Interestingly, unlike Montague's poem on his relationship with his mother, 'The Locket', where he constantly refers to himself, using words such as 'I', 'my' and 'me', there is no further use of 'I' until the final stanza of 'The Cage'.

From this point, the poem takes flight into a series of vivid images that put flesh on this 'least happy man'. Again, it is Montague's use of conversational language that draws us into the poem. It is so easy to read, yet the emotion conveyed by the words makes it a very moving piece. This is not only because the man himself led such an unfulfilling life, but also because of the way in which his son, Montague, was affected. So we read of a man drained of colour by his years working underground. There is the suggestion that the physical paleness of his face represents the sucking out of his life force. He is only a white, half-alive creature, rather like the victim of a vampire. The narrowness and the pointlessness of his life are conveyed in the following three lines with tightly packed phrases like 'the lost years' and 'listening to a subway'. What a way to live!

The tone of the second stanza lifts slightly with Montague's use of the word 'But' and the rest of the opening line, 'But a traditional Irishman'. There seems to be some comfort here. The implication of the 'traditional Irishman' is of a cheerful, social individual who likes a 'drink'. And, as we read down through the second and third stanzas, it seems that Montague's father fits this preconception. He drinks 'neat whiskey' and smiles at his neighbours. However, certain words and phrases used in these stanzas suggest that all is not quite as positive as it seems. Montague's father does not simply leave his work; he is 'released'. This use of the word 'released' is brilliant in that it suggests his father's feelings of being trapped, of being imprisoned by the metal mesh in his ticket-box. Like an animal in a zoo he escapes from his cage, but, sadly, he still carries the effects of his captivity with him into freedom. So, his drinking is not simply for social purposes; it is driven by the determination to forget, to blot out the memories. The terrible and tragic aim of his drinking is described by Montague's pairing of two words, 'brute oblivion'. There is an immense feeling of waste in the fact that this reasonless, unthinking forgetfulness is the only condition that Montague's father 'felt at home in'.

Against this background, the father's 'march down the street' has the brittle quality of pretence about it. Before going out this man has 'picked himself | up', suggesting not only that he had physically fallen down in a drunken condition, but also that he had been 'down' mentally and emotionally. The father's feelings of a rather pathetic pride are conveyed by the fact that his neighbourhood is 'all-white'. It is clearly one of the few things that he can hang on to: he and his neighbourhood are better than those that are non-white.

When Montague's father finally returned to Tyrone in 1952, the poet was in his twenties. The fourth and fifth stanzas describe a walk that the pair took. Montague's father is at home in this place that he has not seen for over twenty years; he remembers the route; it is 'as though | he had never left'. Sadly, his relationship with his son is not so comfortable. There is no sense of companionship between the two men. In fact Montague likens them to the ancient Greek father and son, Odysseus and Telemachus. Odysseus left his wife, Penelope, and his young son, Telemachus, to fight in the Trojan War. You may have seen this war portrayed in the film 'Troy'. After Troy had fallen, Odysseus had many adventures and did not return home for twenty years, by which time

Telemachus was a young man. When he got home Odysseus sent Telemachus into exile, because he had been warned that he should not trust his son. Unfortunately the warning referred to another of Odysseus' sons, who later accidentally killed Odysseus. Montague had just won a scholarship to the USA and was soon to leave Ireland, so his comparison calls up the idea of the father returning as the son leaves. There is also the suggestion that the two men, like Odysseus and Telemachus, are somehow destined by Fate never to live in the same place. In addition, just as Montague uses images from Courtly Love in 'The Locket' to provide an emotional distance from the situation, here he employs images from Ancient Greek mythology for the same reason.

Yet in the final stanza we see that, once again, Montague's unyielding determination to confront reality has enabled him to develop a feeling of sympathy for, and acceptance of, his father as a human being. This acceptance gives Montague the strength to remember his father as he really was: a vulnerable, ageing man with a 'bald head' caged 'behind | the bars of the small booth' where he worked. His father had, indeed, been scarred by injuries that he had received in a car accident. But more than that, Montague clearly believes that he was a man whose life had been irreparably damaged, lastingly marked, by forces outside of his control, the political situation in Northern Ireland. It was this 'car crash' with Destiny that made his father into a 'ghostly' shadow of himself and 'the least happy | man' that Montague had ever known.

THEMES

Once again we see Montague beginning with the details of his own particular life, and then expanding into wider issues. So the main theme of this poem is the nature of Montague's relationship with his father.

Montague's second theme deals with the negative effects of the political situation in Northern Ireland. His father, and his relationship with his father, are representative of the damage that was caused by the Northern difficulties. His father, like so many other Irishmen, was forced to leave his homeland. These men lived lives that that did not make him happy; they lived lives filled with 'lost years'. They were frequently separated from their families for long periods of time and this meant that the effects of the Northern political situation were carried through to the next generation.

DEPICTION OF CHARACTER

Montague makes his father just as real as his mother, but he uses different methods to describe him. He gave very few physical details about his mother, but he tells us quite a lot about how his father looked: a pale, bald man who had a scar on his forehead. Also, Montague directly quoted a number of the things that his mother used to say, but we never hear his father's voice at all. He seems to be a man who was beaten into silence by the life that he led.

However, Montague does use actions to highlight key personality traits. His father spent years trapped underground 'listening to a subway'. He 'drank neat whiskey' and then 'picked himself | up'. Then he would 'march down the street | extending his smile'. His life in Brooklyn was clearly very unhappy, but he disguised his unhappiness in front of his neighbours. Once back in Ireland, he seemed to be much more at home and more relaxed. He could walk 'across fields'. It was as if 'he had never left'.

A SENSE OF PLACE

We have already seen how Montague is able to create vivid images that not only make us see what he is describing, but also enable us to experience them emotionally and intellectually. This ability is particularly evident in 'The Cage', with his contrasting descriptions of Brooklyn and Garvaghey. Because Montague uses lean and condensed language his descriptions create a strong impression. First we encounter Brooklyn's underground world, where the darkness and artificial lights make the workers pale and the subway trains cause the ground to 'shudder'. Then we come up into the light of the 'all-white' neighbourhood, filled with the sound of the bells of St Teresa's church. Montague appeals to the senses of sight and hearing to make us 'feel' that Brooklyn is a hard world filled with noises, metal and people.

Garvaghey, on the other hand, is a much softer, calmer place. There are fields edged with 'hawthorn on the summer | hedges' and 'a bend of the road | which still sheltered | primroses'. Montague's father can 'walk' rather than 'march' here, and he does not have to pretend to smile any more. Again, Montague appeals to the sense of sight; we can 'see' the green fields, the white hawthorn blossom and the yellow of the primroses. As for sounds, in marked contrast to Brooklyn, there are none: just the quiet of the summer countryside.

Windharp

Text of poem: New Explorations Anthology page 248

THE APPEARANCE OF THE POEM

As with 'Killing the Pig', it is worthwhile taking a moment to consider the way that this poem appears on the page. It is essentially one long sentence that is broken up into lines of three or four words. The result is that the shape of the poem reflects the continuous movement of the wind, rising and falling in gusts. In this way, Montague uses the appearance of 'Windharp' to contribute to his realisation of the wind.

A READING OF THE POEM

Montague's writing in this poem is marvellously taut and condensed. Using lines of only three or four words, he evokes the many aspects of the wind, so that we do not merely see, hear and feel the wind, but we also understand the essence of its force and energy. 'Windharp' is like an Impressionist painting, in that it does not seek to represent the wind in a factual sense; instead, Montague drives his writing onwards by his use of a 'stream of consciousness' approach to the images that he creates. As we considered previously, Modernist writers try to reproduce the way in which thoughts develop and connect in a continuous internal processing of life's experiences. This approach enables Montague to create his own personal realisation of the wind. In order to communicate this realisation, Montague presents a series of analogous images that, within his mind, have a similarity to aspects of the wind that he considers essential. Thus if we look at the first line of the poem, 'The sounds of Ireland,' it is clear that Montague is highlighting what he considers to be an essential aspect of the wind: the way in which 'that restless whispering' of the wind acts on the whole countryside of Ireland and produces a variety of sounds. His 'stream of consciousness' then goes on to consider some of these sounds, and Montague portrays them in a series of images: 'seeping out of | low bushes and grass'; 'wrinkling bog pools' and 'scraping tree branches'.

So far, the connections that he makes are pretty understandable. However, Montague begins to move his realisation of the wind onto a deeper, more personal level with the images that he calls up from line 9: 'light hunting cloud, | sound hounding sight'. Here he seems to be using images from fox-hunting to illustrate an aspect of the wind. Montague may be trying to convey the rough-and-tumble connection between light and cloud, sound and sight that exist when the wind blows across the Irish landscape. Remember, the images that the poet uses may have only a partial and personally based correspondence with the original object, and my interpretation need not necessarily be the correct one. Again, he pushes his realisation to even greater personal depths with the next image, of 'a hand ceaselessly | combing and stroking | the landscape'. Montague's linking of the wind to a hand may seem rather puzzling at first, nevertheless, if we allow the two images to float around inside our heads for a while, the connection begins to reveal itself. The wind acts like a hand on the landscape in that it suggests a close and intimate form of physical contact. The wind moves on the countryside like a hand involved in combing and stroking but, instead of hair, the hand combs through trees and fields of grain and it strokes grass on the hillsides or water in a mountain lake. Again, coming from this combing and stroking imagery, the 'stream of consciousness' moves on to the final analogous image: that of a mountain pony. With this image Montague seems to be suggesting that the wind has a positive effect on the countryside, in that it makes the landscape gleam just like the glossy coat of the pony. This could mean that the rippling trees, the waving grass and the water all sparkle with light. Equally, he could be suggesting that the movement caused by the wind brings the countryside to life. It seems to be filled with an energy that is absent when the wind is not blowing. There is the feeling that the landscape of Ireland, like the pony, willingly submits to the wind's actions because they both realise that these actions will be pleasurable, and will make them better than they would have been had the 'combing and stroking' not taken place.

THEMES

The most obvious theme in this poem could be simply the realisation of the wind in a vivid and emotionally affective word-painting. However, there is another theme interwoven with the condensed, yet vibrant images that Montague creates. If we look at these images, we can see that they are all centred on the idea that the wind possesses an energy that has a significant and positive effect on the Irish countryside. If we relate this concept back to the title of the poem, 'Windharp', there is the implication that Montague sees Ireland's countryside as being like a windharp: just as the wind blowing across the windharp's strings creates beautiful notes, notes that would not exist without the intimate interaction between the two, so the wind acting on the landscape of Ireland creates a beauty that would not exist without the intimate interaction between land and moving air. This beauty is not only the concrete beauty of a world in movement it is also the beauty found in the creativity present in this intimate interaction. So, a second, less obvious theme is that of Montague considering the Creative Impulse and the part that the Irish environment plays in this Creative Impulse.

LANGUAGE

As we noted previously, during his college days in Dublin Montague became involved in the Dublin poetic scene. There he met the poet Austin Clarke and was immensely impressed with Clarke's efforts to incorporate many of the old Gaelic poetic devices into his poetry. Old Irish poetry was performed out loud by bards and so it was extremely 'musical' to the ear. This musicality came from the use of such devices as internal rhyme, assonance and rhythm. In 'Windharp', we can see Montague carefully utilising these effects to add to his realisation of the wind. For example, he avoids using the end-of-line rhyme in favour of the much more subtle approach of internal rhyme: '**sound hound**ing sight'. The unexpected appearance of this internal rhyme contributes to the words rolling easily off the tongue, because the human brain likes and finds pleasure in rhyming words. Of course, there is also assonance here, in that both words have the same vowel sound of 'ou'. The echoing effect created by Montague's use of these devices is suggestive of repeated gusts of wind blowing over the Irish landscape.

Similarly, Montague handles the rhythm of this poem very skilfully indeed. The rhythm is grounded in the fact that the poem is one long sentence, interspersed with commas. This creates a continuous, flowing rhythm that captures the wind's movement. Within this rhythm Montague introduces other brief rhythms that reflect the imagery, as in 'that restless whispering', where the 's' sounds and the building up of syllables from 1 (that) to 3 (whispering) create a feeling of air moving.

This elegance in Montague's writing is particularly evident if we make a comparison between the different rhythms used in two lines from this poem:

wrinkling bog pools,

combing and stroking

Both lines consist of only three words, yet the first line has a jagged, edgy rhythm conjuring up ripples on water; while the second line has a soothing rhythm created by the balancing of the two syllable words, 'combing' and 'stroking', on either side of the monosyllabic 'and'.

All Legendary Obstacles

Text of poem: New Explorations Anthology page 251

A READING OF THE POEM

This poem has a marvellously cinematic opening. It is as though we are sitting in front of a wide cinema screen, watching a camera pan from the east coast to the west coast of America. Once again Montague uses his condensed style of writing to create a real sense of place. We can 'see' the 'long imaginary plain' spread out before our eyes; we 'climb over' the hugely 'monstrous ruck of mountains'; and we 'feel' the drenching coldness of 'The hissing drift of winter rain.'

However, in spite of the 'reality' of this scene, there are indications in the first stanza that the poem is not simply about two lovers separated by bad weather and a difficult and arduous train journey. Montague inserts two words, 'legendary' and 'imaginary', into his vivid descriptions that hint at the complexity underlying this poem. The word 'legendary' establishes a connection between the poem and the world of myths and legends, where gods and heroes encounter challenges and 'monstrous' ordeals that are far greater than those of the ordinary, human world. Similarly, 'imaginary' evokes a world that is not restricted by what we know and expect – a world where anything can happen, and usually does.

In the second stanza Montague moves the focus of the poem down onto an individual figure: himself. He has spoken about the circumstances in his life that led to this experience: he was waiting to meet his girlfriend, who was later to become his first wife, after a period of separation when they were based in different colleges in America. Montague's anxiety and uncertainty, evident in his restless 'shifting | . . . from station to bar' contrast with the assurance and the certainty of the trains that 'sail | By', unhindered by the heavy rain.

Finally, in the third stanza, the train that he has been waiting for 'All day' arrives at the station. The time is significant: 'midnight' conjures up images of intense darkness, a time when the supernatural world is very close to our everyday world. We can imagine his girlfriend's face 'pale | Above the negro porter's lamp', glowing in a ghostly manner against the wet blackness of the night. Montague's reaction to her arrival is unexpected. He clearly loves this woman deeply, as he has waited for a whole day for her arrival; however, he is 'too blind with rain | And doubt to speak'. He can only stretch forward 'Until our chilled hands met.' The word 'chilled' implies more than simply the coldness of a wet winter's night. It conveys a sense of emotional tension and apprehensiveness. Montague feels 'doubt' about the situation. But it is not only his hands that are 'chilled'. The implication is that his girlfriend's hands are also cold – perhaps from exhaustion as a result of her arduous journey, or perhaps because she too feels a certain anxiety. The image of Montague reaching up to clasp her hands is suggestive of his trying to draw his girlfriend from one world into another. They are both in an incapacitated state: he is 'blind' and cannot speak; while she is 'pale'. The meeting of their 'chilled hands' suggests the triumph of their hope and their faith in each other because they have bridged the distance that separated them, represented by the gap between the platform and the train.

In the final stanza the focus moves onto his girlfriend, with Montague using 'You' rather than 'I'. We learn that she has also had a difficult time, but it is clear that Montague does not know or understand all that she has endured. This highlights the fact that, no matter how much the two love each other, they will always be two separate people and this unchangeable individuality places a limitation on their love. Her difficulties are summed up in the lines, 'You had been travelling for days | With an old lady'. As we have seen in 'The Locket' and 'The Cage', Montague is very adept at using behaviour to reveal character. Here, the 'old lady' seems to be rather correct and proper in her attitude: like a true lady, she wears gloves and she rubs a 'neat circle' on the window. She watches the two lovers 'Move into the wet darkness'. There is some feeling of optimism about the lovers' relationship when we read that they are 'Kissing', indicating that they are gradually becoming more intimate, that the degree of separation between them is slowly being reduced. However, it is not a totally optimistic ending because the final words of the poem tell us that the two lovers are 'still unable to speak'.

THEME

It is evident that Montague is writing about the theme of love in this poem. However, this is no sugary-sweet consideration of a romantic, idealised love. With the same uncompromising honesty that he used to view his mother and his father, Montague describes the true reality of his love. And again he clothes this strength of vision with an elegance of expression and a finesse of language. In an interview with Dennis O'Driscoll, Montague said of this poem:

> It's a complicated poem: there's a lot of water in it, railway trains in it (I lived close to the old 'El' when I was a boy in Brooklyn). But I don't really want to explicate it, except that the Orpheus myth comes in . . .

If we take each of the points that Montague mentions, we may well arrive at some better understanding of this 'complicated poem'. However, as was discussed previously, we do need to remember that the connections established by the imagery of Modernist poetry can be quite subtle, since they arise out of the poet's personal 'stream of consciousness'.

There is, indeed, 'a lot of water' in 'All Legendary Obstacles'. From the very first stanza the poem vibrates with watery images, and echoes to the sounds of water in lines 4–6, 10–12, 15–16 and 22–24. The connection between love and all this water is not immediately clear. In the first stanza the 'hissing drift of winter rain' could be seen as one of the 'legendary obstacles' that the lovers have to overcome before they can be reunited. Yet if we look at the way that this rain causes the huge rivers, the Sacramento and the San Joaquin, to flood, there is the suggestion of 'Flooding' in an emotional sense. Rather like early Hollywood films used crashing waves to imply intensity and intimacy, the rain-filled rivers rushing through the land could be seen as images of the way in which love sweeps through the human heart and soul. Thus, as he waits at the station, Montague's anxious anticipation and his awareness of all that is making the lovers' reunion difficult are underpinned by the overwhelming nature of his love for this woman.

The image of the 'water dripping | From great flanged wheels' has something of tears being shed about it. The trains that 'sail | By' represent disappointment for Montague because they are not the trains that will deliver his girlfriend to him. We have all waited to meet someone, so we can easily imagine the way in which Montague's excitement increases with the sight of each train coming towards the station and then the crashing distress when each train continues by. The 'great flanged wheels' shed the water as carelessly as they crush Montague's hopes and expectations of love.

'I was too blind with rain' is a clearer representation of the connection between water and love. Montague is in such a heightened emotional state by the time that his girlfriend finally arrives that he is simply unable to function in the normal, expected way: he cannot see properly and he cannot speak. He is almost paralysed by the power of his feelings.

In the final stanza we see the two lovers move away 'into the wet darkness'. There is a positive indication in this movement, in that the water was one of the 'legendary obstacles' facing the lovers and they have now triumphed over it by being reunited. There is a feeling of the 'wet darkness' embracing the two, implying that they willingly surrender themselves to their love. It also hides them from the watching old lady, who seems to be waiting for some act of failure. So, it allows their loving intimacy to be shared in privacy. But there is also a sense of entering into an unknown state. The 'darkness' prevents others from watching the two lovers, but equally it prevents the lovers from seeing where they are going. In this moment they are happy to focus purely on each other and on their love, but there is the implication that there could be something lurking out there in the 'wet darkness' that might threaten their love.

The connection between the images of the trains and the poem's theme of love is somewhat less ambiguous. On the one hand the trains symbolise hope and expectation, because it will be a train that will help the two lovers to overcome the 'legendary obstacles' that face their love. Montague knows that his lover will step down to him from a train, and so each train is greeted with a surge of his love. However, the trains that do not stop cause him to feel an intense disappointment. In this way they too become another obstacle that has to be overcome.

Finally, we must consider the poem's framework of the Classical myth of 'Orpheus and Eurydice'. Orpheus was able to sing so sweetly that savage beasts would follow him, the trees would bow down to him and wild men would become gentle. He fell in love with Eurydice and they were married. But one day, while she was trying to escape from the advances of an unwelcome lover, Eurydice stepped on a snake that bit her and she died. Orpheus went down into the Underworld to try to recover his wife. He played such beautiful music on his lyre and was so brave that Hades, the god of the dead, agreed to release Eurydice back up to the world of the living. Hades set one condition, however, he told Orpheus that he must walk towards daylight without looking back to make sure that his wife was following him. Orpheus managed to do this until he had almost reached daylight: but then he looked back at Eurydice. Instantly, Eurydice died again and was taken back down to the Underworld, while

Orpheus returned to the land of the living alone.

Why, then, should Montague feel that this mythical story was relevant to his situation: waiting for his girlfriend at a train station during bad weather? There is the connection that both Montague and Orpheus are creative individuals. There is also the similarity that both couples are in love and separated by formidable obstacles. But Montague may have chosen to locate his poem within the framework of the Orpheus and Eurydice story because it is Orpheus who fails Eurydice, and the incident that leads to their love being put under threat – the snake bite – is caused by a force outside of the lovers' control. Montague seems to feel anxious about his ability to truly love his girlfriend without letting her down: 'I was too blind with rain | And doubt to speak'. There is also the suggestion that he is anxious that something outside of their control may happen that will lead to the destruction of their perfect love: 'Move into the wet darkness | Kissing, still unable to speak.'

What does Montague communicate about the theme of love in this poem? First, he recognises that being in love is not an easy experience. Frequently there are obstacles to that love that have to be overcome, and there are forces that may seek to damage or destroy that love. Second, he understands that love has no guarantees about it, no matter how much we might wish that it had. He is anxious that he will somehow fail his girlfriend and the love that they share. On the one hand he is enthralled by and celebrates the perfect love that they share, but on the other hand he fears that this perfection will not last. This is an ambiguity that we probably all share about love.

Interestingly, it seems to me that there are similarities between the focus of this poem and U2's song 'I still haven't found what I'm looking for'. Perhaps you might like to listen to it and decide for yourself.

The Same Gesture

Text of poem: New Explorations Anthology page 254

A READING OF THE POEM

We have already seen the way in which Montague's poetry possesses an elegance of expression that is underpinned by a muscularity of focus. This poem is a particularly good example of both of these qualities. The short, poetic line; the sense of order imposed by the five-line stanzas; the condensed, everyday language; the exacting honesty of imagery: all combine to create a masterly piece of writing.

The elegance of the first stanza is evident from the opening words: 'There is a secret room | of golden light'. The simple refinement of these words belies the strength of emotion that underpins them. The image of this wonderful 'secret room' filled with 'golden light' inspires us all to remember a place where we, too, felt safe and warm. But it is at this point that Montague's muscularity of focus kicks in. He is not content to leave us wallowing in our nostalgic memories; instead, he tells us what happens in this apparently idyllic place: 'everything – love, violence, | hatred is possible'. There is something distinctly shocking about these lines. The 'secret room' is not a haven of calm and tranquillity at all, but somewhere that is filled with the unrestrained passion of 'love, violence, | hatred'. However, with the final line of this stanza, consisting of the three simple words 'and, again, love', Montague skilfully reinstates a feeling of peaceful orderliness.

Montague maintains this feeling of orderliness in the following six lines, where he describes their love making as having the elegant ritual of a religious 'rite', or the formalised pattern of movements of 'court music'. Yet, in spite of the apparent detachment of these descriptions, the emotional impact of the lines is inescapable. The couple achieve an 'intimacy of hand | and mind' that produces a 'healing'. What the lovers share is more than a purely physical release; rather, their physical actions, 'the shifting of | hands', enable them to connect in a truly meaningful way.

The level of their intimacy is expressed in lines 12–15. Montague's repetition of words connected with nakedness in these lines communicates the depth and honesty of their relationship. Their nakedness is not simply physical, but also emotional and spiritual. They are each truly themselves and they are each truly of the other, because of the complete honesty that lies at the heart of their meetings in this 'secret room'.

Yet, wonderful as such nakedness is, it cannot last for ever, and in the fourth and fifth stanzas Montague presents us with a series of vivid and dramatic images that represent the lovers coming out of the 'secret room', with its passionate honesty, and back into the humdrum routine of ordinary life. The lovers find themselves obliged to function in the everyday world. They may no longer share that intense and passionate intimacy, but they do still have the memories that they 'must remember'. These memories are so distinct that they ripple through the lovers' everyday actions. So the simple act of changing the gears in a car becomes a reminder of the loving movements and the emotional warmth that they shared. There is an elegant sense of closure in the final three lines of the poem, arising out of the beautiful connection that Montague establishes between them and the opening two lines:

> There is a secret room
> Of golden light . . .
>
> the same gesture as

> eased your snowbound
> heart and flesh.

The 'golden light' of the 'secret room' has succeeded in thawing out the 'snowbound | heart and flesh', just as the sun melts away the ice at midday. In the face of such a magical experience, is it any wonder that the two lovers carry the memories of it with them always?

Theme

Within this poem Montague explores the theme of love, but it is a very specific type of love. It is the love shared by two people in a very particular environment, a secret room. The implication is that their relationship has to be conducted in secret. It cannot be allowed to expand into the whole of their lives and worlds. Perhaps because of the secret and restricted nature of their love, it is very intense. This intensity reveals itself both in the emotions that they experience within the room, 'love, violence, | hatred', and in the way that they view their intimacy as 'a rite | like court music' that eases the 'snowbound | heart and flesh.' It is this balance between raw, passionate emotions and an almost religious, ritualised respect for what they share that gives this poem a greater impact. It is interesting to note that even though this is a deeply personal piece of writing, Montague never uses 'I'. His use of 'we' is indicative of the shared closeness of their connection.

Rhythm and punctuation

We have already noted that there is a skilled elegance about Montague's writing here, in the sense that he uses words in a simple yet graceful manner. His use of rhythm and punctuation play a major part in the creation of this elegance. If we highlight the stressed words in the opening lines of the poem, and read the highlights slightly louder, it is clear that they have a very measured and regular rhythm:

> There **is** a secret **room**
> Of **golden light** . . .

Thus, the meaning of these words is underpinned by the rhythm to create an image of a tranquil, calm environment. This is further reinforced by the lack of punctuation, so that the words run smoothly. But, Montague suddenly destroys this impression in the following lines:

> . . . where
> everything – love, violence,
> hatred is possible;

These words deal with passionate, unrestrained emotions, and as a result Montague deliberately uses a much more irregular rhythm, further broken up by his use of punctuation.

Like dolmens round my childhood . . .
Text of poem: New Explorations Anthology page 257
[*Note: This poem is also prescribed for Ordinary Level 2007 exam*]

A READING OF THE POEM

In the very first line of this poem, Montague establishes the fundamental partnership of images that lies at its heart, the 'dolmens' and 'the old people'. He then goes on to give a series of vivid and realistic 'pen pictures' of some of the old people that he remembers. In 'The Locket' and 'The Cage' we saw how Montague used a variety of methods to suggest character, including physical description, references to actions and behaviour and quoting favourite sayings. He uses a number of these methods once again in 'Like Dolmens Round My Childhood'.

The first stanza describes Jamie MacCrystal by means of his behaviour and actions. His habit of singing to himself suggests a gentle eccentricity, while his kindness and generosity are shown by his regular gift of a penny to the young Montague and his feeding of the birds in winter. Jamie MacCrystal was a nice old man. This makes the description of the terrible incidents that happened after his death all the more shocking, when robbers tore his cottage apart looking for money. The only slightly positive note is the fact that the robbers did not touch poor Jamie MacCrystal's dead body.

In the second stanza we meet Maggie Owens. We learn that she 'was surrounded by animals'. This would seem to indicate that she, too, was a kindly and caring old person. But then Montague tells us that she 'was a well of gossip defiled' and he calls her a 'Fanged chronicler'. Montague's choice of words such as 'defiled' – meaning 'polluted' – and 'Fanged' make it clear that Maggie is not quite as nice as we thought. She liked to gossip, but not just the harmless chit-chat that we all enjoy. Maggie's gossip had a nasty and vindictive quality to it because she liked to 'deride', or make fun of people. However, just as we come to the conclusion that Maggie Owens was a rather unpleasant person, Montague tells us that her 'need to deride' came from the fact that she was 'lonely'. Maggie Owens obviously had a caring side, shown by her concern for animals, but her ability to be caring towards other people had been twisted and destroyed by her terrible loneliness.

The Nialls are the subject of the third stanza. We never learn who the Nialls were, whether they were male or female, brothers or sisters. They lived in a beautiful place with 'heather bells' and 'clumps of foxglove.' Tragically, the Nialls were unable to appreciate this beauty, as they were blind. All they had to make up for their lack of sight is a 'Blind Pension and Wireless'. Montague's description of their 'Dead eyes' that 'serpent-flickered' sounds like a child's view of these old, blind people. The implication is that as a child he was slightly afraid of them, because of their disability. Nevertheless, he was happy to shelter in their cottage and listen to the crickets chirping until the rain passed. We get the feeling that the Nialls never moved far away from their home: their blindness trapped them in a narrow and largely isolated world. Yet, there is a feeling of warmth about the open door, which allowed the young Montague to shelter, and the crickets chirping.

Mary Moore, in the fourth stanza, was a much more active person. She was always out and about tending to her cattle. It is obvious from Montague's description that Mary was fighting a losing battle to maintain her farm. She lived in a 'crumbling gatehouse', her cattle were 'lean' and lived in a 'miry stable'. Her life was one of unending hard work and, because of this, Mary Moore became a hard woman filled with 'fierceness'. However, once again Montague shows us that people are not always as they appear. This fierce, hard-working lady who constantly wore a 'Bag-apron and boots' loved romantic novels. All her longing for love was revealed in her dreams of 'gypsy love-rites'. Sadly, Montague makes it clear that Mary Moore never got to fulfil any of these wonderful dreams.

Finally we encounter Billy Eagleson. At first, Billy seems to be quite a heroic, independent chap. He is 'wild' and this wildness led to him going against the rules of Northern society by marrying a Catholic servant girl. True, he did wait until all his family were dead, so perhaps he was not quite so independent as we first thought. Perhaps he was nothing more than a lonely old man craving some sort of companionship. Nevertheless, because of his marriage, he was rejected by his own religion and his wife's religion. He became an outcast who could be teased and ridiculed by the local gangs of children. His feeble attempts to hit the boys with his 'flailing blackthorn' stick make him seem a rather pathetic figure. But, in spite of enduring rejection by both Protestants and Catholics, Billy still felt moved when the 'Orange drums banged' and the Loyalist men marched in 'bowler and sash' declaring their loyalty to the sovereign.

In the sixth stanza, Montague shifts the focus of the poem onto the 'Curate and doctor': the only two people who seem to show any interest in the old men and women. Whether out of a sense of duty, or a genuine concern for the old, these two are willing 'to attend them'. We see them struggling to reach the isolated homes 'gulping mountain air'. However, the doctor and the curate are not simply calling to visit the old people; they are going to deal with their dead bodies. Here Montague once again describes the true reality of the situation with uncompromising honesty. As the old people largely lived alone, isolated from love and care, so they died alone, without love and care. Occasionally, their bodies are 'found by neighbours', but the 'smokeless hearth' and the phrase 'cast in the mould of death' suggest that the old people were dead for a long time before anyone came to check on them.

It is this uncompromising honesty in describing the harshness of the old people's lives that Montague carries forward into the final stanza. His comment 'Ancient Ireland, indeed!' is written with the strength and contempt of a man who wants to destroy the idealised view of 'Ancient Ireland' being a perfect world. Instead, Montague wants us to recognise and understand the negative aspects of 'Ancient Ireland'. It was a society where superstition was widespread, where feuds were pursued with 'fierceness', where old people were left to live and die in loneliness and isolation. Once Montague realises this, his attitude towards the old people changes: they no longer haunt him in his dreams, because he understands that 'the old people' have a 'permanence' about them. Like the dolmens, the old men and women have a lasting quality in that they are part of Montague's heritage: they are part of the past world that made him what he is.

Theme

Montague uses the individual life-stories of the old people to illustrate the harsh and divided nature of the Northern Ireland society that he grew up in. He feels that we must recognise that Northern Irish society has its foundations in the past, in superstition and feuding. It is only by doing this that we can move on to creating a new and more caring community.

The tone of the poem

The tone, that is the emotion or attitude expressed in the poet's words, tends to change quite a lot in this poem. In his descriptions of the old people there is often a mixture of a tone of affection and sympathy with a tone of anger and contempt. Jamie MacCrystal is written about with affection: ' He tipped me a penny every pension day'. With Maggie Owens and Mary Moore, Montague uses a sympathetic tone as he comes to understand the reasons for their behaviour. Although he is angry and contemptuous about Maggie's love of 'gossip defiled', he understands that it comes from 'her lonely need to deride'. Similarly, Mary's 'fierceness' is only a pretence to hide her longing for the romance of 'gypsy love-rites'. In the final stanza he sees the old people as 'figures of fear and friendliness' because as a child he may have found some of them frightening, but as an adult he came to regard them as friends because he saw them as lonely and isolated human beings.

At times, Montague's tone echoes with his childhood voice. So when he remembers that Maggie Owens was 'reputed a witch', we hear the voice of a small boy who believes that witches really exist. Similarly, his tone is one of giddy excitement as he describes how the boys 'danced around' Billy Eagleson shouting 'To hell with King Billy'. Clearly, most adults would not feel like this about such behaviour, so this tone is the voice of the young boy Montague, who enjoyed youngsters getting away with making fun of an adult.

In the final stanza his tone is filled with anger and contempt for the superstition and harshness of the society of 'Ancient Ireland'. However, it becomes much calmer and more affectionate when he speaks of 'the old people', because he understands the part that they played in his development:

> I felt their shadows pass
>
> Into that dark permanence of ancient forms.

The Wild Dog Rose

Text of poem: New Explorations Anthology page 262

A READING OF THE POEM

Section 1

Montague immediately draws his readers into this poem by vividly describing the journey he makes to visit the 'cailleach', an old woman. His attention to detail really makes his descriptions come alive. We can see the cottage, the misshapen trees and the 'rank thistles'. We can hear the 'savage whingeing cries' of the old woman's dogs.

As with the old people in 'Like dolmens round my childhood . . .' Montague places his childhood attitude to the old woman,' that terrible figure who haunted my childhood', alongside his adult understanding of her as 'a human being | merely, hurt by event.' Indeed, his use of the Irish word 'cailleach' sums up his mixed feelings about her as it can mean 'an old woman' or 'a Witch'. When he first sees the old woman he reverts back to 'the terror of a child'. Indeed, she has a rather witchlike appearance, appearing as 'a moving nest | of shawls and rags' with a 'great hooked nose', 'the staring blue | of the sunken eyes', and 'mottled claws' instead of hands. However, his adult reaction takes over and he is able 'to greet her . . . in friendliness.'

Montague stands and listens to the old woman speaking. It is clear that she goes on at length about her past. Montague listens patiently because he understands that the old woman does not have anyone to talk to, and that it is her loneliness that makes her drone on 'rehearsing the small events of her life.'

Section 2

Montague introduces the important image of 'the dog rose' at the beginning of this section. This flower is very different from the other plants that we have encountered previously in the poem: the trees twisted 'by the mountain winds' and 'the rank thistles | and leathery bracken'. There is something special about the Dog-rose because it 'shines in the hedge'. This could well be because the flowers of the Dog-Rose are either white or pink, with a pale yellow centre: colours that would stand out against the greens and browns of the other plants.

Suddenly, the tone of the poem changes to one of terror and fear as we hear the old woman's story of her attempted rape by 'a drunk'. As she struggles with her attacker, the old woman calls on 'the Blessed Virgin herself | for help' and finally she does manage to escape from the man.

Section 3

The image of the 'dog rose' occurs once again. It still 'shines in the hedge', but here Montague supplies more details about its appearance. The Dog-Rose may seem to be a delicate flower with 'Petals beaten wide by rain' and its 'slender, tangled, arching branch'. Indeed, it even 'sways slightly'. However, for the old woman, the Dog-Rose symbolises 'the Holy Mother of God and | all she suffered.' This capacity for endurance is represented by the fact that the Dog-Rose 'is the only rose without thorns'. Thus, the Dog-Rose is incapable of wounding or causing suffering; it simply persists and withstands. Montague realises that it is these qualities that give the Dog-Rose a strength, a strength that is suggested by the scent of the flower: ' the air is strong with the smell | of that weak flower'. So, although the flower of the Dog-Rose may have a 'crumbling yellow cup' and 'pale bleeding lips | fading to white' and petals that are 'bruised', he understands what the old woman recognises: that this flower has a power, a power that resides in each of its 'heart- | shaped' petals, a power that resides in the figure of the Blessed Virgin, a power that 'shines in the hedge', a power that fills a lonely, frightened old woman with courage to endure in the face of brutality.

THEMES

Montague explains the political aspect to this poem as follows:

> 'Ireland has often been seen as feminine, . . . and her colonisation has aspects of rape – becoming even more complicated when colonial England became Protestant and Ireland remained Roman Catholic, attached to the medieval ethos of the Virgin Mary.'

If we consider the image of the Dog-Rose and the old woman's endurance and strength within this context, they become symbols of the survival of Ireland. Indeed, in the past, the rose was frequently used as a secret code-name for Ireland.

In addition, there is a strong religious element to the poem in the connection that is made between the Dog-Rose and 'the Blessed Virgin'. The old woman's faith in the Blessed Virgin gives her the strength to resist her attacker. Furthermore, in Section 3 the Dog-Rose is described as a 'yellow cup', conjuring up an image of a golden chalice. Both the Blessed Virgin and the chalice symbolise the healing power of faith, the healing power that the old woman has experienced. However, the power that is suggested by the Dog-Rose and the Blessed Virgin may not be totally triumphant, as Montague has pointed out:

> In 'The Wild Dog Rose', as she is being almost raped the woman prays to the Blessed Virgin. The Blessed Virgin is symbolised for her by the wild dog rose, but the end of the poem describes that as a 'weak flower'. This is her comfort. The poem doesn't say that it accepts that comfort, just that she has been able to draw strength from it as people do from whatever they can manage to believe in.

A Welcoming Party

Text of poem: New Explorations Anthology page 268

A READING OF THE POEM

Montague's decision to open this poem with a quotation in German serves to create a context for his writing. The use of the German language signals that this piece is somehow connected to a world beyond Montague's home in Garvaghey. The nature of the question asked provides a further clue, 'Wie war das möglich?', 'How did this happen?' This is the same question that many used after the attack on the World Trade Center in New York. It is a question that expresses the inability of the human mind and heart to understand something terrible.

So, Montague's first stanza begins to describe the 'something terrible' that he encountered. He conveys the setting for his boyhood experience in two brief phrases, 'That final newsreel' and 'at the cinema door'. Once again, Montague's ability to condense the essences of a life experience into a few brief words is evident. He moves on to vividly portray the horror of the scene that is shown in the 'final newsreel of the war'. At this point we do not need to ask 'Which war?'; the German question has made it clear that Montague writes of the brutality of World War II.

The phrase 'Met us at the cinema door' does more than simply tell us that Montague was in a cinema. It also conveys a feeling of these horrible images, not only filling the darkness of the cinema but also the minds of those who were watching them. Montague, with his customary uncompromising honesty, likens these half-alive 'shades' of human beings to insects in a series of deeply disturbing images. They make 'Clicking' noises with 'what remained of their heels' and out of 'nests of bodies like hatching eggs' break 'insectlike hands and legs'. This is the stuff of nightmares, made all the more dreadful by the inhuman wailing, the 'ululation' filling the air. But this is not a nightmare; it is the reality of a Nazi concentration camp.

In the third stanza Montague echoes the movements of a film camera by shifting the focus of his descriptions away from panning across the enormity of the horror to pictures of individual suffering. We see 'a mouth like a burnt glove' ragged and blackened by brutality, and 'upheld hands' that seek some small, kindly response to their suffering, 'the small change' of the souls of the watchers.

Such images overwhelm both the young Montague and his companions. They simply cannot believe that human life can exist in such dehumanised forms and so they ask 'Can those bones live?' He realises that, up until now, he has lived in a world that is on the edge of experience. His world is localised and narrow in its outlook and restricted in its vision; it is 'parochial', a small parish far away from real life.

However, in spite of the shock of this realisation, Montague simply cannot absorb the impact of what he has seen. The 'doves of mercy' are unable to soar, not through any hardness or lack of humanity on the part of Montague, but simply because the scenes that he witnesses are so completely outside his experience, his 'parochial brand of innocence', that he cannot respond to them. Just as we all watched in shock as the Twin Towers collapsed, so Montague is stunned by what he has seen.

The final stanza of the poem may seem to be rather unfeeling in the light of the descriptions that Montague has so vividly portrayed. Yet it is filled with his muscular honesty, his determination to represent things as they are, not things as we would like them to be. The young Montague understands that he has witnessed 'one meaning of total war'. He realises that war is much more than coloured flags on a map, or heroic deeds and shared victories. He has seen a glimpse of the wide world that lies beyond his 'parochial' one. But, once he leaves the cinema, he returns to his own world of the 'Christian school', where he runs to 'belt a football through the air'. He does this because it is all that he can do. He is a young boy, who has little experience of life and, rather like a small child running to his parents for comfort, Montague seeks out the safe normality of his small world. And there is a kind of triumph in this. Just as we went back to the normality of our lives after '9/11', so Montague's return represents the indomitable strength of the human spirit. We know that we will never be quite the same, Montague knows that he will never be quite the same; but what will continue is the human will to live.

THEMES

On one level, this poem can be seen as a consideration of the horrors of war: the dehumanised 'insectlike' figures represent man's inhumanity to man, his capacity for brutality. It traces Montague's boyhood realisation of the true implications of war: 'I learnt one meaning of total war'.

However, Montague also addresses the position of 1940s Ireland on the world stage. As a society struggling to redefine its identity after a shattering War of Independence and civil war, Ireland was economically impoverished and deeply inward-looking. Out of his encounter with the 'newsreel of the war', Montague comes to an understanding of Ireland's position at the outer regions of world events: 'To be always at the periphery of incident'. He also recognises that this isolationism disables the Irish people in that they do not feel part of the greater world.

TONE

Montague uses the conversational language of everyday speech to great effect in this poem, because each familiar word and phrase vibrates with a profound intensity of tone. The opening stanza conveys the setting for the poem, but then we encounter the line 'Clicking what remained of their heels.' The impact of the words 'what remained' is tremendous. Despite the matter-of-fact simplicity of the language, the tone is one of shocked horror.

There is a similar effect with the question, 'Can those bones live?' in the fourth stanza. These four deceptively simple words capture the utter incredulity with which Montague watches the nightmare images. He cannot believe that human life can persist in such dehumanised forms.

There is a tone of frustration in the lines 'To be always at the periphery of incident | Gave my childhood its Irish dimension; drama of unevent'. As he grew older Montague became increasingly resentful of the intellectual isolationism that ruled Ireland, and in 1952 he left Ireland with great relief to study in America.

When Montague remembers his boyhood reaction to what he had seen, in the final six lines of the poem, his tone changes to one of regret, but it is regret tinged with understanding. He knows that his actions of going back to his 'Christian school' in order to 'belt a football through the air' were totally inadequate and represented a failure on his part. In this way, he allowed the 'doves of mercy 'to 'falter'. But the adult Montague can understand that as a young boy, reared in the 'parochial' world of 1940s Ireland, he simply did not have the capacity to respond to such images.

So the various tones that resonate through this poem reveal it to be the adult Montague's acknowledgment of the wide-ranging and lasting effects that the 'newsreel of the war' had on him. As a young boy he was unable to make this acknowledgment; but now, through his adult acknowledgment, he is able to set 'the doves of mercy' flying again.

Developing a personal reaction to John Montague

1. What is the relationship between Montague's poetry and his life? How does his poetry influence his attitude to his life experiences?
2. What themes occur in Montague's poetry? Are they all relevant to your life or are some more relevant than others?
3. How would you describe the language that Montague uses in his poetry? What is your reaction to the type of language that he uses?
4. In your own words, describe the process of 'realisation'. Did you encounter any realisations in your reading of Montague that you found particularly successful?
5. How do you feel about the 'stream of consciousness' approach to imagery? Did it help or hinder your understanding of what Montague was communicating in his poetry?
6. Does Montague's approach to the layout and organisation of his poetry excite your interest, or would you rather he used more traditional formats?
7. Select four words that you feel describe John Montague's poetry. In each case, use references from his work to justify your choice.
8. Consider what aspects of Montague's poetry appeal to you and what aspects you find unappealing.
9. John Montague was born in 1929 in America. What can his poetry say to young adults living in twenty-first-century Ireland?
10. What will you remember from your work on John Montague after you have completed the Leaving Certificate examination?

Questions

1. Read 'The Locket', then answer the following questions:
    1. (a) How did this poem make you feel?
        (b) Describe the kind of relationship that Montague had with his mother. Refer to the poem in your response.
        (c) What picture do you get of John Montague's mother from the poem?
    2. Answer **ONE** of the following:

(a) Do you think that 'The Locket' is a good title for this poem? Explain your answer.

OR

(b) Imagine that you are making a short film based on this poem. Choose **two scenes** and describe the images and music that you would use.

OR

(c) 'And still, mysterious blessing,
I never knew, until you were gone,'
What does Montague discover after his mother has died? Why do you think he calls this discovery a 'mysterious blessing'?

2. Read 'Like dolmens round my childhood . . .', then answer the following questions:
    1. (a) Which **one** of the old people in the poem do you feel the most sympathy for? Explain the reasons for your choice.
       (b) 'Sometimes they were found by neighbours,
       Silent keepers of a smokeless hearth,
       Suddenly cast in the mould of death.'
       From these lines, what do you understand about the way that the old people died?
       (c) How does Montague's attitude to the old people change in the last four lines of the poem?
    2. Answer **ONE** of the following:
       (a) The following list of phrases suggests some of the poet's attitudes to the old people:
       - *He likes them.*
       - *He feels sorry for them.*
       - *He is afraid of them.*

       Choose the phrase from the above list that is closest to your own reading of the poem. Explain your choice, supporting your view by reference to the words of the poem.

OR

       (b) Imagine that you are the curate **or** the doctor in the poem. Describe how you feel about visiting the old people.

OR

       (c) 'Like dolmens round my childhood, the old people.'
       Can you explain the connection between the old people and the dolmens? Do you think that the poem helps you to understand this connection? Give reasons for your answer.
3. 'Introducing John Montague.' Write out the text of a short presentation that you would make to your class group under the above title. Support your

point of view by reference to, or quotation from, the poetry of John Montague that you have studied.
4. *'Dear John Montague . . .'*
   Write a letter to John Montague telling him how you responded to some of his poems on your course. Support the points you make by detailed reference to your chosen poems.
5. 'The poetry of John Montague appeals to his readers because we do not simply read it, we feel it physically and emotionally. Write an essay in which you discuss this statement, quoting from or referring to his poems to support your discussion.
6. 'Poetry never deals with the problems of real life.'
   Imagine that one of your friends has made this comment to you. Respond to the comment, referring to the poems by John Montague on your course.
7. 'The unforgettable John Montague'. You have been asked to submit an article with this title for your school's poetry magazine. Write out your article, supporting your points by quotations from or references to your chosen poems.
8. John Montague looks at life with honesty and understanding. Discuss. Support the points you make by reference to the poetry of Montague that you have studied.
9. 'John Montague: a poet for the twenty-first century.' In response to the above statement, write an essay on the poetry of Montague. Support your points by detailed reference to the poems on your course.
10. What impact did the poetry of John Montague make on you as a reader? In your answer you might like to consider some of the following:
    - *Montague's outlook on life*
    - *his use of language and imagery*
    - *the themes of his poems.*

Bibliography

Brown, Terence, *Northern Voices: Poets from Ulster*, Dublin: Gill and Macmillan 1975.

Corcoran, Neil (editor), *The Chosen Ground: Essays on the Contemporary Poetry of Northern Ireland*, Bridgend, Mid Glamorgan: Seren Books 1992.

Deane, Seamus, *Celtic Revivals: Essays in Modern Irish Literature 1880–1980*, London: Faber 1985.

Dunn, Douglas (compiled by), *Two Decades of Irish Writing: A Critical Survey*, Cheadle: Carcanet Press 1975.

Garratt, Robert F., *Modern Irish Poetry*, Berkeley: University of California Press 1986.

Harmon, Maurice (editor), *Irish Poetry after Yeats*, Dublin: Wolfhound Press 1979.

Johnston, Dillon, *Irish Poetry after Joyce* (second edition), Syracuse: Syracuse University Press 1997.

Lampe, David (editor), *Born in Brooklyn: John Montague's America*, New York: White Wine Press 1991.

Lucy, Sean (editor), *Irish Poets in English*, Cork: The Mercier Press 1973.

Kernowski, Frank, *John Montague*, New Jersey: Associated University Presses Inc. 1975.

Montague, John, *Company: A Chosen Life*, London: Duckworth 2001.

Murrray, Christopher (editor), *Irish University Review: Special John Montague Number*, 19.1 Spring 1989.

The Arts Show: *John Montague*, R.T.É. 7 November 1995.

Quinn, Antoinette (editor), *The Figure in the Cave and Other Essays*, Dublin: Lilliput 1989.

Welch, Robert, *The Structure of Process: John Montague's Poetry*, Coleraine: Cranagh Press 1999.

8 Sylvia PLATH

Ann Hyland

Introduction

Sylvia Plath was born in Boston, Massachusetts, on 27 October 1932 to Aurelia Schober Plath and Otto Plath. Shortly after his son Warren's birth in 1935, Otto Plath fell ill. His condition was treatable, but he refused to consult a doctor. In 1940, following an operation, he died. Neither of the children attended the funeral.

These events had a huge effect on Sylvia's life. Her father's illness deprived her of both parents' attention for much of her early life. His death, which she sometimes saw as suicide because of his refusal to seek medical help, left her feeling bereft. She never came to terms with her grief and anger at his loss, and these feelings resurfaced in her last poems.

Sylvia's childhood taught her the value of being a 'good girl'. Her mother's approval was gained by being quiet, not disturbing her invalid father, reading and writing, and also doing well in school. This she achieved with little difficulty: remarkably intelligent and very ambitious, she always earned high grades. Her writing life began early, and her first poem was published when she was only eight.

She was a brilliant pupil in secondary school, consistently earning A grades. Attractive, vivacious, and active in school clubs, she led a busy social life. She worked hard but loved clothes, dancing, music and dating.

One problem that she refers to in her letters to her mother and in her journals was her anxiety to conceal her academic ability from the boys she dated: she felt (probably rightly) that her popularity would suffer if she upstaged them academically. In the conservative 1940s and 50s girls were meant to be 'nice': that is, genteel, polite, and above all feminine – certainly not ambitious and intellectual, publicly questioning the status quo. There was an all-pervasive pressure to conform to society's expectations.

By the end of her secondary school career she had achieved some success as a writer and artist. A number of her stories had appeared in *Seventeen*, a popular teenage magazine, while some poems and drawings were published in the *Christian Science Monitor*. She had also been introduced to the works of authors who were important influences on her writing: D. H. Lawrence, Virginia

Woolf, Emily Dickinson, Dylan Thomas and W.B. Yeats. In 1950 she entered Smith College, Massachusetts, a prestigious women's university, where her academic and writing success continued. At the end of her third year, in June 1953, she won a guest editorship with a young women's magazine, *Mademoiselle*. This involved living in New York for the month. Her work schedule there was demanding, and she was also expected to fulfil endless social engagements. The whole experience was exhausting.

On her return home to Wellesley she became severely depressed. She was treated with electro-convulsive shock therapy, which seems to have been disastrous: far from curing her, it propelled her into a serious suicide attempt. Her life was saved only because her brother discovered her hidden in the cellar three days after she disappeared. She entered a psychiatric hospital, where she recovered with the help of a sympathetic psychiatrist. This experience formed the basis for her novel *The Bell Jar*, published in 1963.

She resumed her studies in Smith College in January 1954, graduating with first-class honours the following year. She won a Fulbright Scholarship to study literature in Cambridge, England, where she met Ted Hughes, a young English poet ('that big, dark, hunky boy, the only one there huge enough for me'). They fell in love, and they married in June 1956.

On completing her studies in Cambridge she accepted a teaching job in her old university, Smith College, and moved to America with her husband for two years. 'Black Rook in Rainy Weather' and 'The Times are Tidy' date from this period.

Shortly after the couple returned to London, in December 1959, her first collection, *The Colossus and Other Poems,* was published. Their daughter, Frieda, was born in April. The following year they moved to Devon, a move that increased her work load. She devoted much energy to turning their old manor-house into a home and to working the extensive garden that surrounded it, in addition to acting as her own and her husband's literary agent and caring for Frieda.

Her son, Nicholas, was born in January 1962. During this time, despite her many domestic tasks and the work involved in looking after two small children, she was writing. Poems from this period include 'Morning Song', 'Finisterre', 'Mirror', 'Pheasant', 'Elm' and 'Poppies in July'. She also completed *The Bell Jar.*

For some time Sylvia and Ted's relationship had been growing troubled, and they separated in August 1962. She remained in Devon, caring for the children and writing, but suffered poor health and recurring depression. Yet this period saw the flood of creativity that produced the poems that made up her second book, *Ariel,* including 'The Arrival of the Bee Box'. She herself was amazed at what she was writing: ' I am . . . writing like mad – have managed a poem a day before breakfast. All book poems. Terrific stuff, as if domesticity had choked me' (*Letters Home,* 12 October 1962).

In December she moved to London with her children. To her great joy she succeeded in renting a flat where W. B. Yeats had once lived. The winter of 1962/63 was one of the coldest on record in England, which added to the trauma of setting up a new home alone. She had problems with heating, power failures, and getting a telephone. She and the children suffered from severe colds, and she had trouble finding a reliable child-minder. These difficulties exacerbated her depression. Despite this, she continued writing; 'Child' dates from January 1963.

However, her difficult circumstances eventually overwhelmed her. Early on the morning of 11 February she left some milk and food by their beds for the children and sealed the door to their room to ensure their safety. She then took an overdose of sleeping pills, sealed herself in the kitchen and gassed herself.

Sylvia Plath's fame has grown steadily since her death. At first this was mainly because of the dramatic circumstances of her suicide: the fame she had always longed for became hers for the wrong reasons. However, the publication of *Ariel* and the *Complete Poems* showed that she was indeed a poet of genius, whose work deserved recognition for its own sake.

The facts of Sylvia Plath's life are easily told. Less simple to assess is the mass of material that has been written about her since (and because of) her suicide. She is variously seen as
- a brilliant but fragile genius
- an ungrateful daughter who hated her mother
- a loving daughter whose loyalty and affection are reflected in her letters home
- an over-ambitious manic depressive
- a controlling and jealous wife who pushed her husband into a love affair
- a loving wife and mother whose life was destroyed by her husband's betrayal
- a virulent feminist whose marriage break-up and suicide expressed her outrage at the ties of domesticity.

In fact it seems that those who write about Sylvia Plath can use her life story to prove almost anything. One reason for this is that she was married to, and just separated from, a famous poet who went on to become Poet Laureate. Another is the quantity of material she wrote. Apart from the poems there are many short stories, essays, and articles for magazines. She also did radio broadcasts and was the subject of a number of interviews. But perhaps most widely quoted – to support points of view that can be utterly contradictory – are the journals she kept from her earliest days almost to the time of her death, and her thousands of letters to family and friends. And indeed these *Letters Home* (published in 1975) and the *Journals* (1982) tell a lot about her. They reflect her 'exaggerated, high-voltage, bigger-than-life personality and imagination'. They

show a young woman who thought about everything, and longed to live life to its fullest. Here is a tiny sample of her opinions:
- On writing: 'It is as necessary for the survival of my haughty sanity as bread is to my flesh.'
- 'And by the way, everything in life is writable about if you have the outgoing guts to do it, and the imagination to improvise. The worst enemy to creativity is self-doubt.'
- On herself: 'I want, I think, to be omniscient . . . I think I would like to call myself "the girl who wanted to be God".'
- On life: 'God is this all it is, the ricocheting down the corridor of laughter and tears? of self-worship and self-loathing? of glory and disgust?'
- On depression: 'I have been and am battling depression. It is as if my life were magically run by two electric currents: joyous positive and despairing negative – whichever is running at the moment dominates my life, floods it.'
- On children: 'Graduate school and travel abroad are not going to be stymied by any squealing, breast-fed brats.'
- On being a woman: 'Learning of the limitations of a woman's sphere is no fun at all.'
- On marriage: 'I plan not to step into a part on marrying – but to go on living as an intelligent mature human being, growing and learning as I always have.'
- 'I am afraid of getting married. Spare me from cooking three meals a day – spare me from the relentless cage of routine and rote. I want to be free.'
- On having children: 'Children might humanise me. But I must rely on them for nothing. Fable of children changing existence and character as absurd as fable of marriage doing it.'
- On poetry: 'A poem can't take the place of a plum or an apple. But just as painting can re-create, by illusion . . . so a poem, by its own system of illusions, can set up a rich and apparently living world within its particular limits.'
- 'Technically I like it to be extremely musical and lyrical, with a singing sound.'
- On the issues that mattered to her: 'The hurt and wonder of loving; making in all its forms – children, loaves of bread, paintings, buildings; and the conservation of life of all people in all places.'
- On politics: 'I do believe I can counteract McCarthy . . . by living a life of honesty and love . . . it is in a way serving my religion, which is that of humanism, and a belief in the potential of each man to learn and love and grow.'

Regardless of where people stand on her personality and life, all are agreed on Sylvia Plath's unique and distinctive voice, and on the impact she has had on the poetry of the end of the twentieth century. The inscription on her headstone could be read as a metaphor for her life: *Even in the midst of fierce flames, the golden lotus may be planted.*

Black Rook in Rainy Weather
Text of poem: New Explorations Anthology page 350

'If only something would happen!' Something being the revelation that transfigures existence; works a miraculous presto-chango upon the mundane mortal world – turning the toads and cockroaches back into handsome fairy princes. (*Journals,* April 1953)

Sylvia Plath was always aware of the need for inspiration to trigger her creative impulse: she hoped for a moment of insight, a 'miracle', to work a change on the 'mundane mortal world', enabling her to create. She wrote 'Black Rook in Rainy Weather' at a time when she was finding it a struggle to write, despite her conviction that writing was her life's work.

A Reading of the Poem

The growing acceptance of identity as a writer is one theme. The year is at the 'stubborn season of fatigue' – late autumn or winter. The speaker is warily walking, 'trekking' in the rain, when her eye is caught by a black rook hunched above her on a twig. Everything around is dull and low-key: bird, rain, 'spotted leaves', 'mute sky', 'ruinous landscape'. Despite this, the speaker is vaguely expectant: a miracle may occur, a trick of light may 'hallow' (make sacred) something as ordinary as a kitchen table or chair, causing it to glow with heavenly radiance. The muse or inspiration may appear as a 'miracle', a 'celestial burning', transforming what might otherwise be an uneventful life, giving

> A brief respite from fear
> Of total neutrality.

She doesn't know what inspiration may surprise her, or

> . . . flare
> Suddenly at my elbow.

The black rook in the rain may even shine and force her to give it her full attention – 'seize my senses'. Therefore she is watchful: such a miracle has happened before.
    One such miracle would be the inspiration to create something extraordinary from her dull surroundings, to

> Patch together a content
> Of sorts.

She might write, create something wonderful. The 'mute sky' may not grant the desired 'backtalk', but the speaker knows that 'miracles occur'. Waiting for the muse is like

> The long wait for the angel,
> For that rare, random descent.

She is prepared to wait.

Landscape

Plath's poetry is often highly subjective, focusing on her inner self, her feelings and thoughts – even when she appears to be writing about the outside world. She uses her immediate surroundings as a metaphor for her feelings and ideas.

This is evident in her treatment of landscape. One critic has described how her poetic landscapes embody associations between scene and mood; she calls them 'psychic landscapes'. She notes Plath's 'ability to transform realistic objects and scenes into consistent sets of metaphors for her thoughts and emotions'. These concrete objects, however, are clearly realised – made real – by Plath's skilful use of language and imagery.

'Black Rook in Rainy Weather' creates a clear picture: the speaker is out walking doggedly on a wet day when she sees a black rook hunched on a bare tree. Everything around is dull and lifeless: sodden fallen leaves, the dark, rainy day, the 'ruinous landscape'. Having set the scene, the speaker quickly moves to her own fears and limited expectations. She is hopeful that (with luck, maybe, perhaps . . .) even such a dull scene may be transformed. The cause of this transformation – miracle, descent of an angel – would seem to be something that might fire her imagination.

Essentially, the bleak place is a metaphor for the speaker's own bleakness. Her mood, like the scene, might be suddenly transformed by a sudden radiance, a miracle, a flash of inspiration. The mute sky may grant her the 'backtalk' she desires.

Themes

- Hope – the expectation of a sudden change for the better
- Despondency – the grim dullness of 'neutrality'
- Creativity – the miracle of a sudden inspiration
- Miracles – the rareness and randomness of life-enhancing moments of brilliance.

Technique
Use of contrast
There is a strong contrast between the dullness of the landscape and the radiant miracle that may occur. The speaker knows that the most 'obtuse object' – black rook, bleak day, dullness, kitchen chair – can be transformed by a miracle, a 'celestial burning', the 'descent of an angel'.

The difference between actual dullness and possible radiance is strongly marked. Plath underlines the blackness by her choice of adjectives: wet, black, desultory, mute, sceptical, minor, obtuse, wary, dull, ruinous. The verbs too convey dispiritedness: hunches, fall, complain, trek, haul, wait. The repetition of the sound 'rain' in line 3 adds to the general bleakness. In complete contrast to this, the hoped-for change is conveyed in terms of brightness: light, fire, incandescence, radiance, flare, shine. It is linked with the divine: miracle, hallowed, angel.

Language
The language of 'Black Rook in Rainy Weather' includes a mixture of the colloquial and the formal. Almost slangy expressions are used side by side with archaic words (words that have fallen out of use). Particularly striking are the semi-Biblical words: 'hallowed', 'bestowing largesse', 'portent'. These contrast strongly with the everyday sound of 'I can't honestly complain,' 'with luck', 'of sorts'. In your opinion, what is the effect of this?

How convincing do you find the possibility of this miracle? Do you feel that the speaker has already experienced such a moment? Look at her description of the moment – the words used to describe it. Be aware also of the many parenthetical statements: 'although', 'I admit', 'may', 'it could happen', 'with luck', 'of sorts', 'if you care to call' .... There is certainly no doubt of her wariness.

Rhyme and rhythm
Throughout Plath's career she worked painstakingly on technique, rewriting and reworking her poems until they were as close to perfect as she could make them. In earlier poems her attention to technique is sometimes too obvious, almost overshadowing the subject matter, the theme.

'Black Rook in Rainy Weather', one of her earlier poems, is carefully crafted. Before reading the comments below, reread it, paying attention to rhyme (end-rhyme, half-rhyme), consonance (rhyming consonants), assonance, alliteration and rhythm. Note down any patterns you observe.

Perhaps the most striking feature of this poem is the carefully patterned rhyming scheme. There are five end-rhymes, repeated in each stanza: in other words, the rhyming scheme is *abcde, abcde, abcde*. In every stanza there is also internal rhyme: stiff twig; arranging – rearranging – rain; desultory – design; table – chair.

The rhythm is also skilfully worked out. Mostly the poet uses three-beat lines, but in each stanza this is broken by a four-beat or (occasionally) a five-beat line. The variation avoids monotony, and also gives some interesting effects. Look at the opening lines and notice the effect of the pattern: the grouping of stresses –

On the stiff twig up there

Hunches a wet black rook

Arranging and rearranging its feathers in the rain

– slows down the voice, drawing attention to the rigidity of the bird, emphasising the bleakness of the scene.

Commenting on 'Black Rook in Rainy Weather' in a letter to her mother, Plath criticised its 'glassy brittleness'. What do you think she might mean?

The Times Are Tidy
Text of poem: New Explorations Anthology page 354

'The Times Are Tidy' was written in 1958, at the height of the socially, politically and materially self-satisfied era of President Eisenhower. It was a time of complacency, when any challenge to the status quo – the way things were – was quickly silenced. The 'establishment' – the powerful elite – viewed change as unnecessary and as a threat to its survival. The smug satisfaction of this decade in the United States was all-pervasive. Artists in general suffered under the oppression of a culture that saw anything that differed from the norm as a threat. This was the McCarthy decade, when those suspected of socialist or communist sympathies were blacklisted. According to one commentator,

> in 'The Times Are Tidy', Plath uses irony and humour to deflate . . . behaviour she finds questionable. The poem focuses on the collapse of moral standards and the all-pervasive addiction to comfort and conformity which so strongly characterised the 1950s.

SOME IDEAS
The 1950s – the 'tidy times' – are contrasted with the very 'untidy' times of the world of legend, an era when heroes fought dragons, and witches cast spells and

brewed magic potions, risking burning at the stake for their practices.

The 'stuck record' of stanza 1 suggests the tendency of the needle on a worn record to go 'ruh-ruh-ruh' when it sticks. It may symbolise the social boredom and monotony of the time.

The 'watchful cooks' were probably the critics of corrupt political values, who were often dismissed and blacklisted. The corruption or (at best) damaging inactivity of politicians could therefore continue without being too closely observed, allowing the 'mayor's rôtisserie' to turn around 'of its own accord': there was no interference in the continuous political graft and favour-giving.

HUMOUR AND IRONY

Plath used humour in all her writings, sometimes light and amusing, bringing a smile to the reader's face; more often black and biting. She particularly ridiculed what she found self-important or pompous. Her humour is seen in her use of wordplay, entertaining images, and sound effects that sometimes echo nursery rhymes or popular jingles. Very often her humour underlined a serious message.

In 'The Times are Tidy' the decade of smug comfort ('cream an inch thick') and boredom ('stuck record') in which she lived is described ironically. No self-respecting hero would want to live in it: there is 'no career' in adventure; dragons have 'withered to leaf-size'. Witches, with their magic herbs, love potions and talking cats, have been burnt up. Plath sets the present age against the world of legend, of fabulous creatures and mythical heroes.

The final lines are deeply ironic: the very elements that have thrilled children of all ages have disappeared or been forced out. But yet they 'are better for it'. Life may be flat, boring, uneventful, 'a stuck record' – but it is suggested that the 'cream an inch thick' is more than compensation for the lost excitement. The imagination is starved, adventure is dead; but life is rich and comfortable, predictable and safe. Plath seems to suggest the ironic question: what else could children (or even adults) want?

Think of the connotations of 'cream'; note down some of the phrases in which it is used. What point is the poet making here? Do you consider it an apt image with which to conclude this poem?

THEMES
- The political corruption of an era that sees material gain as all that counts
- The collapse of moral standards in public life, where self-seeking, greed and corruption dominate
- Self-righteousness – the justification of the status quo because it benefits the elite
- The death of the spirit of adventure, the failure to challenge the 'dragon' of political smugness and corruption, which threaten to suffocate society.

Morning Song

Text of poem: New Explorations Anthology page 356

Plath wrote 'Morning Song' ten months after the birth of her first child, Frieda, on 1 April 1960. She intended it to be the opening poem of a new collection entitled *Ariel*. The first word of the poem, and therefore of the book, is 'Love', setting a warm, positive tone for the collection. It is one of a number of poems she wrote to or about children and motherhood.

Her attitude towards performing the duties of motherhood was often ambivalent. She was aware of the repetitiveness of the work involved in caring for babies, and the inroads it would make on her time; however, this was the negative side of being a mother: it did not cloud her deep love for her children, which is always clear and unequivocal.

A READING OF THE POEM

The opening image creates a warm, loving mood. The speaker addresses the child directly, affirming that she was conceived in love, set in motion 'like a fat gold watch'. The tone is tender and humorous. The mother then recalls the infant's birth, her first cry establishing her place 'among the elements'.

The new parents talk of her arrival, magnifying it; but they also feel threatened by it. The world is a 'draughty museum' and this 'statue' in its 'nakedness' is vulnerable – making them aware of their own vulnerability – 'shadows our safety'.

The 'bald cry' brings a change of scene, from the intimacy of lines 1 and 2 to the chilly world – the 'museum' – where the parents feel their safety is shadowed. The mother feels displaced, unimportant. Even though her love helped to create this child, she now feels that she is no longer necessary. She compares herself to the cloud that brings rain, creating a pool of water: the cloud is momentarily reflected in the pool before the wind slowly blows it on:

> . . . slow
> Effacement at the wind's hand.

This seems to suggest that she is briefly reflected in her child but is then displaced, effaced. It is as if the mother has nothing more to give: the child is autonomous.

However, this troubling idea gives way to the present reality of the child's need of its mother, the mother's attentiveness to the child. The child's 'moth-breath' is almost imperceptible, but the mother hears it. At the first cry she 'stumbles' from bed, heavy and cow-like in her flowery pink nightdress – a note of self-mockery here. She moves towards the child, whose open mouth is 'clean as a cat's.' This startling image suggests the delicate pinkness of the child's mouth.

As morning breaks, the single cry changes to a 'handful of notes' – echoing the 'bald cry' of stanza 1. The image of the 'vowels [rising] like balloons' suggests the beauty of the sounds, and adds a note of playfulness.

IMAGERY

Plath's images are remarkable for their clarity and unexpectedness. Highly concrete, often drawn from ordinary, everyday things, they catch the reader unawares. The 'fat gold watch' of stanza 1 is simple but vivid, witty and unusual. Its marked rhythm is emphatic:

> like a fat gold watch.

The description of the world as a 'drafty museum' and new babies as 'naked statues' is a most unusual image, one that makes the reader think. It is an image she has used before: it suggests a world that has held on to its past, storing events, people, everything that makes up our life – not a very comfortable place, but perhaps not unsafe for the new 'statue'.

Imagery is effective in contrasting the infant's lightness and delicacy and the mother's clumsiness and heaviness: the baby's 'moth-breath | Flickers' (notice the lightness of the sounds as well as the delicacy of the image), her 'clear vowels rise like balloons'. The mother, however, is portrayed as homely and a little clumsy: she stumbles 'cow-heavy', swathed in a 'floral . . . Victorian nightgown.'

Imagery is also central to the contrast between the first three stanzas and the last three. There is a conscious development in animation: watch, statue, walls, mirror and even cloud are inanimate objects, just things, incapable of independent activity; moth, cat, singer (child) and cow (mother) are living creatures, capable of acting alone. Can you suggest a reason for the change from inanimate to animate? What is the effect on the reader?

FEELINGS

'Morning Song' evokes a number of moods. There seems to be a placid acceptance in stanza 1 ('fat gold watch', the midwife's matter-of-fact action, the 'bald cry [taking] its place among the elements'). However, this changes in stanza 2: the world is now cold – 'a drafty museum' – and the adults seem dwarfed by the place. Their 'voices echo', they are 'blank as walls', and their safety is threatened. Why? Does the baby's nakedness make them feel more vulnerable? Or perhaps the new arrival reminds them that they are now an older generation, facing death?

The sense of unease becomes even stronger in stanza 3. The speaker seems to feel that she has nothing to offer the infant: she is mirrored in the child for a while, before being slowly effaced by the passage of time.

These feelings of dislocation, unimportance and impermanence are quickly dispelled by the present moment, evoked vividly in stanza 4. The baby's gentle breath, the rose-patterned room and the watchful mother in her old-fashioned nightdress create a scene of warmth and intimacy.

The remaining stanzas reflect the growing feeling of connectedness between mother and child: one cry brings her to the child, whose mouth is wide open. The dawn breaks to the baby's clear 'handful of notes'. Intimacy, love, joy and pleasure dominate these stanzas. What do you think Plath may be saying here about motherhood?

What is your final impression of this morning song?

Finisterre

Text of poem: New Explorations Anthology page 358

'Finisterre' (Finistère) is the French name for a region in the west of Brittany. It means 'land's end' – the point where land gives way to sea.

PLATH AND NATURE

Plath wrote many poems that describe a scene or a place – landscape poems. In these she creates a vivid picture of the place described, conveying a strong sense of the atmosphere and mood of the place at a particular time. Also, she frequently uses the scene described to draw the reader into the mood of the speaker. A number of critics have used the term 'psychic landscapes' to describe such poems.

In 'Finisterre' a seemingly ordinary – though wild and remote – place is described in graphic terms that reflect fear, hopelessness and death. The scene actually becomes secondary to the feelings, despite the speaker's detailed, realistic descriptions. The rugged black cliffs extend into the sea, which pounds them with explosive force. The comparison with 'knuckled and rheumatic' hands 'cramped on nothing' is striking. This is quickly followed by a series of unusual metaphors for the rocks: 'faces of the drowned', 'old soldiers', 'messy wars', 'hidden grudges'. The poet personifies them, creating a powerful metaphor for anger, destruction, and death. The mood evoked is sinister and grim.

Stanza 2 opens with a lovely picture of the small, delicate flowers – trefoils, stars, and bells – edging the cliff, almost like embroidery. But the lightness is quickly dispelled: such flowers might have been embroidered by 'fingers . . . close to death'. And this strikes the note for the remainder of the stanza: death is omnipresent. The mists are described as

>   Souls, rolled in the doom-noise of the sea.
>   They bruise the rocks out of existence, then resurrect them.
>   They go up without hope, like sighs.

The speaker walks through them, and they almost suffocate her: 'They stuff my mouth with cotton,' and leave her 'beaded with tears.'

In 'Black Rook in Rainy Weather' Plath also used nature as a vehicle for feelings. What is the impact of this approach?

THE MONUMENT

Our Lady of the Shipwrecked, as described in stanza 3, would certainly be one reason why the souls of stanza 2 go up without hope! She is aloof, self-important, and self-absorbed,

>   . . . three times life size,
>   Her lips sweet with divinity.

She strides towards the horizon, in love with the sea. Far from ignoring those at her feet, she doesn't even appear to know of their presence. The marble sailor is distraught, but gets no attention; the black-clad peasant woman appears to feel that directing her prayers to the praying sailor may be more effective than trying to establish contact with Our Lady of the Shipwrecked.

The monument described here is of a kind not uncommon in Brittany, once a deeply religious region: a kneeling figure looking up to an upright figure, which is looking up to heaven. (Think of the popular statues of Our Lady of Lourdes.) What impression do you form of Plath's response to this monument?

IRONY

There is considerable irony in the description of Our Lady of the Shipwrecked. The statue to whom people pray understands nothing. Her love is for the 'beautiful formlessness of the sea', the source of the shipwrecks she was erected to protect against. She dominates the scene, taking the narrator's – and therefore the reader's – attention away from the underlying horrors of the earlier stanzas. Her pink-tipped cloak, her sweet appearance and her love for the sea seem wildly inappropriate when compared with the doom-laden bay. And how can she love something that has such hideous secrets, hides grudges?

Plath is setting up an ironic contrast here. How effective do you think this is?

There is humorous irony in the final stanza also: in the contrast between the chatty peasants, with their commercial stalls, and the ancient grudging rocks of stanza 1. The only reference the stallholders make to the headland is rather off-hand: 'The Bay of the Dead down there'. The name, however, alerts the reader to one possible explanation for the gloom of the opening stanzas. It also conveys how ordinary it is to those who make their living from tourists. The trinkets on the stall – flapping laces, postcards, necklaces, toy ladies – add to the feeling of ordinariness. It almost seems that, in creating such a homely picture, the narrator is mocking her own over-reaction to the scene in stanza 1.

Another ironic – and humorous – contrast is that between the 'toy ladies' and Our Lady of the Shipwrecked. They are miniature ladies, made from fragile shells – 'trinkets the sea hides' – with no claim to anything other than prettiness. She, on the other hand, is gigantic, made from marble, and is associated with God – 'lips sweet with divinity.' However, she offers no comfort to those who pray to her; whereas the shell ladies are pretty – and available to those who wish to buy them.

The conclusion seems to be deliberately jaunty: 'These are our crêpes. Eat them before they blow cold.' What is the impact of the tone here?

IMAGERY

The strong visual imagery that is a feature of Plath's poetry is evident in 'Finisterre'. Her ability to create 'startling, beautiful phrases and lines' (Ted Hughes) is rightly celebrated. Here the promontories of rock are

> . . . the last fingers, knuckled and rheumatic,
> Cramped on nothing. Black
> Admonitory cliffs

Dark underwater rocks 'hide their grudges under the water.' The notion that mists 'bruise rocks out of existence, then resurrect them' is a remarkable description of the effect of fog.

Can you identify images that you find particularly striking? What is their impact?

SOUND EFFECTS

The poem is written in nine-line stanzas, a heavy, formal structure that is particularly appropriate for conveying the weighty terrors of the opening stanzas.

The language too is heavy and forceful, with harsh sounds: 'admonitory', 'knuckled', 'gloomy', 'dump of rocks', 'sea cannons', 'budge', 'grudge'. Harsh 'k' and 'g' sounds echo through it, as do long vowel sounds: 'exploding', 'faces', 'drowned', 'gloomy', 'old'. The pounding rhythm of these lines echoes the pounding of the cannoning sea.

Contrast this with the lightness of stanza 4. The same nine-line stanza is used, but the effect is quite different. How does the writer achieve this? Look at colour, sound effects, rhythm, line length, use of dialogue.

THEMES
- A rather grim seascape
- The failure of formal religion to answer people's needs
- Hidden unhappiness and hopelessness
- Fear of the unknown.

CONCLUDING NOTE
In general, 'Finisterre' is a remarkable re-creation of a scene and of a mood. The narrator's progress through the place is reflected in what she sees, hears and feels: sea, sounds, weather, rocks, flowers, monument, stallholders. All of it is coloured by Plath's unique imagination.

Mirror

Text of poem: New Explorations Anthology page 362

Commentaries on 'Mirror' are immensely varied. At one extreme it has been described as 'silly adolescent scribbling which simply informs the reader that Plath is like everyone else, searching the reaches for what she really is' – an unusually dismissive attitude. At the other extreme it is considered to be a wonderfully complex meditation on the conflict between woman as creative writer and woman in the socially acceptable role of wife, homemaker and mother. In between there is a wealth of opinions.

The variety of interpretations shows how 'Mirror' touches the life experience of many people. Ironically, the poem has become a mirror in which each reader sees his or her concerns reflected – making one wonder if this was Plath's intention.

Before you read the following notes it would help you if you were to arrive at your own understanding of what Plath is saying. It might be useful to make notes about your response to the poem as a whole, or to individual images or ideas.

BACKGROUND NOTE
In her personal life, Sylvia Plath frequently questioned who she was. Expectations for a young woman in the late 1950s were limiting: appearance was important, as was marrying suitably and being a good wife, homemaker and mother. For Plath, with her fierce ambition to be a successful writer, such a world was deeply threatening. She certainly loved to look well, enjoyed dating, wanted to marry, have a home and have children – but not at the cost of her writing.

From early in her life she returns frequently in her *Journals* to her fear that marriage would oblige her to bury her creative genius in order to attend to the daily round of housework and baby-minding, which was the lot of most married women in that era.

> Will I be a secretary – a self-rationalising housewife, secretly jealous of my husband's ability to grow intellectually & professionally while I am impeded – will I submerge my embarrassing desires & aspirations, refuse to face myself, and go either mad or become neurotic?

Women writers had an even harder struggle than most: their work was often seen as 'nice', a neat accomplishment – but not necessary. These concerns may have helped to inspire this poem.

A READING OF THE POEM

The 'I' persona of stanza 1 is identified as a mirror only through the title and the named functions. Without the title, this stanza would read like a children's riddle poem. The reader, however, has little difficulty in guessing the identity of 'I'. How much of the poem would you need to read to identify it?

Having identified itself as a mirror, it then informs the reader in stanza 2 that it is a lake. The shift in meaning forces the reader to question the other elements of the poem. This *duality* (doubleness) is echoed in many places and adds to the difficulty of giving a definitive reading.

Stanza 1 seems clear and unambiguous at first reading. Short, simple statements set out the precision, truthfulness and objectivity of 'I'. However, these statements raise many questions when examined closely. Why does a mirror need to explain that it is without preconceptions? 'unmisted by dislike'? 'not cruel, only truthful'? If it is as objective and exact as it claims, why does it 'think' (an inexact statement) that a wall could be part of its heart? Can a mirror have a heart? How does this fit in with its own notion that it is exact?

Perhaps because of these contradictions and the almost childlike certainties, the tone of this stanza is light and breezy. The wittiness of the riddle format, the precise details, the simplicity and the fast rhythm all add a humorous note. Even the self-importance of the mirror – a little god – is amusing, as is the wordplay on 'I' and 'eye'.

The opening statement of the second stanza – 'Now I am a lake' – adds a new dimension, causing the reader to revise the first reading of stanza 1. Is the mirror choosing an image to describe itself as it is in the mind of the woman 'who bends over me'? This woman is not just looking at the superficial reflection: she is 'searching my reaches for what she really is.' A silver, exact, four-square mirror has no reaches: it is flat, two-dimensional. It can only reflect back the surface image: there is no depth, no murkiness, no darkness. Yet the woman sees there something that makes her turn away, escape what she sees or suspects by looking 'to those liars, the candles or the moon.'

The 'truth' follows her – 'I see her back and reflect it faithfully' – and her tears and agitation are the mirror's reward. Despite this she returns: the truth she finds in the mirror is important to her. 'Each morning' in the mirror she sees her face, sees that

> she has drowned a young girl, and in me an old woman
> Rises towards her, like a terrible fish.

One simple interpretation of this is that she sees her youth 'drowning', and watches with horror the approach of old age – which she views as monstrous, a terrible fish.

This raises other questions. Why 'drowning'? This implies suffocation, sudden loss, not the gradual fading of youth. The old woman and the terrible fish are terrifying – and certainly don't come from the mirror. They rise up from the murky depths of the lake, the darkness, the reaches of the woman's subconscious.

The frightening truths that rise from the depths are what the woman meets when she searches for 'what she really is' – her true identity. This is not the pretty, docile, smiling, youthful woman that society admires: it is something frightening, dark, ugly, terrible – and true.

THEMES
- Knowing oneself
- Ageing
- Identity: the double self
- Fear
- The human condition.

TWO-SIDEDNESS
A poem is not necessarily part of the life story of the poet, nor of those around her; the 'I' persona is not the poet narrating her life experiences. However, those experiences inform the poet's work; they are the raw material from which she shapes her poetry.

You may find it helpful, therefore, when studying this poem to look back at Plath's life. Of particular relevance to 'Mirror' is the fact that she spent long years striving to achieve high ambitions: a consistent 'alpha' (A grade) pupil through school and university, she always strove to give of her best. It often appears, though, that she judged her best not just by her own very high standard but also by the far more unpredictable standard of winning the recognition and approval of others. This was true of her work and of her life: she seemed to need constant affirmation of her worth. One consequence of this was a pleasant, smiling appearance, the 'all-American girl' image – 'a maddening docility', according to Robert Lowell, whose writing class she attended – which often concealed so-called negative emotions such as anger, disappointment, resentment, jealousy and hatred.

In several of Plath's poems she presents a double image, two sides of a person: in 'In Plaster' (1961), for example, the speaker – the body encased in plaster, a metaphor here for the inner self – talks about the plaster cast that she has had to wear and recognises its whiteness, its coldness, and its utter dependence on what it encases. When the clean white plaster is removed this ugly, hairy, old, yellow person within will be revealed; but the speaker is determined to 'manage without' the plaster. In this way what appears clean, bright and pleasant is in fact only cheap plaster; the true self may be ugly – but it is the real self.

> I used to think we might make a go of it together –
> After all it was a kind of marriage, being so close.
> Now I see it must be one or the other of us.
> She may be a saint and I may be ugly and hairy,
> But she'll soon find out that doesn't matter a bit.

What similarities do you see between this and 'Mirror'?

Revealing one's true identity

A committed poet, Plath knew the importance of speaking from the heart. But speaking from the heart means saying things others might not approve of, expressing socially unacceptable feelings. It means revealing one's true identity, and risking rejection. 'Mirror' could be read as an expression of this conflict. At this time in her life Plath's style and subject matter were undergoing a change, which eventually gave birth to her most powerful and controversial poems, many of which voice sentiments that a lot of people experience but don't talk about.

The mirror could be seen as a metaphor for her 'golden girl' image – silver, exact, reflecting back what others projected, not creating any controversy. But the lake has hidden depths, and when these are searched, murkiness, darkness, terror and ugliness are revealed – and the demure young lady is drowned. This mirror therefore has a bright side and a dark side, like Plath herself – like all who share the human condition.

Pheasant

Text of poem: New Explorations Anthology page 364

'Pheasant' is a wonderful evocation of the beauty and vitality of a bird that is under threat of death. Read it through a few times just for enjoyment.

Get a sense of the speaker's attitude to the bird (note how this is conveyed). Her relationship with 'you' also colours the poem; the tension generated by the opening lines is sustained to the end, and underlined by the closing plea. Pay particular attention to her use of clear images, precise detail, language, colour and contrast to paint a picture of what she sees now, and remembers from last winter.

A READING OF THE POEM

The opening line is the narrator's heartfelt plea to 'you' not to kill the pheasant this morning, as he had said he would.

The pheasant is pictured in strong, visual language: the narrator is startled by

> The jut of that odd, dark head, pacing
> Through the uncut grass on the elm's hill.

She values it for its sheer beauty, its vitality. The bird seems to her to be at home on the hill – 'simply in its element.' It is kingly – visiting 'our court' (possibly a play on the name of Plath's home, Green Court). Last winter it had also visited during snowy weather, leaving its tail-track and its large footprint, which differed from the 'crosshatch' of smaller birds.

Returning to the present, she captures its appearance in a few graphic words – 'green and red', 'a good shape', 'so vivid', 'a little cornucopia', 'brown as a leaf' – as it 'unclaps' its wings and flies up into the elm, where 'it is easy.'

The narrator feels that she is the trespasser: she disturbed the pheasant as it sunned itself in the narcissi. She turns again to 'you', pleading once again for its life: 'Let be, let be.'

VOICE

One strength of this poem lies in the personal voice of the narrator. It is as if the reader is looking in on a moment of her life – eavesdropping on her words to 'you'. The tone is intimate, immediate. Her plea is clear and unambiguous: 'Do not kill it.'

Her response to the pheasant is equally immediate: it rings absolutely true; there is no doubting the sincerity of her admiration. Can you pinpoint how this effect is achieved?

The pheasant is described in a concrete, detailed manner. There is indeed nothing 'mystical' about it: it is so vivid, so alive that this alone should be reason enough to let it be. Plath captures the vividness in a few well-chosen details: movement (jut, pacing, unclaps), colour (dark, green, red, brown), and shape (print of its big foot, tail-track). Its very sense of being at home here gives it a kingliness: it paces the hill, 'in its element', 'visits us', settles in the elm where it 'is easy', making the narrator feel she trespasses 'stupidly.'

Her statement that

> . . . it isn't
> As if I thought it had a spirit

suggests the idea that it has indeed a spirit, that she feels some mystical connection with it. Everything she says gives the impression that it has a superior claim to this place, and a right to live.

Mood

The pleas that open and close the poem suggest tension between 'I' and 'you'. Her spirited defence of the pheasant is sparked by her recollection that 'you said you would kill it this morning.' The abruptness makes the statement sound like an accusation.

These words, and her defensiveness, suggest another scene, not described here. Why has 'you' threatened to kill the bird? Why are they in conflict about it? Do the final words suggest defeat or victory? While there are no answers to these questions in the poem, looking at the possibilities can help you to determine the tone of the poem.

Themes
- Tension
- The rights of wild creatures
- The mystery of beauty.

Technique

Verse form

The verse form of this poem is *terza rima,* a form that Plath used frequently. This is an Italian term meaning 'third rhyme', and it is based on three-line stanzas, where the first and third lines rhyme. Often the end-sound of the second line becomes the rhyme of lines 1 and 3 in the next stanza, and so on, creating the sound-pattern *aba, bcb, cdc* . . . The stanzas are therefore interlaced.

This verse form is an effective one for building a narrative: it creates a series of short, interlaced vignettes. In this poem each stanza traces some aspect of the pheasant's appearance or its actions, with the grammatical sentence often carrying the thought through the break into the next stanza. This creates an almost casual flow, despite the formal structure of the poem.

Rhyme

A glance through the poem will show that *terza rima* is used consistently, though the rhymes often depend on *consonance* (rhyming final consonants) rather than on the more traditional and more obvious end-rhyme.

The effect of this muted rhyming pattern is a subtle music, an effect Plath strove to achieve in all her poetry. The singing quality of the poem is helped by her use of assonance and repetition. Again a quick look at any stanza reveals examples. In stanza 1, for example, there is

> . . . kill it this morning.
> . . . kill it. It startles . . . still.

Can you find other examples?

Rhythm
Pay attention also to the 'voice-rhythm' of the lines, the way many lines echo the rhythm of normal speech. While this creates an impression of ease and simplicity, it is in fact a highly skilful achievement, requiring mastery of technique.

STYLE
While Plath's attention to technique is evident when one studies 'Pheasant' closely, it does not stand out or impose itself on the reader. Form here serves the content: it draws attention to what the poet is saying, or adds to the beauty of the poem. It is not simply an end in itself.

Compare this with her technique in earlier poems, such as 'Black Rook in Rainy Weather'. Can you explain the difference? A look at the poet's level of engagement with her topic might be a good starting-point.

Elm
Text of poem: New Explorations Anthology page 366

Sylvia Plath dedicated 'Elm' to her friend Ruth Fainlight, an American poet. This is one of the first poems in which the distinctive voice of Plath's later poetry is heard. She always drew on her own experiences for material for her poems; but these late poems reflect a level of intensity not found in 'Finisterre' or 'Black Rook in Rainy Weather'. They also have a freedom, a lack of constraint and natural flow quite unlike the careful patterning of her earlier poems.

Some critics have linked the deep fear and rage expressed in 'Elm' with the growing tensions in Plath's marriage at the time of writing. These possibly triggered a renewal of the unresolved grief caused by the loss of her father at the age of eight, and of the depression that had caused her to have a nervous breakdown at the age of twenty. Part of the treatment for depression at that time was electric shock treatment, most probably the source of the image of scorching burning filaments used here and in other poems.

But it is important to emphasise that while these factors clearly influenced Plath's choice of theme and style, she is not writing about her life. A poem is an artistic creation, a work of art, which may be inspired by external events but is not a documentary about those events.

'Elm' is a complex poem. It is best perhaps to listen attentively to it several times to tune in to its deeply felt emotions, its energy. Try not to concentrate too much on understanding or interpreting individual lines or stanzas: respond rather to the general effect, the rich images, the sounds, the rhythm and, above all, the feelings that infuse it.

A READING OF THE POEM

The speaker seems to be quoting the words she imagines the elm is directing to her. The elm – speaking as 'I' throughout – taunts 'you', the speaker, the source of the fear released in the poem, for her fear of the unknown. 'I know the bottom . . . I do not fear it,' she claims – unlike 'you', who fears it. 'You' hear the sea – or perhaps the voice of nothingness, a voice she is familiar with since her madness.

'You' foolishly seeks love – a 'shadow' that has galloped away. The elm will mimic that galloping sound all night, driving you to near-death: 'Till your head is a stone, your pillow a little turf'.

The taunting voice of the elm then describes some of the nightmarish horrors she knows, horrors that suggest a nervy, exhausted state:
- the sound of poisons, rain, 'this big hush', and its fruit, 'tin-white like arsenic'
- sunsets – atrocities that 'scorch to the root', making its 'filaments burn and stand'
- the wind, a destructively violent force that leaves nothing unharmed, will 'tolerate no bystanding', causing the elm to shriek
- the merciless moon, a symbol of barrenness, whose cruel radiance burns; when freed from the elm, this moon is flat – like a woman who has had radical surgery.

The frenzied violence of the verbs – scorch, burn, stand, break up, fly, shriek, drag, scathe – eases off in the next stanzas. The elm challenges 'you' for releasing the bad dreams that now 'possess and endow me.' The distinction between 'you' and the elm – so clear at first – is blurred. 'You' now seems to inhabit the elm – perhaps it is the dark, fearful side of the elm.

The elm turns from external violence to inner terror – a 'cry' that

> . . . flaps out
> Looking, with its hooks, for something to love.

She feels a terrifying 'dark thing', with its 'soft, feathery turnings', that sleeps in her, something that is also wicked, malignant. These 'soft feathery turnings' sound even more sinister than the wild violence of the earlier stanzas.

Silent inward terror gives way to a less claustrophobic tone. Looking outwards again, the elm watches 'clouds pass and disperse.' They may be the 'faces of love', and – like the love that went off like a horse in stanza 2 – they are irretrievable, gone for ever. The taunting voice that earlier mocked 'you' for her need for love has changed. The elm too seems to feel bereft (or possibly angry?): '. . . I agitate my heart'.

She now changes from the confident, knowing, fearless voice of the early stanzas to a fearful, petrified being, 'incapable of more knowledge.' This sounds as if she knows at some level what she could learn (does in fact 'know the bottom') but does not want to truly understand.

The cry, the dark thing, is now a face, 'so murderous in its strangle of branches', a creature whose 'snaky acids hiss' and freeze the will. The elm is now struggling with 'slow, isolate faults', which are self-destructive, potentially fatal, 'that kill, that kill, that kill.'

Language

Plath's language in this poem is extraordinarily rich. The opening is simple and direct. 'I know the bottom, she says. I know it with my great tap-root'. Indeed many lines in the poem are written in the same simple, unvarnished style:

> 'Love is a shadow'.
> 'I let her go. I let her go'
> 'This is rain now, this big hush.'
> 'I am terrified by this dark thing | That sleeps in me;'
> 'Its snaky acids hiss.'

It is this directness that strikes the reader most forcibly on a first reading.

The tactile quality that is so often noted in Plath's poetry is evident here: words like 'stone', 'turf', 'arsenic', 'burn and stand', 'scathes', 'soft, feathery turnings' evoke things we can feel or hear or touch or taste. Every line of the poem contains concrete language – words, phrases and images that pile up to create a vibrant and powerful effect. It is as if each sensation, each feeling, each moment described is etched out. This has a powerful impact on the reader; the effect is cumulative until the final

> . . . isolate, slow faults
> That kill, that kill, that kill.

Imagery

While her experience is conveyed through metaphors, these are not used for their cleverness. The images used are powerful, conveying depth of feeling in richly evocative terms.

Re-examine the images that you find most striking. Notice the sparseness of the language: many of the statements are simple and clear, depending on strong verbs and nouns for their impact.

The central metaphor, the elm, is drawn from her immediate surroundings. 'The house in Devon was overshadowed by a giant wych-elm, flanked by two others in a single mass, growing on the shoulder of a moated prehistoric mound' (Ted Hughes). It features in a number of her poems, including 'Pheasant'; the bird settled in it, 'easy'. In 'Elm', however, there is no ease. Indeed the first draft of this poem opened with the lines 'She is not easy, she is not peaceful.'

Many of the images used here recur in other Plath poems: sea, horse, moon, scorching, clouds, acid, colours. By reusing the same images throughout her work she has created a series of symbols that echo and link up with each other, gaining an additional force from repeated use.

THEMES

Like 'Mirror', 'Elm' has been read and interpreted in innumerable ways. Some themes are:

- the 'stigma of selfhood' (Plath wrote these words at the top of the first draft of this poem) – the awful fear of being oneself
- despair and frustration
- the paralysis of fear
- the loss of love
- jealousy
- dissatisfaction
- the threat of madness
- exhaustion.

TECHNIQUE
Form

The close observance of writing rules – technique or form – sometimes made Plath's poems seem over-controlled. As her work developed she moved away from such tight control towards a freer style. 'Elm' is a good example of her success in overcoming what she herself called a 'clever, too brittle and glassy tone', a move that enabled her 'to speak straight out, and of real experience, not just in metaphorical conceits'. It is remarkably open and intense, reflecting feelings that come from the deepest self.

Rhythm and rhyme

Written in *tercets* (three-line stanzas), this poem flows with the poet's feelings. There is no attempt at a rhyming scheme. What difference do you think this makes? The lines are free-flowing and varied in length. Can you suggest why this is?

There is, however, consistent use of internal rhyme: assonance, alliteration, repetition. Even in its wildest moments, this poem sings. Commenting on her later poems, Plath said: 'I speak them to myself . . . I say them aloud.' Can you find any evidence of this attention to sound effects in 'Elm'? Listen to it again, and pay close attention to the impact of sound effects, sentence length, one-liners and direct speech.

Note
This poem benefits from repeated readings. Trying to make sense of each individual line or stanza will only confuse you. Listening to it and re-reading it several times will enable you to tap into the energy and the powerful emotions that infuse it.

Poppies in July
Text of poem: New Explorations Anthology page 370

A reading of the poem
The first part of 'Poppies in July' presents the physical appearance of the poppies: their intense red colour, the wrinkly petals, their light, flickering movement in the wind, their 'little bloody skirts!' However, the metaphors used go well beyond simple description: the poet is indirectly telling a 'story', rather than merely describing flowers.

Firstly, the poppies are associated with fire – usually a metaphor for vitality or life force in Plath's poetry. Here the fire is like 'hell flames', normally connected with intense pain. However, the speaker does not know whether they hurt her: 'Do you do no harm?' They do not burn the speaker – or if they do, she doesn't feel the pain. This suggests a state beyond pain, a sense of numbness. She is exhausted; this may be caused by the sheer vividness of the poppies. They are fully alive, but she is apparently unable to experience life. They seem to plunge her into despair at something that is happening to her in her life. Her pain is underlined by the references to blood: they look like

> . . . the skin of a mouth.
> A mouth just bloodied.

or 'little bloody skirts'. The flowers are personified, given human characteristics. The 'I' persona can't be like the poppies, it seems: she can't feel their burning, share their vitality. She is not fired by any life force or vitality. She can't bleed: 'If my mouth could marry a hurt like that!' Even her state of not feeling pain seems to distress her. It's not that she is not in pain: she just can't feel it, which brings its own anguish. *Husband having an affair*

She turns from the appearance to the hidden properties of the poppies in the second part of the poem – their 'fumes', their 'opiates' (opium is extracted from the seeds of the white poppy), which can cause sleep, oblivion. She longs for the 'dulling and stilling' state they could induce in her.

The red poppies, a symbol of life, colourful and vivid, could help the speaker to escape into the dull, colourless world of oblivion, away from the exhaustion caused by the intensity of life, by the agony of just being. She longs for non-being.

Tone

There is a strong contrast between the vividness and vitality of the poppies and the dull, lacklustre mood of the speaker. She watches them, sees their 'flames', but 'cannot touch' them; even though she puts her 'hands among the flames', 'nothing burns.' She feels exhausted simply watching them: her mood seems directly opposite to the mood she attributes to the poppies.

She gives the impression that she can't participate in life – can't bleed, can't sleep, can't 'marry a hurt'. These lines suggest the feeling of desperation that leads her to yearn for oblivion:

> Dulling and stilling.
> But colorless. Colorless.

Background

'Poppies in July' is one of a series of poems where the 'I' persona turns in on herself, dealing with some deep-seated grief; she does not disclose the source and nature of this, but the feeling is strongly conveyed. She longs for oblivion, but does not explain why. However, on reading the poem we get the sense that life itself is too much for her.

A companion poem to this one, called 'Poppies in October', written some months later, is quite different in tone. Here the blazing red of the poppies – 'brighter than sunrise' – is

> a gift
> A love gift
> Utterly unasked for.

This underlines the sense that it is not the poppies that generate the sense of grief and hopelessness, the desire for oblivion: it comes from within the speaker; but it is only temporary.

Comparing three poems

'Pheasant', 'Elm' and 'Poppies in July' were written around the same time (in April and July 1962). In each poem the speaker is engaging in a struggle with some threatening force beyond herself. Each seems to re-create or suggest a scene in the drama of tensions within her life – a scene involving suspicion, hurt, jealousy and anger.

Re-read the three of them together, and note how the mood of the speaker seems to progress. In 'Pheasant' she is quite rational, though fearful for the pheasant. Her plea is logical and ordered and based on very ordinary claims: the beauty of the pheasant, its kingliness, colours, right to be in this place. At the same time the reader is aware of her tension right through the poem, and of the note of possible surrender in the final line: 'Let be, let be.'

In 'Elm' the speaker has lost love; it has galloped away and is irretrievable. The anguish experienced is expressed in a series of harsh, brilliant metaphors, conveying deep feelings of rage, terror, anguish and finally exhaustion.

'Poppies in July' reflects that same exhaustion: the vividness and movement of the flowers make the speaker feel exhausted. There is a sense of deep pain: 'hell flames', 'mouth just bloodied', 'bloody skirts'. She longs for oblivion, for non-being.

The Arrival of the Bee Box

Text of poem: New Explorations Anthology page 372

[Note: This poem is also prescribed for Ordinary Level 2007 exam]

THE BEE POEMS

Over one week, in October 1962, Sylvia Plath wrote a cycle of five poems, generally called the 'bee poems', set in the world of bee-keeping. All five are written in five-line stanzas, and they form a unit in that they move logically through the various phases of bee-keeping.

These poems grew from her own experience. Her father's speciality was bees: he studied them throughout his life, and wrote two highly regarded books on the subject. Given her lifelong obsession with her father, it is not surprising that Plath should have found it an interesting topic. Indeed, one of her earlier poems was entitled 'The Bee-Keeper's Daughter'.

After the birth of her son Plath decided to keep bees, and she turned to the local bee-keepers' society for help in setting up her hives. Each of the poems in the cycle deals with a practical element of bee-keeping, drawing on the poet's initiation into this skill. But each one is also a metaphor for something in life: it is as if through these poems she found a way of defining her identity, coming to terms with elements of life.

THE STORY OF THE POEM

The story of 'The Arrival of the Bee Box' is straightforward: the narrator has taken delivery of a bee box ordered some time before. She describes its appearance, and also the appalling noise that comes from it. This she finds threatening, but also fascinating: she 'can't keep away from it.' Looking through the little grid, she sees only 'swarmy' darkness. She considers sending them back, or possibly even starving them. These considerations don't sound very convincing, however; she quickly goes on to wonder how hungry they are, and whether they will attack her when she unlocks the box. There are flowers in the garden that should attract them away from her when they fly out. She concludes by apparently deciding to free them tomorrow: 'The box is only temporary.'

THEMES
- Freedom and repression
- Self-expression
- Being oneself
- Control.

METAPHOR
Metaphor is the use of a word or phrase that describes one thing with the purpose of explaining or giving an understanding of something else. In describing the arrival of the bee box and her reactions, Plath explores a number of themes through a series of rich metaphors.

The bee box
The bee box itself is presented as something solid, ordinary: a 'clean wood box', 'square as a chair' and very heavy. The language here is direct and wholesome: even the rhyme of 'square' and 'chair' seems to underline its homely quality. However, this ordinariness quickly changes. The next line brings in a sinister note – or possibly it is merely humorous: this could be the coffin of a midget or a square baby were it not for the noise coming from it.

The box clearly means more to the speaker than a practical way of transporting bees. It immediately suggests death ('coffin') and threat ('dangerous'). Discovering that a familiar object is sinister and threatening is truly frightening: it seems to remove the feeling of safety one has around everyday things. She is fascinated and frightened. It contains, locks in, something she wants to keep in but also wants to release.

The bee box can be seen as a metaphor for containment, imprisonment or repression; this repression could come from concern for outward appearances, form, doing the right thing, trying to be what others expect, to behave in an acceptable way, saying the correct words, not being yourself, denying your true self. This is a form of repression, of boxing in something so that others will accept what they think you are. Remembering Plath's concerns about her life and her art, can you see why this seems an apt interpretation?

The bees
The sense of something sinister is heightened in stanza 2. The threat comes from the contents of the box – the bees, their noise, their clamour, their apparent anger.

Plath uses three metaphors to describe the hidden bees, each of them an image of power and oppression:
- They are like tiny shrunken African hands, packed for export: black, clambering – like slaves in a slave-ship. She has power over them: she could free them, but wonders how.
- They are like a Roman mob, safe individually but 'my god, together!' The exclamation mark (unusual in Plath's poems) suggests many possibilities. Not being an autocrat, a Caesar, she feels she can't control them.
- They are just maniacs – thus also locked away, mad, a threat to others unless controlled by someone else.

Some critics see these as metaphors for the narrator's voice. If the box is external appearances, the bees may be seen as the speaker's inner life, feelings, real self or core of identity. This true self, her authentic voice, is locked in by convention. Her repressed words are 'a din', 'a noise that appals', 'unintelligible syllables', 'furious Latin.' Suppressed by rigid outer form or convention, they are unintelligible, formless and fearsome.

Her dread of releasing these words and ideas is so great that she wonders about getting rid of them, starving them: 'I need feed them nothing'; but the idea is half-hearted. Can you see anything in the structure of this statement that might imply that she doesn't fully mean it?

She fears that she herself may suffer if she releases the bees (or words):

> 'It is the noise that appals me . . .'
> 'I have simply ordered a box of maniacs.'
> 'I wonder if they would forget me'
> 'They might ignore me immediately'

In what way do you think she would be hurt by her own words? by her own poetry? by releasing her imaginative powers?

Tree
The narrator then imagines herself turning into a tree to avoid their anger. The reference to Daphne connects her (the speaker) with other women – she is not alone in her fear. The references to the 'blond' flowers of the laburnum and the 'petticoats of the cherry' also connect her with women.

How might her silence, her repression of her real self be echoed in the lives of other women at that time?

INTERPRETING THE POEM
This is only one interpretation of this rich metaphorical poem. There are others: look back at 'Mirror' and 'Elm'. Do you see anything that connects with them? Note the resemblances and the differences. As with many poems, 'reading in' one meaning can be simplistic, blocking the way to other possible interpretations and ideas.

TECHNIQUE
Wordplay and sound effects
There are several examples of Plath's clever wordplay and witty sound effects in this poem: the short *'i'* sound of 'din in it' combined with the repeated *'n'* seems to mimic the bees' buzzing; the almost unpronounceable 'unintelligible syllables' echoes the meaning of the words.

She also uses internal rhyme (square – chair – square – there), and also repetition (grid . . . grid – dark . . . dark – black . . . black). These are effective: sometimes they underline a point or highlight a word; always they make the poem sing.

The five-line stanza used in 'The Arrival of the Bee Box' is similar to that used in all five bee poems. There is, however, one difference in this poem: there is an additional single line at the end of the poem:

> The box is only temporary.

It is almost as if it has escaped – has been freed – from the form of the poem.

NOTE
This is a complex and rich poem, one that will benefit from several readings. As it is part of a cycle of five poems, reading it together with the other four may add to your understanding.

Child

Text of poem: New Explorations Anthology page 375
[*Note: This poem is also prescribed for Ordinary Level 2007 exam*]

A READING OF THE POEM
This simple poem is almost like a lullaby. The mother addresses her child, wanting to fill his eye,

> the one absolutely beautiful thing

with wonders.

The tone at first is clear and bright. She longs to fill his vision with colour, ducks, newness and flowers. He is like a flower-stalk without wrinkle, or a pool that reflects the beauty of the world. However, the tone changes in the final stanza; the narrator turns away from the child and his world to

> this troublous
> Wringing of hands.

She sees another world that is the direct opposite of the light and flower-filled world of the child,

> . . . this dark
> Ceiling without a star.

This could perhaps be a reflection of her fears for the child in a world that is often antagonistic to beauty and dangerous for the helpless. It might also refer to her own feelings of unhappiness and depression. There is a marked contrast between the joyful, limpid quality of the first three stanzas and the dark, unlit, enclosed space of the last line. What effect has this on the reader? What is your response to the poem?

PLATH AND CHILDREN

'Child' is one of a number of poems that Plath wrote about children, in particular her own children and her relationship with them. It is an eloquent love poem, reflecting a strong connection with them and with the world she would like to show to them. However, in most of these poems the poet turns from the tender joy and lightness of her child's world to anxiety; the conclusion here creates a strong sense of darkness, chilliness. There is a suggestion that she fears threatening forces that may hurt the child.

STYLE

'Child' is written in the three-line stanza form, one that Plath used often in her later poems. Here it seems particularly appropriate. The sort stanzas are clear and uncluttered, the rhythm quick and light. Most lines have two or three beats, giving the poem an easy, flowing movement.

The theme is simple: love, childhood joys, motherhood, and also fear and anxiety about the bleakness that may threaten the child, the 'troublous wringing of hands'.

The language is concrete: the narrator lists simple objects that bring joy to children: colours and ducks, the zoo of the new, flowers and water. Her fear too is worded in concrete terms: 'wringing of hands', 'dark ceiling without a star.'

Compare this poem in tone, theme and style with 'Morning Song'.

Overview of the poems

This is a brief look at the selection of poems by Sylvia Plath that you have studied. The points made here represent one interpretation of her work. It is important that you develop your own response to each poem; where this differs from the suggestions given here, trust your own judgment. Reread the poem, and validate your opinion.

BACKGROUND

Plath wrote incessantly during her short life: poetry, short stories, articles, essays and one semi-autobiographical novel. Her writings were first published in magazines on both sides of the Atlantic; later they appeared in book form.

She considered poems written before 1956 as 'juvenilia'. Her first published book, *The Colossus,* includes only poems written after this date, among them two of the poems you have studied, 'Black Rook in Rainy Weather' and 'The Times are Tidy'. Her remaining poems were published after her death in three collections: *Ariel and Other Poems, Crossing the Water* and *Winter Trees.*

Her last poems are generally seen as Plath's outstanding achievement. Here she truly found her voice, expressing herself in a distinctive, unique style. She was aware of this herself: while writing them, she informed her mother:

> I am a writer . . . I am a genius of a writer; I have it in me. I am writing the best poems of my life; they will make my name . . . (*Letters Home,* 16 October 1962).

Her husband describes these poems equally glowingly:

> Her real self showed itself in her writing . . . . When a real self finds language and manages to speak, it is surely a dazzling event. (Ted Hughes, foreword to *The Journals of Sylvia Plath,* 1982)

READING PLATH'S POEMS

There is a widespread tendency to interpret Plath's work as autobiographical, to read her poems as if they tell her life story. While it is quite obvious – and probably inevitable – that a writer's life will influence what she writes, it is important to understand that poetry is art. Writing about this issue, Ted Hughes pointed out that the reader must learn 'to distinguish between a subjective work that was trying to reach an artistic form using a real event as its basis, and a documentary of some event that did happen'.

Some critics read her later poems exclusively in the light of her suicide. They argue that she signals her suicide (intentionally or otherwise) in a number of her last poems, through various references to despair, rage, loss, separation or death. That is by no means as obvious as these critics claim. Many of these poems are the work of a woman who is coming into her own, recognising her own needs, using her own voice, finding her true self. Look back, for example, at 'The Arrival of the Bee Box'. This is about facing and releasing the fears that are hidden beneath the surface – not about a woman who is contemplating death.

It is important to read the poems as they stand. Looking for signs of what was to happen afterwards in her life is to predetermine how the poems should be read, not actually attending to the poem itself.

THEMES AND ISSUES IN THE PRESCRIBED POEMS
The writer's identity
In 'Black Rook in Rainy Weather' (1956), one theme is the poet's identity as a writer. The speaker, surrounded by wintry bleakness, longs for the miracle that will transform this into something radiant. That miracle is the creative impulse, the imagination that will change an otherwise uneventful period. For the speaker, this miracle was of vital importance.

Motherhood
Plath wrote many poems dealing with all aspects of pregnancy, childbirth and motherhood, at a time when writers, especially poets, rarely touched on such topics. Her best-known work on the theme, 'Poem for Three Voices', evokes powerfully the variety of emotions experienced by women around pregnancy, miscarriage, motherhood and adoption. Her poems on this theme are remarkable for their lyricism (song-like quality), depth of feeling, and tenderness.

> What did my fingers do before they held him?
> What did my heart do, with its love?

However, being a realist, she also reflected the other side of being a mother: the drudgery, the anxieties, and the level to which a mother is bound to her child.

> I have never seen a thing so clear . . .
> It is a terrible thing to be so open: it is as if my heart
> Put on a face and walked into the world.

Both attitudes are seen in 'Morning Song'. The mother's life is shadowed by the child's arrival, but is enriched by the joy of love. 'Child' also reflects the simple pleasure she derives from her child; his eye is the one absolutely beautiful thing that she longs to fill with the beauty of the world. But there is also an underlying threat to the child's safety, which distresses her.

Identity

Plath frequently returned to the issue of double identity in her writing. The subject of her undergraduate dissertation in Smith College was 'The Magic Mirror: A Study of the Double in Dostoevsky Novels'. Her interest in what appears on the surface and what is hidden is reflected in 'Mirror'. Here, the depths hide something frightening and sinister, something the woman would prefer to avoid but cannot escape.

'Elm' also deals with doubleness: the apparent calm of the elm in the opening stanzas, and the hidden terrors that surface as she talks.

A similar preoccupation is at the heart of 'The Arrival of the Bee Box'. The practical, square box is a simple container: apparently there are no mysteries here. However, it conceals something sinister, but also fascinating.

Nature

Plath's abiding interest in the world around her, her interest in nature, is reflected in many poems. Her descriptions are remarkable for their concrete, precise detail.

'Finisterre' paints a graphic picture of the scene before her eyes, conveying the harshness of the sea, the bleakness of the rocks, the delicacy of the flowers on the cliff and the effect of the mist.

'Black Rook in Rainy Weather' is strong in visual details, accurately portraying a scene on a wet, wintry day.

Her painterly style creates graphic images in 'Pheasant': the bird itself, the flowers, the hill and elm in the background, the earlier scene where the snow was marked with the 'crosshatch' footprints of various birds.

Through unusual images, 'Poppies in July' captures the vivid colour and fluid movement of the poppies' petals.

'Pheasant' reflects her stance against the destruction of nature, a concern that features in many of her poems.

Psychic landscapes

While Plath's descriptions of landscapes and seascapes are striking, the scene is at times simply the backdrop to the mood of the speaker.

'Black Rook in Rainy Weather' is strong in visual detail, but the place does not really matter. What comes across as significant is the mood of the speaker, the sense of tentative expectancy. The landscape is almost a backdrop.

In 'Finisterre', the place is identified by the title. The landscape is captured in a series of wonderful images. Many of these are personified: cliffs are 'admonitory', rocks hide their grudges, the sea wages war and mists are without hope. The place assumes an atmosphere that is oddly human.

TECHNIQUE
Style
Plath's style changed considerably during her career, but there are certain features that mark all her work:
- remarkable use of language
- unusual and striking imagery
- humour.

Language
Plath's 'crackling verbal energy' is apparent in her poems' biting precision of word and image. Her writing has been variously praised for its tactile quality, power, incisiveness, control, taut originality and luminosity. Joyce Carol Oates observed that 'the final memorable poems ['Elm', 'Poppies in July' and 'The Arrival of the Bee Box', among others] . . . read as if they've been chiselled with a fine surgical implement out of arctic ice.' In her *Journals*, Plath constantly urges herself to develop a 'diamond-edged', 'gem-bright' style. This she certainly achieved. Part of her technique was to reuse certain words in many poems, which thus took on an almost symbolic meaning: smiles, hooks, element, dissatisfaction, vowels, shriek, horse, sea.

'Black Rook in Rainy Weather' is a good example of her earlier control of language and form. In it the language is clear and precise, creating a series of carefully worked out pictures.

'Pheasant' is a later example of her skilled control of descriptive language. The form here is less dominant, and the poet's feelings are reflected in the personal voice that speaks throughout. The words are simple, the descriptions are vivid, and the poem is crystal clear. It is a good example of Plath's descriptive powers at their best.

'Elm' shows her powerful response to loss, pain and terror. The feeling of despair, for example, is conveyed through a number of highly charged nouns and verbs.

Imagery
Certain images recur in Plath's poetry, taking on a symbolic meaning that gains added force through repeated use.
- The moon symbolises barrenness, coldness and the negation of life. In 'Elm' it is merciless, cruel and barren, associated with pain and suffering.
- The mirror often symbolises the hidden alter ego (the 'other self'), as in 'Mirror'.
- The horse is a symbol of vitality. In 'Elm', love gallops off like a horse.
- Blood symbolises vitality, life force and creativity, as in 'Poppies in July'. In a later poem, Plath states:

> The blood jet is poetry,
> There is no stopping it

- The sea is often associated with undefined menace or hidden threat, as is so graphically evident in 'Finisterre'.

She uses many other images, however, that are not symbolic, images that add to the vividness and immediacy of what she is describing. One of the most distinctive features of her work is her use of metaphors, many of which are visual. Examples abound:
- Mists are 'souls', which 'bruise the rocks out of existence' ('Finisterre').
- The pheasant is 'brown as a leaf', a 'little cornucopia' ('Pheasant').
- Poppies are 'little hell flames', 'wrinkly and clear red, like the skin of a mouth | A mouth just bloodied', 'little bloody skirts' ('Poppies in July').
- The bee box is 'square as a chair', a 'midget's coffin' ('The Arrival of the Bee Box').
- Bees are like 'African hands, | Minute and shrunk for export' ('The Arrival of the Bee Box').
- A life of boring regularity is like a 'stuck record' ('The Times are Tidy').
- The baby's mouth opens 'clean as a cat's' ('Morning Song').
- Her crying is 'a handful of notes', which rise 'like balloons' ('Morning Song').

Plath attached great importance to colours, often identifying them with specific attributes. The repeated use of colour to suggest certain qualities links her poems to one another, giving added force to her meaning.
- Red signifies vitality, life force: the red poppies are animated, vital, unlike the colourless life of the narrator. The pheasant's vitality is envisaged largely through its vivid colouring.
- Green too signifies the positive, creativity, life force: the pheasant is red and green.
- Black is associated with death, anger, depression, aggression and destruction: the black headland that opens 'Finisterre' underlines the sinister mood.
- The depressed mood of the speaker in 'Black Rook in Rainy Weather' is conveyed through the repetition of black and the dominating presence of the rook.
- Surprisingly, white too is sinister: the white faces of the dead, the white mists in 'Finisterre'.

Humour

Running through her work is Plath's humour, sharp and ironic at times, at other times mocking and black. She uses ironic humour to challenge self-importance, to mock what she found ridiculous and pompous, and often to mock herself.

'The Times are Tidy' ridicules the politicians and the life of the 1950s. The smug satisfaction of this decade was all-pervasive. Plath ironically contrasts this era with that of dragon-slayers and witches (created by myth-makers). The rich cream – wealth and material possessions – is an ironic substitute for adventure and excitement. The inch-thick cream suggests fat cats 'creaming' it.

In 'Finisterre' the ironic description of the monument shows how remote formal religion is from the concerns of ordinary people. The giant statue of Our Lady of the Shipwrecked ignores the plight of the little people at her feet. The introduction of the shell-toy women makes the reader wonder whether they don't offer more comfort than their gigantic marble sister.

In 'Morning Song' she uses gentle self-irony, creating an amusing picture of the mother in the small details given: she stumbles from her bed, cow-like in her flowery nightdress.

'Mirror' opens with the mirror's unintentionally comic description of itself, giving the poem an ironic twist.

PLATH'S ROMANTICISM

Sylvia Plath was a lyric poet in the Romantic tradition. She wrote poems that drew on her own experience of life and explored a range of emotions from love and joy to terror and despair. Like the Romantics, she looked inwards rather than outwards; her experience is gauged by what she has lived through.

'Elm' is perhaps the most striking example of this. It is one of a number of poems she wrote around the same time, expressing agonising emotions. Some of these emotions were quite 'acceptable', provided they were not shown too openly: the grief and loneliness expressed in 'Elm', for example. However, less acceptable was the intensity with which she voiced them; it was considered 'over the top', too revealing. She also voiced the other, far less 'acceptable' feelings (those not talked about in public) here and in other poems: gleeful destructiveness and hatred ('Daddy') or intense resentment ('The Zoo-Keeper's Wife').

The writer and critic Joyce Carol Oates sees in these poems the seeds of Plath's eventual suicide.

> Her poems have that heart-breaking quality about them that has made Sylvia Plath our acknowledged Queen of Sorrows, the spokeswoman for our most private, most helpless nightmares; her poetry is as deathly as it is impeccable; it enchants us almost as powerfully as it must have enchanted her.

Not everyone agrees with this estimate, however. Janice Markey sees Plath's writings as life-affirming:

The enduring success and greatness of Plath's work lies in its universal appeal and in an innovative, effective presentation. Plath was the first writer in modern times to write about women with a new aggressive confidence and clarity, and the first to integrate this confidence and clarity in a sane, honest and compassionate vision.

Forming a personal view or response

1. What did you like best about Sylvia Plath's poems?
2. Choose one poem that you enjoyed and identify what appealed to you about it.
3. In what way is Plath different from the other poets on your course?
4. Plath's poetry reflects many facets of life. Which of these did you find most interesting?
5. What did you learn about Plath as a person from studying her poetry?
6. Is there anything you particularly like or dislike about her poetry?
7. Are the themes and issues in her poetry relevant to young people today?
8. Plath's unique and distinctive voice has often been praised. Do you find her voice – her way of writing, of expressing her ideas – unique?
9. Is there any particular image or description that remains with you from reading Plath's poetry? If so, identify why it impressed you.

Questions

1. 'Sylvia Plath created a language for herself that was utterly and startlingly original.' How true is this statement of the poems by Plath that you have studied?
2. Discuss Plath's treatment of nature in her poems. Support your discussion by quotation from or reference to the poems by her that you have studied.
3. 'Plath's poetry is a reflection of the era in which she lived.' Discuss this statement, supporting your discussion by quotation from or reference to the poems by Plath that you have studied.
4. Write a short essay on the aspects of Sylvia Plath's poems (content or style) that you found most interesting. Support your discussion by reference to or quotation from the poems by Plath that you have studied.
5. 'Sylvia Plath: a personal response'. Using this title, write an essay on the poetry of Plath, supporting your points by quotation from or reference to the poems on your course.
6. 'Sylvia Plath's taut language and startling images make her poems unique.' Discuss this statement, supporting your discussion by quotation from or reference to the poems by Plath that you have studied.

7. 'Sylvia Plath's poetry reflects a wide range of emotions.' Discuss this statement, concentrating on at least two different emotions that are evident in her poetry.
8. 'Despite the seriousness of her themes, Plath uses humour to devastating effect at times.' Discuss this statement, supporting your discussion by quotation from or reference to the poems by Plath that you have studied.
9. 'Recurring themes of loneliness, separation and pain mark the poetry of Sylvia Plath.' Discuss this statement, supporting your discussion by quotation from or reference to the poems by Plath that you have studied.
10. 'The use of brilliant and startling imagery gives a surreal quality to the poems of Sylvia Plath.' Discuss this statement, supporting your discussion by quotation from or reference to the poems by Plath that you have studied.

Ordinary Level, 2007 Examination

Explanatory note

Candidates taking the Ordinary (Pass) level exam in 2007 have a choice of questions when dealing with the prescribed poems. They can answer either (*a*) a question on one of the poems by a poet prescribed for Higher Level for the 2007 exam, or (*b*) a question from a list of other prescribed poems (i.e. the alternative poems discussed on pages 306–25).

(*a*) The poems by Higher level poets that may also be answered by Ordinary level candidates in the 2007 exam are as follows:

Donne	The Flea (p. 2)	**Kavanagh**	Shancoduff (p. 150)
	Song: Go, and catch a falling star (p. 4)		A Christmas Childhood (p. 157)
Yeats	The Lake Isle of Innisfree (p. 49)		On Raglan Road (p. 162)
	The Wild Swans at Coole (p. 54)	**Bishop**	The Fish (p. 173)
			Filling Station (p. 194)
	An Irish Airman Foresees his Death (p. 57)	**Montague**	The Locket (p. 240)
			The Cage (p. 244)
Frost	'Out, Out –' (p. 102)		Like dolmens round my childhood. . . (p. 257)
	The Road Not Taken (p. 104)		
	Acquainted With the Night (p. 108)	**Plath**	The Arrival of the Bee Box (p. 372)
			Child (p. 375)
Eliot	Preludes (p. 124)		
	Aunt Helen (p. 128)		

(*b*) The alternative poems that Ordinary level candidates sitting the exam in 2007 may choose to study instead are discussed on pages 306–25.

Contributors
Carole Scully
John McCarthy
John G. Fahy
David Keogh
Bernard Connolly

Ordinary Level, 2007 Examination
Alternative poems

Henry Vaughan
Peace
Text of the poem: New Explorations Anthology page 467

A reading of the poem
The poet addresses his soul and describes heaven as 'a Countrie | Far beyond the stars', guarded by a sentry 'All skilfull in the wars'. Peace sits 'crown'd with smiles' above the clamour and danger that characterise life on Earth. Christ is portrayed as a military commander commanding the angelic troops. He is the soul's friend, who for motives of 'pure love' descended to the earth to die 'for thy sake'. If the soul could 'get but thither' to Christ, in heaven 'there growes the flowre of peace'. Peace is symbolised by the 'Rose that cannot wither' and as a fortress offering security. The soul is exhorted to cease its wanderings: 'Leave then thy foolish ranges' and to embrace Christ, who 'never changes' and is 'Thy God, thy life, thy Cure.' This poem is perhaps best understood as a dramatic sermon in which Christ offers mankind peace. Peace is defined in terms of military security with Christ as the warrior prince, and offering an end to aimless wandering. In his poem 'Man' Vaughan refers to the human condition: 'Man is the shuttle . . . God ordered motion but ordained no rest'. In 'Peace', rest – 'ease' – replaces restlessness – 'foolish ranges' – in the poet's view of heaven, protected by 'one who never changes'.

Imagery
Vaughan's use of imagery in the poem is striking, as heaven is 'a Countrie | Far beyond the stars'. Christ is presented as a warrior; he 'Commands the Beauteous files', offering protection; he is 'skilfull in the wars'. Associated with this warlike image is 'the flowre of peace', which is 'The Rose that cannot wither'.

Christ/peace is a 'fortresse', offering an end to aimless wandering: 'thy foolish ranges'. Vaughan weaves the various strands of imagery together to dramatic effect, to convey a moral lesson, as the soul is exhorted – 'O my soul awake!' – to embrace Christ's peace.

Muscular language
Vaughan writes with vigour, as the brisk rhythm of the short lines, with their forceful beat, builds up to the pause at the semicolon in line 16. The following

line is in the imperative, as the soul is instructed to act on the knowledge gained: 'Leave then thy foolish ranges;'. Triplication in the final line enhances the rhetorical effect of the punctuation, with pauses after the key words 'Thy God, thy life, thy Cure.' The poem possesses a hymn-like quality, with its alternate lines rhyming and its simplicity of language.

Christina Rossetti
Remember

Text of poem: New Explorations Anthology page 473

STRUCTURE

This poem is written in the Sonnet form. It is made up of fourteen lines. The first eight lines are divided by the rhymes at the ends of the lines and the punctuation into two groups of four, known as quatrains. The final six lines are called a sestet.

A READING OF THE POEM

Rossetti opens the poem by telling her companion to 'remember' her when they are no longer together. She emphasises the idea of separation by repeating the words 'gone' and 'away' and adding in the word 'far'. She uses two vivid images to help the reader to understand the effects that this parting will have on the couple: they will no longer be able to hold hands or to turn around to be together. So, in the first quatrain, the couple are seen as being forced to give up their close physical intimacy and, instead, to be 'far away' from each other.

In the second quatrain, she uses the phrase 'remember me' twice as if she is growing increasingly agitated. These lines also develop our understanding of just how close the couple's relationship is. They speak together of their 'future' in detail. We realise that they are not only physically close, but also intellectually and emotionally close: they share their thoughts and hopes and dreams. This conversation contrasts with the terrible quietness of 'the silent land' that Rossetti imagines in the second line of the poem. The feeling that the couple are helpless to resist this separation is suggested in the phrase 'It will be late to counsel then or pray'.

The sestet reveals just how much Rossetti cares for her companion. Although she has repeated her hope that she will be remembered in the first eight lines of the poem, she now reveals her concern that her partner should not feel sad nor grieve for her going. In the final two lines of the poem she makes it clear that her desire to be remembered after she is gone is not as strong as her desire for her partner to be happy without her. In words that are simple yet deeply moving, she says that she would rather her companion forgot about her and be happy than remember her and be sad.

Edward Thomas
Adlestrop
Text of poem: New Explorations Anthology page 476

A READING OF THE POEM
The opening of this poem is quietly understated. Thomas simply speaks to the reader, explaining how the name 'Adlestrop' triggers a memory for him.

His description of his brief stop at Adlestrop is communicated with a deceptive simplicity. In the first stanza, he relates how he came to be in Adlestrop: 'the express-train drew up there | Unwontedly', adding that it was 'late June'. In the second stanza, we hear how his gaze lingered first on the station: 'No one left and no one came | On the bare platform.' Idly, Thomas noted the name of Adlestrop on the signpost. But then, his gaze moved beyond the station out to the English countryside surrounding it and, suddenly, 'Adlestrop' was no longer 'only the name'. The third stanza gives a wonderful sense of the view that stretched out before Thomas. Our eyes move with his from the 'willows, willow-herb, and grass' in the foreground, to the 'haycocks' further beyond, and then farther still, up to the 'high cloudlets in the sky.' In the fourth stanza, we learn that the beauty and harmony of the moment were increased, for Thomas, by the singing of a blackbird 'Close by' and 'Farther and farther, all the birds | Of Oxfordshire and Gloucestershire.'

THEME
Although Thomas can be classed as a 'War Poet', in that he wrote his poetry around the time of the First World War, he did not concentrate on writing about the war. Rather, he wrote of the unique beauty of the English countryside and of his great love for it.

In 'Adlestrop', Thomas describes a brief moment when he encountered this natural beauty and responded with admiration and appreciation. The fact that the First World War, with all its horrors, had begun, simply served to make such a view and such a feeling all the more precious.

LANGUAGE AND RHYME
Thomas uses the language of everyday speech in this poem. However, this in no way limits the effectiveness of his images. For instance, in the second stanza, we see how his skilful arrangement of familiar words in familiar patterns successfully communicates the experience of stopping unexpectedly and briefly on a train journey. Similarly, the third stanza graphically conveys the breathtaking view that was stretched out before him.

Such simplicity should never be regarded as commonplace or easily achieved. It is somewhat surprising to realise that Thomas' poem has a rhyme scheme, as the words seem to flow naturally. He has succeeded in managing the conversational language with such expertise that the rhyme is subtle and in no way interrupts the flow of the words and thoughts.

IMAGERY
Thomas creates a series of images that evoke the scene so distinctly, it is as if we too are sitting on the train. He achieves this by building a strong sensory element into his images. His reference to the 'heat' appeals to the sense of touch. He brings hearing into play with the hissing steam, the person clearing his throat and the songs of the birds. Finally, sight ranges from the 'bare platform' to the Adlestrop sign and, then, to the 'willows, willow-herb', the 'haycocks' and 'the high cloudlets'.

W.H. Auden
Funeral Blues
Text of poem: New Explorations Anthology page 482

ORIGINS OF THE POEM
It is sometimes difficult to trace the origins of certain Auden poems, because he had the habit of revising his material frequently, incorporating some poems in longer works and generally rewriting. A version of 'Stop All the Clocks' (the first two verses as here, with two others) first appeared in the drama Auden wrote and produced jointly with Christopher Isherwood in 1936, *The Ascent of F6*. In this satirical fable about politics and leadership the song is a 'spoof' of a dirge for a dead political leader. It is a tongue-in-cheek lament, making fun of the gullibility of the public, who insist on making heroes of flawed human beings.

The present version appeared in the collection *Another Time* (1940) and was entitled 'Funeral Blues', one of 'Four Cabaret Songs for Miss Heidi Anderson'. At the time of composition Heidi Anderson was engaged to Auden's friend and collaborator, the Irish poet Louis MacNeice. The music for these was composed by Benjamin Britten.

READING OF THE POEM
This poem can be read either as an elegy or as a satire. If we read it as an elegy we tend to concentrate on the two final stanzas and focus on the depth of feeling, that intense sense of loss that finds expression in the outpouring of unbridled grief:

> He was my North, my South, my East and West . . .
> The stars are not wanted now: put out every one . . .

If we read it as an elegy, these exaggerated sentiments are an attempt to communicate the depth of pain and the fearful grief felt by the speaker. If we read it as a satire, we take our cue from the first two stanzas in particular and view the poem as a satirical treatment of public mourning, as a lament with exaggerated sentiments and imagery that succeeds in ridiculing the practice of the public funeral and is critical of the outpouring of popular grief for a public figure.

STYLE

On first reading this poem one is struck by the ludicrous imagery and the wildly exaggerated emotions. The reader may not be sure whether this is comic or tragic. But if we consider the poem's origins as a blues song it may help our understanding. The critic John Fuller sees the poem as 'a good pastiche of the stoical lament and flamboyant imagery of the traditional blues lyric'. In other words, the style is a mixture of features from the lament and the blues lyric, and Auden has exaggerated these. So, we find an overstatement of the usual blues sentiment in lamenting a dead lover. This exaggerated feeling is carried in the imagery, which varies from the stately and solemn –

> Silence the pianos and with muffled drum
> Bring out the coffin, let the mourners come

– to the comic 'Put the crêpe bows round the white necks of the public doves.' We find the blues style also in the use of clichés:

> He was my North, my South, my East and West,
> My working week and my Sunday rest.

Banal and much-used metaphors such as these help convey the notion that these feelings are felt by everybody, by ordinary people. They foster the idea that this grief is universal. Blues rhythms too are suggested in the metre. We get these long, rolling sentences, for example in the third stanza; and then the division of some lines into two introduces a counter-rhythm and a regular beat: 'I thought that love would last for ever: I was wrong.'

THE SATIRE

The satirical effect is created through exaggeration. The realistic sounds, silences and colours of a funeral are evoked in the first two stanzas: stop all the clocks, silence the pianos, muffled drum, aeroplanes moaning, crêpe bow, black cotton gloves. The long *o* and *u* sounds help create the atmosphere of mourning: phone, bone, drum, come. But it all goes over the top into melodrama, through the use of extremes: 'Prevent the dog from barking' and 'Let aeroplanes circle moaning overhead | Scribbling in the sky the message: He is Dead.' The flamboyant American advertising culture is quite inappropriate for conveying the announcement of a death; this bad taste heightens the sense of satire. The somewhat hysterical tone of the opening ('Stop all the clocks, cut off the telephone') adds to the melodrama, as do the extremes of feeling in

> Pour away the ocean and sweep up the wood.
> For nothing now can ever come to any good.

But do you think there might be a hint of real grief and sorrow behind this melodramatic exaggeration? Consider, for instance, the third stanza. Could line 1 be read as meaning 'He was the whole world to me,' line 2 as 'He was always in my thoughts, both at work and leisure,' and line 3 as 'He was at the centre of all my moods, happy or depressed' (noon or midnight)?

It might be useful to list (in your own words) the speaker's feelings for the dead person; then examine the final stanza in some detail. Why do you think he chooses the references he does? Why the sun, moon, and stars? Why does he feel he will no longer need the ocean or the wood? Could these have been their favourite places?

Do you find that the two final stanzas prompt you to consider that this poem communicates genuine feeling and depth of emotion?

Edwin Morgan
Strawberries
Text of poem: New Explorations Anthology page 490

A READING OF THE POEM
Morgan begins his poem by focusing on the strawberries that were eaten by the couple on this remembered afternoon. He regards the strawberries as special: 'There were never strawberries | like the ones we had | that sultry afternoon', just as 'that sultry afternoon' was special.

His description of the two people is one of intimacy and closeness. They sit on a step 'facing each other', knees interlocked. There is a feeling of commitment and belonging in the phrase 'your knees held in mine'. The eating of the strawberries reinforces this sense of physical intimacy. The actions of the couple mirror each other: 'we dipped them in sugar'. They look not at the strawberries as they eat, but at each other.

The sensuality of the strawberries, evident in such phrases as 'strawberries glistening' and 'we dipped them in sugar', captures the simmering sensuality that crackles between the lovers. It becomes clear that the eating of the strawberries is, in reality, an introduction to another type of sensual intimacy that the couple anticipates sharing. They eat the strawberries 'not hurrying', drawing out this anticipation, savouring the expectation and the promise of this moment. The tension builds with each mouthful until the plates are empty and 'laid on the stone'. The image of the 'two forks crossed' is reflected in the poet's moving towards his companion: 'and I bent towards you'. The sweetness of the strawberries dipped in sugar becomes the sweetness of his companion's presence, and both merge in the taste of his lover's lips. The hot sunlight that shone on the 'strawberries glistening' now shines on the couple in their sensual 'forgetfulness' as they create a 'heat intense'. The remembered moment is so intense for Morgan that it comes out of the past and into the present, as he urges his lover 'lean back again let me love you'.

The poem closes on the spectacular images of 'summer lightening' flashing on the 'Kilpatrick hills' and a rain-storm cleaning the forgotten plates. These could be seen as representing the intensity of the couple's loving. However, there is an undercurrent of destruction and danger about the 'lightening'. Could Morgan be suggesting that although this sensual, intense love shared by the couple was incredibly special, it also carried danger with it, because it made the lovers emotionally vulnerable to each other? Does the storm that washed the plates represent the ending of their love?

THEME

Morgan writes about the theme of love in an intensely sensual and physical way. He uses the eating of the strawberries to suggest a sense of anticipation and close intimacy. Similarly, the heat of the sun indicates the intensity of their relationship. However, he seems to sound a cautionary note about such love with the images of the lightning and the storm.

STRUCTURE

Interestingly, this poem is written as one unpunctuated piece. Morgan tries to represent, on the page, the continuous movement of his memories of 'that sultry afternoon'. His words and phrases glide smoothly from one image to another, capturing the way in which remembered thoughts of an incident flow, without full stops or commas.

Morgan's use of the past and present tenses cleverly communicates the way in which past memories can become so vivid that they take over the present moment. So the past tense, used for eating the strawberries, suddenly becomes the present as he holds his lover and says, 'lean back again let me love you' and urges that they surrender to 'forgetfulness'.

Howard Nemerov
Wolves in the Zoo
Text of the poem: New Explorations Anthology page 492

A READING OF THE POEM

The first line of this poem is a surprising one: Nemerov describes the wolves as being like 'big dogs badly drawn'. This comparison makes the wolves appear much less frightening. It is hard to be afraid of a pack of oddly shaped dogs. After all, dogs were one of the first animals that man domesticated and we know them as 'man's best friend'.

Nemerov continues to challenge the accepted view of wolves as savage beasts. The sign on the wolves' cage states that there is 'No evidence' that wolves killed humans. Similarly, he tells us that the story of babies being thrown out of sleds in Siberia to slow down attacking packs of wolves is untrue. Most importantly of all, he questions the truth of the wolf's portrayal in the popular children's story 'Little Red Riding Hood'.

Nemerov presents us with a different side to wolves. It seems that rather than humans being the victims of wolves, it is the wolves that are the victims at the hands of humans. He states that all the untrue tales told about wolves gradually became accepted as true facts, just like the facts that are contained in 'history'. Because of this bad press humans came to see wolves as a threat, a threat that had to be destroyed or controlled. As a result, two breeds of wolf are nearing extinction.

In the final stanza of the poem, Nemerov leaves us with a sad scene. Those wolves that have not been killed by man have been forced to surrender to him. Along with the proud peacock and the majestic tiger, the wolves live a life in captivity, held in cages simply to amuse or entertain human beings. We have been shown the terrible damage that can be caused by man's unquestioning acceptance of attitudes and behaviour.

LANGUAGE

Nemerov uses conversational language to express his thoughts on the wolves. It is as if we are having a chat with him. This makes his writing come alive. We do not have to struggle with complicated poetic language or rhymes that make the meaning hard to understand. Instead, Nemerov uses simple but very effective words to encourage us to look again at the wolves' situation.

Denise Levertov
What Were They Like?
Text of poem from New Explorations Anthology page 498

This is a direct, angry, political poem about the Vietnam War. The poet sets up a question-and-answer session. Six questions are asked, and then later they are answered. The tension is felt all through the poem. There is a boiling anger, yet the speaker in the poem is trying her best to be reserved and cautious.

The questions come first, and seem to be coming from an anthropologist who is trying to find information about a lost society. They seem to be harmless, but when they are balanced by the answers their significance becomes obvious. The questions refer to innocuous items like 'lanterns of stone', 'opening of buds', 'laughter', 'ornament', 'poetry' and 'speech and singing'. But when we hear the tenor of the responses, we know these things to be very important indeed.

In the first answer, the speaker turns the metaphor of stone from referring to their lanterns to referring to their hearts. In fact the thought of even asking about lanterns seems anathema to the speaker. She implies that it cannot matter about light when you have no heart.

Next she explains that without life or the beginnings of life there was no place for flowering beauty, never mind celebrations of that. The third answer is perhaps the most terrifying and bleak: yet also the plainest.

> Sir, laughter is bitter to the burned mouth.

It is obvious from the fourth answer that ornament is only an afterthought, when you consider that the people barely had bodies to put the ornament on.

In the fifth answer she explains that the victors often write history. There is nothing in these people's immediate history that they would want to celebrate. Even Nature was destroyed for them. They could not look in pools of water and see themselves any longer. Their language had been reduced to the language of the panicked:

> When bombs smashed those mirrors
> there was time only to scream.

Again, the speaker tells us that singing can no longer be heard from these people, who have been frightened into silence. She gives us the most beautiful image in the poem when she tells us that when they did sing 'their singing resembled | the flight of moths in moonlight.' This encapsulates the great, unified beauty that they were once capable of. She reminds us then of the fact that all that beauty is now irrelevant, for there is nothing left to see or hear.

This is a hauntingly powerful poem that tells the story of a forgotten people.

Patricia Beer
The Voice
Text of poem: New Explorations Anthology page 501

A READING OF THE POEM

Patricia Beer's poem opens conversationally: 'When God took my aunt's baby boy, a merciful neighbour | Gave her a parrot.' The reference to the parrot is unexpected and sets the tone for some wry observations from the poet. A dramatic turning point in the unnamed aunt's life is referred to matter-of-factly: 'And turned her back on the idea of other babies.' Her difficult financial circumstances are suggested by the fact that she 'could not have afforded' the parrot. In her house the parrot 'looked unlikely' because of his bright coloration; the only other colour there was the old-fashioned, cheap 'local pottery' with quaint dialect inscriptions, 'Du ee help yourself to crame, me handsome'. Beer describes how the parrot 'said nothing', while speculating entertainingly on what sounds might have issued from him, 'From pet-shop gossip or a sailor's oath . . . tom-tom, war-cry or wild beast roaring.' The aunt teaches him 'nursery rhymes morning after morning'; he learns to speak in a Devon accent. Beer associates the parrot with the aunt's lost child: 'He sounded like a farmer, as her son might have.' In a telling phrase, 'He fitted in.'

Beer mixes humour and pathos, as the parrot becomes ill: 'he got confused, and muddled up | His rhymes. Jack Horner ate his pail of water . . . I wept'. There is some of Beer's characteristic wry humour to be observed in 'He had never seemed puzzled by the bizarre events | He spoke of' and clever phrasing in 'And tumbled after.' Ironically when the aunt died, 'widowed, childless, pitied | And patronised', the poet is left with no memory of her voice, 'But I can still hear his'.

LANGUAGE

Beer captures the rhythms and idioms of colloquial speech: 'When God took my aunt's baby boy' and 'And turned her back on the idea of other babies.' Her style is direct: 'But I can still hear his', while displaying a playful sense of humour as she echoes the nursery rhyme: 'Said 'Broke his crown' and 'Christmas pie'. And tumbled after.' Her use of dialect helps to suggest the character of the aunt's house and decorations: 'With the local pottery which carried messages | Like "Du ee help yourself to crame, me handsome"'. Beer sums up the aunt's life most succinctly: 'My aunt died the next winter, widowed, childless, pitied | And patronised.' The alliterating *w* and *p* sounds help make the line memorable, like the *h* sounds in the final line: 'I can still hear his.'

Tone

As the poem opens the poet seems detached: 'When God took . . . a merciful neighbour gave her a parrot.' There are flashes of humour as she describes the aunt's pottery and 'her jokes; she used to say turds and whey'. The parrot's confusion in his final illness is humorously illustrated; she also suggests her feelings: 'I wept'.

The final stanza allows a rather different perspective, as Beer reflects on the unnamed aunt's life, 'widowed, childless, pitied | And patronised.' She is far more sensitive to the woman's suffering and concludes ironically with the poignant observation, 'She would not have expected it to be remembered | After so long.' In a poem about voices the aunt has no voice and no name. The colourful parrot's voice is still heard.

Richard Murphy
The Reading Lesson
Text of Poem: New Explorations Anthology page 508

Critical commentary

'The Reading Lesson' is based on a dialogue between two people. The speaker in the poem is a reading teacher who is trying to help a fourteen-year-old traveller boy to read. The poem describes the boy's struggle to come to grips with the world of letters and the teacher's frustration at his lack of progress, and it also shows the rest of society's reaction to their attempts. The poem uses images that are part of the boy's world to describe the struggle that goes on between them.

The boy either doesn't want to read or he is finding it so hard that he has almost given up. The first metaphor that is introduced by the poet to describe the situation is the dog hunting the hare. This gives the reader an image of a great wild chase – that he is trying to trap and tie down the boy's wild nature and bring it to a passive trap. There is a sense here, understood by both the teacher and the boy, that if he is 'tamed' he may lose something in the trade-off between them. The hunt is brought up to a climax when the teacher finally becomes so frustrated that he challenges the boy with a stern question. The teacher may think he is being rhetorical, but the boy takes him very literally and gives an equally stern reply:

> 'Don't you want to learn to read?'
> 'I'll be the same man whatever I do.'

The teacher compares this riposte to an animal that has been cornered and comes out with his teeth bared on his release.

The second verse continues with the nature imagery. The poet uses a mule, a goat and a snipe to describe the way the boy looks at the page. He explains that the atmosphere is tense and says that if there is

> 'A sharp word, and he'll mooch
> Back to his piebald mare and bantam cock.'

He finishes by explaining that his task is as difficult as catching mercury.

The third verse shows us that they have all but given up; the boy will not be using his fingers to follow words on a page, but he will use them to go hawking scrap or even going pickpocketing. The teacher says that the boy could easily revert to the stereotype that the chuckling neighbour ascribes to him. The neighbour says that the boy is untameable, that he will always have a yearning to escape and go back to being his natural, wild self as soon as he has the chance.

The final verse finishes with some images that are specific to travellers. He says that books are something that the boy feels will restrict him and stop him from making his own way. They are as restrictive and separate from him as the idea of settling on a small farm to live for the rest of his life. He says that his life will be one of petty theft and poaching. He ends by comparing this book learning to the wren. The wren became The King Of All Birds by being clever enough to sit on the back of an eagle and therefore fly the highest in the sky. To the boy, that is how unobtainable to him books are.

Fleur Adcock
For Heidi with Blue Hair
Text of Poem: New Explorations Anthology page 514

Issues

This poem deals with adolescent assertiveness and the right to choose one's own dress code, hairstyle, and so on. These issues often become symbolic of individual freedoms and rights in the conflict between the teenager and authority, whether at school or at home. This conflict between youth culture and school culture has been elevated to the status of a 'battle' in this poem.

On a broader scale we might view the poem as demonstrating the conflict between different outlooks, attitudes, or philosophies – liberalism versus the need to conform. The more relaxed tolerance of the father is pitted against the rather snooty conformism of the school. But the school is not really very authoritarian, as the teachers give in, probably taking the home background into account.

Tone

For the most part, the poem is written in humorous or mock-serious tone. The humour is brought about through the contrast between the formality of the language and the relative insignificance of the event. Examine, for instance, the formal expression and complex structure of the language in the headmistress's telephone call (stanza 2). There is also a sense of the ridiculous in the witty, repartee-style comment 'you wiped your eyes, I also not in a school colour.' The rebellious, trend-setting ending adds to the sense of mischief and lets us see where the poet's sympathies lie: with the teenager and in support of the subversive. The exuberant colours add to the lightness of atmosphere here.

The one bleak note sounded concerns the reference to the mother's death, 'that shimmered behind the arguments.' 'Shimmered' suggests a vague, ill-defined, ghost-like presence and captures well the background thoughts on the mother's death, which nobody has had the courage to formulate into words. Would this be happening if her mother was alive? Should we indulge this child a bit because of her loss?

Capturing character

Adcock is particularly good at evoking the essence of characters in a spare yet effective way. The kind, liberal father is supportive of his daughter, however ridiculous her looks. He believes in 'dialogue' – talking things out: 'She discussed it with me first.' And we have the image of rebellious, defiant Heidi, reduced to tears – not so tough really! And we recognise her desperation as she tries a range of separate excuses: the cost, and the indelible nature of the dye. The teachers are well captured, however briefly: 'the teachers twittered.' We get an image of nice old dears, genteel, ladylike disapproval and all the connotations about the type of school that this conjures up.

The success of the portraiture depends to a good degree on Adcock's sharp ear for dialogue. She had a real feel for the style of conversation. She captures the father's defensive terse tones: 'She discussed . . . we checked . . .' and the headmistress's long-winded, slightly grand style, conveyed in the complex syntax of the second stanza. We can hear her careful, measured statement: '. . . not specifically forbidden.' And she captures the casual, pushy, argumentative style of the teenager Heidi: 'And anyway, Dad . . .'

Sharon Olds
The Present Moment
Text of poem: New Explorations Anthology page 527

A READING OF THE POEM

This thoughtful meditation concerns issues of ageing and of how we perceive the ageing process. A daughter sees her father in hospital, where he is terminally ill, and she tries to reconcile the image she once had of her father as somebody who was strong physically and mentally with the frail figure who lies before her. Through the poem she gives a powerful description of what illness does to people, of how it can ravage the body and the mind at the same time in a ruthless manner.

She combines the body and the mind at the start of the poem. She shows how the father has gone in such a short time from being someone who was active to being just a passive entity on the edge of existence. The first instance comes when she sees him just lying on his hospital bed. He is now motionless, facing towards the wall. This is becoming her dominant image of him now, instead of the image that she had of him before he entered the hospital and he 'sat up and put on his reading glasses'. At that stage he was actively reading, taking things in, his eyes alive as the 'lights in the room multiplied in the lenses.'

She uses the image of food to show the changes he has gone through. He now is dependent on food that will pass through him for energy, not for taste. He eats 'dense, earthen food, like liver', which is pure tasteless fuel – not something more unusual and aesthetic, like pineapple with its exotic connotations.

She follows this by noticing the changes to his body over the years. He is none of the more appealing figures that he used to be. She goes in reverse chronological order through his phases of life. She describes him as a portly man with a 'torso packed with extra matter'. As a young man he was a 'smooth-skinned, dark-haired boy'.

She admits to not knowing him obviously when he was a baby, but she notes his dependence back then, when he would 'drink from a woman's | body'. Once again he is being fed. And his 'steady | gaze' now is again like when he was just born: where sleep brings only relief to him now, just as it did then.

She finishes with a metaphor of a swimmer, only her father is swimming towards death: and want as she might to help him, she is helpless. She can only look on while he continues in his struggle.

Paul Durcan
Going Home to Mayo, Winter, 1949

Text of poem: New Explorations Anthology page 531

A READING OF THE POEM

The poem deals directly with the contrast between urban life and rural culture, between present and past. The village is a romantic, welcoming place, with an old-fashioned, magical charm about it – 'all oil-lamps and women'. It has a gentle, feminine identity, in contrast to the hard, powerful, masculine city: 'blocks after blocks of so-called "new" tenements'. The country is a known place, a place of heritage, where they belonged: 'my father's mother's house'. This is in marked contrast to the impersonal 'alien, foreign city of Dublin'.

The village is an exotic place, particularly to a child. There is the novelty of the unusual: 'my bedroom over the public bar below'. It is all beautifully chaotic, with an animal wildness, a naturalness, that is quaintly appealing.

> And in the morning cattle-cries and cock-crows:
> Life's seemingly seamless garment gorgeously rent
> By their screeches and bellowings.

Contrast this with the rigid divisions and barren orderliness of the city, with its 'railings and palings and asphalt and traffic-lights'.

The village is a place that fostered intimacy between father and son:

> I walked with my father in the high grass down by the river
> Talking with him – an unheard-of thing in the city.

The city is associated with loneliness, isolation, and death. The tenements are seen as graveyards, with 'thousands of crosses of loneliness' that somehow become a reminder of actual death for the father. For him, death is more real, perhaps because it is more immediate – and so the shape of the grave is more clearly defined as 'the narrowing grave'. But the city carries an aura of death even for the child, for whom death is less immediate and obvious: 'In the wide, wide cemetery of the boy's childhood.' Perhaps there is a hint, too, that the city proved the cemetery of the boy's dreams.

The poet displays a yearning for the village of Turlough that is almost religious in its intensity. Like a religious exile, he is 'going home', with all the excitement and anticipation that entails. Consequently he is deeply disappointed when he realises that it is a temporary stay, that 'home was not home'. Turlough means life and excitement for him; the city means exile and death.

A CHILD'S VIEW OF THE WORLD

Part I communicates a child's view of life, a magical world full of possibilities:

> 'Daddy, Daddy,' I cried, 'Pass out the moon.'

The journey becomes a symbolic quest for the promised land: names of towns are reeled off as in a religious litany. And in this magic place, all is transformed, and children are no longer treated as inferior.

> I walked with my father in the high grass down by the river
> Talking with him . . .

FATHER AND SON

The relationship with his father provided a good deal of grief for Paul Durcan, but we see little of that here. The portrait of the father is typically masculine, associated with driving, energy, direction and with going places. There is a hint of aloofness, in that the intimacy of conversation is unusual, 'unheard-of thing in the city'. Yet on this occasion father and son collaborate on the quest ('no matter how hard he drove he could not pass out the moon'). An interlude of closeness and cooperation is provided by the return to the village; it is as if the ideal relationship is attainable only in this hallowed place.

IMAGERY

The image of a journey, which is central to the poem, achieves a certain symbolic significance here. It is both a real journey and a magical quest for origins, for the perfect place, for happiness. The drive through the night has its counter-image in the 'daylight nightmare of Dublin city' and so helps to link both halves of the poem, the perfect dream and the hard-working reality. The images evoking rural life have a biblical quality to them: 'oil-lamps and women', 'cattle-cries and cock-crows'; and the metaphor of most obvious biblical significance, 'Life's seemingly seamless garment gorgeously rent.' The effect is to suggest that this is a good and holy place, as well as a place obviously teeming with life.

In contrast, pictures of the city are cold, non-human, and divisive rather than fostering life: railings and palings, blocks of flats; and in some surreal way they become associated with crosses and death.

Paddy Bushe
Jasmine
Text of poem: New Explorations Anthology page 538

CRITICAL COMMENTARY
This poem is about the decay of a father as he gets older and starts losing his memory, possibly through Alzheimer's Syndrome or maybe just through senility. The father has been taken from his children by his illness. The poem discusses how that makes the children feel.

The father asks the simple question, 'What colour is jasmine?' The question does not pose a difficulty for his son. What does cause a difficulty is the idea of how that question raised itself to the mind of the father in the first place. They are not sure how the question made its way to their father's mind, or where it was going to next:

> . . . we couldn't recognise the road
> your question had travelled, nor sound the extent
> of the blue void to which it would return.

We get the feeling that the question stopped them in their tracks as the ward had to come back to normality and the 'hum | of conscientious care.'

They decide that thinking about that question in a literal way isn't an option. So they 'took the long way home'.

In the final couplet the poet ties the metaphor to the rest of the poem. He asks that the question may bring his father to a kind of peace, just as a climbing plant such as jasmine can pull a broken piece of trellising together. It can climb among the broken pieces and allow them to stay tied to the wall even if they have come away. This is what he wishes for his father: that he will be able to keep himself together.

The poet creates the mood in this poem by using sensuous language. The language is designed to appeal to the senses by using soft *s* sounds. There is an atmosphere of compassion and of wonder.

Colour is also used to give life to the poem; as well as the colours in the flower itself, he also uses the 'blue from your wheelchair' and the 'blue void' to this end most effectively.

The poem ends in an upbeat fashion. The poet is toasting his father by beginning the couplet with a salutary 'And may . . .'

Overall this is a poem that is searching for understanding. It is one that is still asking questions about the significance of what occurred. There is almost a sense of hope from not knowing the answers, yet knowing that there is still activity in the father's mind.

Paul Muldoon
Anseo
Text of poem: New Explorations Anthology page 541

CRITICAL COMMENTARY

'Anseo' describes how things happen in cycles and how the abused can often become the abuser.

The initial scene is a typical Irish primary school. The poet describes the roll-call system by which everybody would answer 'Anseo' as their name was called out. This word 'was the first word of Irish I spoke', as was the case and possibly still is for many Irish schoolchildren. The poet remembers what would happen at the start of every class, when the teacher would call out the last name on the roll – which belonged to Joseph Mary Plunkett Ward. This name is significant for a number of reasons. Joseph Mary Plunkett was one of the leaders of the Easter Rising in 1916. The Mary part of it is also significant, in so far as it is usually a name associated with girls rather than boys, and certainly not with a military leader – which the 1916 leader was and that this boy was about to become.

Finally, the name is also important because it gives the teacher a chance to make a pun on the boy's name. Every day he would ask the same question: 'And where's our little Ward–of–court?' There was a sense of expectancy around this question; the other students would look at each other to see the reaction to it. The teacher was obviously having fun at Ward's expense.

In the second verse we see the twisted nature of the teacher, as he would send Ward out to find his own stick to be beaten with. The teacher would refuse different options, until he got the right one to beat him with. This is the sort of ritual that Ward was seeing and, as we see later on, he was learning from it as well. The poet gives us fine detail as he outlines exactly the trouble that Ward would go to when he was preparing his own tormentor. We can almost imagine Ward taking pride in his work or being given a lecture about it from the teacher. We can see the engraving being like a commemoration on a gift:

> Its twist of red and yellow lacquers
> Sanded and polished,
> And altogether so delicately wrought
> That he had engraved his initials on it.

The poet then brings us further along in time. Joseph Mary Plunkett Ward is now doing what his part namesake had also done. He is leading a secret IRA battalion and had obviously risen through the ranks. There are many contradictions in his life when we see that

> He was living in the *open*,
> In a *secret* camp

He is no longer the boy who is being bullied and victimised. Instead he is 'Making things happen.' He has become an important person in a vicious world. He has also learned from his old schoolteacher. He calls a roll, just like in primary school. One feels the punishment for not answering the roll call this time could be much more severe than getting beaten by a hazel-wand.

He is now the one in the position of authority. He is able to put people in their place and tell them what to do. People have fear of him now.

Muldoon makes a simple point in a clever way and uses the simple Irish word 'Anseo' to illustrate it. He says that power must be used carefully. He also says that if not cared for properly, the bullied can become the bully.

Carol Ann Duffy
Valentine

Text of poem: New Explorations Anthology page 548

A READING OF THE POEM

This is a love poem, but it is not a straightforward, romantic love poem. Indeed in the first line we see that the poet is putting great emphasis on the fact that her love (the emotion and the person) is not ordinary, and therefore she is not going to give a traditional gift for St Valentine's Day, like a 'red rose or a satin heart'; instead she is going to give her lover an onion.

The rest of the poem explains why she feels she should give an onion to her lover. The onion becomes an *extended metaphor*. She points out that the onion can give light in a time of darkness, just like the moon. She examines the erotic nature of an onion. She compares the onion to a lover who brings out the truth regardless of the price. She says that a love affair, like an onion, can make the protagonists see sides of themselves that they'd rather not see. She talks about its taste, which is difficult to shift; but, like the taste of an onion, a love affair can eventually end as well. Then she compares the inside of an onion to a wedding ring; but then she says that this is lethal.

All these images are harsh, and in a way they are cold. The poet seems to be bringing a 'wake-up call' to her lover. The implication could be that they have not got a traditional romantic relationship, and therefore to give a traditional romantic present would be the wrong thing to do and would be dishonest.

At the end she adds her own caution: getting too close is dangerous; love can be 'lethal'.

TONE

She uses a forceful, matter-of-fact tone. There is little ambiguity. Note her use of the definite 'I will' and 'I give,' instead of 'It could' or 'I offer.' There is a sense of 'these are the facts; if you don't like them – tough'; though there is a little hint of teasing in the poem as well.

STRUCTURE AND LANGUAGE

She uses very few formal traditional poetic devices, though she is careful with her use of sound, especially in such lines as

> Its fierce kiss will stay on your lips.

The metre in the poem seems to be purpose-built. She varies her line lengths a lot, even giving one word to one line. What do you think the significance of these small lines is?

Simon Armitage
It Ain't What You Do, It's What It Does To You
Text of poem: New Explorations Anthology page 555

This is a beautifully simple poem about the difference people can make and about how people can be important, even if they are not living exotic lives. The poet sets up four exotic scenarios and contrasts them with four seemingly banal instances, giving each equal credence. This poem could easily be compared with Patrick Kavanagh's poem 'Epic' in the way that it contrasts the local with the universal.

The first contrast is between a Bohemian travelling across the USA, living 'with only a dollar to spare, one pair | of busted Levis and a Bowie knife', and simply living with 'thieves in Manchester'. The banality of the place Manchester, which is local and drab, compared to the living-on-the-edge lifestyle in the States, is also emphasised by the simplicity of the line.

Next, he tells us that he doesn't get his spiritual wholeness from one of the wonders of the world, but from the energy used in skimming stones across an old lake in northern England. He finds himself at one with the energy of the Black Moss, instead of with the glamorous Taj Mahal. He points out here that what is important is the feeling it gives him, rather than the location.

Finally he refers to two different actions. The first is daring and brave – getting ready to take a parachute jump where life and limb are seemingly risked. The second is simply caring for a mentally handicapped boy in a help centre. He obviously feels that the latter is more important. He goes on to assess what this does to him, and finds that it gives him a 'tightness in the throat' and a 'tiny cascading sensation'. He thinks that these feelings give him a purpose in life. They give him a 'sense of something else'.